HERODOTUS
BOOK VI

Edited with Introduction,
and Commentary by
E.I. McQUEEN

Bristol Classical Press

First published in 2000 by
Bristol Classical Press
an imprint of
Gerald Duckworth & Co. Ltd
61 Frith Street
London W1D 3JL
e-mail: inquiries@duckworth-publishers.co.uk
Website: www.ducknet.co.uk

Reprinted 2001

A catalogue record for this book is available
from the British Library

ISBN 1-85399-586-X

Printed in Great Britain by
Antony Rowe Ltd, Eastbourne

Contents

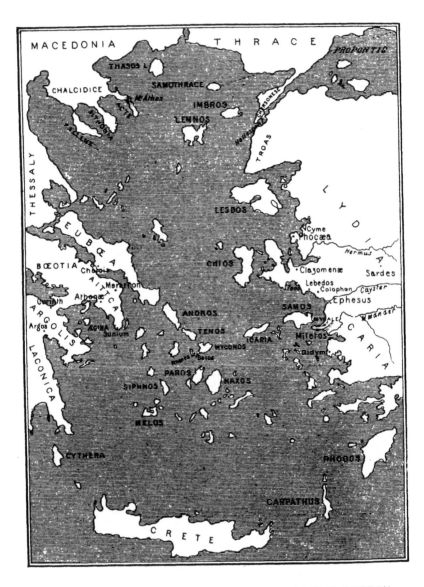

THE IONIAN CITIES AND THE ISLANDS OF THE AEGEAN

Preface

The aim of the present edition is to introduce A-level students and undergraduates to reading Herodotus in the original language. The subject matter of Book 6, the Ionian Revolt, the Marathon campaign and some of the more interesting and significant episodes in the history of both Athens and Sparta renders it particularly attractive for this purpose. Yet there has been no English edition since that of E.S. Shuckburgh, originally published by Cambridge University Press in 1889 and more recently available in the Bristol Classical Press reprint of 1984. Shuckburgh's edition, though still extremely useful, suffers from two major drawbacks which make it less helpful than it could be for the modern student. Firstly a vast amount of research has been done in the field of Greek history since its appearance, which needs to be taken into account in a modern commentary; and secondly, the work, aimed as it was at students who had been taught Greek by traditional methods, could assume a much greater knowledge of Greek grammar and syntax than is likely to be possessed by most contemporary students of the language. The former handicap was partially rectified with the appearance of *A Commentary on Herodotus* by W.W. How and J. Wells (Oxford, 1912) but, excellent as this two-volume work was, it too has been overtaken by recent advances in our historical knowledge. Nevertheless the debt of the present commentary to both Shuckburgh and to Howe and Wells cannot be overestimated.

The text printed here is that of Shuckburgh's edition; the few places where there is any serious doubt about what Herodotus himself wrote are indicated in the commentary. Shuckburgh's text originally used line-numbers; these have been replaced by the more commonly used paragraph/sub-section numbers, as found in the Oxford Classical Text (*OCT*) of K. Hude (3rd edn., 1927); it is to these that the commentary refers.

In the grammatical and syntactical notes I have provided references, for the benefit of students who require further information, to the relevant sections of W.W. Goodwin's *Greek Grammar*, which is the most readily available book on the subject in print at the present day (most recent edn. Bristol, 1998). For reasons of length and cost, I have made the introduction as brief as possible, and in the bibliography I have restricted myself to the books in English which are of major importance for the study of Herodotus and of the period of Greek History covered in Book 6. References to relevant articles in learned journals will be found, where appropriate, in the commentary as well as in the bibliographies included in the individual works which I list.

In the treatment of oracular pronouncements from Delphi, two books are cited in the notes, the two volume *The Delphic Oracle* by H.W. Parke and

D.E.W. Wormell (Blackwell, Oxford, 1956) and J. Fontenrose, *The Delphic Oracle: its Responses and Operations*, Berkeley, Los Angeles and London, 1978. Numbers cited in the commentary refer in the case of Parke and Wormell to the catalogue of oracular responses printed in Vol. 2 of that work, and in the case of Fontenrose to the responses gathered together at the end of the work. The citation of a page number referes to the discussion of particular responses that appears in the main body of the book. In the case of Parke and Wormell, page citations (as opposed to citations prefixed by 'no.'), refer to Volume I of that work.

In the commentary, the term 'the King' with upper case K invariably refers to the king of Persia (the 'Great King'), as opposed to 'the king' in lower case, which refers to all other monarchs mentioned in the text (e.g. rulers of Sparta).

Introduction

Life of Herodotus

The traditional date for the birth of Herodotus, 484 (Aulus Gellius 15.23), may not be too wide of the mark, though it perhaps rests on no more than two suppositions: firstly, that he was around forty at the time of the foundation of Thurii in 444/3; and secondly, that he was one of the original colonists of the city. His birthplace of Halicarnassus, one of the more cosmopolitan cities of Asia Minor, was in the historian's day an Ionian city, though one with a strong admixture of Dorian and Carian elements. Indeed the existence of Carian names in Herodotus' own family (his father Lyxes and his relative Panyassis) attests to the presence of some Carian blood within it. His family, which was of sufficient importance to play a part in the politics of the city, was also cultured enough to produce in Panyassis a well-known epic poet. The opposition of the family to Lygdamis, the hellenised Carian ruler of the city, resulted in the exile (c.460) of its more prominent members – Herodotus included – to the island of Samos, where the historian acquired most of his information on the Samian tyranny (3.39-59, 121-6, 139-49) and presumably his letter of introduction to Archias, the Samian *proxenos* at Sparta (3.55, cf. Plutarch, *Moralia* 860c). He may subsequently have been reconciled to Lygdamis, only to be sent into exile for a second time (c.450). On this occasion he came to the Greek mainland where he spent some time in Athens, perhaps in the hope of obtaining Athenian citizenship; but if so, his hopes were dashed and he had to be content with citizenship of Thurii, the colony founded by the Athenians in Italy in 444/3. He may have moved there either at the time of its foundation or at a later date.

The date of his death is unknown, though he certainly survived at least into the early years of the Peloponnesian War, as is indicated by passages such as 7.233.2 (the Theban attack on Plataea in 431); 6.91 (the expulsion of the Aeginetans, also in 431); and 7.137.2 (the execution of the Spartan envoys captured by the Athenians on their way to Persia in 430). Parts of his work were already sufficiently famous at Athens to be parodied by Aristophanes: his Preface in *Acharnians* (523 ff.) in 425; his descriptions of the walls of Babylon (1.178.3-179.3) and of the construction of the Great Pyramid at Giza (2.124-7) in *Birds* (1124 ff.) in 414.

At some time in his life Herodotus undertook a wide range of travels in the course of which he amassed much of the information which he reproduces in the *Histories*. Unless, as some schoars maintain (see the section of the bibliography headed *The Liar School*), Herodotus deliberately fed his readers with false information, his text attests visits to Lydia (implied at 1.93), Babylon (implied at 1.181.2), Egypt (2.3, 2.5-13, 2.29, 2.75, 2.91, 2.125, 2.143, 2.148, 2.156, 3.12), Cyrene (2.32.4, 2.181.5), Syria (2.106-10), Tyre (2.44.1), the Black Sea area (2.104.1, 4.24, 4.76.6, 4.81.2, 4.82, 4.86); as well as, in the Greek world, to Samos (3.60.4), Thasos (2.44.4), Delphi (1.51), Thessaly (implied at 7.129), Thebes (5.59), Athens (5.77.3), Tegea (1.66.4), Sparta (3.55.2), Zacynthus (4.195.2), Proconnesus and Cyzicus (4.14), Croton (5.45) and Metapontum (4.15).

The date of his travels cannot be determined, nor is it possible to say whether he undertook only one long sojourn abroad or made several journeys of shorter duration at various times in his life. A visit to Macedonia is implied at 5.17 and doubtfully attested in the Suda, which has an entry to the effect that the logographer Hellanicus spent some time 'at the court of Amyntas along with Herodotus, in the times of Euripides and Sophocles'. There is some confusion in this statement; for, of the three Macedonian kings named Amyntas, the first ruled in the sixth century before Herodotus was born, and the second and third in the fourth, after his death. Scholars who wish to salvage something from this confusion emend the text to read *Alexander* (i.e. Alexander I, king from the 490s until c.454) or *Perdiccas* (i.e. Perdiccas II, who ruled from c.425-13), though *Archelaus*, king from 413-399, who unlike Alexander and Perdiccas **did** have a reputation for inviting intellectuals to his court, and who undoubtedly entertained Euripides amongst others, might be a likelier candidate, if we could be sure that Herodotus survived into the penultimate decade of the century.

The only other recorded events of his life concern the public recitations he gave from his work in progress. Unlike Thucydides, who aimed his history at readers of some intelligence (1.22.4), both Herodotus and the logographers sought to entertain audiences with public recitations from their work, and could hope to earn a fee if their readings met with approval. Traditions survive of recitations given by Herodotus at Corinth (Dio Chrysostom 37.103), Thebes (Plut. *Mor.* 864D), Athens (Plut. *Mor.* 862B = Diyllus, Frag. 3J) and Olympia (Lucian, *Herodotus* 1-2; Suda s.v. Thucydides). In Athens he is said to have received a fee of 10 talents, on a motion proposed by one Anytus, but if the proposer is to be identified with the prosecutor of Socrates, the story is to be rejected on chronological grounds. At Olympia, the young Thucydides was supposedly in the audience and burst into tears under the influence of strong emotion, though whether the emotion in question was one of rapture or disgust is unstated.

Herodotus Book VI

The sixth book of Herodotus' *Histories*, Janus-like, looks both backwards and forwards. The principal topics covered are the Ionian Revolt and the Marathon campaign, which form two episodes in the long conflict between East and West, Asia and Greece which figures so prominently in the Preface to Book 1. The two episodes follow naturally on both from the Persian conquest of Ionia in 545 (1.141-77), of Samos c.517 (3.139-49) and of the north Aegean seaboard c. 513-11 (4.143-4; 5.11-27), and from the antecedents to the Ionian revolt itself narrated in chapters 28-38 and 97-126 of Book 5. At the same time the events covered in Book 6 look forward to Xerxes' invasion of Greece in 480-79, the subject of Books 7-9 – to which the sixth book serves as a prologue. Structurally the book falls into four parts: the Ionian Revolt and its aftermath (1-47); the third instalment of Spartan history (48-84), picking up from 1.65-9 and 5.39-54; the third instalment of Athenian history (85-94, 122-40), resumed from 1.59-64 and 5.55-78; and the expedition of Datis including the Marathon campaign (95-121). In the course of the book Herodotus' narrative ranges over a vast geographical area from Sicily and Magna Graecia in the west (21-24) to Ampe on the Persian Gulf (20) and Ardericca in Susiana (119.2) in the east. Nevertheless his literary skills were such that he was able to smooth over the many transitions that the assemblage of such a huge quantity of heterogeneous material inevitably produced, while seeming to create the appearance of a harmonious and well integrated whole.

As is the case with the work as a whole, Herodotus gathered most of his information for Book 6 in the course of his travels, his main sources being autopsy and hearsay evidence. There was plenty for him to see, and no shortage of individuals for him to meet who were only too willing to respond to the questions he posed in his attempts to arrive at a correct understanding and interpretation of what he had learned from personal observation. His lack of fluency in the Persian tongue (as demonstrated, for example, by the erroneous translations he provides for the meaning of the names of Persian kings in chapter 98) was perhaps less of a handicap in Book 6 than elsewhere, but the accuracy of his information was variable. Unlike Thucydides, who chose to write on contemporary history, Herodotus in his choice of theme was always at the mercy of his informants. Though aware of the superiority of autopsy over word of mouth (see, e.g., 2.99.1), he lacked not only Thucydides' conviction (1.1.3, 20.1, 21.1) that the oral tradition can often be unreliable, but also his awareness (1.22.3) that informants are prone to err as a result of bias or faulty memory.

Though the events of Book 6 took place before Herodotus was born, they were not so remote that he was unable to find surviving participants in the actual events he describes. Yet in Book 6 he is more reticent than usual in naming his sources of information. In chapter 105, the tale of Philippides' meeting with the god Pan is ascribed to the runner in person, but as he died shortly afterwards, Herodotus can only be citing him at second hand. Similarly, though Epizelus himself is quoted for the story of his supernatural encounter at Marathon (chapter 117), the historian makes it clear that he did not hear the tale direct from the horse's mouth. Far too often, he is content to refer to his authorities in vague terms such as 'the Spartans say' (52.1, 53.1, 84.1), 'the Parians say' (134.1), 'the Athenians say' (137.3). The identity of such informants is unclear, and some scholars (the so-called 'liar school', for which see the bibliography p. xiv) accuse him of having fabricated the material himself. If however we are prepared to concede him some degree of honesty, we must assume that he is referring to the oral tradition current in the cities or among the peoples in question.

Beyond this we can only speculate. Much of his information on the Ionian Revolt is likely to have been obtained from his fellow citizens at Halicarnassus and from elsewhere in Ionia and the adjacent islands. In the case of Samos, the favourable treatment accorded to the tyrant Maeandrius (3.142) suggests that Herodotus may have talked with some of his descendants while in exile there in the 450s (see G. Shipley, *A History of Samos 810-188 BC*, Oxford, 1987, pp. 104-5), though the discreditable story of Maeandrius' attempt to bribe Cleomenes of Sparta (3.148) is likely to have emanated from a Spartan source. While at Sparta, the historian certainly met and conversed with Archias son of Samius and probable grandson of the Archias who was killed in the course of the attempt to overthrow Polycrates (3.55.2, cf. Plut. *Moralia*. 860c). This individual may well be one of his authorities for the material on Spartan history in chapters 48-84. The prominence given elsewhere in the *Histories* both to Gorgo, daughter of Cleomenes and widow of Leonidas (5.51.8-9; 7.239), and to the exiled Eurypontid king Demaratus, who fell foul of Cleomenes (6.50 ff.; 7.3, 209, 234-9), may indicate that Herodotus met informants who had moved in elevated Spartan circles. In the case of Demaratus, Herodotus could have met some of the descendants who were living in Asia Minor in his day (see note on 70.2).

For his account of Athenian history, the historian will have relied on information acquired during his residence there, including tales current in the great noble families of the Philaidae (34-40, 109-10), Alcmeonidae (121-123.4) and Ceryces (122, if genuine), while the inclusion of such unflattering material as the demise of Miltiades (133-6) or the greed of Alcmeon (125) shows him no less ready to add information from the hostile traditions of rival clans to the eulogistic tales told by each family about its own members. Such material seems to have been adulterated with elements derived ultimately from folk-tales, which had come in the course of time to be attached to historical individuals. Thus the story of the wooing of Agariste, influenced no doubt by that of the wooing of Helen ([Hesiod], *Eoiae*, Frag.

196-204; Euripides, *Iphigeneia at Aulis* 49-71; Apollodorus 3.10.8; Hyginus, *Fab*. 81) has similarities to folk-tales current in various forms in many different countries. The closest parallel to the Herodotean story is the Indian tale of the Dancing Peacock, narrated in Appendix XIV of R.W. Macan's 1895 edition of the book.

Though there is nothing in Book 6 comparable to the the more obviously Delphic passages of Book 1 (chs 14, 20, 51), Herodotus' citations from oracular pronouncements in Book 6 (chs 19, 34, 52, 77, 86, 135, 139) may owe as much to his familiarity with Delphi and its priesthood as to the oral tradition. Epigraphical material, though frequently mentioned elsewhere in the work, is completely absent from the sixth book. Of his predecessors and contemporaries the logographers, only Hecataeus of Miletus is named (2.143; 5.36 and 125-6), and is cited at 6.137, alongside 'the Athenians themselves' as an authority for the Athenian occupation of Lemnos. No attempt is made to evaluate the alternatives given, thus leaving the readership free, as so often in Herodotus, to determine the truth of the matter by themselves.

Bibliography

Commentaries

Macan, R.W., *Herodotus: The Fourth, Fifth and Sixth Books* (London, 1885; reprinted New York, 1973).

Shuckburgh, E.S., *Herodotus, Book VI* (Cambridge, 1889; reprinted by Bristol Classical Press, 1984).

How, W.W. and Wells, J., *A Commentary on Herodotus*, 2 vols. (Oxford, 1912) – the only complete commentary in English.

English Translations

Four twentieth-century translations are currently in print. These are, in order of publication:

A.D. Godley's translation in the Loeb Classical Library (1921-4) – now somewhat dated.

A. de Selincourt, *Herodotus, The Histories*: originally published by Penguin in 1954 and currently available in a revised edition with new introduction and notes by John Marincola (1996). The translation is eminently readable, though at times somewhat free and therefore less helpful than it could have been to students of the original language.

David Greene, *Herodotus: The History*, published in 1987 by the University of Chicago Press. This translation has a useful introduction and is less readable but more literal than the Penguin.

Robin Waterfield, *Herodotus: The Histories*, published 1998 in the Oxford World's Classics Series. This translation, which has the merit of being both readable and scholarly, comes provided with short appendices on Greek Clothing and on Weights and Measures, as well as with some useful and comparatively detailed explanatory notes compiled by Carolyn Dewald, and glossaries of Greek terms and foreign words occurring in the text.

General books on Herodotus

Benardete, Seth, *Herodotean Enquiries* (The Hague, 1969).

Boedeker, Deborah, ed., *Herodotus and the Invention of History*, Arethusa, vol. 20 (Buffalo, 1970).

Evans, J.A.S., *Herodotus, Explorer of the Past* (Princeton, 1981).

————*Herodotus* (Boston, 1982).

Flory, S., *The Archaic Smile of Herodotus* (Detroit, 1987).

Fornara, C.W., *Herodotus: an Interpretative Essay* (Oxford, 1971).

Gould, John, *Herodotus* (London, 1989; reprinted by Bristol Classical Press, 2000).

Hart, John, *Herodotus and Greek History* (London and New York, 1982).

Hartog, F., *The Mirror of Herodotus; the Representation of the Other in the Writing of History*, translated by Janet Lloyd (Berkeley, Los Angeles and London, 1988).

Hohti, Paavo, *The Interrelation of Speech and Action in the Histories of Herodotus*, Commentationes Humanarum Litterarum 57 (Helsinki, 1976).

Hunter, Virginia, *Past and Process in Herodotus and Thucydides* (Princeton, 1982).

Immerwahr, Henry R., *Form and Thought in Herodotus*, American Philological Association Monograph 23 (Cleveland, 1966).

Lang, Mabel, *Herodotean Narrative and Discourse*, Martin Classical Lectures, vol. 28 (Cambridge Mass. and London, 1984).

Lateiner, D., *The Historical Method of Herodotus* (Toronto, 1989).

Long, Timothy, *Repetition and Variation in the Short Stories of Herodotus*, (Frankfurt, 1987).

Myres, J.L., *Herodotus, Father of History* (Oxford, 1953).

Powell, J.E., *The History of Herodotus* (Cambridge, 1939).

Romm, James, *Herodotus* (New Haven and London, 1998).

Thompson, Norma, *Herodotus and the Origin of the Political Community: Arion's Leap* (New Haven and London, 1996).

Waters, K.H., *Herodotos on Tyrants and Despots: a Study in Objectivity*, Historia, Einzeischrift 15 (Wiesbaden, 1971).

————*Herodotos the Historian: his Problems, Methods and Originality* (London and Sydney, 1985).

Wood, Henry, *The Histories of Herodotus; an Analysis of the Formal Structure* (Paris, 1972).

The Liar School

This name has been given to a group of scholars who have cast doubt on Herodotus' veracity in matters such as his claims to have visited every single place for which he cites personal autopsy, or in connection with citations like 'the Egyptians say' – which these scholars regard as little more than fabrications of the historian himself. The founder and leading light in the 'liar school' is Detlev Fehling, whose book *Herodotus and his 'Sources': Citation, Invention and Narrative Art*, originally published in German in 1971, was reissued in an English translation by J.G.Howie as vol. 21 of Arca, Classical and Medieval Texts, Papers and Monographs (Francis Cairns Publications, 1989).

Also to be placed in the 'Liar School' is O. Kimball Armayor, who has written a series of articles and a book which likewise call into question Herodotus' good faith:

'Did Herodotus Ever Go to the Black Sea?', *HSCP* 82 (1978) pp. 45-68.

'Herodotus' Catalogues of the Persian Empire in the Light of the Monuments and the Greek Literary Tradition', *TAPA* 108 (1978) pp. 1-8.

'Did Herodotus Ever Go to Egypt?', *JARCE* 15 (1980) pp. 59-77.

'Sesostris and Herodotus' Autopsy of Thrace, Colchis, Inland Asia Minor and the Levant', *HSCP* 84 (1980) pp. 51-74.

Herodotus' Autopsy of the Fayoum, Lake Moeris and the Labyrinth of Egypt (Amsterdam, 1985).

Stephanie West's article 'Herodotus' Epigraphic Interests', *CQ*, 35 (1985) pp. 278-305) establishes her place as a third member of this group.

For an attempted refutation of these writers from a primarily archaeological viewpoint, see W.K. Pritchett, *The Liar School of Herodotus* (Amsterdam, 1993). For an alternative approach to refutation which takes account of factors such as time (proximity or remoteness from Herodotus' own day), place (proximity to or distance from the Greek world) and cultural transfer (from a non-Greek to a Greek culture), see G.S. Shrimpton and K.M. Gillis, 'Herodotus' Source Citations', in G.S. Shrimpton, *History and Memory in Ancient Greece* (Montreal & Kingston, London and Buffalo, 1997) Appendix 1, pp. 229-65.

Books On Greek (and Persian) History 500-481

Balcer, J.M., *Sparda by the Bitter Sea: Imperial Interaction in Western Anatolia*, Brown Judaic Studies, 52 (Chico, California, 1984).

——*The Persian Conquest of the Greek States 545-450 BC.* (Konstanz, 1995) chs 7-9.

——*A Prosopographical Study of the Ancient Persians Royal and Noble c. 550-450 BC.* (Lewiston, Queenston and Lampeter, 1993).

Brosius, Maria, *Women in Ancient Persia (559-331 BC.)* (Oxford, 1996).

Burn, A.R., *Persia and the Greeks*, ed. 2, with postscript by D.M. Lewis (London, 1984).

——'Persia and the Greeks', in *The Cambridge History of Iran*, vol. 2 (Cambridge, 1983) ch. 6, pp. 292-331.

Cartledge, Paul, *Sparta and Laconia: a Regional History* (London, 1979) ch. 9.

Cook, J.M., *The Persian Empire* (London, Melbourne and Toronto, 1983) ch. 9.

Dandamev, M.A., *A Political History of the Achaemenid Empire*, translated by W. Vogelsang (Leiden, New York, Copenhagen and Cologne, 1989) chs 17-19.

Figueira, T.J., *Aegina: Society and Politics* (New York, 1981).

——*Excursions in Epichoric History: Aeginetan Essays* (Lanham, Maryland, 1993) chs 2-5.

Forrest, W.G., *A History of Sparta 950-192 BC.*, second edn. (London, 1980; reprinted by Bristol Classical Press, 2000).

Green, Peter, *The Greco-Persian Wars* (Berkeley, Los Angeles and London, 1996) Parts 1 and 2.

Hammond, N.G.L., *Studies in Greek History* (Oxford, 1973) pp. 170-250.

Hignett, C., *Xerxes' Invasion of Greece* (Oxford, 1963) pp. 55-74 (the Marathon Campaign).

Huxley, G.L., *Early Sparta* (London, 1962).

——*The Early Ionians* (London, 1966); the Ionian Revolt is covered in ch. 16.

Jones, A.H.M., *Sparta* (London, 1967); the reign of Cleomenes I is covered in ch. 12.

Kelly, Thomas, *A History of Argos to 500 BC.* (Minneapolis, 1976) ch. 8.

Lazenby, J.F., *The Defence of Greece 490-479 BC.* (Warminster. 1993) ch. 3 (the Marathon campaign).

Lloyd, Alan, *Marathon: The Story of Civilisation on Collision Course* (New York, 1973).

Roebuck, Carl, *Ionian Trade and Colonization* (New York, 1959).

Tomlinson, R.A., *Argos and the Argolid* (London, 1972) especially ch. 8.

Abbreviations

Grammatical

abs.	absolute		*masc.*	masculine gender
acc.	accusative case		*midd.*	middle voice
act.	active voice		*neg.*	negative
adj.	adjective		*neut.*	neuter gender
adv.	adverb		*nom.*	nominative case
aor.	aorist tense		*opt.*	optative mood
art.	article		*part.*	participle
comp.	comparative degree		*pass.*	passive voice
conj.	conjunction		*perf.*	perfect tense
dat.	dative case		*pers.*	personal
def.	definite		*plup.*	pluperfect tense
dem.	demonstrative		*plur.*	plural number
fem.	feminine gender		*prep.*	preposition
fut.	future tense		*pres.*	present tense
gen.	genitive case		*pron.*	pronoun
imp.	imperative mood		*rel.*	relative
imperf.	imperfect tense		*sing.*	singular number
impers.	impersonal		*subj.*	subjunctive mood
ind.	indicative mood		*superl.*	superlative degree
indef.	indefinite		*trans.*	transitive
indic.	indicative mood		*verb.*	verbal
inf.	infinitive		*voc.*	vocative case
intrans.	intransitive			

Bibliographical

Burn *PG*   A.R. Burn, *Persia and the Greeks*, ed. 2 with postcript by D.M. Lewis (London, 1984).

Davies *APF*   J.K. Davies, *Athenian Propertied Families 680-300 B.C.* (Oxford 1971).

Denniston *GP*   J.D. Denniston, *Greek Particles*, ed. 2 (Oxford 1954; Rpr. Bristol Classical Press, 1996).

Develin *AO*   Robert Develin, *Athenian Officials 684-321 B.C.* (Cambridge, 1989).

Fontenrose *DO*   J. Fontenrose, *The Delphic Oracle: its Responses and Operations* (Berkeley, Los Angeles and London, 1978).

Goodwin   W.W. Goodwin, *Greek Grammar* (Bristol Classical Press, 1998).

How and Wells   W.W. How and J. Wells, *A Commentary on Herodotus* (Oxford, 1912).

ML   R. Meiggs and D.M. Lewis, *A Selection of Greek Historical Inscriptions*, ed. 2 (Oxford, 1988).

OCT   K. Hude (ed.), *Herodoti Historiae*, in the Oxford Classical Texts series (Oxford, 1927).

PW   H.W. Parke and D.E.W. Wormell, *The Delphic Oracle* Vol. 1 *The History*. Vol. 2, *The Oracular Responses* (Blackwell, Oxford, 1956).

Poralla, *PL*   P. Poralla and A.S. Bradford, *A Prosopography of Lacedaemonians from the Earliest Times to the Death of Alexander the Great*, ed. 2 (Chicago, 1985).

Tod *GHI*   M.N. Tod, *A Selection of Greek Historical Inscriptions*, Vol. 2 (Oxford, 1948).

ΗΡΟΔΟΤΟΥ ΕΡΑΤΩ.

BOOK VI.

Histiaios comes from Susa to Sardis. Artaphernes hints that he knows the origin of the Ionian revolt.

I. Ἀρισταγόρης μέν νυν Ἰωνίην ἀποστήσας 1
οὕτω τελευτᾷ. Ἱστιαῖος δὲ ὁ Μιλήτου τύραννος
μεμετιμένος ὑπὸ Δαρείου παρῆν ἐς Σάρδις. ἀπιγ-
μένον δὲ αὐτὸν ἐκ τῶν Σούσων εἴρετο Ἀρταφέρνης
ὁ Σαρδίων ὕπαρχος, κατὰ κοῖόν τι δοκέοι Ἴωνας
ἀπεστάναι· ὁ δὲ οὔτε εἰδέναι ἔφη, ἐθώυμαζέ τε τὸ
γεγονὸς ὡς οὐδὲν δῆθεν τῶν παρεόντων πρηγμάτων
ἐπιστάμενος. ὁ δὲ Ἀρταφέρνης ὁρέων αὐτὸν τεχνά- 2
ζοντα εἶπε, εἰδὼς τὴν ἀτρεκείην τῆς ἀποστάσιος·
"Οὕτω τοι, Ἱστιαῖε, ἔχει κατὰ ταῦτα τὰ πρήγματα·
"τοῦτο τὸ ὑπόδημα ἔρραψας μὲν σύ, ὑπεδήσατο δὲ
"Ἀρισταγόρης."

Histiaios therefore flies to Chios, forfeiting his promise of conquering Sardinia.

II. Ἀρταφέρνης μὲν ταῦτα ἐς τὴν ἀπόστασιν 1
ἔχοντα εἶπε. Ἱστιαῖος δὲ δείσας ὡς συνιέντα Ἀρταφέρνεα ὑπὸ τὴν πρώτην ἐπελθοῦσαν νύκτα ἀπέδρη
ἐπὶ θάλασσαν, βασιλέα Δαρεῖον ἐξηπατηκώς· ὃς

Σαρδὼ νῆσον τὴν μεγίστην ὑποδεξάμενος κατεργάσεσθαι ὑπέδυνε τῶν Ἰώνων τὴν ἡγεμονίην τοῦ πρὸς
Δαρεῖον πολέμου. διαβὰς δὲ ἐς Χίον ἐδέθη ὑπὸ   2
Χίων, καταγνωσθεὶς πρὸς αὐτῶν νεώτερα πρήσσειν
πρήγματα ἐς ἑωυτοὺς ἐκ Δαρείου. μαθόντες μέντοι
οἱ Χῖοι τὸν πάντα λόγον, ὡς πολέμιος εἴη βασιλέι,
ἔλυσαν αὐτόν.

*He falsely reports a scheme of the king's to transfer the
Ionians to Phoenikia.*

III. Ἐνθαῦτα δὴ εἰρωτεόμενος ὑπὸ τῶν Ἰώνων
ὁ Ἱστιαῖος, κατ᾽ ὅ τι προθύμως οὕτω ἐπέστειλε τῷ
Ἀρισταγόρῃ ἀπίστασθαι ἀπὸ βασιλέος καὶ κακὸν
τοσοῦτο εἴη Ἴωνας ἐξεργασμένος, τὴν μὲν γενομένην
αὐτοῖσι αἰτίην οὐ μάλα ἐξέφαινε, ὁ δὲ ἔλεγέ σφι, ὡς
βασιλεὺς Δαρεῖος ἐβουλεύσατο Φοίνικας μὲν ἐξαναστήσας ἐν τῇ Ἰωνίῃ κατοικίσαι, Ἴωνας δὲ ἐν τῇ
Φοινίκῃ, καὶ τούτων εἵνεκεν ἐπιστείλειε. οὐδέν τι
πάντως ταῦτα βασιλέος βουλευσαμένου ἐδειμάτου
τοὺς Ἴωνας.

A plot discovered in Sardis.

IV. Μετὰ δὲ ὁ Ἱστιαῖος δι᾽ ἀγγέλου ποιεύμενος   1
Ἑρμίππου ἀνδρὸς Ἀταρνείτεω τοῖσι ἐν Σάρδισι
ἐοῦσι Περσέων ἔπεμπε βιβλία ὡς προλελεσχηνευμένων αὐτῷ ἀποστάσιος πέρι. ὁ δὲ Ἕρμιππος, πρὸς
τοὺς μὲν ἀπεπέμφθη, οὐ διδοῖ, φέρων δὲ ἐνεχείρισε
τὰ βιβλία Ἀρταφέρνεῖ. ὁ δὲ μαθὼν ἅπαν τὸ γινό-   2
μενον ἐκέλευε τὸν Ἕρμιππον τὰ μὲν παρὰ τοῦ
Ἱστιαίου δοῦναι φέροντα τοῖσί περ ἔφερε, τὰ δὲ
ἀμοιβαῖα τὰ παρὰ τῶν Περσέων ἀντιπεμπόμενα

Ἱστιαίῳ ἑωυτῷ δοῦναι. τούτων δὲ γενομένων φανε-
ρῶν ἀπέκτεινε ἐνθαῦτα πολλοὺς Περσέων ὁ Ἀρταφέρνης.

*Histiaios after vainly trying to recover Miletos goes to
Byzantium.*

V. Περὶ Σάρδις μὲν δὴ ἐγένετο ταραχή. Ἱστιαῖον   1
δὲ ταύτης ἀποσφαλέντα τῆς ἐλπίδος Χῖοι κατῆγον ἐς
Μίλητον αὐτοῦ Ἱστιαίου δεηθέντος. οἱ δὲ Μιλήσιοι,
ἄσμενοι ἀπαλλαχθέντες καὶ Ἀρισταγόρεω, οὐδαμῶς
πρόθυμοι ἦσαν ἄλλον τύραννον δέκεσθαι ἐς τὴν
χώρην, οἷα ἐλευθερίης γευσάμενοι. καὶ δὴ, νυκτὸς   2
γὰρ ἐούσης βίη ἐπειρᾶτο κατιὼν ὁ Ἱστιαῖος ἐς τὴν
Μίλητον, τιτρώσκεται τὸν μηρὸν ὑπό τευ τῶν Μιλησίων. ὁ μὲν δὴ ὡς ἀπωστὸς τῆς ἑωυτοῦ γίνεται,
ἀπικνέεται ὀπίσω ἐς τὴν Χίον· ἐνθεῦτεν δὲ, οὐ γὰρ
ἔπειθε τοὺς Χίους ὥστε ἑωυτῷ δοῦναι νέας, διέβη ἐς
Μυτιλήνην καὶ ἔπεισε Λεσβίους δοῦναί οἱ νέας. οἱ   3
δὲ πληρώσαντες ὀκτὼ τριήρεας ἔπλωον ἅμα Ἱστιαίῳ
ἐς Βυζάντιον, ἐνθαῦτα δὲ ἱζόμενοι τὰς ἐκ τοῦ Πόντου
ἐκπλωούσας τῶν νεῶν ἐλάμβανον, πλὴν ἢ ὅσοι αὐτῶν
Ἱστιαίῳ ἔφασαν ἑτοῖμοι εἶναι πείθεσθαι.

B.C. 495.   *The Persians prepare to attack Miletos.*

VI. Ἱστιαῖος μέν νυν καὶ Μυτιληναῖοι ἐποίευν
ταῦτα, ἐπὶ δὲ Μίλητον αὐτὴν ναυτικὸς πολλὸς καὶ
πεζὸς ἦν στρατὸς προσδόκιμος· συστραφέντες γὰρ
οἱ στρατηγοὶ τῶν Περσέων καὶ ἐν ποιήσαντες στρατόπεδον ἤλαυνον ἐπὶ τὴν Μίλητον, τὰ ἄλλα πολίσ-
ματα περὶ ἐλάσσονος ποιησάμενοι. τοῦ δὲ ναυτικοῦ
Φοίνικες μὲν ἦσαν προθυμότατοι, συνεστρατεύοντο

δὲ καὶ Κύπριοι νεωστὶ κατεστραμμένοι καὶ Κίλικές
τε καὶ Αἰγύπτιοι.

*The Ionians in council decide not to resist by land, but to
prepare a large fleet.*

VII. Οἱ μὲν δὴ ἐπὶ τὴν Μίλητον καὶ τὴν ἄλλην
Ἰωνίην ἐστράτευον, Ἴωνες δὲ πυνθανόμενοι ταῦτα
ἔπεμπον προβούλους σφέων αὐτῶν ἐς Πανιώνιον.
ἀπικομένοισι δὲ τούτοισι ἐς τοῦτον τὸν χῶρον καὶ
βουλευομένοισι ἔδοξε πεζὸν μὲν στρατὸν μὴ συλλέ-
γειν ἀντίξοον Πέρσῃσι, ἀλλὰ τὰ τείχεα ῥύεσθαι
αὐτοὺς Μιλησίους, τὸ δὲ ναυτικὸν πληροῦν ὑπολει-
πομένους μηδεμίαν τῶν νεῶν, πληρώσαντας δὲ συλλέ-
γεσθαι τὴν ταχίστην ἐς Λάδην, προναυμαχήσοντας
Μιλήτου· ἡ δὲ Λάδη ἐστὶ νῆσος σμικρὴ ἐπὶ τῇ πόλι
τῇ Μιλησίων κειμένη.

The Ionian forces.

VIII. Μετὰ δὲ ταῦτα πεπληρωμένῃσι τῇσι νηυσὶ 1
παρῆσαν οἱ Ἴωνες, σὺν δέ σφι καὶ Αἰολέων οἳ Λέσβον
νέμονται· ἐτάσσοντο δὲ ὧδε· τὸ μὲν πρὸς τὴν ἠῶ
εἶχον κέρας αὐτοὶ Μιλήσιοι, νέας παρεχόμενοι ὀγδώκοντα, εἴχοντο δὲ τούτων Πριηνέες δυώδεκα νηυσὶ
καὶ Μυούσιοι τρισὶ νηυσί, Μυουσίων δὲ Τήιοι εἴχοντο
ἑπτακαίδεκα νηυσί, Τηίων δὲ εἴχοντο Χῖοι ἑκατὸν
νηυσί· πρὸς δὲ τούτοισι Ἐρυθραῖοί τε ἐτάσσοντο καὶ 2
Φωκαιέες, Ἐρυθραῖοι μὲν ὀκτὼ νέας παρεχόμενοι,
Φωκαιέες δὲ τρεῖς· Φωκαιέων δὲ εἴχοντο Λέσβιοι
νηυσὶ ἑβδομήκοντα· τελευταῖοι δὲ ἐτάσσοντο ἔχοντες
τὸ πρὸς ἑσπέρην κέρας Σάμιοι ἑξήκοντα νηυσί. πάντων δὲ τούτων ὁ σύμπας ἀριθμὸς ἐγένετο τρεῖς καὶ
πεντήκοντα καὶ τριηκόσιαι τριήρεες.

*The expelled Ionian tyrants urged to detach their several
countrymen from the insurgents.*

IX. Αὗται μὲν Ἰώνων ἦσαν· τῶν δὲ βαρβάρων 1
τὸ πλῆθος τῶν νεῶν ἦσαν ἑξακόσιαι. ὡς δὲ καὶ αὗται
ἀπίκατο πρὸς τὴν Μιλησίην καὶ ὁ πεζός σφι ἅπας
παρῆν, ἐνθαῦτα οἱ Περσέων στρατηγοὶ πυθόμενοι τὸ
πλῆθος τῶν Ἰάδων νεῶν καταρρώδησαν, μὴ οὐ δυνατοὶ
γένωνται ὑπερβαλέσθαι, καὶ οὕτω οὔτε τὴν Μίλητον
οἷοί τε ἔωσι ἐξελεῖν μὴ οὐκ ἐόντες ναυκράτορες, πρός
τε Δαρείου κινδυνεύσωσι κακόν τι λαβεῖν. ταῦτα 2
ἐπιλεγόμενοι, συλλέξαντες τῶν Ἰώνων τοὺς τυράννους, οἳ ὑπ᾽ Ἀρισταγόρεω μὲν τοῦ Μιλησίου καταλυ-
θέντες τῶν ἀρχέων ἔφευγον ἐς Μήδους, ἐτύγχανον δὲ
τότε συστρατευόμενοι ἐπὶ τὴν Μίλητον,—τούτων τῶν
ἀνδρῶν τοὺς παρεόντας συγκαλέσαντες ἔλεγόν σφι
τάδε· "Ἄνδρες Ἴωνες, νῦν τις ὑμέων εὖ ποιήσας 3
"φανήτω τὸν βασιλέος οἶκον· τοὺς γὰρ ἑωυτοῦ ἕκαστος
"ὑμέων πολιήτας πειράσθω ἀποσχίζων ἀπὸ τοῦ λοιποῦ
"συμμαχικοῦ. προϊσχόμενοι δὲ ἐπαγγείλασθε τάδε,
"ὡς πείσονταί τε ἄχαρι οὐδὲν διὰ τὴν ἀπόστασιν, οὐδέ
"σφι οὔτε τὰ ἱρὰ οὔτε τὰ ἴδια ἐμπεπρήσεται, οὐδὲ
"βιαιότερον ἕξουσι οὐδὲν, ἢ πρότερον εἶχον· εἰ δὲ 4
"ταῦτα μὲν οὐ ποιήσουσι, οἱ δὲ πάντως διὰ μάχης
"ἐλεύσονται, τάδε σφι λέγετε ἐπηρεάζοντες, τά πέρ
"σφεας κατέξει, ὡς ἐσσωθέντες τῇ μάχῃ ἐξανδρα-
"ποδιεῦνται, καὶ ὥς σφεων τοὺς παῖδας ἐκτομίας
"ποιήσομεν, τὰς δὲ παρθένους ἀνασπάστους ἐς Βάκ-
"τρα, καὶ ὡς τὴν χώρην ἄλλοισι παραδώσομεν."

They fail to do so.

X. Οἱ μὲν δὴ ἔλεγον ταῦτα, τῶν δὲ Ἰώνων οἱ

τύραννοι διέπεμπον νυκτὸς ἕκαστος ἐς τοὺς ἑωυτοῦ
ἐξαγγελλόμενος. οἱ δὲ Ἴωνες, ἐς τοὺς καὶ ἀπίκοντο
αὗται αἱ ἀγγελίαι, ἀγνωμοσύνῃ τε διεχρέοντο καὶ οὐ
προσίεντο τὴν προδοσίην, ἑωυτοῖσί τε ἕκαστοι ἐδόκεον
μούνοισι ταῦτα τοὺς Πέρσας ἐξαγγέλλεσθαι. ταῦτα
μὲν νῦν ἰθέως ἀπικομένων ἐς τὴν Μίλητον τῶν
Περσέων ἐγίνετο.

Dionysios of Phokaia put in command of the Ionian fleet.

XI. Μετὰ δὲ τῶν Ἰώνων συλλεχθέντων ἐς τὴν   1
Λάδην ἐγίνοντο ἀγοραί. καὶ δή κού σφι καὶ ἄλλοι
ἠγορεύοντο, ἐν δὲ δὴ καὶ ὁ Φωκαιεὺς στρατηγὸς
Διονύσιος λέγων τάδε· "Ἐπὶ ξυροῦ γὰρ ἀκμῆς ἔχεται   2
" ἡμῖν τὰ πρήγματα, ἄνδρες Ἴωνες, ἢ εἶναι ἐλευθέροισι
" ἢ δούλοισι, καὶ τούτοισι ὡς δρηπέτῃσι· νῦν ὦν ὑμεῖς,
" ἢν μὲν βούλησθε ταλαιπωρίας ἐνδέκεσθαι, τὸ παρα-
" χρῆμα μὲν πόνος ὑμῖν ἔσται, οἷοί τε δὲ ἔσεσθε ὑπερ-
" βαλόμενοι τοὺς ἐναντίους εἶναι ἐλεύθεροι· εἰ δὲ
" μαλακίῃ τε καὶ ἀταξίῃ διαχρήσεσθε, οὐδεμίαν ὑμέων
" ἔχω ἐλπίδα μὴ οὐ δώσειν ὑμέας δίκην βασιλέι τῆς
" ἀποστάσιος. ἀλλ' ἐμοί τε πείθεσθε καὶ ἐμοὶ ὑμέας   3
" αὐτοὺς ἐπιτρέψατε· καὶ ὑμῖν ἐγὼ θεῶν τὰ ἴσα νεμόν-
" των ὑποδέκομαι ἢ οὐ συμμίξειν τοὺς πολεμίους ἢ
" συμμίσγοντας πολλὸν ἐλασσωθήσεσθαι." Ταῦτα
ἀκούσαντες οἱ Ἴωνες ἐπιτράπουσι σφέας αὐτοὺς τῷ
Διονυσίῳ.

Discontent at the severity of the discipline of Dionysios.

XII. Ὁ δὲ ἀνάγων ἑκάστοτε ἐπὶ κέρας τὰς νέας,   1
ὅκως τοῖσι ἐρέτῃσι χρήσαιτο διέκπλοον ποιεύμενος
τῇσι νηυσὶ δι' ἀλληλέων καὶ τοὺς ἐπιβάτας ὁπλίσειε,
τὸ λοιπὸν τῆς ἡμέρης τὰς νέας ἔχεσκε ἐπ' ἀγκυρέων,

παρεῖχέ τε τοῖσι Ἴωσι πόνον δι' ἡμέρης. μέχρι μέν 2
νυν ἡμερέων ἑπτὰ ἐπείθοντό τε καὶ ἐποίευν τὸ κελευό-
μενον, τῇ δὲ ἐπὶ ταύτῃσι οἱ Ἴωνες, οἷα ἀπαθέες ἐόντες
πόνων τοιούτων τετρυμένοι τε ταλαιπωρίῃσί τε καὶ
ἡλίῳ, ἔλεξαν πρὸς ἑωυτοὺς τάδε· "Τίνα δαιμόνων 3
"παραβάντες τάδε ἀναπίμπλαμεν; οἵτινες παρα-
"φρονήσαντες καὶ ἐκπλώσαντες ἐκ τοῦ νόου ἀνδρὶ
"Φωκαιέϊ ἀλαζόνι, παρεχομένῳ νέας τρεῖς, ἐπιτρέψ-
"αντες ἡμέας αὐτοὺς ἔχομεν· ὁ δὲ παραλαβὼν ἡμέας
"λυμαίνεται λύμῃσι ἀνηκέστοισι, καὶ δὴ πολλοὶ μὲν
"ἡμέων ἐς νούσους πεπτώκασι, πολλοὶ δὲ ἐπίδοξοι
"τὠυτὸ τοῦτο πείσεσθαί εἰσι· πρό τε τούτων τῶν
"κακῶν ἡμῖν γε κρέσσον καὶ ὁτιῶν ἄλλο παθεῖν ἐστι,
"καὶ τὴν μέλλουσαν δουληΐην ὑπομεῖναι, ἥ τις ἔσται,
"μᾶλλον ἢ τῇ παρεούσῃ συνέχεσθαι. φέρετε, τοῦ
"λοιποῦ μὴ πειθώμεθα αὐτοῦ." Ταῦτα ἔλεξαν, καὶ 4
μετὰ ταῦτα αὐτίκα πείθεσθαι οὐδεὶς ἤθελε, ἀλλ' οἷα
στρατιὴ, σκηνάς τε πηξάμενοι ἐν τῇ νήσῳ ἐσκιητροφέοντο καὶ ἐσβαίνειν οὐκ ἐθέλεσκον ἐς τὰς νέας οὐδ'
ἀναπειρᾶσθαι.

The Samians accept the Persian terms.

XIII. Μαθόντες δὲ ταῦτα τὰ γινόμενα ἐκ τῶν 1
Ἰώνων οἱ στρατηγοὶ τῶν Σαμίων, ἐνθαῦτα δὴ παρ'
Αἰάκεος τοῦ Συλοσῶντος ἐκείνους τοὺς πρότερον ἔπεμπε λόγους ὁ Αἰάκης κελευόντων τῶν Περσέων, δεόμενός
σφεων ἐκλιπεῖν τὴν Ἰώνων συμμαχίην, οἱ Σάμιοι ὦν
ὁρέοντες ἅμα μὲν ἐοῦσαν ἀταξίην πολλὴν ἐκ τῶν Ἰώνων
ἐδέκοντο τοὺς λόγους, ἅμα δὲ κατεφαίνετό σφι εἶναι
ἀδύνατα τὰ βασιλέος πρήγματα ὑπερβαλέσθαι, εὖ
τε ἐπιστάμενοι, ὡς, εἰ καὶ τὸ παρεὸν ναυτικὸν ὑπερβα-

λοίατο τοῦ Δαρείου, ἄλλο σφι παρέσται πενταπλήσιον. προφάσιος ὢν ἐπιλαβόμενοι, ἐπεί τε τάχιστα 2
εἶδον τοὺς Ἴωνας οὐ βουλομένους εἶναι χρηστούς, ἐν
κέρδεϊ ἐποιεῦντο περιποιῆσαι τά τε ἱρὰ τὰ σφέτερα καὶ
τὰ ἴδια. ὁ δὲ Αἰάκης, παρ᾽ ὅτευ τοὺς λόγους ἐδέκοντο
οἱ Σάμιοι, παῖς μὲν ἦν Συλοσῶντος τοῦ Αἰάκεος,
τύραννος δὲ ἐὼν Σάμου ὑπὸ τοῦ Μιλησίου Ἀρισταγόρεω ἀπεστέρητο τὴν ἀρχὴν κατά περ οἱ ἄλλοι τῆς
Ἰωνίης τύραννοι.

Battle of Lade B.C. 495.

XIV. Τότε ὦν ἐπεὶ ἐπέπλωον οἱ Φοίνικες, οἱ 1
Ἴωνες ἀντανῆγον καὶ αὐτοὶ τὰς νέας ἐπὶ κέρας. ὡς
δὲ καὶ ἀγχοῦ ἐγένοντο καὶ συνέμισγον ἀλλήλοισι, τὸ
ἐνθεῦτεν οὐκ ἔχω ἀτρεκέως συγγράψαι, οἵ τινες τῶν
Ἰώνων ἐγένοντο ἄνδρες κακοὶ ἢ ἀγαθοὶ ἐν τῇ ναυμαχίῃ
ταύτῃ· ἀλλήλους γὰρ καταιτιῶνται. λέγονται δὲ 2
Σάμιοι ἐνθαῦτα κατὰ τὰ συγκείμενα πρὸς τὸν Αἰάκεα
ἀειράμενοι τὰ ἱστία ἀποπλῶσαι ἐκ τῆς τάξιος ἐς τὴν
Σάμον, πλὴν ἕνδεκα νεῶν. τούτων δὲ οἱ τριήραρχοι
παρέμενον καὶ ἐναυμάχεον ἀνηκουστήσαντες τοῖσι
στρατηγοῖσι· καί σφι τὸ κοινὸν τῶν Σαμίων ἔδωκε 3
διὰ τοῦτο τὸ πρῆγμα ἐν στήλῃ ἀναγραφῆναι πατρόθεν
ὡς ἀνδράσι ἀγαθοῖσι γενομένοισι, καὶ ἔστι αὕτη ἡ
στήλη ἐν τῇ ἀγορῇ. ἰδόμενοι δὲ καὶ Λέσβιοι τοὺς
προσεχέας φεύγοντας τὠυτὸ ἐποίευν τοῖσι Σαμίοισι·
ὡς δὲ καὶ οἱ πλεῦνες τῶν Ἰώνων ἐποίευν τὰ αὐτὰ
ταῦτα. XV. Τῶν δὲ παραμεινάντων ἐν τῇ ναυμαχίῃ 1
περιέφθησαν τρηχύτατα Χῖοι ὡς ἀποδεικνύμενοί τε
ἔργα λαμπρὰ καὶ οὐκ ἐθελοκακέοντες· παρείχοντο μὲν
γάρ, ὥσπερ καὶ πρότερον εἰρέθη, νέας ἑκατὸν καὶ ἐπ᾽

ἑκάστης αὐτέων ἄνδρας τεσσεράκοντα τῶν ἀστῶν
λογάδας ἐπιβατεύοντας· ὁρέοντες δὲ τοὺς πολλοὺς τῶν
συμμάχων προδιδόντας οὐκ ἐδικαίευν γενέσθαι τοῖσι
κακοῖσι αὐτῶν ὁμοῖοι, ἀλλὰ μετ᾽ ὀλίγων συμμάχων
μεμουνωμένοι διεκπλώοντες ἐναυμάχεον, ἐς ὃ τῶν πολεμίων ἑλόντες νέας συχνὰς ἀπέβαλον τῶν σφετέρων
νεῶν τὰς πλεῦνας. XVI. Χῖοι μὲν δὴ τῆσι λοιπῆσι
τῶν νεῶν ἀποφεύγουσι ἐς τὴν ἑωυτῶν· ὅσοισι δὲ τῶν
Χίων ἀδύνατοι ἦσαν αἱ νέες ὑπὸ τρωμάτων, οὗτοι δὲ
ὡς ἐδιώκοντο, καταφυγγάνουσι πρὸς τὴν Μυκάλην.
νέας μὲν δὴ αὐτοῦ ταύτῃ ἐποκείλαντες κατέλιπον, οἱ
δὲ πεζῇ ἐκομίζοντο διὰ τῆς ἠπείρου. ἐπεὶ δὲ ἐσέβαλον
ἐς τὴν Ἐφεσίην κομιζόμενοι οἱ Χῖοι, νυκτός τε ἀπίκατο
ἐς αὐτὴν καὶ ἐόντων τῆσι γυναιξὶ αὐτόθι θεσμοφορίων·
ἐνθαῦτα δὴ οἱ Ἐφέσιοι, οὔτε προακηκοότες ὡς εἶχε περὶ
τῶν Χίων, ἰδόντες τε στρατὸν ἐς τὴν χώρην ἐσβεβλη-
κότα, πάγχυ σφέας καταδόξαντες εἶναι κλῶπας καὶ
ἰέναι ἐπὶ τὰς γυναῖκας, ἐξεβοήθεον πανδημεὶ καὶ ἔκτεινον τοὺς Χίους. XVII. Οὗτοι μέν νυν τοιαύτῃσι
περιέπιπτον τύχῃσι· Διονύσιος δὲ ὁ Φωκαιεὺς ἐπείτε
ἔμαθε τῶν Ἰώνων τὰ πρήγματα διεφθαρμένα, νέας
ἑλὼν τρεῖς τῶν πολεμίων ἀπέπλωε ἐς μὲν Φώκαιαν
οὐκέτι, εὖ εἰδὼς ὡς ἀνδραποδιεῖται σὺν τῇ ἄλλῃ
Ἰωνίῃ, ὁ δὲ ἰθέως ὡς εἶχε ἔπλωε ἐς Φοινίκην, γαύλους
δὲ ἐνθαῦτα καταδύσας καὶ χρήματα λαβὼν πολλὰ
ἔπλωε ἐς Σικελίην, ὁρμεόμενος δὲ ἐνθεῦτεν ληιστὴς
κατεστήκεε Ἑλλήνων μὲν οὐδενός, Καρχηδονίων δὲ
καὶ Τυρσηνῶν.

Fall of Miletos.

XVIII. Οἱ δὲ Πέρσαι ἐπείτε τῇ ναυμαχίῃ
ἐνίκων τοὺς Ἴωνας, τὴν Μίλητον πολιορκέοντες ἐκ.

γῆς καὶ θαλάσσης καὶ ὑπορύσσοντες τὰ τείχεα καὶ
παντοίας μηχανὰς προσφέροντες αἱρέουσι κατ' ἄκρης
ἕκτῳ ἔτεϊ ἀπὸ τῆς ἀποστάσιος τῆς Ἀρισταγόρεω, καὶ
ἠνδραποδίσαντο τὴν πόλιν ὥστε συμπεσεῖν τὸ πάθος
τῷ χρηστηρίῳ τῷ ἐς Μίλητον γενομένῳ.

An oracle fulfilled by the destruction of the Milesians.

XIX. Χρεομένοισι γὰρ Ἀργείοισι ἐν Δελφοῖσι   1
περὶ σωτηρίης τῆς πόλιος τῆς σφετέρης ἐχρήσθη
ἐπίκοινον χρηστήριον, τὸ μὲν ἐς αὐτοὺς τοὺς Ἀργείους
φέρον, τὴν δὲ παρενθήκην ἔχρησε ἐς Μιλησίους. τὸ   2
μέν νυν ἐς αὐτοὺς Ἀργείους ἔχον, ἐπεὰν κατὰ τοῦτο
γένωμαι τοῦ λόγου, τότε μνησθήσομαι, τὰ δὲ τοῖσι
Μιλησίοισι οὐ παρεοῦσι ἔχρησε, ἔχει ὧδε·

Καὶ τότε δή, Μίλητε, κακῶν ἐπιμήχανε ἔργων,
πολλοῖσιν δεῖπνόν τε καὶ ἀγλαὰ δῶρα γενήσῃ,
σαὶ δ' ἄλοχοι πολλοῖσι πόδας νίψουσι κομήταις,
νηοῦ δ' ἡμετέρου Διδύμοις ἄλλοισι μελήσει.

τότε δὴ ταῦτα τοὺς Μιλησίους κατελάμβανε, ὅτε γε   3
ἄνδρες μὲν οἱ πλεῦνες ἐκτείνοντο ὑπὸ τῶν Περσέων
ἐόντων κομητέων, γυναῖκες δὲ καὶ τέκνα ἐν ἀνδραπόδων
λόγῳ ἐγίνοντο, ἱρὸν δὲ τὸ ἐν Διδύμοισι, ὁ νηός τε καὶ
τὸ χρηστήριον, συληθέντα ἐνεπίμπρατο. τῶν δ' ἐν
τῷ ἱρῷ τούτῳ χρημάτων πολλάκις μνήμην ἑτέρωθι
τοῦ λόγου ἐποιησάμην.

Merciful treatment of the survivors.

XX. Ἐνθεῦτεν οἱ ζωγρηθέντες τῶν Μιλησίων
ἤγοντο ἐς Σοῦσα. βασιλεὺς δέ σφεας Δαρεῖος κακὸν
οὐδὲν ἄλλο ποιήσας κατοίκισε ἐπὶ τῇ Ἐρυθρῇ καλεομένῃ θαλάσσῃ, ἐν Ἄμπῃ πόλι, παρ' ἣν Τίγρης ποτα-
μὸς παρρρέων ἐς θάλασσαν ἐξίει. τῆς δὲ Μιλησίης

χώρης αὐτοὶ μὲν οἱ Πέρσαι εἶχον τὰ περὶ τὴν πόλιν καὶ τὸ πεδίον, τὰ δὲ ὑπεράκρια ἔδοσαν Καρσὶ Πηδασεῦσι ἐκτῆσθαι.

Grief at Athens shewn by the fining of Phrynichos.

XXI. Παθοῦσι δὲ ταῦτα Μιλησίοισι πρὸς Περ- 1
σέων οὐκ ἀπέδοσαν τὴν ὁμοίην Συβαρῖται, οἳ Λᾶον τε καὶ Σκίδρον οἴκεον τῆς πόλιος ἀπεστερημένοι. Συβάριος γὰρ ἁλούσης ὑπὸ Κροτωνιητέων Μιλήσιοι πάντες ἡβηδὸν ἀπεκείραντο τὰς κεφαλὰς καὶ πένθος μέγα προσεθήκαντο· πόλιες γὰρ αὗται μάλιστα δὴ τῶν ἡμεῖς ἴδμεν ἀλλήλῃσι ἐξεινώθησαν. οὐδὲν ὁμοίως 2
καὶ Ἀθηναῖοι· Ἀθηναῖοι μὲν γὰρ δῆλον ἐποίησαν ὑπεραχθεσθέντες τῇ Μιλήτου ἁλώσι τῇ τε ἄλλῃ πολλαχῇ, καὶ δὴ καὶ ποιήσαντι Φρυνίχῳ δρᾶμα Μιλήτου ἅλωσιν καὶ διδάξαντι ἐς δάκρυά τε ἔπεσε τὸ θέητρον, καὶ ἐζημίωσάν μιν ὡς ἀναμνήσαντα οἰκήια κακὰ χιλίῃσι δραχμῇσι, καὶ ἐπέταξαν μηκέτι μηδένα χρᾶσθαι τούτῳ τῷ δράματι.

The richer Samians, disapproving of the action of their leaders, abandon their country and sail to Sicily, and seize the town of Zankle.

XXII. Μίλητος μέν νυν Μιλησίων ἠρήμωτο, 1
Σαμίων δὲ τοῖσί τι ἔχουσι τὸ μὲν ἐς τοὺς Μήδους ἐκ τῶν στρατηγῶν τῶν σφετέρων ποιηθὲν οὐδαμῶς ἤρεσκε, ἐδόκεε δὲ μετὰ τὴν ναυμαχίην αὐτίκα βουλευομένοισι, πρὶν ἤ σφι ἐς τὴν χώρην ἀπικέσθαι τὸν τύραννον Αἰάκεα, ἐς ἀποικίην ἐκπλώειν μηδὲ μένοντας Μήδοισί τε καὶ Αἰάκεϊ δουλεύειν. Ζαγκλαῖοι γὰρ οἱ 2
ἀπὸ Σικελίης τὸν αὐτὸν χρόνον τοῦτον πέμποντες ἐς τὴν Ἰωνίην ἀγγέλους ἐπεκαλέοντο τοὺς Ἴωνας ἐς

Καλὴν ἀκτὴν, βουλόμενοι αὐτόθι πόλιν κτίσαι Ἰώνων·
ἡ δὲ Καλὴ αὕτη ἀκτὴ καλεομένη ἐστὶ μὲν Σικελῶν,
πρὸς δὲ Τυρσηνίην τετραμμένη τῆς Σικελίης· τούτων
ὦν ἐπικαλεομένων οἱ Σάμιοι μοῦνοι Ἰώνων ἐστάλησαν, σὺν δέ σφι Μιλησίων οἱ ἐκπεφευγότες. XXIII.
Ἐν ᾧ τοιόνδε δή τι συνήνεικε γενέσθαι· Σάμιοι γὰρ   1
κομιζόμενοι ἐς Σικελίην ἐγίνοντο ἐν Λοκροῖσι τοῖσι
Ἐπιζεφυρίοισι, καὶ Ζαγκλαῖοι αὐτοί τε καὶ ὁ βασιλεὺς
αὐτῶν, τῷ οὔνομα ἦν Σκύθης, περικατέατο πόλιν τῶν
Σικελῶν ἐξελεῖν βουλόμενοι, μαθὼν δὲ ταῦτα ὁ   2
Ῥηγίου τύραννος Ἀναξίλεως, ὥστε ἐὼν διάφορος
τοῖσι Ζαγκλαίοισι, συμμίξας τοῖσι Σαμίοισι ἀναπείθει, ὡς χρεὺν εἴη Καλὴν μὲν ἀκτὴν, ἐπ᾽ ἣν
ἔπλωον, ἐᾶν χαίρειν, τὴν δὲ Ζάγκλην σχεῖν ἐοῦσαν
ἐρῆμον ἀνδρῶν. πειθομένων δὲ τῶν Σαμίων καὶ   3
σχόντων τὴν Ζάγκλην ἐνθαῦτα οἱ Ζαγκλαῖοι ὡς
ἐπύθοντο ἐχομένην τὴν πόλιν ἑωυτῶν, ἐβοήθεον αὐτῇ
καὶ ἐπεκαλέοντο Ἱπποκράτεα τὸν Γέλης τύραννον·
ἦν γὰρ δή σφι οὗτος σύμμαχος. ἐπείτε δὲ αὐτοῖσι   4
καὶ ὁ Ἱπποκράτης σὺν τῇ στρατιῇ ἧκε βοηθέων,
Σκύθην μὲν τὸν μούναρχον τῶν Ζαγκλαίων ὡς ἀποβαλόντα τὴν πόλιν ὁ Ἱπποκράτης πεδήσας, καὶ τὸν
ἀδελφεὸν αὐτοῦ Πυθογένεα, ἐς Ἴνυκον πόλιν ἀπέ-
πεμψε, τοὺς δὲ λοιποὺς Ζαγκλαίους κοινολογησάμενος
τοῖσι Σαμίοισι καὶ ὅρκους δοὺς καὶ δεξάμενος προέ-
δωκε. μισθὸς δέ οἱ ἦν εἰρημένος ὅδε ὑπὸ τῶν Σαμίων,   5
πάντων τῶν ἐπίπλων καὶ ἀνδραπόδων τὰ ἡμίσεα
λαβεῖν τῶν ἐν τῇ πόλι, τὰ δ᾽ ἐπὶ τῶν ἀγρῶν πάντα
Ἱπποκράτεα λαγχάνειν. τοὺς μὲν δὴ πλεῦνας τῶν   6
Ζαγκλαίων αὐτὸς ἐν ἀνδραπόδων λόγῳ εἶχε δήσας,
τοὺς δὲ κορυφαίους αὐτῶν τριηκοσίους ἔδωκε τοῖσι

Σαμίοισι κατασφάξαι. οὐ μέντοι οἵ γε Σάμιοι ἐποίησαν ταῦτα. XXIV. Σκύθης δὲ ὁ τῶν Ζαγκλαίων 1
μούναρχος ἐκ τῆς Ἰνύκου ἐκδιδρήσκει ἐς Ἱμέρην, ἐκ δὲ
ταύτης παρῆν ἐς τὴν Ἀσίην καὶ ἀνέβη παρὰ βασιλέα
Δαρεῖον. καί μιν ἐνόμισε Δαρεῖος πάντων ἀνδρῶν
δικαιότατον εἶναι, ὅσοι ἐκ τῆς Ἑλλάδος παρ' ἑωυτὸν
ἀνέβησαν. καὶ γὰρ παραιτησάμενος βασιλέα ἐς 2
Σικελίην ἀπίκετο καὶ αὖτις ἐκ τῆς Σικελίης ὀπίσω
παρὰ βασιλέα, ἐς ὃ γήραϊ μέγα ὄλβιος ἐὼν ἐτελεύτησε
ἐν Πέρσῃσι. Σάμιοι δὲ ἀπαλλαχθέντες Μήδων ἀπονητὶ πόλιν καλλίστην Ζάγκλην περιεβεβλέατο.

Results of the fall of Miletos.

XXV. Μετὰ δὲ τὴν ναυμαχίην τὴν ὑπὲρ Μιλήτου 1
γενομένην Φοίνικες κελευσάντων Περσέων κατῆγον
ἐς Σάμον Αἰάκεα τὸν Συλοσῶντος ὡς πολλοῦ τε ἄξιον
γενόμενον σφίσι καὶ μεγάλα κατεργασάμενον. καὶ 2
Σαμίοισι μούνοισι τῶν ἀποστάντων ἀπὸ Δαρείου διὰ
τὴν ἔκλειψιν τῶν νεῶν τὴν ἐν τῇ ναυμαχίῃ οὔτε ἡ
πόλις οὔτε τὰ ἱρὰ ἐνεπρήσθη. Μιλήτου δὲ ἁλούσης
αὐτίκα Καρίην ἔσχον οἱ Πέρσαι, τὰς μὲν ἐθελοντὴν
τῶν πολίων ὑποκυψάσας, τὰς δὲ ἀνάγκῃ προσηγάγοντο.

Histiaios, hearing of the fall of Miletos, leaves Byzantium and seizes Chios.

XXVI. Ταῦτα μὲν δὴ οὕτω ἐγίνετο, Ἱστιαίῳ δὲ 1
τῷ Μιλησίῳ ἐόντι περὶ Βυζάντιον καὶ συλλαμβάνοντι
τὰς Ἰώνων ὁλκάδας ἐκπλωούσας ἐκ τοῦ Πόντου ἐξαγ-
γέλλεται τὰ περὶ Μίλητον γενόμενα. τὰ μὲν δὴ περὶ
Ἑλλήσποντον ἔχοντα πρήγματα ἐπιτράπει Βισάλτῃ

Ἀπολλοφάνεος παιδὶ Ἀβυδηνῷ, αὐτὸς δὲ ἔχων Λεσβίους ἐς Χίον ἔπλωε, καὶ Χίων φρουρῇ οὐ προσιεμένῃ
μιν συνέβαλε ἐν Κοίλοισι καλεομένοισι τῆς Χίης
χώρης. τούτων τε δὴ ἐφόνευσε συχνοὺς, καὶ τῶν 2
λοιπῶν Χίων, οἷα δὴ κεκακωμένων ἐκ τῆς ναυμαχέης,
ὁ Ἱστιαῖος ἔχων τοὺς Λεσβίους ἐπεκράτησε, ἐκ Πο-
λίχνης τῆς Χίων ὁρμεόμενος.

Two previous disasters to the Chians.

XXVII. Φιλέει δέ κως προσημαίνειν, εὖτ᾽ ἂν 1
μέλλῃ μεγάλα κακὰ ἢ πόλι ἢ ἔθνεϊ ἔσεσθαι· καὶ γὰρ
Χίοισι πρὸ τούτων σημήϊα μεγάλα ἐγένετο. τοῦτο 2
μέν σφι πέμψασι ἐς Δελφοὺς χορὸν νεηνιέων ἑκατὸν
δύο μοῦνοι τούτων ἀπενόστησαν, τοὺς δὲ ὀκτώ τε καὶ
ἐνενήκοντα αὐτῶν λοιμὸς ὑπολαβὼν ἀπήνεικε· τοῦτο
δὲ ἐν τῇ πόλι τὸν αὐτὸν τοῦτον χρόνον, ὀλίγῳ πρὸ
τῆς ναυμαχίης, παισὶ γράμματα διδασκομένοισι ἐνέ-
πεσε ἡ στέγη, ὥστε ἀπ᾽ ἑκατὸν καὶ εἴκοσι παίδων εἷς
μοῦνος ἀπέφυγε. ταῦτα μέν σφι σημήϊα ὁ θεὸς 3
προέδεξε, μετὰ δὲ ταῦτα ἡ ναυμαχίη ὑπολαβοῦσα ἐς
γόνυ τὴν πόλιν ἔβαλε, ἐπὶ δὲ τῇ ναυμαχίῃ ἐπεγένετο
Ἱστιαῖος Λεσβίους ἄγων· κεκακωμένων δὲ τῶν Χίων,
καταστροφὴν εὐπετέως αὐτῶν ἐποιήσατο.

*Histiaios thence goes to Thasos, Lesbos, and the plain of
the Kaïkos in Mysia, where he is captured by Har-
pagos and put to death B.C. 494.*

XXVIII. Ἐνθεῦτεν δὲ ὁ Ἱστιαῖος ἐστρατεύετο 1
ἐπὶ Θάσον ἄγων Ἰώνων καὶ Αἰολέων συχνούς. περι-
κατημένῳ δέ οἱ Θάσον ἦλθε ἀγγελίη, ὡς οἱ Φοίνικες
ἀναπλώουσι ἐκ τῆς Μιλήτου ἐπὶ τὴν ἄλλην Ἰωνίην.

πυθόμενος δὲ ταῦτα Θάσον μὲν ἀπόρθητον λείπει,
αὐτὸς δὲ ἐς τὴν Λέσβον ἠπείγετο ἄγων πᾶσαν τὴν
στρατιήν. ἐκ Λέσβου δὲ λιμαινούσης οἱ τῆς στρατιῆς 2
πέρην διαβαίνει, ἐκ τοῦ Ἀταρνέος ὡς ἀμήσων τὸν
σῖτον τόν τε ἐνθεῦτεν καὶ τὸν ἐκ Καΐκου πεδίου τὸν
τῶν Μυσῶν. ἐν δὲ τούτοισι τοῖσι χωρίοισι ἐτύγχανε
ἐὼν Ἅρπαγος ἀνὴρ Πέρσης, στρατηγὸς στρατιῆς οὐκ
ὀλίγης, ὅς οἱ ἀποβάντι συμβαλὼν αὐτόν τε Ἱστιαίου
ζωγρίῃ ἔλαβε καὶ τὸν στρατὸν αὐτοῦ τὸν πλέω διέφ-
θειρε. XXIX. Ἐζωγρήθη δὲ ὁ Ἱστιαῖος ὧδε· ὡς 1
ἐμάχοντο οἱ Ἕλληνες τοῖσι Πέρσῃσι ἐν τῇ Μαλήνῃ
τῆς Ἀταρνείτιδος χώρης, οἱ μὲν συνέστασαν χρόνον
ἐπὶ πολλὸν, ἡ δὲ ἵππος ὕστερον ὁρμηθεῖσα ἐπιπίπτει
τοῖσι Ἕλλησι· τό τε δὴ ἔργον τῆς ἵππου τοῦτο
ἐγένετο, καὶ τετραμμένων τῶν Ἑλλήνων ὁ Ἱστιαῖος
ἐλπίζων οὐκ ἀπολέεσθαι ὑπὸ βασιλέος διὰ τὴν παρε-
οῦσαν ἁμαρτάδα φιλοψυχίην τοιήνδε τινὰ ἀναιρέεται·
ὡς φεύγων τε κατελαμβάνετο ὑπ᾿ ἀνδρὸς Πέρσεω καὶ 2
ὡς καταιρεόμενος ὑπ᾿ αὐτοῦ ἔμελλε συγκεντηθήσεσθαι,
Περσίδα γλῶσσαν μετεὶς καταμηνύει ἑωυτὸν, ὡς εἴη
Ἱστιαῖος ὁ Μιλήσιος. XXX. Εἰ μέν νυν, ὡς ἐζω- 1
γρήθη, ἀνήχθη ἀγόμενος παρὰ βασιλέα Δαρεῖον, ὁ δὲ
οὔτ᾿ ἂν ἔπαθε κακὸν οὐδὲν δοκέειν ἐμοί, ἀπῆκέ τ᾿ ἂν
αὐτῷ τὴν αἰτίην· νῦν δέ μιν αὐτῶν τε τούτων εἵνεκεν,
καὶ ἵνα μὴ διαφυγὼν αὖτις μέγας παρὰ βασιλέι
γένηται, Ἀρταφέρνης τε ὁ Σαρδίων ὕπαρχος καὶ ὁ
λαβὼν Ἅρπαγος, ὡς ἀπίκετο ἀγόμενος ἐς Σάρδις, τὸ
μὲν αὐτοῦ σῶμα αὐτοῦ ταύτῃ ἀνεσταύρωσαν, τὴν δὲ
κεφαλὴν ταριχεύσαντες ἀνήνεικαν παρὰ βασιλέα
Δαρεῖον ἐς Σοῦσα. Δαρεῖος δὲ πυθόμενος ταῦτα καὶ 2
ἐπαιτιησάμενος τοὺς ταῦτα ποιήσαντας, ὅτι μιν οὐ

ζώοντα ἀνήγαγον ἐς ὄψιν τὴν ἑωυτοῦ, τὴν κεφαλὴν
τὴν Ἰστιαίου λούσαντάς τε καὶ περιστείλαντας εὖ
ἐνετείλατο θάψαι ὡς ἀνδρὸς μεγάλως ἑωυτῷ τε καὶ
Πέρσῃσι εὐεργέτεω.

After wintering at Miletos (B.C. 494—493) *the Persian
fleet reduce Chios, Lesbos, and Tenedos. The Persian
drag-net.*

XXXI. Τὰ μὲν περὶ Ἰστιαῖον οὕτω ἔσχε. ὁ   1
δὲ ναυτικὸς στρατὸς ὁ Περσέων χειμερίσας περὶ
Μίλητον τῷ δευτέρῳ ἔτεϊ ὡς ἀνέπλωσε, αἱρέει
εὐπετέως τὰς νήσους τὰς πρὸς τῇ ἠπείρῳ κειμένας,
Χίον καὶ Λέσβον καὶ Τένεδον. ὅκως δὲ λάβοι τινὰ
τῶν νήσων, ὡς ἑκάστην αἱρέοντες οἱ βάρβαροι ἐσαγήνευον τοὺς ἀνθρώπους. σαγηνεύουσι δὲ τόνδε   2
τὸν τρόπον· ἀνὴρ ἀνδρὸς ἁψάμενος τῆς χειρὸς ἐκ
θαλάσσης τῆς βορηΐης ἐπὶ τὴν νοτίην διήκουσι,
καὶ ἔπειτεν διὰ πάσης τῆς νήσου διέρχονται ἐκθηρεύ-
οντες τοὺς ἀνθρώπους. αἵρεον δὲ καὶ τὰς ἐν τῇ
ἠπείρῳ πόλιας τὰς Ἰάδας κατὰ ταὐτά,- πλὴν οὐκ
ἐσαγήνευον τοὺς ἀνθρώπους· οὐ γὰρ οἷά τ᾽ ἦν.
XXXII. Ἐνθαῦτα Περσέων οἱ στρατηγοὶ οὐκ ἐψεύσαντο τὰς ἀπειλὰς, τὰς ἐπηπείλησαν τοῖσι Ἴωσι
στρατοπεδευομένοισι ἐναντία σφίσι. ὡς γὰρ δὴ ἐπεκράτησαν τῶν πολίων, παῖδάς τε τοὺς εὐειδεστάτους
ἐκλεγόμενοι ἐξέταμνον καὶ ἐποίευν ἀντὶ τοῦ εἶναι
ἐνόρχιας εὐνούχους, καὶ παρθένους τὰς καλλιστευού-
σας ἀνασπάστους παρὰ βασιλέα· ταῦτά τε δὴ ἐποίευν,
καὶ τὰς πόλιας ἐνεπίμπρασαν αὐτοῖσι τοῖς ἱροῖσι.
οὕτω δὴ τὸ τρίτον Ἴωνες κατεδουλώθησαν, πρῶτον
μὲν ὑπὸ Λυδῶν, δὶς δὲ ἐπεξῆς τότε ὑπὸ Περσέων.

B.C. 493. *Then they take the cities of the European coast of the Hellespont up to Byzantium (the Byzantines and Kalchedonians retreating into the Euxine and settling at Mesambria), then Proconnesos and Artake, then the Thracian Chersonese.*

XXXIII. Ἀπὸ δὲ Ἰωνίης ἀπαλλασσόμενος ὁ 1
ναυτικὸς στρατὸς τὰ ἐπ' ἀριστερὰ ἐσπλώοντι τοῦ
Ἑλλησπόντου αἴρεε πάντα· τὰ γὰρ ἐπὶ δεξιὰ αὐτοῖσι
τοῖσι Πέρσῃσι ὑποχείρια ἦν γεγονότα κατ' ἤπειρον.
Εἰσὶ δὲ ἐν τῇ Εὐρώπῃ αἴδε τοῦ Ἑλλησπόντου· Χερσόνησός τε, ἐν τῇ πόλιες συχναὶ ἔνεισι, καὶ Πέρινθος
καὶ τὰ τείχεα τὰ ἐπὶ Θρηΐκης καὶ Σηλυβρίη τε καὶ
Βυζάντιον. Βυζάντιοι μέν νυν καὶ οἱ πέρηθε Καλ- 2
χηδόνιοι οὐδ' ὑπέμειναν ἐπιπλώοντας τοὺς Φοίνικας,
ἀλλ' οἴχοντο ἀπολιπόντες τὴν σφετέρην ἔσω ἐς τὸν
Εὔξεινον πόντον, καὶ ἐνθαῦτα πόλιν Μεσαμβρίην
οἴκησαν· οἱ δὲ Φοίνικες κατακαύσαντες ταύτας τὰς
χώρας τὰς καταλεχθείσας τράπονται ἐπί τε Προκόννησον καὶ Ἀρτάκην, πυρὶ δὲ καὶ ταύτας νείμαντες
ἔπλωον αὖτις ἐς τὴν Χερσόνησον ἐξαιρήσοντες τὰς
ἐπιλοίπους τῶν πολίων, ὅσας πρότερον προσσχόντες
οὐ κατέσυραν. ἐπὶ δὲ Κύζικον οὐδὲ ἔπλωσαν ἀρχήν· 3
αὐτοὶ γὰρ Κυζικηνοὶ ἔτι πρότερον τοῦ Φοινίκων
ἐσπλόου ἐγεγόνεσαν ὑπὸ βασιλέϊ Οἰβάρεϊ τῷ Μεγα-
βάζου ὁμολογήσαντες, τῷ ἐν Δασκυλείῳ ὑπάρχῳ.
τῆς δὲ Χερσονήσου, πλὴν Καρδίης πόλιος, τὰς ἄλλας
πάσας ἐχειρώσαντο οἱ Φοίνικες.

Miltiades son of Kypselos, invited by the Dolonki, becomes tyrant of the Chersonese [before B.C. 546], and fortifies it.

XXXIV. Ἐτυράννευε δὲ αὐτέων μέχρι τότε 1

Μιλτιάδης ὁ Κίμωνος τοῦ Στησαγόρεω, κτησαμένου
τὴν ἀρχὴν ταύτην πρότερον Μιλτιάδεω τοῦ Κυψέλου
τρόπῳ τοιῷδε· εἶχον Δόλογκοι Θρήϊκες τὴν Χερσόνησον ταύτην. οὗτοι ὦν οἱ Δόλογκοι πιεσθέντες
πολέμῳ ὑπὸ Ἀψινθίων ἐς Δελφοὺς ἔπεμψαν τοὺς
βασιλέας περὶ τοῦ πολέμου χρησομένους. ἡ δὲ 2
Πυθίη σφι ἀνεῖλε οἰκιστὴν ἐπάγεσθαι ἐπὶ τὴν χώρην
τοῦτον, ὃς ἄν σφεας ἀπιόντας ἐκ τοῦ ἱροῦ πρῶτος ἐπὶ
ξείνια καλέσῃ. ἰόντες δὲ οἱ Δόλογκοι τὴν ἱρὴν ὁδὸν
διὰ Φωκέων τε καὶ Βοιωτῶν ἤϊσαν καί σφεας ὡς οὐδεὶς
ἐκάλεε, ἐκτράπονται ἐπ᾽ Ἀθηνέων. XXXV. Ἐν δὲ 1
τῇσι Ἀθήνῃσι τηνικαῦτα εἶχε μὲν τὸ πᾶν κράτος
Πεισίστρατος, ἀτὰρ ἐδυνάστευε καὶ Μιλτιάδης ὁ Κυψέλου, ἐὼν οἰκίης τεθριπποτρόφου, τὰ μὲν ἀνέκαθεν
ἀπ᾽ Αἰακοῦ τε καὶ Αἰγίνης γεγονώς, τὰ δὲ νεώτερα
Ἀθηναῖος, Φιλαίου τοῦ Αἴαντος παιδὸς, γενομένου
πρώτου τῆς οἰκίης ταύτης Ἀθηναίου. οὗτος ὁ Μιλ- 2
τιάδης κατήμενος ἐν τοῖσι προθύροισι τοῖσι ἑωυτοῦ,
ὁρέων τοὺς Δολόγκους παριόντας ἐσθῆτα ἔχοντας οὐκ
ἐγχωρίην καὶ αἰχμὰς προσεβώσατο, καί σφι προσ-
ελθοῦσι ἐπηγγείλατο καταγωγὴν καὶ ξείνια. οἱ δὲ
δεξάμενοι καὶ ξεινισθέντες ὑπ᾽ αὐτοῦ ἐξέφαινον πᾶν
τὸ μαντήιον, ἐκφήναντες δὲ ἐδέοντο αὐτοῦ τῷ θεῷ
μιν πείθεσθαι. Μιλτιάδεα δὲ ἀκούσαντα παραυτίκα 3
ἔπεισε ὁ λόγος οἷα ἀχθόμενόν τε τῇ Πεισιστράτου
ἀρχῇ καὶ βουλόμενον ἐκποδὼν εἶναι. αὐτίκα δὲ
ἐστάλη ἐς Δελφοὺς ἐπειρησόμενος τὸ χρηστήριον,
εἰ ποιέῃ τά περ αὐτοῦ οἱ Δόλογκοι προσεδέοντο.
XXXVI. Κελευούσης δὲ καὶ τῆς Πυθίης, οὕτω δὴ 1
Μιλτιάδης ὁ Κυψέλου, Ὀλύμπια ἀναραιρηκὼς πρότερον τούτων τεθρίππῳ, τότε παραλαβὼν Ἀθηναίων

πάντα τὸν βουλόμενον μετέχειν τοῦ στόλου ἔπλωε
ἅμα τοῖσι Δολόγκοισι, καὶ ἔσχε τὴν χώρην. καί μιν
οἱ ἐπαγαγόμενοι τύραννον κατεστήσαντο. ὁ δὲ πρῶτον   2
μὲν ἀπετείχισε τὸν ἰσθμὸν τῆς Χερσονήσου ἐκ Καρδίης πόλιος ἐς Πακτύην, ἵνα μὴ ἔχοιέν σφεας οἱ
Ἀψίνθιοι δηλέεσθαι ἐσβάλλοντες ἐς τὴν χώρην. εἰσὶ
δὲ οὗτοι στάδιοι ἕξ τε καὶ τριήκοντα τοῦ ἰσθμοῦ·
ἀπὸ δὲ τοῦ ἰσθμοῦ τούτου ἡ Χερσόνησος ἔσω πᾶσά
ἐστι σταδίων εἴκοσι καὶ τετρακοσίων τὸ μῆκος.
XXXVII. Ἀποτειχίσας ὦν τὸν αὐχένα τῆς Χερ-   1
σονήσου ὁ Μιλτιάδης καὶ τοὺς Ἀψινθίους τρόπῳ
τοιούτῳ ὠσάμενος, τῶν λοιπῶν πρώτοισι ἐπολέμησε
Λαμψακηνοῖσι. καί μιν οἱ Λαμψακηνοὶ λοχήσαντες
αἱρέουσι ζωγρίῃ. ἦν δὲ ὁ Μιλτιάδης Κροίσῳ τῷ Λυδῷ
ἐν γνώμῃ γεγονώς· πυθόμενος ὦν ὁ Κροῖσος ταῦτα
πέμπων προηγόρευε τοῖσι Λαμψακηνοῖσι μετιέναι
Μιλτιάδεα, εἰ δὲ μὴ, σφέας πίτυος τρόπον ἠπείλεε
ἐκτρίψειν. πλανωμένων δὲ τῶν Λαμψακηνῶν ἐν τοῖσι   2
λόγοισι, τί ἐθέλει τὸ ἔπος εἶναι, τό σφι ἠπείλησεν ὁ
Κροῖσος, πίτυος τρόπον ἐκτρίψειν, μόγις κοτὲ μαθὼν
τῶν τις πρεσβυτέρων εἶπε τὸ ἐὸν, ὅτι πίτυς μούνη
δενδρέων πάντων ἐκκοπεῖσα βλαστὸν οὐδένα μετίει,
ἀλλὰ πανώλεθρος ἐξαπόλλυται. δείσαντες ὦν οἱ
Λαμψακηνοὶ Κροῖσον λύσαντες μετῆκαν Μιλτιάδεα.

*Miltiades son of Kypselos is succeeded by his nephew Stesa-
goras son of Kimon, who having been assassinated
was succeeded by his brother Miltiades son of Kimon
[between B.C. 527—514].*

XXXVIII. Οὗτος μὲν δὴ διὰ Κροῖσον ἐκφεύγει,   1
μετὰ δὲ τελευτᾷ ἄπαις, τὴν ἀρχήν τε καὶ τὰ χρήματα

παραδοὺς Στησαγόρῃ τῷ Κίμωνος ἀδελφεοῦ παιδὶ
ὁμομητρίου. καὶ οἱ τελευτήσαντι Χερσονησῖται θύουσι, ὡς νόμος οἰκιστῇ, καὶ ἀγῶνα ἱππικόν τε καὶ
γυμνικὸν ἐπιστᾶσι, ἐν τῷ Λαμψακηνῶν οὐδενὶ ἐγγίνεται ἀγωνίζεσθαι. πολέμου δὲ ἐόντος πρὸς Λαμψα- 2
κηνοὺς καὶ Στησαγόρην κατέλαβε ἀποθανεῖν ἄπαιδα,
πληγέντα τὴν κεφαλὴν πελέκεϊ ἐν τῷ πρυτανηΐῳ
πρὸς ἀνδρὸς αὐτομόλου μὲν τῷ λόγῳ, πολεμίου δὲ καὶ
ὑποθερμοτέρου τῷ ἔργῳ. XXXIX. Τελευτήσαντος 1
δὲ καὶ Στησαγόρεω τρόπῳ τοιῷδε ἐνθαῦτα Μιλτιάδεα
τὸν Κίμωνος, Στησαγόρεω δὲ τοῦ τελευτήσαντος
ἀδελφεὸν, καταλαμψόμενον τὰ πρήγματα ἐπὶ Χερσονήσου ἀποστέλλουσι τριήρεϊ οἱ Πεισιστρατίδαι, οἵ
μιν καὶ ἐν Ἀθήνῃσι ἐποίευν εὖ, ὡς οὐ συνειδότες
δῆθεν τοῦ πατρὸς [Κίμωνος] αὐτοῦ τὸν θάνατον, τὸν
ἐγὼ ἐν ἄλλῳ λόγῳ σημανέω ὡς ἐγένετο. Μιλτιάδης 2
δὲ ἀπικόμενος ἐς τὴν Χερσόνησον εἶχε κατ᾽ οἴκους,
τὸν ἀδελφεὸν Στησαγόρην δηλαδὴ ἐπιτιμέων. οἱ δὲ
Χερσονησῖται πυνθανόμενοι ταῦτα συνελέχθησαν ἀπὸ
πασέων τῶν πολίων οἱ δυναστεύοντες πάντοθεν,
κοινῷ δὲ στόλῳ ἀπικόμενοι ὡς συλλυπηθησόμενοι
ἐδέθησαν ὑπ᾽ αὐτοῦ. Μιλτιάδης τε δὴ ἴσχει τὴν
Χερσόνησον πεντακοσίους βόσκων ἐπικούρους, καὶ
γαμέει Ὀλόρου τοῦ Θρηΐκων βασιλέος θυγατέρα
Ἡγησιπύλην.

In B.C. 495 *Miltiades was expelled from the Chersonese by
the Scythians, but returned. In* B.C. 493 *he fled to
Athens for fear of the Phoenikian fleet of Darius.*

XL. Οὗτος δὲ ὁ Κίμωνος Μιλτιάδης νεωστὶ μὲν 1
ἐληλύθεε ἐς τὴν Χερσόνησον, κατελάμβανε δέ μιν

ἐλθόντα ἄλλα τῶν κατεχόντων πρηγμάτων χαλεπώτερα. τρίτῳ μὲν γὰρ ἔτεϊ τούτων Σκύθας ἐκφεύγει·
Σκύθαι γὰρ οἱ νομάδες ἐρεθισθέντες ὑπὸ βασιλέος
Δαρείου συνεστράφησαν καὶ ἤλασαν μέχρι τῆς Χερσονήσου ταύτης. τούτους ἐπιόντας οὐκ ὑπομείνας ὁ
Μιλτιάδης ἔφευγε ἀπὸ Χερσονήσου, ἐς ὃ οἵ τε Σκύθαι
ἀπηλλάχθησαν καί μιν οἱ Δόλογκοι κατήγαγον ὀπίσω.
ταῦτα μὲν δὴ τρίτῳ ἔτεϊ πρότερον ἐγεγόνεε τῶν τότε
μιν κατεχόντων, XLI. τότε δὲ πυνθανόμενος εἶναι 1
τοὺς Φοίνικας ἐν Τενέδῳ, πληρώσας τριήρεας πέντε
χρημάτων τῶν παρεόντων ἀπέπλωε ἐς τὰς Ἀθήνας.
καὶ ὥσπερ ὡρμήθη ἐκ Καρδίης πόλιος, ἔπλωε διὰ τοῦ
Μέλανος κόλπου παραμείβετό τε τὴν Χερσόνησον,
καὶ οἱ Φοίνικές οἱ περιπίπτουσι τῇσι νηυσί. αὐτὸς 2
μὲν δὴ Μιλτιάδης σὺν τῇσι τέσσερσι τῶν νεῶν καταφεύγει ἐς Ἴμβρον, τὴν δέ οἱ πέμπτην τῶν νεῶν
κατεῖλον διώκοντες οἱ Φοίνικες. τῆς δὲ νεὸς ταύτης
ἔτυχε τῶν Μιλτιάδεω παίδων ὁ πρεσβύτατος ἄρχων
Μητίοχος, οὐκ ἐκ τῆς Ὀλόρου τοῦ Θρήϊκος ἐὼν
θυγατρός, ἀλλ' ἐξ ἄλλης. καὶ τοῦτον ἅμα τῇ νηῒ 3
εἷλον οἱ Φοίνικες, καί μιν πυθόμενοι ὡς εἴη Μιλτιάδεω
παῖς, ἀνήγαγον παρὰ βασιλέα, δοκέοντες χάριτα
μεγάλην καταθήσεσθαι, ὅτι δὴ Μιλτιάδης γνώμην
ἀπεδέξατο ἐν τοῖσι Ἴωσι πείθεσθαι κελεύων τοῖσι
Σκύθῃσι, ὅτε οἱ Σκύθαι προσεδέοντο λύσαντας τὴν
σχεδίην ἀποπλώειν ἐς τὴν ἑωυτῶν. Δαρεῖος δὲ, ὡς οἱ 4
Φοίνικες Μητίοχον τὸν Μιλτιάδεω ἀνήγαγον, ἐποίησε
κακὸν μὲν οὐδὲν Μητίοχον, ἀγαθὰ δὲ συχνά· καὶ γὰρ
οἶκον καὶ κτῆσιν ἔδωκε καὶ Περσίδα γυναῖκα, ἐκ
τῆς οἱ τέκνα ἐγένετο, τὰ ἐς Πέρσας κεκοσμέαται.
Μιλτιάδης δὲ ἐξ Ἴμβρου ἀπικνέεται ἐς τὰς Ἀθήνας.

B.C. 493. *Reorganisation of Ionia.*

XLII. Καὶ κατὰ τὸ ἔτος τοῦτο ἐκ τῶν Περσέων 1
οὐδὲν ἔτι πλέον ἐγένετο τούτων ἐς νεῖκος φέρον Ἴωσι,
ἀλλὰ τάδε μὲν χρήσιμα κάρτα τοῖσι Ἴωσι ἐγένετο
τούτου τοῦ ἔτεος· Ἀρταφέρνης ὁ Σαρδίων ὕπαρχος
μεταπεμψάμενος ἀγγέλους ἐκ τῶν πολίων συνθήκας
σφίσι αὐτοῖσι τοὺς Ἴωνας ἠνάγκασε ποιέεσθαι, ἵνα
δωσίδικοι εἶεν καὶ μὴ ἀλλήλους φέροιέν τε καὶ
ἄγοιεν. ταῦτά τε ἠνάγκασε ποιέειν, καὶ τὰς χώρας 2
σφέων μετρήσας κατὰ παρασάγγας, τοὺς καλέουσι οἱ
Πέρσαι τὰ τριήκοντα στάδια, κατὰ δὴ τούτους
μετρήσας φόρους ἔταξε ἑκάστοισι, οἳ κατὰ χώρην
διατελέουσι ἔχοντες ἐκ τούτου τοῦ χρόνου αἰεὶ ἔτι
καὶ ἐς ἐμὲ ὡς ἐτάχθησαν ἐξ Ἀρταφέρνεος, ἐτάχθησαν
δὲ σχεδὸν κατὰ τὰ αὐτὰ τὰ καὶ πρότερον εἶχον.

B.C. 492. *Mardonius made Satrap of Asia Minor, establishes democracy in the Ionian cities, and proceeds
from the Hellespont to coast along the European shore.*

XLIII. Καί σφι ταῦτα μὲν εἰρηναῖα ἦν, ἅμα δὲ 1
τῷ ἔαρι τῶν ἄλλων καταλελυμένων στρατηγῶν ἐκ
βασιλέος Μαρδόνιος ὁ Γωβρύεω κατέβαινε ἐπὶ
θάλασσαν, στρατὸν πολλὸν μὲν κάρτα πεζὸν ἅμα
ἀγόμενος, πολλὸν δὲ ναυτικόν, ἡλικίην τε νέος ἐὼν
καὶ νεωστὶ γεγαμηκὼς βασιλέος Δαρείου θυγατέρα
Ἀρταζώστρην. ἄγων δὲ τὸν στρατὸν τοῦτον ὁ 2
Μαρδόνιος ἐπείτε ἐγένετο ἐν τῇ Κιλικίῃ, αὐτὸς μὲν
ἐπιβὰς ἐπὶ νεὸς ἐκομίζετο ἅμα τῇσι ἄλλῃσι νηυσί,
στρατιὴν δὲ τὴν πεζὴν ἄλλοι ἡγεμόνες ἦγον ἐπὶ τὸν
Ἑλλήσποντον. ὡς δὲ παραπλώων τὴν Ἀσίην ἀπίκετο 3

ὁ Μαρδόνιος ἐς τὴν Ἰωνίην, ἐνθαῦτα μέγιστον θῶυμα
ἐρέω τοῖσι μὴ ἀποδεκομένοισι Ἑλλήνων Περσέων
τοῖσι ἑπτὰ Ὀτάνεα γνώμην ἀποδέξασθαι, ὡς χρεὸν
εἴη δημοκρατέεσθαι Πέρσας· τοὺς γὰρ τυράννους
τῶν Ἰώνων καταπαύσας πάντας ὁ Μαρδόνιος δημοκρατίας κατίστα ἐς τὰς πόλιας. ταῦτα δὲ ποιήσας 4
ἠπείγετο ἐς τὸν Ἑλλήσποντον. ὡς δὲ συνελέχθη μὲν
χρῆμα πολλὸν νεῶν, συνελέχθη δὲ καὶ πεζὸς στρατὸς
πολλὸς, διαβάντες τῇσι νηυσὶ τὸν Ἑλλήσποντον
ἐπορεύοντο διὰ τῆς Εὐρώπης, ἐπορεύοντο δὲ ἐπί τε
Ἐρέτριαν καὶ Ἀθήνας.

The fleet of Mardonius is wrecked on Mt Athos;

XLIV. Αὗται μὲν ὧν σφι πρόσχημα ἦσαν τοῦ 1
στόλου, ἀτὰρ ἐν νόῳ ἔχοντες ὅσας ἂν πλείστας
δύναιντο καταστρέφεσθαι τῶν Ἑλληνίδων πολίων,
τοῦτο μὲν δὴ τῇσι νηυσὶ Θασίους οὐδὲ χεῖρας ἀνταειραμένους κατεστρέψαντο, τοῦτο δὲ τῷ πεζῷ Μακεδόνας πρὸς τοῖσι ὑπάρχουσι δούλους προσεκτήσαντο·
τὰ γὰρ ἐντὸς Μακεδόνων ἔθνεα πάντα σφι ἤδη ἦν
ὑποχείρια γεγονότα. ἐκ μὲν δὴ Θάσου διαβαλόντες 2
πέρην ὑπὸ τὴν ἤπειρον ἐκομίζοντο μέχρι Ἀκάνθου,
ἐκ δὲ Ἀκάνθου ὁρμεόμενοι τὸν Ἄθων περιέβαλλον.
ἐπιπεσὼν δέ σφι περιπλώουσι βορῆς ἄνεμος μέγας
τε καὶ ἄπορος κάρτα τρηχέως περιέσπε πλήθεϊ
πολλὰς τῶν νεῶν ἐκβάλλων πρὸς τὸν Ἄθων. λέγεται 3
γὰρ κατὰ τριηκοσίας μὲν τῶν νεῶν τὰς διαφθαρείσας
εἶναι, ὑπὲρ δὲ δύο μυριάδας ἀνθρώπων· ὥστε γὰρ
θηριωδεστάτης ἐούσης τῆς θαλάσσης ταύτης τῆς
περὶ τὸν Ἄθων οἱ μὲν ὑπὸ τῶν θηρίων διεφθείροντο
ἁρπαζόμενοι, οἱ δὲ πρὸς τὰς πέτρας ἀρασσόμενοι· οἱ

δὲ αὐτῶν νέειν οὐκ ἠπιστέατο καὶ κατὰ τοῦτο
διεφθείροντο, οἱ δὲ ῥίγεϊ.

and the army much damaged by the Brygi, whom however
he finally subdues.

XLV. Ὁ μὲν δὴ ναυτικὸς στρατὸς οὕτω ἔπρησ- 1
σε. Μαρδονίῳ δὲ καὶ τῷ πεζῷ στρατοπεδευομένῳ
ἐν Μακεδονίῃ νυκτὸς Βρύγοι Θρήϊκες ἐπεχείρησαν.
καί σφεων πολλοὺς φονεύουσι οἱ Βρύγοι, Μαρδόνιον
δὲ αὐτὸν τρωματίζουσι. οὐ μέντοι οὐδὲ αὐτοὶ δουλο-
σύνην διέφυγον πρὸς Περσέων· οὐ γὰρ δὴ πρότερον
ἀπανέστη ἐκ τῶν χωρέων τούτων Μαρδόνιος, πρὶν
ἤ σφεας ὑποχειρίους ἐποιήσατο. τούτους μέντοι 2
καταστρεψάμενος ἀπῆγε τὴν στρατιὴν ὀπίσω, ἅτε
τῷ πεζῷ τε προσπταίσας πρὸς τοὺς Βρύγους καὶ
τῷ ναυτικῷ μεγάλως περὶ Ἄθων. οὗτος μέν νυν
ὁ στόλος αἰσχρῶς ἀγωνισάμενος ἀπηλλάχθη ἐς τὴν
Ἀσίην.

B.C. 491. *The Thasians deprived of their fleet, and ordered
to dismantle their fortifications.*

XLVI. Δευτέρῳ δὲ ἔτεϊ τούτων ὁ Δαρεῖος πρῶτα 1
μὲν Θασίους διαβληθέντας ὑπὸ τῶν ἀστυγειτόνων,
ὡς ἀπόστασιν μηχανῷατο, πέμψας ἄγγελον ἐκέλευέ
σφεας τὸ τεῖχος περιαιρέειν καὶ τὰς νέας ἐς Ἄβδηρα
κομίζειν. οἱ γὰρ δὴ Θάσιοι οἷα ὑπὸ Ἱστιαίου τε τοῦ 2
Μιλησίου πολιορκηθέντες καὶ προσόδων ἐουσέων
μεγάλων ἐχρέοντο τοῖσι χρήμασι ναῦς τε ναυπηγεύμενοι μακρὰς καὶ τεῖχος ἰσχυρότερον περιβαλλόμενοι. ἡ δὲ πρόσοδός σφι ἐγίνετο ἐκ τε τῆς
ἠπείρου καὶ ἀπὸ τῶν μετάλλων. ἐκ μέν γε τῶν ἐκ 3

Σκαπτησύλης τῶν χρυσέων μετάλλων τὸ ἐπίπαν
ὀγδώκοντα τάλαντα προσήϊε, ἐκ δὲ τῶν ἐν αὐτῇ.
Θάσῳ ἐλάσσω μὲν τούτων, συχνὰ δὲ οὕτω, ὥστε τὸ
ἐπίπαν Θασίοισι ἐοῦσι καρπῶν ἀτελέσι προσήϊε
ἀπό τε τῆς ἠπείρου καὶ τῶν μετάλλων ἔτεος ἐκάστου
διηκόσια τάλαντα, ὅτε δὲ τὸ πλεῖστον προσῆλθε,
τριηκόσια. XLVII. Εἶδον δὲ καὶ αὐτὸς τὰ μέταλλα 1
ταῦτα, καὶ μακρῷ ἦν αὐτῶν θωυμασιώτατα τὰ οἱ
Φοίνικες ἀνεῦρον οἱ μετὰ Θάσου κτίσαντες τὴν νῆσον
ταύτην, ἥτις νῦν ἐπὶ τοῦ Θάσου τούτου τοῦ Φοίνικος
τὸ οὔνομα ἔσχε. τὰ δὲ μέταλλα τὰ Φοινικικὰ ταῦτα 2
ἐστὶ τῆς Θάσου μεταξὺ Αἰνύρων τε χώρου καλεομένου
καὶ Κοινύρων, ἀντίον δὲ Σαμοθρηΐκης, οὖρος μέγα
ἀνεστραμμένον ἐν τῇ ζητήσι.

*Darius sends envoys to demand earth and water of the
Greek cities.*

XLVIII. Τοῦτο μὲν νύν ἐστι τοιοῦτο. οἱ δὲ 1
Θάσιοι τῷ βασιλέι κελεύσαντι καὶ τὸ τεῖχος τὸ
σφέτερον κατεῖλον καὶ τὰς νέας τὰς πάσας ἐκόμισαν
ἐς Ἄβδηρα.

Μετὰ δὲ τοῦτο ἀπεπειρᾶτο ὁ Δαρεῖος τῶν Ἑλλήνων, ὅ τι ἐν νόῳ ἔχοιεν, κότερα πολεμέειν ἑωυτῷ ἢ
παραδιδόναι σφέας αὐτούς. διέπεμπε ὦν κήρυκας 2
ἄλλους ἄλλῃ τάξας ἀνὰ τὴν Ἑλλάδα, κελεύων
αἰτέειν βασιλέι γῆν τε καὶ ὕδωρ. τούτους μὲν δὴ ἐς
τὴν Ἑλλάδα ἔπεμπε, ἄλλους δὲ κήρυκας διέπεμπε ἐς
τὰς ἑωυτοῦ δασμοφόρους πόλιας τὰς παραθαλασσίους,
κελεύων νέας τε μακρὰς καὶ ἱππαγωγὰ πλοῖα ποιέεσθαι.

*Many of the continental towns obey, and all the islands.
The Athenians use this as a pretext for accusing the
Aeginetans to the Spartans.*

XLIX. Οὗτοί τε δὴ παρεσκευάζοντο ταῦτα, καὶ   1
τοῖσι ἥκουσι ἐς τὴν Ἑλλάδα κήρυξι πολλοὶ μὲν
ἠπειρωτέων ἔδοσαν τὰ προΐσχετο αἰτέων ὁ Πέρσης,
πάντες δὲ νησιῶται ἐς τοὺς ἀπικοίατο αἰτήσοντες.
οἵ τε δὴ ἄλλοι νησιῶται διδοῦσι γῆν τε καὶ ὕδωρ
Δαρείῳ, καὶ δὴ καὶ Αἰγινῆται. ποιήσασι δέ σφι   2
ταῦτα ἰθέως Ἀθηναῖοι ἐπεκέατο, δοκέοντες ἐπὶ σφίσι
ἔχοντας τοὺς Αἰγινήτας δεδωκέναι, ὡς ἅμα τῷ Πέρσῃ
ἐπὶ σφέας στρατεύωνται. καὶ ἅσμενοι προφάσιος
ἐπελάβοντο, φοιτέοντές τε ἐς τὴν Σπάρτην κατηγόρεον τῶν Αἰγινητέων τὰ πεποιήκοιεν προδόντες τὴν
Ἑλλάδα.

*The Spartan king Kleomenes goes to Aegina to arrest the
medizers, but his authority is undermined by the other
king Demaratus.*

L. Πρὸς ταύτην δὲ τὴν κατηγορίην Κλεομένης ὁ   1
Ἀναξανδρίδεω βασιλεὺς ἐὼν Σπαρτιητέων διέβη ἐς
Αἴγιναν, βουλόμενος συλλαβεῖν Αἰγινητέων τοὺς
αἰτιωτάτους· ὡς δὲ ἐπειρᾶτο συλλαμβάνων, ἄλλοι   2
τε δὴ αὐτῷ ἐγίνοντο ἀντίξοοι τῶν Αἰγινητέων, ἐν δὲ
δὴ καὶ Κρῖος ὁ Πολυκρίτου μάλιστα, ὃς οὐκ ἔφη
αὐτὸν οὐδένα ἄξειν χαίροντα Αἰγινητέων· ἄνευ γάρ
μιν Σπαρτιητέων τοῦ κοινοῦ ποιέειν ταῦτα ὑπ᾽
Ἀθηναίων ἀναγνωσθέντα χρήμασι· ἅμα γὰρ ἄν μιν
τῷ ἑτέρῳ βασιλέι ἐλθόντα συλλαμβάνειν. ἔλεγε δὲ   3
ταῦτα ἐξ ἐπιστολῆς τῆς Δημαρήτου. Κλεομένης δὲ
ἀπελαυνόμενος ἐκ τῆς Αἰγίνης εἴρετο τὸν Κρῖον ὅ τι

οἱ εἴη τὸ οὔνομα· ὁ δέ οἱ τὸ ἐὸν ἔφρασε. ὁ δὲ
Κλεομένης πρὸς αὐτὸν ἔφη· "Ἤδη νῦν καταχαλκοῦ
ὦ κριὲ τὰ κέρεα, ὡς συνοισόμενος μεγάλῳ κακῷ."

Origin of the double kingship in Sparta.
[Digression to c. 60.]

LI. Ἐν δὲ τῇ Σπάρτῃ τοῦτον τὸν χρόνον
ὑπομένων Δημάρητος ὁ Ἀρίστωνος διέβαλλε τὸν
Κλεομένεα, ἐὼν βασιλεὺς καὶ οὗτος Σπαρτιητέων,
οἰκίης δὲ τῆς ὑποδεεστέρης, κατ' ἄλλο μὲν οὐδὲν
ὑποδεεστέρης (ἀπὸ γὰρ τοῦ αὐτοῦ γεγόνασι), κατὰ
πρεσβυγενείην δέ κως τετίμηται μᾶλλον ἢ Εὐρυσθέ-
νεος. LII. Λακεδαιμόνιοι γὰρ ὁμολογέοντες οὐδενὶ 1
ποιητῇ λέγουσι αὐτὸν Ἀριστόδημον τὸν Ἀριστομάχου
τοῦ Κλεοδαίου τοῦ Ὕλλου βασιλεύοντα ἀγαγεῖν
σφέας ἐς ταύτην τὴν χώρην, τὴν νῦν ἐκτέαται, ἀλλ'
οὐ τοὺς Ἀριστοδήμου παῖδας. μετὰ δὲ χρόνον οὐ 2
πολλὸν Ἀριστοδήμῳ τεκεῖν τὴν γυναῖκα, τῇ οὔνομα
εἶναι Ἀργείην· θυγατέρα δὲ αὐτὴν λέγουσι εἶναι
Αὐτεσίωνος τοῦ Τισαμενοῦ τοῦ Θερσάνδρου τοῦ
Πολυνείκεος· ταύτην δὲ τεκεῖν δίδυμα, ἐπιδόντα δὲ
τὸν Ἀριστόδημον τὰ τέκνα νούσῳ τελευτᾶν. Λακε- 3
δαιμονίους δὲ τοὺς τότε ἐόντας βουλεῦσαι κατὰ νόμον
βασιλέα τῶν παίδων τὸν πρεσβύτερον ποιήσασθαι·
οὐκ ὦν δή σφεας ἔχειν, ὁκότερον ἕλωνται, ὥστε καὶ
ὁμοίων καὶ ἴσων ἐόντων· οὐ δυναμένους δὲ γνῶναι, ἢ
καὶ πρὸ τούτου, ἐπειρωτᾶν τὴν τεκοῦσαν. τὴν δὲ 4
οὐδὲ αὐτὴν φάναι διαγινώσκειν· εἰδυῖαν μὲν καὶ τὸ
κάρτα λέγειν ταῦτα, βουλομένην δὲ εἴ κως ἀμφότεροι
γενοίατο βασιλέες. τοὺς ὦν δὴ Λακεδαιμονίους
ἀπορέειν, ἀπορέοντας δὲ πέμπειν ἐς Δελφοὺς ἐπειρη-

σομένους, ὅ τι χρήσωνται τῷ πρήγματι. τὴν δὲ 5
Πυθίην κελεύειν σφέας ἀμφότερα τὰ παιδία ἡγήσα-
σθαι βασιλέας, τιμᾶν δὲ μᾶλλον τὸν γεραίτερον. τὴν
μὲν δὴ Πυθίην ταῦτά σφι ἀνελεῖν, τοῖσι δὲ Λακεδαιμονίοισι ἀπορέουσι οὐδὲν ἔσσον, ὅκως ἐξεύρωσι
αὐτῶν τὸν πρεσβύτερον, ὑποθέσθαι ἄνδρα Μεσσήνιον, τῷ οὔνομα εἶναι Πανίτην. ὑποθέσθαι δὲ 6
τοῦτον τὸν Πανίτην τάδε τοῖσι Λακεδαιμονίοισι,
φυλάξαι τὴν γειναμένην, ὁκότερον τῶν παίδων
πρότερον λούει καὶ σιτίζει· καὶ ἢν μὲν κατὰ ταῦτὰ
φαίνηται αἰεὶ ποιεῦσα, τοὺς δὲ πᾶν ἕξειν ὅσον τι καὶ
δίζηνται καὶ ἐθέλουσι ἐξευρεῖν, ἢν δὲ πλανᾶται καὶ
ἐκείνη ἐναλλὰξ ποιεῦσα, δῆλά σφι ἔσεσθαι, ὡς οὐδὲ
ἐκείνη πλέον οὐδὲν οἶδε, ἐπ' ἄλλην τέ σφεας τρά-
πεσθαι ὁδόν. ἐνθαῦτα δὴ τοὺς Σπαρτιήτας κατὰ τὰς 7
τοῦ Μεσσηνίου ὑποθήκας φυλάξαντας τὴν μητέρα
τῶν Ἀριστοδήμου παίδων λαβεῖν κατὰ τὰ αὐτὰ
τιμῶσαν τὸν πρότερον καὶ σίτοισι καὶ λουτροῖσι, οὐκ
εἰδυῖαν τῶν εἵνεκεν ἐφυλάσσετο. λαβόντας δὲ τὸ
παιδίον τὸ τιμώμενον πρὸς τῆς γειναμένης ὡς ἐὸν
πρότερον τρέφειν ἐν τῷ δημοσίῳ· καί οἱ οὔνομα
τεθῆναι Εὐρυσθένεα, τῷ δὲ Προκλέα. τούτους ἀν- 8
δρωθέντας αὐτούς τε ἀδελφεοὺς ἐόντας λέγουσι
διαφόρους εἶναι τὸν πάντα χρόνον τῆς ζόης ἀλλήλοισι, καὶ τοὺς ἀπὸ τούτων γενομένους ὡσαύτως
διατελέειν.

Variations of the legend.

LIII. Ταῦτα μὲν Λακεδαιμόνιοι λέγουσι μοῦνοι 1
Ἑλλήνων· τάδε δὲ κατὰ τὰ λεγόμενα ὑπ' Ἑλλήνων
ἐγὼ γράφω· τούτους γὰρ δὴ τοὺς Δωριέων βασιλέας

μέχρι μὲν Περσέος τοῦ Δανάης, τοῦ θεοῦ ἀπεόντος,
καταλεγομένους ὀρθῶς ὑπ' Ἑλλήνων καὶ ἀποδεικ-
νυμένους ὥς εἰσι Ἕλληνες· ἤδη γὰρ τηνικαῦτα ἐς
Ἕλληνας οὗτοι ἐτέλεον. ἔλεξα δὲ μέχρι Περσέος 2
τοῦδε εἵνεκεν, ἀλλ' οὐκ ἀνέκαθεν ἔτι ἔλαβον, ὅτι οὐκ
ἔπεστι ἐπωνυμίη Περσέϊ οὐδεμία πατρὸς θνητοῦ,
ὥσπερ Ἡρακλέϊ Ἀμφιτρύων· ἤδη ὦν ὀρθῷ λόγῳ
χρεομένῳ μέχρι τοῦ Περσέος ὀρθῶς εἴρηταί μοι, ἀπὸ
δὲ Δανάης τῆς Ἀκρισίου καταλέγοντι τοὺς ἄνω αἰεὶ
πατέρας αὐτῶν φαινοίατο ἂν ἐόντες οἱ τῶν Δωριέων
ἡγεμόνες Αἰγύπτιοι ἰθαγενέες. LIV. Ταῦτα μέν
νυν κατὰ τὰ Ἕλληνες λέγουσι γεγενεηλόγηται· ὡς δὲ
ὁ Περσέων λόγος λέγεται, αὐτὸς ὁ Περσεὺς ἐὼν
Ἀσσύριος ἐγένετο Ἕλλην, ἀλλ' οὐκ οἱ Περσέος
πρόγονοι· τοὺς δὲ Ἀκρισίου γε πατέρας ὁμολο-
γέοντας κατ' οἰκηϊότητα Περσέϊ οὐδέν, τούτους δὲ
εἶναι, κατά περ Ἕλληνες λέγουσι, Αἰγυπτίους. LV.
Καὶ ταῦτα μέν νυν περὶ τούτων εἰρήσθω. ὅ τι δὲ
ἐόντες Αἰγύπτιοι, καὶ ὅ τι ἀποδεξάμενοι ἔλαβον τὰς
Δωριέων βασιληΐας, ἄλλοισι γὰρ περὶ αὐτῶν εἴρηται,
ἐάσομεν αὐτά· τὰ δὲ ἄλλοι οὐ κατελάβοντο, τούτων
μνήμην ποιήσομαι.

Functions and honours of the Spartan kings: (1) *in war,*

LVI. Γέρεά τε δὴ τάδε τοῖσι βασιλεῦσι Σπαρτιῆται δεδώκασι· ἱρωσύνας δύο, Διός τε Λακεδαίμονος καὶ Διὸς οὐρανίου, καὶ πόλεμόν γε ἐκφέρειν
ἐπ' ἢν ἂν βούλωνται χώρην, τούτου δὲ μηδένα εἶναι
Σπαρτιητέων διακωλυτήν, εἰ δὲ μή, αὐτὸν ἐν τῷ ἄγεϊ
ἐνέχεσθαι· στρατευομένων δὲ πρώτους ἰέναι τοὺς
βασιλέας, ὑστάτους δὲ ἀπιέναι· ἑκατὸν δὲ ἄνδρας

λογάδας ἐπὶ στρατιῆς φυλάσσειν αὐτούς· προβάτοισι
δὲ χρᾶσθαι ἐν τῇσι ἐξοδίῃσι, ὁκόσοισι ἂν ἐθέλωσι,
τῶν δὲ θυομένων ἁπάντων τὰ δέρματά τε καὶ τὰ νῶτα
λαμβάνειν σφέας.

(2) *in peace,*

LVII. Ταῦτα μὲν τὰ ἐμπολέμια, τὰ δὲ ἄλλα τὰ   1
εἰρηναῖα κατὰ τάδε σφι δέδοται· ἢν θυσίη τις
δημοτελὴς ποιέηται, πρώτους ἐπὶ τὸ δεῖπνον ἵζειν
τοὺς βασιλέας καὶ ἀπὸ τούτων πρῶτον ἄρχεσθαι,
διπλήσια νέμοντας ἑκατέρῳ τὰ πάντα ἢ τοῖσι
ἄλλοισι δαιτυμόνεσι· καὶ σπονδαρχίας εἶναι τούτων, καὶ τῶν τυθέντων τὰ δέρματα. νεομηνίας   2
δὲ ἀνὰ πάσας καὶ ἑβδόμας ἱσταμένου τοῦ μηνὸς
δίδοσθαι ἐκ τοῦ δημοσίου ἱρήιον τέλεον ἑκατέρῳ ἐς
Ἀπόλλωνος καὶ μέδιμνον ἀλφίτων καὶ οἴνου τετάρτην
Λακωνικὴν, καὶ ἐν τοῖσι ἀγῶσι πᾶσι προεδρίας
ἐξαιρέτους· καὶ προξείνους ἀποδεικνύναι τούτοισι
προσκεῖσθαι τοὺς ἂν ἐθέλωσι τῶν ἀστῶν, καὶ
Πυθίους αἱρέεσθαι δύο ἑκάτερον· οἱ δὲ Πύθιοί εἰσι
θεοπρόποι ἐς Δελφούς, σιτεόμενοι μετὰ τῶν βασιλέων
τὰ δημόσια· μὴ ἐλθοῦσι δὲ τοῖσι βασιλεῦσι ἐπὶ τὸ   3
δεῖπνον ἀποπέμπεσθαί σφι ἐς τὰ οἰκία ἀλφίτων τε
δύο χοίνικας ἑκατέρῳ καὶ οἴνου κοτύλην, παρεοῦσι δὲ
διπλήσια πάντα δίδοσθαι· τὠυτὸ δὲ τοῦτο καὶ πρὸς
ἰδιωτέων κληθέντας ἐπὶ δεῖπνον τιμᾶσθαι· τὰς δὲ   4
μαντηΐας τὰς γινομένας τούτους φυλάσσειν, συνει-
δέναι δὲ καὶ τοὺς Πυθίους· δικάζειν δὲ μούνους τοὺς
βασιλέας τοσάδε μοῦνα· πατρούχου τε παρθένου
πέρι, ἐς τὸν ἱκνέεται ἔχειν, ἢν μή περ ὁ πατὴρ αὐτὴν
ἐγγυήσῃ. καὶ ὁδῶν δημοσίεων πέρι· καὶ ἤν τις θετὸν   5

παῖδα ποιέεσθαι ἐθέλῃ, βασιλέων ἐναντίον ποιέεσθαι·
καὶ παρίζειν βουλεύουσι τοῖσι γέρουσι, ἐοῦσι δυῶν
δέουσι τριήκοντα. ἢν δὲ μὴ ἔλθωσι, τοὺς μάλιστά
σφι τῶν γερόντων προσήκοντας ἔχειν τὰ τῶν
βασιλέων γέρεα, δύο ψήφους τιθεμένους, τρίτην δὲ
τὴν ἑωυτῶν.

(3) honours after death.

LVIII. Ταῦτα μὲν ζώουσι τοῖσι βασιλεῦσι   1
δέδοται ἐκ τοῦ κοινοῦ τῶν Σπαρτιητέων, ἀποθανοῦσι
δὲ τάδε· ἱππέες περιαγγέλλουσι τὸ γεγονὸς κατὰ
πᾶσαν τὴν Λακωνικήν, κατὰ δὲ τὴν πόλιν γυναῖκες
περιιοῦσαι λέβητα κροτέουσι. ἐπεὰν ὦν τοῦτο
γένηται τοιοῦτο, ἀνάγκη ἐξ οἰκίης ἑκάστης ἐλευθέρους
δύο καταμιαίνεσθαι, ἄνδρα τε καὶ γυναῖκα· μὴ
ποιήσασι δὲ τοῦτο ζημίαι μεγάλαι ἐπικέαται. νόμος   2
δὲ τοῖσι Λακεδαιμονίοισι κατὰ τῶν βασιλέων τοὺς
θανάτους ἐστὶ ὡυτὸς καὶ τοῖσι βαρβάροισι τοῖσι ἐν
τῇ Ἀσίῃ· τῶν γὰρ ὦν βαρβάρων οἱ πλεῦνες τὠυτῷ
νόμῳ χρέονται κατὰ τοὺς θανάτους τῶν βασιλέων.
ἐπεὰν γὰρ ἀποθάνῃ βασιλεὺς Λακεδαιμονίων, ἐκ
πάσης δέει Λακεδαίμονος, χωρὶς Σπαρτιητέων, ἀριθμῷ
τῶν περιοίκων ἀναγκαστοὺς ἐς τὸ κῆδος ἰέναι· τούτων   3
ὦν καὶ τῶν εἱλωτέων καὶ αὐτῶν Σπαρτιητέων ἐπεὰν
συλλεχθέωσι ἐς τὠυτὸ πολλαὶ χιλιάδες, σύμμιγα
τῇσι γυναιξὶ κόπτονταί τε προθύμως καὶ οἰμωγῇ
διαχρέονται ἀπλέτῳ, φάμενοι τὸν ὕστατον αἰεὶ ἀπο-
γενόμενον τῶν βασιλέων, τοῦτον δὴ γενέσθαι ἄριστον.
ὃς δ' ἂν ἐν πολέμῳ τῶν βασιλέων ἀποθάνῃ, τούτῳ
δὲ εἴδωλον σκευάσαντες ἐν κλίνῃ εὖ ἐστρωμένῃ
ἐκφέρουσι. ἐπεὰν δὲ θάψωσι, ἀγορὴ δέκα ἡμερέων

οὐκ ἵσταταί σφι, οὐδ᾽ ἀρχαιρεσίη συνίζει, ἀλλὰ πενθέουσι ταύτας τὰς ἡμέρας.

Analogies with the Persians,

LIX. Συμφέρονται δὲ ἄλλο τόδε τοῖσι Πέρσῃσι· ἐπεὰν ἀποθανόντος τοῦ βασιλέος ἄλλος ἐνίστηται βασιλεύς, οὗτος ὁ ἐσιὼν ἐλευθεροῖ ὅστις τι Σπαρτιητέων τῷ βασιλέϊ ἢ τῷ δημοσίῳ ὤφειλε. ἐν δ᾽ αὖ Πέρσῃσι ὁ κατιστάμενος βασιλεὺς τὸν προοφειλόμενον φόρον μετίει τῇσι πόλισι πάσῃσι.

and with the Egyptians.

LX. Συμφέρονται δὲ καὶ τάδε Αἰγυπτίοισι Λακεδαιμόνιοι· οἱ κήρυκες αὐτῶν καὶ αὐληταὶ καὶ μάγειροι ἐκδέκονται τὰς πατρωΐας τέχνας, καὶ αὐλητής τε αὐλητέω γίνεται καὶ μάγειρος μαγείρου καὶ κῆρυξ κήρυκος· οὐ κατὰ λαμπροφωνίην ἐπιτιθέμενοι ἄλλοι σφέας παρακληΐουσι, ἀλλὰ κατὰ τὰ πάτρια ἐπιτελέουσι.

[Resuming from c. 50. B.C. 491.] *On his return from Aegina Kleomenes determines to depose Demaratos.*

LXI. Ταῦτα μὲν δὴ οὕτω γίνεται. τότε δὲ τὸν 1 Κλεομένεα ἐόντα ἐν τῇ Αἰγίνῃ καὶ κοινὰ τῇ Ἑλλάδι ἀγαθὰ προεργαζόμενον ὁ Δημάρητος διέβαλε, οὐκ Αἰγινητέων οὕτω κηδόμενος, ὡς φθόνῳ καὶ ἄγῃ χρεόμενος. Κλεομένης δὲ νοστήσας ἀπ᾽ Αἰγίνης ἐβούλευε τὸν Δημάρητον παῦσαι τῆς βασιληΐης, διὰ πρῆγμα τοιόνδε ἐπίβασιν ἐς αὐτὸν ποιεύμενος·

The story of King Ariston and the beautiful wife of his friend Agetos.

Ἀρίστωνι βασιλεύοντι ἐν Σπάρτῃ καὶ γήμαντι

γυναῖκας δύο παῖδες οὐκ ἐγίνοντο. καὶ οὐ γάρ 2
συνεγινώσκετο αὐτὸς τούτων εἶναι αἴτιος, γαμέει
τρίτην γυναῖκα. ὧδε δὲ γαμέει. ἦν οἱ φίλος τῶν
Σπαρτιητέων ἀνήρ, τῷ προσεκέετο τῶν ἀστῶν
μάλιστα ὁ Ἀρίστων. τούτῳ τῷ ἀνδρὶ ἐτύγχανε
ἐοῦσα γυνὴ καλλίστη μακρῷ τῶν ἐν Σπάρτῃ
γυναικῶν, καὶ ταῦτα μέντοι καλλίστη ἐξ αἰσχίστης
γενομένη. ἐοῦσαν γάρ μιν τὸ εἶδος φλαύρην ἡ 3
τροφὸς αὐτῆς, οἷα ἀνθρώπων τε ὀλβίων θυγατέρα
καὶ δυσειδέα ἐοῦσαν, πρὸς δὲ καὶ ὁρέουσα τοὺς
γονέας συμφορὴν τὸ εἶδος αὐτῆς ποιευμένους, ταῦτα
ἕκαστα μαθοῦσα ἐπιφράζεται τοιάδε· ἐφόρεε αὐτὴν
ἀνὰ πᾶσαν ἡμέρην ἐς τὸ τῆς Ἑλένης ἱρόν· τὸ
δ' ἐστὶ ἐν τῇ Θεράπνῃ καλευμένῃ, ὕπερθε τοῦ
Φοιβηίου ἱροῦ· ὅκως δὲ ἐνείκειε ἡ τροφός, πρός τε
τὤγαλμα ἵστα καὶ ἐλίσσετο τὴν θεὸν ἀπαλλάξαι τῆς
δυσμορφίης τὸ παιδίον. καὶ δή κοτε ἀπιούσῃ ἐκ τοῦ 4
ἱροῦ τῇ τροφῷ γυναῖκα λέγεται ἐπιφανῆναι, ἐπι-
φανεῖσαν δὲ ἐπείρεσθαί μιν, ὅ τι φέρει ἐν τῇ ἀγκάλῃ,
καὶ τὴν φράσαι, ὡς παιδίον φορέει· τὴν δὲ κελεῦσαί
οἱ δέξαι· τὴν δὲ οὐ φάναι· ἀπειρῆσθαι γάρ οἱ ἐκ τῶν
γειναμένων μηδενὶ ἐπιδεικνύναι· τὴν δὲ πάντως
ἑωυτῇ κελεύειν ἐπιδέξαι· ὁρέουσαν δὲ τὴν γυναῖκα 5
περὶ πολλοῦ ποιευμένην ἰδέσθαι, οὕτω δὴ τὴν
τροφὸν δέξαι τὸ παιδίον· τὴν δὲ καταψῶσαν τοῦ
παιδίου τὴν κεφαλὴν εἶπαι, ὡς καλλιστεύσει πασέων
τῶν ἐν Σπάρτῃ γυναικῶν. ἀπὸ μὲν δὴ ταύτης τῆς
ἡμέρης μεταπεσεῖν τὸ εἶδος. γαμέει δὲ δή μιν ἐς
γάμου ὥρην ἀπικομένην Ἄγητος ὁ Ἀλκείδεω, οὗτος
δὴ ὁ τοῦ Ἀρίστωνος φίλος. LXII. Τὸν δὲ Ἀρί- 1
στωνα ἔκνιζε ἄρα τῆς γυναικὸς ταύτης ὁ ἔρως·

μηχανᾶται δὴ τοιάδε· αὐτός τε τῷ ἑταίρῳ, τοῦ ἦν ἡ
γυνὴ αὕτη, ὑποδέκεται δωτίνην δώσειν τῶν ἑωυτοῦ
πάντων ἕν, τὸ ἂν αὐτὸς ἐκεῖνος ἕληται, καὶ τὸν
ἑταῖρον ἑωυτῷ ἐκέλευε ὡσαύτως τὴν ὁμοίην διδόναι.
ὁ δὲ οὐδὲν φοβηθεὶς ἀμφὶ τῇ γυναικὶ, ὁρέων ἐοῦσαν
καὶ Ἀρίστωνι γυναῖκα, καταινέει ταῦτα· ἐπὶ τούτοισι
δὲ ὅρκους ἐπήλασαν. μετὰ δὲ αὐτός τε ὁ Ἀρίστων 2
ἔδωκε τοῦτο, ὅ τι δὴ ἦν, τὸ εἵλετο τῶν κειμηλίων τῶν
Ἀρίστωνος ὁ Ἄγητος, καὶ αὐτὸς τὴν ὁμοίην ζητέων
φέρεσθαι παρ' ἐκείνου, ἐνθαῦτα δὴ τοῦ ἑταίρου τὴν
γυναῖκα ἐπειρᾶτο ἀπάγεσθαι. ὁ δὲ πλὴν τούτου
μούνου τὰ ἄλλα ἔφη καταινέσαι. ἀναγκαζόμενος
μέντοι τῷ τε ὅρκῳ καὶ τῆς ἀπάτης τῇ παραγωγῇ
ἀπίει ἀπάγεσθαι.

*Ariston marries the woman as his third wife. She bears
Demaratos, whose paternity is doubted.*

LXIII. Οὕτω μὲν δὴ τὴν τρίτην ἐσηγάγετο 1
γυναῖκα ὁ Ἀρίστων, τὴν δευτέρην ἀποπεμψάμενος,
ἐν δέ οἱ χρόνῳ ἐλάσσονι καὶ οὐ πληρώσασα τοὺς
δέκα μῆνας ἡ γυνὴ αὕτη τίκτει τοῦτον δὴ τὸν
Δημάρητον. καί τίς οἱ τῶν οἰκετέων ἐν θώκῳ κατη- 2
μένῳ μετὰ τῶν ἐφόρων ἐξαγγέλλει, ὥς οἱ παῖς γέγονε.
ὁ δὲ ἐπιστάμενός τε τὸν χρόνον, τῷ ἠγάγετο τὴν
γυναῖκα, καὶ ἐπὶ δακτύλων συμβαλλόμενος τοὺς
μῆνας εἶπε ἀπομόσας "οὐκ ἂν ἐμὸς εἴη·" τοῦτο
ἤκουσαν μὲν οἱ ἔφοροι, πρῆγμα μέντοι οὐδὲν ἐποιήσαντο τὸ παραυτίκα, ὁ δὲ παῖς αὔξετο, καὶ τῷ
Ἀρίστωνι τὸ εἰρημένον μετέμελε· παῖδα γὰρ τὸν
Δημάρητον ἐς τὰ μάλιστά οἱ ἐνόμισε εἶναι. Δημά- 3
ρητον δὲ αὐτῷ οὔνομα ἔθετο διὰ τόδε· πρότερον

τούτων πανδημεὶ Σπαρτιῆται Ἀρίστωνι, ὡς ἀνδρὶ
εὐδοκιμέοντι διὰ πάντων δὴ τῶν βασιλέων τῶν ἐν τῇ
Σπάρτῃ γενομένων, ἀρὴν ἐποιήσαντο παῖδα γενέσθαι·
διὰ τοῦτο μέν οἱ τὸ οὔνομα Δημάρητος ἐτέθη.
LXIV. Χρόνου δὲ προϊόντος Ἀρίστων μὲν ἀπέθανε,
Δημάρητος δὲ ἔσχε τὴν βασιληίην. ἔδεε δὲ, ὡς οἶκε,
ἀνάπυστα γενόμενα ταῦτα καταπαῦσαι Δημάρητον
τῆς βασιληίης, δι' ἃ Κλεομένει διεβλήθη μεγάλως
πρότερόν τε ὁ Δημάρητος ἀπαγαγὼν τὴν στρατιὴν ἐξ
Ἐλευσῖνος καὶ δὴ καὶ τότε ἐπ' Αἰγινητέων τοὺς
μηδίσαντας διαβάντος Κλεομένεος.

*Kleomenes agrees with Leotychides to make him king, in
place of his cousin Demaratos, whom Leotychides had
also a private reason for hating.*

LXV. Ὁρμηθεὶς ὦν ἀποτίνυσθαι ὁ Κλεομένης   1
συντίθεται Λευτυχίδῃ τῷ Μενάρεος τοῦ Ἄγιος, ἐόντι
οἰκίης τῆς αὐτῆς Δημαρήτῳ, ἐπ' ᾧ τε, ἢν αὐτὸν
καταστήσῃ βασιλέα ἀντὶ Δημαρήτου, ἕψεταί οἱ ἐπ'
Αἰγινήτας. ὁ δὲ Λευτυχίδης ἦν ἐχθρὸς τῷ Δημαρήτῳ   2
μάλιστα γεγονὼς διὰ πρῆγμα τοιόνδε· ἁρμοσαμένου
Λευτυχίδεω Πέρκαλον τὴν Χίλωνος τοῦ Δημαρμένου
θυγατέρα ὁ Δημάρητος ἐπιβουλεύσας ἀποστερέει
Λευτυχίδην τοῦ γάμου, φθάσας αὐτὸς τὴν Πέρκαλον
ἁρπάσας καὶ σχὼν γυναῖκα· κατὰ τοῦτο μὲν τῷ Λευτυ-   3
χίδῃ ἡ ἔχθρη ἡ ἐς τὸν Δημάρητον ἐγεγόνεε, τότε δὲ ἐκ
τῆς Κλεομένεος προθυμίης ὁ Λευτυχίδης κατόμνυται
Δημαρήτου, φὰς αὐτὸν οὐκ ἰκνεομένως βασιλεύειν
Σπαρτιητέων, οὐκ ἐόντα παῖδα Ἀρίστωνος. μετὰ δὲ
τὴν κατωμοσίην ἐδίωκε ἀνασώζων ἐκεῖνο τὸ ἔπος, το
εἶπε Ἀρίστων τότε, ὅτε οἱ ἐξήγγειλε ὁ οἰκέτης παῖδα

γεγονέναι, ὁ δὲ συμβαλόμενος τοὺς μῆνας ἀπώμοσε,
φὰς οὐκ ἑωυτοῦ εἶναι. τούτου δὴ ἐπιβατεύων τοῦ 4
ῥήματος ὁ Λευτυχίδης ἀπέφαινε τὸν Δημάρητον
οὔτε ἐξ Ἀρίστωνος γεγονότα οὔτε ἰκνεομένως βασιλεύοντα Σπάρτης, τοὺς ἐφόρους μάρτυρας παρε-
χόμενος κείνους, οἳ τότε ἔτυχον πάρεδροί τε ἐόντες
καὶ ἀκούσαντες ταῦτα Ἀρίστωνος.

*The Spartans agree to refer the matter of the paternity of
Demaratos to the oracle at Delphi. Kleomenes secures
a decision against Demaratos by an intrigue, which
cost the Pythia her office.*

LXVI. Τέλος δὲ ἐόντων περὶ αὐτῶν νεικέων 1
ἔδοξε Σπαρτιήτῃσι ἐπείρεσθαι τὸ χρηστήριον τὸ ἐν
Δελφοῖσι, εἰ Ἀρίστωνος εἴη παῖς ὁ Δημάρητος.
ἀνοίστου δὲ γενομένου ἐκ προνοίης τῆς Κλεομένεος ἐς 2
τὴν Πυθίην ἐνθαῦτα προσποιέεται Κλεομένης Κόβωνα
τὸν Ἀριστοφάντου, ἄνδρα ἐν Δελφοῖσι δυναστεύοντα
μέγιστον, ὁ δὲ Κόβων Περίαλλαν τὴν πρόμαντιν
ἀναπείθει, τὰ Κλεομένης ἐβούλετο λέγεσθαι, λέγειν.
οὕτω δὴ ἡ Πυθίη ἐπειρωτώντων τῶν θεοπρόπων
ἔκρινε μὴ Ἀρίστωνος εἶναι Δημάρητον παῖδα. ὑστέρῳ
μέντοι χρόνῳ ἀνάπυστα ἐγένετο ταῦτα, καὶ Κόβων
τε ἔφυγε ἐκ Δελφῶν καὶ Περίαλλα ἡ πρόμαντις
ἐπαύσθη τῆς τιμῆς.

*Demaratos remained in Sparta for a time ; but, on receiv-
ing an insult from Leotychides, determines to put an
end to his uncertainty.*

LXVII. Κατὰ μὲν δὴ τὴν Δημαρήτου κατά- 1
παυσιν τῆς βασιληίης οὕτω ἐγένετο, ἔφευγε δὲ
Δημάρητος ἐκ Σπάρτης ἐς Μήδους ἐκ τοιοῦδε ὀνείδεος·

μετὰ τῆς βασιληίης τὴν κατάπαυσιν ὁ Δημάρητος
ἦρχε αἱρεθεὶς ἀρχήν. ἦσαν μὲν δὴ γυμνοπαιδίαι, 2
θηωμένου δὲ τοῦ Δημαρήτου ὁ Λευτυχίδης, γεγονὼς
ἤδη αὐτὸς βασιλεὺς ἀντ᾽ ἐκείνου, πέμψας τὸν θερά-
ποντα ἐπὶ γέλωτί τε καὶ λάσθῃ εἰρώτα τὸν Δημάρητον, ὁκοῖόν τι εἴη τὸ ἄρχειν μετὰ τὸ βασιλεύειν·
ὁ δὲ ἀλγήσας τῷ ἐπειρωτήματι εἶπε φὰς "αὐτὸς μὲν 3
"ἀμφοτέρων ἤδη πεπειρῆσθαι, ἐκεῖνον δὲ οὔ, τὴν
"μέντοι ἐπειρώτησιν ταύτην ἄρξειν Λακεδαιμονίοισι
"ἢ μυρίης κακότητος ἢ μυρίης εὐδαιμονίης." ταῦτα
δὲ εἴπας καὶ κατακαλυψάμενος ἤιε ἐκ τοῦ θεήτρου ἐς
τὰ ἑωυτοῦ οἰκία, αὐτίκα δὲ παρασκευασάμενος ἔθυε
τῷ Διὶ βοῦν, θύσας δὲ τὴν μητέρα ἐκάλεσε.

*He therefore solemnly appeals to his mother to tell him
the truth.*

LXVIII.   Ἀπικομένῃ δὲ τῇ μητρὶ ἐσθεὶς ἐς τὰς 1
χεῖράς οἱ τῶν σπλάγχνων κατικέτευε λέγων τοιάδε·
"Ὦ μῆτερ, θεῶν σε τῶν τε ἄλλων καταπτόμενος
"ἱκετεύω καὶ τοῦ ἑρκείου Διὸς τοῦδε φράσαι μοι τὴν
"ἀληθείην, τίς μεύ ἐστι πατὴρ ὀρθῷ λόγῳ. Λευτυ- 2
"χίδης μὲν γὰρ ἔφη ἐν τοῖσι νείκεσι λέγων κυέουσάν
"σε ἐκ τοῦ προτέρου ἀνδρὸς οὕτω ἐλθεῖν παρὰ Ἀρίσ-
"τωνα, οἱ δὲ καὶ τὸν ματαιότερον λόγον λέγοντες φασί
"σε ἐλθεῖν παρὰ τῶν οἰκετέων τὸν ὀνοφορβὸν, καὶ ἐμὲ
"εἶναι ἐκείνου παῖδα. ἐγὼ ὦν σε μετέρχομαι τῶι 3
"θεῶν εἰπεῖν τώληθές· οὔτε γὰρ, εἴ περ πεποίηκάς
"τι τῶν λεγομένων, μούνη δὴ πεποίηκας, μετὰ πολ-
"λέων δὲ, ὅ τε λόγος πολλὸς ἐν Σπάρτῃ, ὡς Ἀρίστωνι
"σπέρμα παιδοποιὸν οὐκ ἐνῆν· τεκεῖν γὰρ ἄν οἱ καὶ
"τὰς προτέρας γυναῖκας."

His mother's explanation. He is the son of the Hero
Astrabakos, or of Ariston.

LXIX. Ὁ μὲν δὴ τοιαῦτα ἔλεγε, ἡ δὲ ἀμείβετο 1
τοισίδε· "Ὦ παῖ, ἐπείτε με λιτῇσι μετέρχεαι εἰπεῖν
"τὴν ἀληθείην, πᾶν ἐς σὲ κατειρήσεται τὠληθές. ὥς
"με ἠγάγετο Ἀρίστων ἐς ἑωυτοῦ, νυκτὶ τρίτῃ ἀπὸ τῆς
"πρώτης ἦλθέ μοι φάσμα εἰδόμενον Ἀρίστωνι, συνευ-
"νηθὲν δὲ τοὺς στεφάνους τοὺς εἶχε ἐμοὶ περιετίθει.
"καὶ τὸ μὲν οἰχώκεε, ἦκε δὲ μετὰ ταῦτα Ἀρίστων. 2
"ὡς δέ με εἶδε ἔχουσαν στεφάνους, εἰρώτα, τίς εἴη ὁ
"μοι δούς. ἐγὼ δὲ ἐφάμην ἐκεῖνον· ὁ δὲ οὐκ ὑπεδέκετο·
"ἐγὼ δὲ κατωμνύμην φαμένη αὐτὸν οὐ καλῶς ποιέειν
"ἀπαρνεύμενον· ὀλίγῳ γάρ τι πρότερον ἐλθόντα καὶ
"συνευνηθέντα δοῦναί μοι τοὺς στεφάνους. ὁρέων δέ 3
"με κατομνυμένην ὁ Ἀρίστων ἔμαθε, ὡς θεῖον εἴη τὸ
"πρῆγμα. καὶ τοῦτο μὲν οἱ στέφανοι ἐφάνησαν ἐόντες
"ἐκ τοῦ ἡρωΐου τοῦ παρὰ τῇσι θύρῃσι τῇσι αὐλείῃσι
"ἱδρυμένου, τὸ καλέουσι Ἀστραβάκου, τοῦτο δὲ οἱ
"μάντιες τὸν αὐτὸν τοῦτον ἥρωα ἀναίρεον εἶναι. οὕτω,
"ὦ παῖ, ἔχεις πᾶν, ὅσον τι καὶ βούλεαι πυθέσθαι.
"ἢ γὰρ ἐκ τοῦ ἥρωος τούτου γέγονας, καί τοι πατήρ 4
"ἐστι Ἀστράβακος ὁ ἥρως, ἢ Ἀρίστων· ἐν γάρ σε τῇ
"νυκτὶ ταύτῃ ἀναιρέομαι. τῇ δέ σευ μάλιστα κατάπ-
"τονται οἱ ἐχθροὶ, λέγοντες, ὡς αὐτὸς ὁ Ἀρίστων, ὅτε
"αὐτῷ σὺ ἠγγέλθης γεγενημένος, πολλῶν ἀκουόντων
"οὐ φήσειέ σε ἑωυτοῦ εἶναι, τὸν χρόνον γὰρ, τοὺς δέκα
"μῆνας, οὐδέκω ἐξήκειν, ἀϊδρείῃ τῶν τοιούτων ἐκεῖνος
"τοῦτο ἀπέρριψε τὸ ἔπος. τίκτουσι γὰρ γυναῖκες καὶ 5
"ἐννεάμηνα καὶ ἑπτάμηνα, καὶ οὐ πᾶσαι δέκα μῆνας
"ἐκτελέσασαι· ἐγὼ δὲ σὲ, ὦ παῖ, ἑπτάμηνον ἔτεκον.
"ἔγνω δὲ καὶ αὐτὸς ὁ Ἀρίστων οὐ μετὰ πολλὸν

" χρόνον, ὡς ἀγνοίη τὸ ἔπος ἐκβάλοι τοῦτο. λόγους δὲ
" ἄλλους περὶ γενέσιος τῆς σεωυτοῦ μὴ δέκεο· τὰ γὰρ
" ἀληθέστατα πάντα ἀκήκοας. ἐκ δὲ ὀνοφορβῶν αὐτῷ
" τε Λευτυχίδῃ καὶ τοῖσι ταῦτα λέγουσι τίκτοιεν αἱ
" γυναῖκες παῖδας."

*He flies to Elis, thence to Zakynthos, and thence to the
Court of Darius, who receives him with great liberality.*

LXX. Ἡ μὲν δὴ ταῦτα ἔλεγε, ὁ δὲ πυθόμενός   1
τε τὰ ἐβούλετο καὶ ἐπόδια λαβὼν ἐπορεύετο ἐς Ἦλιν,
τῷ λόγῳ φὰς, ὡς ἐς Δελφοὺς χρησόμενος τῷ χρηστηρίῳ πορεύεται. Λακεδαιμόνιοι δὲ ὑποτοπηθέντες
Δημάρητον δρησμῷ ἐπιχειρέειν ἐδίωκον. καί κως   2
ἔφθη ἐς Ζάκυνθον διαβὰς ὁ Δημάρητος ἐκ τῆς
Ἤλιδος. ἐπιδιαβάντες δὲ οἱ Λακεδαιμόνιοι αὐτοῦ τε
ἅπτοντο καὶ τοὺς θεράποντας αὐτὸν ἀπαιρέονται.
μετὰ δὲ, οὐ γὰρ ἐξεδίδοσαν αὐτὸν οἱ Ζακύνθιοι,
ἐνθεῦτεν διαβαίνει ἐς τὴν Ἀσίην παρὰ βασιλέα
Δαρεῖον. ὁ δὲ ὑπεδέξατό τε αὐτὸν μεγαλωστὶ καὶ
γῆν τε καὶ πόλις ἔδωκε. οὕτω ἀπίκετο ἐς τὴν Ἀσίην   3
Δημάρητος καὶ τοιαύτη χρησάμενος τύχῃ, ἄλλα τε
Λακεδαιμονίοισι συχνὰ ἔργοισί τε καὶ γνώμῃσι ἀπο-
λαμπρυνθεὶς, ἐν δὲ δὴ καὶ Ὀλυμπιάδα σφι ἀνελόμενος τεθρίππῳ προσέβαλε, μοῦνος τοῦτο πάντων δὴ
τῶν γενομένων βασιλέων ἐν Σπάρτῃ ποιήσας.

*Leotychides succeeded Demaratos at Sparta. Zeuxidemos
died in the lifetime of his father Leotychides, leaving a
son Archidamos. Leotychides married again and had
a daughter, Lampito, who married her nephew Archidamos.*

LXXI. Λευτυχίδης δὲ ὁ Μενάρεος Δημαρήτου   1

καταπαυθέντος διεδέξατο τὴν βασιληίην. καὶ οἱ
γίνεται παῖς Ζευξίδημος, τὸν δὴ Κυνίσκον μετεξέτεροι Σπαρτιητέων ἐκάλεον. οὗτος ὁ Ζευξίδημος οὐκ
ἐβασίλευσε Σπάρτης· πρὸ Λευτυχίδεω γὰρ τελευτᾷ,
λιπὼν παῖδα Ἀρχίδημον. Λευτυχίδης δὲ στερηθεὶς 2
Ζευξιδήμου γαμέει δευτέρην γυναῖκα Εὐρυδάμην,
ἐοῦσαν Μενίου μὲν ἀδελφεὴν, Διακτορίδεω δὲ θυγατέρα, ἐκ τῆς οἱ ἔρσεν μὲν γίνεται οὐδὲν, θυγάτηρ δὲ
Λαμπιτώ, τὴν Ἀρχίδημος ὁ Ζευξιδήμου γαμέει δόντος
αὐτῷ Λευτυχίδεω.

At a later period (about B.C. 478) Leotychides was convicted
of taking a bribe in Thessaly and banished, and died
in Tegea.

LXXII. Οὐ μὲν οὐδὲ Λευτυχίδης κατεγήρα ἐν 1
Σπάρτῃ, ἀλλὰ τίσιν τοιήνδε τινὰ Δημαρήτῳ ἐξέτισε·
ἐστρατήγησε Λακεδαιμονίοισι ἐς Θεσσαλίην, παρεὸν
δέ οἱ ὑποχείρια πάντα ποιήσασθαι ἐδωροδόκησε
ἀργύριον πολλόν. ἐπ᾽ αὐτοφώρῳ δὲ ἁλοὺς αὐτοῦ ἐν 2
τῷ στρατοπέδῳ, ἐπικατήμενος χειρίδι πλέῃ ἀργυρίου,
ἔφυγε ἐκ Σπάρτης ὑπὸ δικαστήριον ὑπαχθείς, καὶ τὰ
οἰκία οἱ κατεσκάφη· ἔφυγε δὲ ἐς Τεγέην καὶ ἐτελεύτησε ἐν ταύτῃ.

B.C. 491. Kleomenes and Leotychides make a joint expedition
into Aegina. The Aeginetans thereupon give ten
hostages who are deposited in Attica.

LXXIII. Ταῦτα μὲν δὴ ἐγένετο χρόνῳ ὕστερον· 1
τότε δὲ ὡς. τῷ Κλεομένεϊ ὡδώθη τὸ ἐς τὸν Δημάρητον πρῆγμα, αὐτίκα παραλαβὼν Λευτυχίδην ἤιε
ἐπὶ τοὺς Αἰγινήτας, δεινόν τινά σφι ἔγκοτον διὰ τὸν
προπηλακισμὸν ἔχων. οὕτω δὴ οὔτε οἱ Αἰγινῆται 2

ἀμφοτέρων τῶν βασιλέων ἡκόντων ἐπ' αὐτοὺς ἐδικαίευν ἔτι ἀντιβαίνειν, ἐκεῖνοί τε ἐπιλεξάμενοι ἄνδρας
δέκα Αἰγινητέων τοὺς πλείστου ἀξίους καὶ πλούτῳ
καὶ γένεϊ ἦγον, καὶ ἄλλους καὶ δὴ καὶ Κρῖόν τε τὸν
Πολυκρίτου καὶ Κάσαμβον τὸν Ἀριστοκράτεος, οἵ
περ εἶχον μέγιστον κράτος· ἀγαγόντες δέ σφεας ἐς
γῆν τὴν Ἀττικὴν παραθήκην παρατίθενται ἐς τοὺς
ἐχθίστους Αἰγινήτῃσι Ἀθηναίους.

*The falseness of Kleomenes' dealing in regard to Demaratos
becoming known, Kleomenes fled, and after a time
raised a party in Arcadia against Sparta.*

LXXIV. Μετὰ δὲ ταῦτα Κλεομένεα ἐπάϊστον 1
γενόμενον κακοτεχνήσαντα ἐς Δημάρητον δεῖμα ἔλαβε
Σπαρτιητέων, καὶ ὑπεξέσχε ἐς Θεσσαλίην. ἐνθεῦτεν
δὲ ἀπικόμενος ἐς τὴν Ἀρκαδίην νεώτερα ἔπρησσε
πρήγματα, συνιστὰς τοὺς Ἀρκάδας ἐπὶ τῇ Σπάρτῃ,
ἄλλους τε ὅρκους προσάγων σφι ἦ μὲν ἕψεσθαί
σφεας αὐτῷ τῇ ἂν ἐξηγῆται, καὶ δὴ καὶ ἐς Νώνακριν
πόλιν πρόθυμος ἦν τῶν Ἀρκάδων τοὺς προεστεῶτας
ἀγινέων ἐξορκοῦν τὸ Στυγὸς ὕδωρ. ἐν δὲ ταύτῃ τῇ 2
πόλι λέγεται εἶναι ὑπ' Ἀρκάδων τὸ Στυγὸς ὕδωρ,
καὶ δὴ καὶ ἔστι τοιόνδε τι· ὕδωρ ὀλίγον φαινόμενον
ἐκ πέτρης στάζει ἐς ἄγκος, τὸ δὲ ἄγκος αἱμασιῆς τις
περιθέει κύκλος. ἡ δὲ Νώνακρις, ἐν τῇ ἡ πηγὴ αὕτη
τυγχάνει ἐοῦσα, πόλις ἐστὶ τῆς Ἀρκαδίης πρὸς
Φενεῷ.

*The Spartans in terror restore him to his office; but he
presently became insane, and whilst in confinement
mangled himself in a horrible manner: which the*

various Greek states accounted for as a divine visitation for acts of sacrilege.

LXXV. Μαθόντες δὲ Λακεδαιμόνιοι Κλεομένεα   1
ταῦτα πρήσσοντα κατῆγον αὐτὸν δείσαντες ἐπὶ τοῖσι
αὐτοῖσι ἐς Σπάρτην, τοῖσι καὶ πρότερον ἦρχε. κατελ-
θόντα δὲ αὐτὸν αὐτίκα ὑπέλαβε μανιὰς νοῦσος, ἐόντα
καὶ πρότερον ὑπομαργότερον· ὅκως γάρ τεῳ ἐντύχοι
Σπαρτιητέων, ἐνέχραυε ἐς τὸ πρόσωπον τὸ σκῆπτρον.
ποιεῦντα δὲ αὐτὸν ταῦτα καὶ παραφρονήσαντα ἔδησαν   2
οἱ προσήκοντες ἐν ξύλῳ· ὁ δὲ δεθεὶς τὸν φύλακον
μουνωθέντα ἰδὼν τῶν ἄλλων αἴτεε μάχαιραν, οὐ
βουλομένου δὲ τὰ πρῶτα τοῦ φυλάκου διδόναι
ἠπείλεε τά μιν λυθεὶς ποιήσει, ἐς ὃ δείσας τὰς
ἀπειλὰς ὁ φύλακος (ἦν γὰρ τῶν τις εἰλωτέων) διδοῖ
οἱ μάχαιραν. Κλεομένης δὲ παραλαβὼν τὸν σίδηρον   3
ἤρχετο ἐκ τῶν κνημέων ἑωυτὸν λωβώμενος· ἐπιτάμνων
γὰρ κατὰ μῆκος τὰς σάρκας προέβαινε ἐκ τῶν
κνημέων ἐς τοὺς μηρούς, ἐκ δὲ τῶν μηρῶν ἔς τε τὰ
ἰσχία καὶ τὰς λαπάρας, ἐς ὃ ἐς τὴν γαστέρα ἀπίκετο
καὶ ταύτην καταχορδεύων ἀπέθανε τρόπῳ τοιούτῳ,
ὡς μὲν οἱ πολλοὶ λέγουσι Ἑλλήνων, ὅτι τὴν Πυθίην
ἀνέγνωσε τὰ περὶ Δημάρητον γενόμενα λέγειν, ὡς δὲ
Ἀθηναῖοι λέγουσι, διότι ἐς Ἐλευσῖνα ἐσβαλὼν ἔκειρε
τὸ τέμενος τῶν θεῶν, ὡς δὲ Ἀργεῖοι, ὅτι ἐξ ἱροῦ
αὐτῶν τοῦ Ἄργου Ἀργείων τοὺς καταφυγόντας ἐκ
τῆς μάχης καταγινέων κατέκοπτε καὶ αὐτὸ τὸ ἄλσος
ἐν ἀλογίῃ ἔχων ἐνέπρησε.

His impieties in the invasion of Argos [about B.C. 510].

LXXVI. Κλεομένεϊ γὰρ μαντευομένῳ ἐν Δελ-   1
φοῖσι ἐχρήσθη Ἄργος αἱρήσειν. ἐπείτε δὲ Σπαρ-

τιήτας ἄγων ἀπίκετο ἐπὶ ποταμὸν Ἐρασῖνον, ὃς
λέγεται ῥέειν ἐκ τῆς Στυμφηλίδος λίμνης (τὴν γὰρ
δὴ λίμνην ταύτην ἐς χάσμα ἀφανὲς ἐκδιδοῦσαν ἀναφαίνεσθαι ἐν Ἄργεϊ, τὸ ἐνθεῦτεν δὲ τὸ ὕδωρ ἤδη
τοῦτο ὑπ᾽ Ἀργείων Ἐρασῖνον καλέεσθαι), ἀπικόμενος
δ᾽ ὦν ὁ Κλεομένης ἐπὶ τὸν ποταμὸν τοῦτον ἐσφαγιάζετο αὐτῷ. καὶ οὐ γὰρ ἐκαλλιέρεε οὐδαμῶς διαβαίνειν   2
μιν, ἄγασθαι μὲν ἔφη τοῦ Ἐρασίνου οὐ προδιδόντος
τοὺς πολιήτας, Ἀργείους μέντοι οὐδ᾽ ὣς χαιρήσειν.
μετὰ δὲ ταῦτα ἐξαναχωρήσας τὴν στρατιὴν κατήγαγε
ἐς Θυρέην, σφαγιασάμενος δὲ τῇ θαλάσσῃ ταῦρον
πλοίοισί σφεας ἤγαγε ἔς τε τὴν Τιρυνθίην χώρην καὶ
Ναυπλίην.

He kills a number of Argives at Tiryns by a ruse;

LXXVII. Ἀργεῖοι δ᾽ ἐβοήθεον πυνθανόμενοι   1
ταῦτα ἐπὶ θάλασσαν. ὡς δὲ ἀγχοῦ μὲν ἐγίνοντο τῆς
Τιρυνθος, χώρῳ δὲ ἐν τούτῳ τῷ κέεται Ἡσίπεια
οὔνομα, μεταίχμιον οὐ μέγα ἀπολιπόντες ἵζοντο
ἀντίοι τοῖσι Λακεδαιμονίοισι. ἐνθαῦτα δὴ οἱ Ἀργεῖοι
τὴν μὲν ἐκ τοῦ φανεροῦ μάχην οὐκ ἐφοβέοντο, ἀλλὰ
μὴ δόλῳ αἱρεθέωσι. καὶ γὰρ δή σφι ἐς τοῦτο τὸ   2
πρῆγμα εἶχε τὸ χρηστήριον, τὸ ἐπίκοινα ἔχρησε ἡ
Πυθίη τούτοισί τε καὶ Μιλησίοισι, λέγον ὧδε·

Ἀλλ᾽ ὅταν ἡ θήλεια τὸν ἄρσενα νικήσασα
ἐξελάσῃ, καὶ κῦδος ἐν Ἀργείοισιν ἄρηται,
πολλὰς Ἀργείων ἀμφιδρυφέας τότε θήσει.
ὥς ποτέ τις ἐρέει καὶ ἐπεσσομένων ἀνθρώπων·
δεινὸς ὄφις τριέλικτος ἀπώλετο δουρὶ δαμασθείς.

Ταῦτα δὴ πάντα συνελθόντα τοῖσι Ἀργείοισι φόβον   3

παρεῖχε. καὶ δή σφι πρὸς ταῦτα ἔδοξε τῷ κήρυκι
τῶν πολεμίων χρᾶσθαι, δόξαν δέ σφι ἐποίευν τοιόνδε·
ὅκως ὁ Σπαρτιήτης κῆρυξ προσημαίνοι τι Λακεδαιμονίοισι, ἐποίευν καὶ οἱ Ἀργεῖοι τὠυτὸ τοῦτο.
LXXVIII. Μαθὼν δὲ ὁ Κλεομένης ποιεῦντας τοὺς 1
Ἀργείους ὁκοῖόν τι ὁ σφέτερος κῆρυξ σημήνειε,
παραγγέλλει σφι, ὅταν σημήνῃ ὁ κῆρυξ ποιέεσθαι
ἄριστον, τότε ἀναλαβόντας τὰ ὅπλα χωρέειν ἐς τοὺς
Ἀργείους. ταῦτα καὶ ἐγένετο ἐπιτελέα ἐκ τῶν Λακε- 2
δαιμονίων· ἄριστον γὰρ ποιευμένοισι τοῖσι Ἀργείοισι
ἐκ τοῦ κηρύγματος ἐπεκέατο, καὶ πολλοὺς μὲν
ἐφόνευσαν αὐτῶν, πολλῷ δ' ἔτι πλεῦνας ἐς τὸ ἄλσος
τοῦ Ἄργου καταφυγόντας περιιζόμενοι ἐφύλασσον.

*and massacres a large number who had taken refuge in
the sacred enclosure of Argos, and burnt the Grove.*

LXXIX. Ἐνθεῦτεν δὲ ὁ Κλεομένης ἐποίεε 1
τοιόνδε· ἔχων αὐτομόλους ἄνδρας καὶ πυνθανόμενος
τούτων ἐξεκάλεε πέμπων κήρυκα, οὐνομαστὶ λέγων
τῶν Ἀργείων τοὺς ἐν τῷ ἱρῷ ἀπεργμένους, ἐξεκάλεε δὲ
φὰς αὐτῶν ἔχειν τὰ ἄποινα· ἄποινα δέ ἐστι Πελοποννησίοισι δύο μνέαι τεταγμέναι κατ' ἄνδρα αἰχμάλωτον
ἐκτίνειν. κατὰ πεντήκοντα δὴ ὦν τῶν Ἀργείων ὡς
ἑκάστους ἐκκαλεύμενος ὁ Κλεομένης ἔκτεινε. ταῦτα 2
δέ κως γινόμενα ἐλελήθεε τοὺς λοιποὺς τοὺς ἐν τῷ
τεμένεϊ· ἅτε γὰρ πυκνοῦ ἐόντος τοῦ ἄλσεος οὐκ ὥρων
οἱ ἐντὸς τοὺς ἐκτὸς ὅ τι ἔπρησσον, πρίν γε δὴ αὐτῶν
τις ἀναβὰς ἐπὶ δένδρος κατεῖδε τὸ ποιεύμενον. οὐκ
ὦν δὴ ἔτι καλεόμενοι ἐξήϊσαν. LXXX. Ἐνθαῦτα
δὴ ὁ Κλεομένης ἐκέλευε πάντα τινὰ τῶν εἰλωτέων
περινέευ ὕλῃ τὸ ἄλσος, τῶν δὲ πειθομένων ἐνέπρησε

τὸ ἄλσος. καιομένου δὲ ἤδη ἐπείρετο τῶν τινὰ
αὐτομόλων, τίνος εἴη θεῶν τὸ ἄλσος, ὁ δὲ ἔφη Ἄργου
εἶναι· ὁ δὲ ὡς ἤκουσε, ἀναστενάξας μέγα εἶπε· "᾽Ω
"Ἄπολλον χρηστήριε, ἦ μεγάλως με ἠπάτηκας φά-
" μενος Ἄργος αἱρήσειν· συμβάλλομαι δ' ἐξήκειν μοι
" τὸ χρηστήριον."

*He then sent his army back to Sparta, and went to the
temple of Here, between Mycenae and Argos; had the
priest dragged out; and offered sacrifice himself.*

LXXXI. Μετὰ δὲ ταῦτα ὁ Κλεομένης τὴν μὲν
πλέω στρατιὴν ἀπῆκε ἀπιέναι ἐς Σπάρτην, χιλίους
δὲ αὐτὸς λαβὼν τοὺς ἀριστέας ἤϊε ἐς τὸ Ἡραῖον
θύσων. βουλόμενον δὲ αὐτὸν θύειν ἐπὶ τοῦ βωμοῦ ὁ
ἱρεὺς ἀπηγόρευε, φὰς οὐκ ὅσιον εἶναι ξείνῳ αὐτόθι
θύειν. ὁ δὲ Κλεομένης τὸν ἱρέα ἐκέλευε τοὺς εἵλωτας
ἀπὸ τοῦ βωμοῦ ἀπάγοντας μαστιγῶσαι, καὶ αὐτὸς
ἔθυσε· ποιήσας δὲ ταῦτα ἀπῆϊε ἐς τὴν Σπάρτην.

*On his return to Sparta he is accused of having spared
Argos for a bribe.*

LXXXII. Νοστήσαντα δέ μιν ὑπῆγον οἱ ἐχθροὶ
ὑπὸ τοὺς ἐφόρους, φάμενοί μιν δωροδοκήσαντα οὐκ
ἑλεῖν τὸ Ἄργος, παρεὸν εὐπετέως μιν ἑλεῖν. ὁ δέ
σφι ἔλεξε, οὔτε εἰ ψευδόμενος οὔτε εἰ ἀληθέα λέγων,
ἔχω σαφηνέως εἶπαι, ἔλεξε δ' ὧν φάμενος, ἐπείτε δὴ
τὸ τοῦ Ἄργου ἱρὸν εἷλε, δοκέειν οἱ ἐξεληλυθέναι τὸν
τοῦ θεοῦ χρησμὸν, πρὸς ὧν ταῦτα οὐ δικαιοῦν πειρᾶν
τῆς πόλιος, πρίν γε δὴ ἱροῖσι χρήσηται καὶ μάθῃ,
εἴτε οἱ ὁ θεὸς παραδιδοῖ εἴτε οἱ ἐμποδὼν ἕστηκε·

καλλιερευμένῳ δὲ ἐν τῷ Ἡραίῳ ἐκ τοῦ ἀγάλματος 2
τῶν στηθέων φλόγα πυρὸς ἐκλάμψαι, μαθεῖν δὲ
αὐτὸς οὕτω τὴν ἀτρεκείην, ὅτι οὐκ αἱρέει τὸ Ἄργος·
εἰ μὲν γὰρ ἐκ τῆς κεφαλῆς τοῦ ἀγάλματος ἐξέλαμψε,
αἱρέειν ἂν κατ᾽ ἄκρης τὴν πόλιν, ἐκ τῶν στηθέων δὲ
λάμψαντος πᾶν οἱ πεποιῆσθαι, ὅσον ὁ θεὸς ἐβούλετο
γενέσθαι. ταῦτα δὲ λέγων πιστά τε καὶ οἰκότα ἐδόκεε
Σπαρτιήτῃσι λέγειν, καὶ διέφυγε πολλὸν τοὺς διώκοντας.

The effect of the invasion upon Argos.

LXXXIII. Ἄργος δὲ ἀνδρῶν ἐχηρώθη οὕτω, 1
ὥστε οἱ δοῦλοι αὐτῶν ἔσχον πάντα τὰ πρήγματα
ἄρχοντές τε καὶ διέποντες, ἐς ὃ ἐπήβησαν οἱ τῶν
ἀπολομένων παῖδες. ἔπειτά σφεας οὗτοι ἀνακτώ-
μενοι ὀπίσω ἐς ἑωυτοὺς τὸ Ἄργος ἐξέβαλον· ἐξω-
θεύμενοι δὲ οἱ δοῦλοι μάχῃ ἔσχον Τίρυνθα. τέως μὲν 2
δή σφι ἦν ἄρθμια ἐς ἀλλήλους, ἔπειτα δὲ ἐς τοὺς
δούλους ἦλθε ἀνὴρ μάντις Κλέανδρος, γένος ἐὼν
Φιγαλεὺς ἀπ᾽ Ἀρκαδίης· οὗτος τοὺς δούλους ἀνέγνωσε
ἐπιθέσθαι τοῖσι δεσπότῃσι. ἐκ τούτου δὲ πόλεμός
σφι ἦν ἐπὶ χρόνον συχνὸν, ἐς ὃ δὴ μόγις οἱ Ἀργεῖοι
ἐπεκράτησαν.

Another account of the origin of Kleomenes' madness.

LXXXIV. Ἀργεῖοι μὲν νυν διὰ ταῦτα Κλεο- 1
μένεά φασι μανέντα ἀπολέσθαι κακῶς, αὐτοὶ δὲ
Σπαρτιῆταί φασι ἐκ δαιμονίου μὲν οὐδενὸς μανῆναι
Κλεομένεα, Σκύθῃσι δὲ ὁμιλήσαντά μιν ἀκρητοπότην
γενέσθαι καὶ ἐκ τούτου μανῆναι. Σκύθας γὰρ τοὺς 2
νομάδας, ἐπείτε σφι Δαρεῖον ἐσβαλεῖν ἐς τὴν χώρην,

μετὰ ταῦτα μεμονέναι μιν τίσασθαι, πέμψαντας δὲ
ἐς Σπάρτην συμμαχίην τε ποιέεσθαι, καὶ συντίθεσθαι,
ὡς χρεὸν εἴη αὐτοὺς μὲν τοὺς Σκύθας παρὰ Φᾶσιν
ποταμὸν πειρᾶν ἐς τὴν Μηδικὴν ἐσβαλεῖν, σφέας δὲ
τοὺς Σπαρτιήτας κελεύειν ἐξ Ἐφέσου ὁρμεομένους
ἀναβαίνειν καὶ ἔπειτα ἐς τὠυτὸ ἀπαντᾶν. Κλεομένεα 3
δὲ λέγουσι ἡκόντων τῶν Σκυθέων ἐπὶ ταῦτα ὁμιλέειν
σφι μεζόνως, ὁμιλέοντα δὲ μᾶλλον τοῦ ἱκνεομένου
μαθεῖν τὴν ἀκρητοποσίην παρ' αὐτῶν· ἐκ τούτου δὲ
μανῆναί μιν νομίζουσι Σπαρτιῆται. ἔκ τε τοῦ, ὡς
αὐτοὶ λέγουσι, ἐπεὰν ζωρότερον βούλωνται πιεῖν,
"ἐπισκύθισον" λέγουσι. οὕτω δὴ Σπαρτιῆται τὰ περὶ
Κλεομένεα λέγουσι· ἐμοὶ δὲ δοκέει τίσιν ταύτην ὁ
Κλεομένης Δημαρήτῳ ἐκτῖσαι.

Resuming from c. 75. *The Aeginetans appeal to the
Spartans against the forcible taking of the ten hostages
by Leotychides. The Spartans decide to give up Leotychides; as a compromise he is sent to Athens to demand
back the hostages.*

LXXXV. Τελευτήσαντος δὲ Κλεομένεος, ὡς 1
ἐπύθοντο Αἰγινῆται, ἔπεμπον ἐς Σπάρτην ἀγγέλους
καταβωσομένους Λευτυχίδεω περὶ τῶν ἐν Ἀθήνῃσι
ὁμήρων ἐχομένων. Λακεδαιμόνιοι δὲ δικαστήριον
συναγαγόντες ἔγνωσαν περιυβρίσθαι Αἰγινήτας ὑπὸ
Λευτυχίδεω, καί μιν κατέκριναν ἔκδοτον ἄγεσθαι ἐς
Αἴγιναν ἀντὶ τῶν ἐν Ἀθήνῃσι ἐχομένων ἀνδρῶν.
μελλόντων δὲ ἄγειν τῶν Αἰγινητέων τὸν Λευτυχίδην 2
εἶπέ σφι Θεασίδης ὁ Λεωπρέπεος, ἐὼν ἐν τῇ Σπάρτῃ
δόκιμος ἀνήρ· "Τί βούλεσθε ποιέειν, ἄνδρες Αἰγι-
"νῆται; τὸν βασιλέα τῶν Σπαρτιητέων ἔκδοτον

" γενόμενον ὑπὸ τῶν πολιητέων ἄγειν; εἰ νῦν ὀργῇ
" χρεόμενοι ἔγνωσαν οὕτω Σπαρτιῆται, ὅκως ἐξ ὑστέ-
" ρης μή τι ὑμῖν, ἢν ταῦτα πρήσσητε, πανώλεθρον
" κακὸν ἐς τὴν χώρην ἐσβάλωσι." ταῦτα ἀκούσαντες   3
οἱ Αἰγινῆται ἔσχοντο τῆς ἀγωγῆς, ὁμολογίῃ δὲ ἐχρήσαντο τοιῇδε, ἐπισπόμενον Λευτυχίδην ἐς Ἀθήνας
ἀποδοῦναι Αἰγινήτῃσι τοὺς ἄνδρας.

The Athenians refuse to give them up.

LXXXVI. Ὡς δὲ ἀπικόμενος Λευτυχίδης ἐς
τὰς Ἀθήνας ἀπαίτεε τὴν παραθήκην, οἱ Ἀθηναῖοι
προφάσιας εἷλκον οὐ βουλόμενοι ἀποδοῦναι, φάντες
δύο σφέας ἐόντας βασιλέας παραθέσθαι καὶ οὐ
δικαιοῦν τῷ ἑτέρῳ ἄνευ τοῦ ἑτέρου ἀποδιδόναι. οὐ   α 1
φαμένων δὲ ἀποδώσειν τῶν Ἀθηναίων ἔλεξέ σφι
Λευτυχίδης τάδε·

The Speech of Leotychides. Story of Glaukos.

"Ὦ Ἀθηναῖοι, ποιέετε μὲν ὁκότερα βούλεσθε
" αὐτοί· καὶ γὰρ ἀποδιδόντες ποιέετε ὅσια, καὶ μὴ
" ἀποδιδόντες τὰ ἐναντία τούτων· ὁκοῖον μέντοι τι ἐν
" τῇ Σπάρτῃ συνηνείχθη γενέσθαι περὶ παρακαταθή-   2
" κης, βούλομαι ὑμῖν εἶπαι. λέγομεν ἡμεῖς οἱ Σπαρτι-
" ῆται γενέσθαι ἐν τῇ Λακεδαίμονι κατὰ τρίτην γενεὴν
" τὴν ἀπ' ἐμέο Γλαῦκον Ἐπικύδεος παῖδα. τοῦτον
" τὸν ἄνδρα φαμὲν τά τε ἄλλα πάντα περιήκειν τὰ
" πρῶτα, καὶ δὴ καὶ ἀκούειν ἄριστα δικαιοσύνης πέρι
" πάντων, ὅσοι τὴν Λακεδαίμονα τοῦτον τὸν χρόνον
" οἴκεον. συνενειχθῆναι δέ οἱ ἐν χρόνῳ ἱκνεομένῳ τάδε   3
" λέγομεν, ἄνδρα Μιλήσιον ἀπικόμενον ἐς Σπάρτην
" βούλεσθαί οἱ ἐλθεῖν ἐς λόγους, προϊσχόμενον τοιάδε·

" ' Εἰμὶ μὲν Μιλήσιος, ἥκω δὲ τῆς σῆς, Γλαῦκε, δικαιο-
" ' σύνης βουλόμενος ἀπολαῦσαι. ὡς γὰρ δὴ ἀνὰ πᾶσαν 4
" ' μὲν τὴν ἄλλην Ἑλλάδα, ἐν δὲ καὶ περὶ Ἰωνίην τῆς
" ' σῆς δικαιοσύνης ἦν λόγος πολλὸς, ἐμεωυτῷ λόγους
" ' ἐδίδουν καὶ ὅτι ἐπικίνδυνός ἐστι αἰεί κοτε ἡ Ἰωνίη,
" ' ἡ δὲ Πελοπόννησος ἀσφαλέως ἱδρυμένη, καὶ διότι
" ' χρήματα οὐδαμὰ τοὺς αὐτοὺς ἔστι ὁρᾶν ἔχοντας.
" ' ταῦτά τε ὦν ἐπιλεγομένῳ καὶ βουλευομένῳ ἔδοξέ 5
" ' μοι τὰ ἡμίσεα πάσης τῆς οὐσίης ἐξαργυρώσαντα
" ' θέσθαι παρὰ σὲ, εὖ ἐξεπισταμένῳ, ὥς μοι κείμενα
" ' ἔσται παρὰ σοὶ σόα. σὺ δή μοι καὶ τὰ χρήματα δέξαι
" ' καὶ τάδε τὰ σύμβολα σῷζε λαβών· ὃς δ᾽ ἂν ἔχων
" ' ταῦτα ἀπαιτέῃ, τούτῳ ἀποδοῦναι.' Ὁ μὲν δὴ ἀπὸ β1
" Μιλήτου ἥκων ξεῖνος τοσαῦτα ἔλεξε, Γλαῦκος δὲ
" ἐδέξατο τὴν παρακαταθήκην ἐπὶ τῷ εἰρημένῳ λόγῳ.
" χρόνου δὲ πολλοῦ διελθόντος ἦλθον ἐς τὴν Σπάρτην·
" τούτου τοῦ παραθεμένου τὰ χρήματα οἱ παῖδες, ἐλ-
" θόντες δὲ ἐς λόγους τῷ Γλαύκῳ καὶ ἀποδεικνύντες τὰ
" σύμβολα ἀπαίτεον τὰ χρήματα. ὁ δὲ διωθέετο ἀντυ-
" ποκρινόμενος τοιάδε· Οὔτε μέμνημαι τὸ πρῆγμα, οὔτε 2
" ' με περιφέρει οὐδὲν εἰδέναι τούτων τῶν ὑμεῖς λέγετε,
" ' βούλομαί τε ἀναμνησθεὶς ποιέειν πᾶν τὸ δίκαιον·
" ' καὶ γὰρ εἰ ἔλαβον, ὀρθῶς ἀποδοῦναι, καὶ εἴ γε ἀρχὴν
" ' μὴ ἔλαβον, νόμοισι τοῖσι Ἑλλήνων χρήσομαι ἐς
" ' ὑμέας. ταῦτα ὦν ὑμῖν ἀναβάλλομαι κυρώσειν ἐς
" ' τέταρτον μῆνα ἀπὸ τοῦδε.' Οἱ μὲν δὴ Μιλήσιοι συμ- χ1
" φορὴν ποιεύμενοι ἀπαλλάσσοντο ὡς ἀπεστερημένοι
" τῶν χρημάτων, Γλαῦκος δὲ ἐπορεύετο ἐς Δελφοὺς
" χρησόμενος τῷ χρηστηρίῳ. ἐπειρωτέοντα δὲ αὐτὸν
" τὸ χρηστήριον, εἰ ὅρκῳ τὰ χρήματα ληίσηται, ἡ
" Πυθίη μετέρχεται τοισίδε τοῖσι ἔπεσι·

" 'Γλαῦκ' Ἐπικυδείδη, τὸ μὲν αὐτίκα κέρδιον οὕτως, 2
" 'ὅρκῳ νικῆσαι καὶ χρήματα ληΐσσασθαι.
" 'ὄμνυ', ἐπεὶ θάνατός γε καὶ εὔορκον μένει ἄνδρα.
" 'ἀλλ' Ὅρκου παΐς ἐστὶν ἀνώνυμος, οὐδ' ἔπι χεῖρες,
" 'οὐδὲ πόδες· κραιπνὸς δὲ μετέρχεται, εἰσόκε πᾶσαν
" 'συμμάρψας ὀλέσει γενεὴν καὶ οἶκον ἅπαντα.
" 'ἀνδρὸς δ' εὐόρκου γενεὴ μετόπισθεν ἀμείνων.'
" ταῦτα ἀκούσας ὁ Γλαῦκος συγγνώμην τὸν θεὸν
" παραιτέετο αὐτῷ σχεῖν τῶν ῥηθέντων. ἡ δὲ Πυθίη
" ἔφη τὸ πειρηθῆναι.τοῦ θεοῦ καὶ τὸ ποιῆσαι ἴσον
" δύνασθαι. Γλαῦκος μὲν δὴ μεταπεμψάμενος τοὺς δ
" Μιλησίους ξείνους ἀποδιδοῖ σφι τὰ χρήματα. τοῦ
" δὲ εἵνεκεν ὁ λόγος ὅδε, ὦ Ἀθηναῖοι, ὡρμήθη λέγεσθαι
" ἐς ὑμέας, εἰρήσεται· Γλαύκου νῦν οὔτε τι ἀπόγονόν
" ἐστι οὐδὲν οὔτ' ἱστίη οὐδεμία νομιζομένη εἶναι
" Γλαύκου, ἐκτέτριπταί τε πρόρριζος ἐκ Σπάρτης.
" οὕτω ἀγαθὸν μηδὲ διανοέεσθαι περὶ παρακαταθήκης
" ἄλλο γε ἢ ἀποδιδόναι." Λευτυχίδης μὲν εἴπας ταῦτα,
ὥς οἱ οὐδὲ οὕτω ἐσήκουον οἱ Ἀθηναῖοι, ἀπαλλάσσετο.

*The Aeginetans retaliate on Athens by seizing the Sacred
vessel off Sunium.*

LXXXVII. Οἱ δὲ Αἰγινῆται, πρὶν τῶν πρότερον
ἀδικημάτων δοῦναι δίκας, τῶν ἐς Ἀθηναίους ὕβρισαν
Θηβαίοισι χαριζόμενοι, ἐποίησαν τοιόνδε· μεμφόμενοι
τοῖσι Ἀθηναίοισι καὶ.ἀξιοῦντες ἀδικέεσθαι, ὡς τιμωρησόμενοι τοὺς Ἀθηναίους παρεσκευάζοντο. καὶ ἦν
γὰρ δὴ τοῖσι Ἀθηναίοισι πεντετηρὶς ἐπὶ Σουνίῳ,
λοχήσαντες ὦν τὴν θεωρίδα νέα εἷλον πλήρεα ἀνδρῶν
τῶν πρώτων Ἀθηναίων, λαβόντες δὲ τοὺς ἄνδρας
ἔδησαν.

The Athenians intrigue with Nikodromos who was heading a popular movement in Aegina to betray the island to them,

LXXXVIII. Ἀθηναῖοι δὲ παθόντες ταῦτα πρὸς Αἰγινητέων οὐκέτι ἀνεβάλλοντο μὴ οὐ τὸ πᾶν μηχανήσασθαι ἐπ' Αἰγινήτῃσι. καὶ ἦν γὰρ Νικό- δρομος Κνοίθου καλεόμενος ἐν τῇ Αἰγίνῃ ἀνὴρ δόκιμος, οὗτος μεμφόμενος μὲν τοῖσι Αἰγινήτῃσι προτέρην ἑωυτοῦ ἐξέλασιν ἐκ τῆς νήσου, μαθὼν δὲ τότε τοὺς Ἀθηναίους ἀναρτημένους ἔρδειν Αἰγινήτας κακῶς, συντίθεται Ἀθηναίοισι προδοσίην Αἰγίνης, φράσας ἐν τῇ τε ἡμέρῃ ἐπιχειρήσει, καὶ ἐκείνους ἐς τὴν ἥκειν δεήσει βοηθέοντας.

but fail because of the difficulty of getting ships in time.

LXXXIX. Μετὰ ταῦτα καταλαμβάνει μὲν κατὰ συνεθήκατο Ἀθηναίοισι ὁ Νικόδρομος τὴν παλαιὴν καλεομένην πόλιν, Ἀθηναῖοι δὲ οὐ παραγίνονται ἐς δέον· οὐ γὰρ ἔτυχον ἐοῦσαι νέες σφι ἀξιόμαχοι τῇσι Αἰγινητέων συμβαλεῖν. ἐν ᾧ ὦν Κορινθίων ἐδέοντο χρῆσαί σφι νέας, ἐν τούτῳ διεφθάρη τὰ πρήγματα. οἱ δὲ Κορίνθιοι, ἦσαν γὰρ σφίσι τοῦτον τὸν χρόνον φίλοι ἐς τὰ μάλιστα, Ἀθηναίοισι διδοῦσι δεομένοισι εἴκοσι νέας, διδοῦσι δὲ πενταδράχμους ἀποδόμενοι· δωρεὴν γὰρ ἐν τῷ νόμῳ οὐκ ἐξῆν δοῦναι. ταύτας τε δὴ λαβόντες οἱ Ἀθηναῖοι καὶ τὰς σφετέρας, πληρώ- σαντες ἑβδομήκοντα νέας τὰς ἁπάσας, ἔπλωον ἐπὶ τὴν Αἴγιναν καὶ ὑστέρησαν ἡμέρῃ μιῇ τῆς συγκειμένης.

Nikodromos escapes, and is settled at Sunium.

XC. Νικόδρομος δὲ, ὡς οἱ Ἀθηναῖοι ἐς τὸν καιρὸν

οὐ παρεγίνοντο, ἐς πλοῖον ἐσβὰς ἐκδιδρήσκει ἐκ τῆς
Αἰγίνης, σὺν δέ οἱ καὶ ἄλλοι ἐκ τῶν Αἰγινητέων
ἔσποντο, τοῖσι Ἀθηναῖοι Σούνιον οἰκῆσαι ἔδοσαν.
ἐνθεῦτεν δὲ οὗτοι ὁρμεόμενοι ἔφερόν τε καὶ ἦγον τοὺς
ἐν τῇ νήσῳ Αἰγινήτας.

Sacrilege of the Aeginetan oligarchical party.

XCI. Ταῦτα μὲν δὴ ὕστερον ἐγίνετο, Αἰγινητέων 1
δὲ οἱ παχέες ἐπαναστάντος τοῦ δήμου σφι ἅμα
Νικοδρόμῳ ἐπεκράτησαν, καὶ ἔπειτά σφεας χειρωσάμενοι ἐξῆγον ἀπολέοντες. ἀπὸ τούτου δὲ καὶ ἄγος
σφι ἐγένετο, τὸ ἐκθύσασθαι οὐχ οἷοί τε ἐγίνοντο
ἐπιμηχανεόμενοι, ἀλλ' ἔφθησαν ἐκπεσόντες πρότερον
ἐκ τῆς νήσου ἤ σφι ἵλεων γενέσθαι τὴν θεόν. ἐπ- 2
τακοσίους γὰρ δὴ τοῦ δήμου ζωγρήσαντες ἐξῆγον ὡς
ἀπολέοντες, εἷς δέ τις τούτων ἐκφυγὼν τὰ δεσμὰ
καταφεύγει πρὸς πρόθυρα Δήμητρος θεσμοφόρου,
ἐπιλαβόμενος δὲ τῶν ἐπισπαστήρων εἴχετο. οἱ
δὲ ἐπεί τέ μιν ἀποσπάσαι οὐκ οἷοί τε ἀπέλκοντες
ἐγίνοντο, ἀποκόψαντες αὐτοῦ τὰς χεῖρας ἦγον οὕτω,
χεῖρες δὲ ἐκεῖναι ἐμπεφυκυῖαι ἦσαν τοῖσι ἐπισπάστροισι.

*Sea fight between the Athenians and Aeginetans. The
Aeginetans being beaten vainly apply for help to Argos.*

XCII. Ταῦτα μέν νυν σφέας αὐτοὺς οἱ Αἰγινῆται 1
ἐργάσαντο, Ἀθηναίοισι δὲ ἥκουσι ἐναυμάχησαν νηυσὶ
ἑβδομήκοντα, ἑσσωθέντες δὲ τῇ ναυμαχίῃ ἐπεκαλέοντο
τοὺς αὐτοὺς καὶ πρότερον, Ἀργείους. καὶ δή σφι
οὗτοι μὲν οὐκέτι βοηθέουσι, μεμφόμενοι, ὅτι Αἰγιναῖαι
νέες ἀνάγκῃ λαμφθεῖσαι ὑπὸ Κλεομένεος ἔσχον τε ἐς

τὴν Ἀργολίδα χώρην καὶ συναπέβησαν Λακεδαιμο-
νίοισι· συναπέβησαν δὲ καὶ ἀπὸ Σικυωνιέων νεῶν
ἄνδρες τῇ αὐτῇ ταύτῃ ἐσβολῇ. καί σφι ὑπ' Ἀργείων 2
ἐπεβλήθη ζημίη, χίλια τάλαντα ἐκτῖσαι, πεντακόσια
ἑκατέρους. Σικυώνιοι μέν νυν συγγνόντες ἀδικῆσαι
ὡμολόγησαν ἑκατὸν τάλαντα ἐκτίσαντες ἀζήμιοι εἶναι,
Αἰγινῆται δὲ οὔτε συνεγινώσκοντο, ἦσάν τε αὐθαδέστεροι. διὰ δὴ ὧν σφι ταῦτα δεομένοισι ἀπὸ μὲν
τοῦ δημοσίου οὐδεὶς Ἀργείων ἔτι ἐβοήθεε, ἐθελονταὶ
δὲ ἐς χιλίους· ἦγε δὲ αὐτοὺς στρατηγὸς Εὐρυβάτης,
πεντάεθλον ἐπασκήσας. τούτων οἱ πλεῦνες οὐκ 3
ἀπενόστησαν ὀπίσω, ἀλλ' ἐτελεύτησαν ὑπ' Ἀθηναίων
ἐν Αἰγίνῃ· αὐτὸς δὲ ὁ στρατηγὸς Εὐρυβάτης μουνο-
μαχίην ἐπασκέων τρεῖς μὲν ἄνδρας τρόπῳ τοιούτῳ
κτείνει, ὑπὸ δὲ τοῦ τετάρτου Σωφάνεος τοῦ Δεκελέος
ἀποθνῄσκει.

They however defeat the Athenian fleet.

XCIII. Αἰγινῆται δὲ ἐοῦσι ἀτάκτοισι Ἀθηναίοισι συμβαλόντες τῇσι νηυσὶ ἐνίκησαν, καί σφεων
νέας τέσσερας αὐτοῖσι ἀνδράσι εἷλον.

B.C. 490. *Darius pushes on his design of invading Greece,
urged on by the Peisistratidae. He deposes Mardonius
from the command, and appoints Datis and Artaphernes. The object is the destruction of Athens and
Eretria.*

XCIV. Ἀθηναίοισι μὲν δὴ πόλεμος συνῆπτο 1
πρὸς Αἰγινήτας· ὁ δὲ Πέρσης τὸ ἑωυτοῦ ἐποίεε ὥστε
ἀναμιμνήσκοντός τε ἀεὶ τοῦ θεράποντος μεμνῆσθαί
μιν τῶν Ἀθηναίων καὶ Πεισιστρατιδέων προσκατη-

μένων καὶ διαβαλλόντων Ἀθηναίους, ἅμα δὲ βουλόμενος ὁ Δαρεῖος ταύτης ἐχόμενος τῆς προφάσιος
καταστρέφεσθαι τῆς Ἑλλάδος τοὺς μὴ δόντας αὐτῷ
γῆν τε καὶ ὕδωρ. Μαρδόνιον μὲν δὴ φλαύρως πρή-   2
ξαντα τῷ στόλῳ παραλύει τῆς στρατηγίης, ἄλλους
δὲ στρατηγοὺς ἀποδέξας ἀπέστελλε ἐπί τε Ἐρέτριαν
καὶ Ἀθήνας, Δᾶτίν τε ἐόντα Μῆδον γένος καὶ
Ἀρταφέρνεα τὸν Ἀρταφέρνεος παῖδα, ἀδελφιδέον
ἑωυτοῦ· ἐντειλάμενος δὲ ἀπέπεμπε ἐξανδραποδί-
σαντας Ἀθήνας καὶ Ἐρέτριαν ἀγαγεῖν ἑωυτῷ ἐς
ὄψιν τὰ ἀνδράποδα.

The Persian army musters on the Aleïan plain in Kilikia.
The fleet takes all on board and sails to Naxos,
where they burn the temples and town.

XCV. Ὡς δὲ οἱ στρατηγοὶ οὗτοι οἱ ἀποδεχ-   1
θέντες πορευόμενοι παρὰ βασιλέος ἀπίκοντο τῆς
Κιλικίης ἐς τὸ Ἀλήιον πεδίον, ἅμα ἀγόμενοι πεζὸν
στρατὸν πολλόν τε καὶ εὖ ἐσκευασμένον, ἐνθαῦτα
στρατοπεδευομένοισι ἐπῆλθε μὲν ὁ ναυτικὸς πᾶς
στρατὸς ὁ ἐπιταχθεὶς ἑκάστοισι, παρεγένοντο δὲ καὶ
αἱ ἱππαγωγοὶ νέες, τὰς τῷ προτέρῳ ἔτεϊ προεῖπε
τοῖσι ἑωυτοῦ δασμοφόροισι Δαρεῖος ἑτοιμάζειν. ἐσβα-   2
λόμενοι δὲ τοὺς ἵππους ἐς ταύτας καὶ τὸν πεζὸν
στρατὸν ἐσβιβάσαντες ἐς τὰς νέας, ἔπλωον ἑξακο-
σίῃσι τριήρεσι ἐς τὴν Ἰωνίην. ἐνθεῦτεν δὲ οὐ παρὰ
τὴν ἤπειρον εἶχον τὰς νέας ἰθὺ τοῦ τε Ἑλλησπόντου
καὶ τῆς Θρηίκης, ἀλλ᾽ ἐκ Σάμου ὁρμεόμενοι παρά τε
Ἰκάριον καὶ διὰ νήσων τὸν πλόον ἐποιεῦντο, ὡς μὲν
ἐμοὶ δοκέειν, δείσαντες μάλιστα τὸν περίπλοον τοῦ
Ἄθω, ὅτι τῷ προτέρῳ ἔτεϊ ποιεύμενοι ταύτῃ τὴν

κομιδὴν μεγάλως προσέπταισαν· πρὸς δὲ καὶ ἡ
Νάξος σφέας ἠνάγκαζε, πρότερον οὐκ ἀλοῦσα.
XCVI. Ἐπεὶ δὲ ἐκ τοῦ Ἰκαρίου πελάγεος προσ-
φερόμενοι προσέμιξαν τῇ Νάξῳ (ἐπὶ ταύτην γὰρ δὴ
πρώτην ἐπεῖχον στρατεύεσθαι οἱ Πέρσαι), μεμνημένοι
τῶν πρότερον οἱ Νάξιοι πρὸς τὰ οὔρεα οἴχοντο
φεύγοντες· οὐδὲ ὑπέμειναν. οἱ δὲ Πέρσαι ἀνδραπο-
δισάμενοι τοὺς κατέλαβον αὐτῶν, ἐνέπρησαν καὶ τὰ
ἱρὰ καὶ τὴν πόλιν, ταῦτα δὲ ποιήσαντες ἐπὶ τὰς
ἄλλας νήσους ἀνήγοντο.

*The Delians fly to Tenos. The Persians anchor at Rhenaea,
and endeavour to induce the Delians to return. They
treat the sacred places with reverence.*

XCVII. Ἐν ᾧ δὲ οὗτοι ταῦτα ἐποίευν, οἱ Δήλιοι   1
ἐκλιπόντες καὶ αὐτοὶ τὴν Δῆλον οἴχοντο φεύγοντες ἐς
Τῆνον. τῆς δὲ στρατιῆς καταπλωούσης ὁ Δᾶτις
προπλώσας οὐκ ἔα τὰς νέας πρὸς τὴν Δῆλον προσορ-
μίζεσθαι, ἀλλὰ πέρην ἐν τῇ Ῥηναίῃ, αὐτὸς δὲ πυθόμενος ἵνα ἦσαν οἱ Δήλιοι, πέμπων κήρυκα ἠγόρευέ
σφι τάδε· "Ἄνδρες ἱροί, τί φεύγοντες οἴχεσθε, οὐκ   2
"ἐπιτήδεα καταγνόντες κατ᾽ ἐμεῦ; ἐγὼ γὰρ καὶ αὐτὸς
"ἐπὶ τοσοῦτό γε φρονέω καί μοι ἐκ βασιλέος ὧδε
"ἐπέσταλται, ἐν τῇ χώρῃ οἱ δύο θεοὶ ἐγένοντο, ταύτην
"μηδὲν σίνεσθαι, μήτε αὐτὴν τὴν χώρην μήτε τοὺς
"οἰκήτορας αὐτῆς. νῦν ὦν καὶ ἄπιτε ἐπὶ τὰ ὑμέτερα
"αὐτῶν καὶ τὴν νῆσον νέμεσθε." Ταῦτα μὲν ἐπεκη-
ρυκεύσατο τοῖσι Δηλίοισι, μετὰ δὲ λιβανωτοῦ τριηκόσια τάλαντα κατανήσας ἐπὶ τοῦ βωμοῦ ἐθυμίησε.

An earthquake at Delos,—an omen of the troubles to come on Greece.

XCVIII. Δᾶτις μὲν δὴ ταῦτα ποιήσας ἔπλεε 1
ἅμα τῷ στρατῷ ἐπὶ τὴν Ἐρέτριαν πρῶτα, ἅμα
ἀγόμενος καὶ Ἴωνας καὶ Αἰολέας, μετὰ δὲ τοῦτον
ἐνθεῦτεν ἐξαναχθέντα Δῆλος ἐκινήθη, ὡς ἔλεγον
Δήλιοι, καὶ πρῶτα καὶ ὕστατα μέχρι ἐμεῦ σεισθεῖσα.
καὶ τοῦτο μέν κου τέρας ἀνθρώποισι τῶν μελλόντων
ἔσεσθαι κακῶν ἔφαινε ὁ θεός. ἐπὶ γὰρ Δαρείου τοῦ 2
Ὑστάσπεος καὶ Ξέρξεω τοῦ Δαρείου καὶ Ἀρταξέρξεω
τοῦ Ξέρξεω, τριῶν τούτων ἐπεξῆς γενεέων ἐγένετο
πλέω κακὰ τῇ Ἑλλάδι ἢ ἐπὶ εἴκοσι ἄλλας γενεὰς
τὰς πρὸ Δαρείου γενομένας, τὰ μὲν ἀπὸ τῶν Περσέων
αὐτῇ γενόμενα, τὰ δὲ ἀπ᾽ αὐτῶν τῶν κορυφαίων περὶ
τῆς ἀρχῆς πολεμεόντων. οὕτω οὐδὲν ἦν ἀεικὲς 3
κινηθῆναι Δῆλον τὸ πρὶν ἐοῦσαν ἀκίνητον. [καὶ ἐν
χρησμῷ ἦν γεγραμμένον περὶ αὐτῆς ὧδε·

κινήσω καὶ Δῆλον, ἀκίνητόν περ ἐοῦσαν.]

δύναται δὲ κατὰ Ἑλλάδα γλῶσσαν ταῦτα τὰ
οὐνόματα, Δαρεῖος ἐρξίης, Ξέρξης ἀρήιος, Ἀρταξέρξης
μέγας ἀρήιος. τούτους μὲν δὴ τοὺς βασιλέας ὧδε
ἂν ὀρθῶς κατὰ γλῶσσαν τὴν σφετέρην Ἕλληνες
καλέοιεν.

The Persian fleet touches at Karystos on the South of Euboea. The Karystians yield.

XCIX. Οἱ δὲ βάρβαροι ὡς ἀπῆραν ἐκ τῆς 1
Δήλου, προσίσχον πρὸς τὰς νήσους, ἐνθεῦτεν δὲ
στρατιήν τε παρελάμβανον καὶ ὁμήρους τῶν νησιω-
τέων παῖδας ἐλάμβανον. ὡς δὲ περιπλέοντες τὰς 2

νήσους προσέσχον καὶ ἐς Κάρυστον, οὐ γὰρ δή σφι
οἱ Καρύστιοι οὔτε ὁμήρους ἐδίδοσαν οὔτε ἔφασαν ἐπὶ
πόλις ἀστυγείτονας στρατεύεσθαι, λέγοντες Ἐρέτριάν
τε καὶ Ἀθήνας, ἐνθαῦτα τούτους ἐπολιόρκεόν τε καὶ
τὴν γῆν σφέων ἔκειρον, ἐς ὃ καὶ οἱ Καρύστιοι
παρέστησαν ἐς τῶν Περσέων τὴν γνώμην.

*The Eretrians send to Athens for help. There is a division
of opinion in Eretria, which is betrayed on the 7th
day by Euphorbos and Philagros.*

C. Ἐρετριέες δὲ πυνθανόμενοι τὴν στρατιὴν τὴν   1
Περσικὴν ἐπὶ σφέας ἐπιπλέουσαν Ἀθηναίων ἐδεήθησαν σφίσι βοηθοὺς γενέσθαι. Ἀθηναῖοι δὲ οὐκ
ἀπείπαντο τὴν ἐπικουρίην, ἀλλὰ τοὺς τετρακισχιλίους κληρουχέοντας τῶν ἱπποβοτέων Χαλκιδέων τὴν
χώρην, τούτους σφι διδοῦσι τιμωρούς. τῶν δὲ
Ἐρετριέων ἦν ἄρα οὐδὲν ὑγιὲς βούλευμα, οἳ μετε-
πέμποντο μὲν Ἀθηναίους, ἐφρόνεον δὲ διφασίας ἰδέας.
οἱ μὲν γὰρ αὐτῶν ἐβουλεύοντο ἐκλιπεῖν τὴν πόλιν ἐς   2
τὰ ἄκρα τῆς Εὐβοίης, ἄλλοι δὲ αὐτῶν ἴδια κέρδεα
προσδεκόμενοι παρὰ τοῦ Πέρσεω οἴσεσθαι προδοσίην
ἐσκευάζοντο. μαθὼν δὲ τούτων ἑκάτερα ὡς εἶχε   3
Αἰσχίνης ὁ Νόθωνος, ἐὼν τῶν Ἐρετριέων τὰ πρῶτα,
φράζει τοῖσι ἥκουσι τῶν Ἀθηναίων πάντα τὰ
παρεόντα σφι πρήγματα, προσεδέετό τε ἀπαλλάσσεσθαί σφεας ἐς τὴν σφετέρην, ἵνα μὴ προσαπόλωνται. οἱ δὲ Ἀθηναῖοι ταῦτα Αἰσχίνῃ συμβου-
λεύσαντι πείθονται. CI. Καὶ οὗτοι μὲν διαβάντες   1
ἐς Ὠρωπὸν ἔσωζον σφέας αὐτούς, οἱ δὲ Πέρσαι
πλέοντες κατέσχον τὰς νέας τῆς Ἐρετρικῆς χώρης
κατὰ Ταμύνας καὶ Χοιρέας καὶ Αἰγίλια, κατασχόντες

δὲ ἐς ταῦτα τὰ χωρία αὐτίκα ἵππους τε ἐξεβάλλοντο
καὶ παρεσκευάζοντα ὡς προσοισόμενοι τοῖσι ἐχθροῖσι.
οἱ δὲ Ἐρετριέες ἐπεξελθεῖν μὲν καὶ μαχέσασθαι οὐκ 2
ἐποιεῦντο βουλήν, εἴ κως δὲ διαφυλάξαιεν τὰ τείχεα,
τούτου σφι ἔμελε πέρι, ἐπεί τε ἐνίκα μὴ ἐκλιπεῖν τὴν
πόλιν. προσβολῆς δὲ γινομένης καρτερῆς πρὸς τὸ
τεῖχος ἔπιπτον ἐπὶ ἓξ ἡμέρας πολλοὶ μὲν ἀμφοτέρων,
τῇ δὲ ἑβδόμῃ Εὔφορβός τε ὁ Ἀλκιμάχου καὶ
Φίλαγρος ὁ Κυνέω, ἄνδρες τῶν ἀστῶν δόκιμοι, προδι-
δοῦσι τοῖσι Πέρσῃσι. οἱ δὲ ἐσελθόντες ἐς τὴν πόλιν 3
τοῦτο μὲν τὰ ἱρὰ συλήσαντες ἐνέπρησαν, ἀποτινύμενοι
τῶν ἐν Σάρδισι κατακαυθέντων ἱρῶν, τοῦτο δὲ τοὺς
ἀνθρώπους ἠνδραποδίσαντο κατὰ τὰς Δαρείου ἐντολάς.

The Persian fleet then sails to Marathon on the Attic coast.

CII. Χειρωσάμενοι δὲ τὴν Ἐρέτριαν καὶ ἐπι-
σχόντες ὀλίγας ἡμέρας ἔπλεον ἐς τὴν Ἀττικήν,
κατέργοντές τε πολλὸν καὶ δοκέοντες ταὐτὰ τοὺς
Ἀθηναίους ποιήσειν, τὰ καὶ τοὺς Ἐρετριέας ἐποίησαν,
καὶ ἦν γὰρ ὁ Μαραθὼν ἐπιτηδεώτατον χωρίον τῆς
Ἀττικῆς ἐνιππεῦσαι καὶ ἀγχοτάτω τῆς Ἐρετρίης, ἐς
τοῦτό σφι κατηγέετο Ἱππίης ὁ Πεισιστράτου.

The Athenians send out an army to defend their country
under their ten Strategi, the tenth being Miltiades.
Previous history of Miltiades.

CIII. Ἀθηναῖοι δὲ ὡς ἐπύθοντο ταῦτα, ἐβοήθεον 1
καὶ αὐτοὶ ἐς τὸν Μαραθῶνα. ἦγον δέ σφεας στρατηγοὶ δέκα, τῶν ὁ δέκατος ἦν Μιλτιάδης, τοῦ τὸν
πατέρα Κίμωνα τὸν Στησαγόρεω κατέλαβε φυγεῖν

ἐξ Ἀθηνέων Πεισίστρατον τὸν Ἱπποκράτεος. καὶ 2
αὐτῷ φεύγοντι Ὀλυμπιάδα ἀνελέσθαι τεθρίππῳ
συνέβη, καὶ ταύτην μὲν τὴν νίκην ἀνελόμενόν μιν
τὠυτὸ ἐξενείκασθαι τῷ ὁμομητρίῳ ἀδελφεῷ Μιλτιάδῃ. μετὰ δὲ τῇ ὑστέρῃ Ὀλυμπιάδι τῇσι αὐτῇσι
ἵπποισι νικῶν παραδιδοῖ Πεισιστράτῳ ἀνακηρυχθῆναι, καὶ τὴν νίκην παρεὶς τούτῳ κατῆλθε ἐπὶ τὰ 3
ἑωυτοῦ ὑπόσπονδος. καί μιν ἀνελόμενον τῇσι αὐτῇσι
ἵπποισι ἄλλην Ὀλυμπιάδα κατέλαβε ἀποθανεῖν ὑπὸ
τῶν Πεισιστράτου παίδων οὐκέτι περιεόντος αὐτοῦ
Πεισιστράτου· κτείνουσι δὲ οὗτοί μιν κατὰ τὸ πρυτανήϊον νυκτὸς ὑπείσαντες ἄνδρας. τέθαπται δὲ
Κίμων πρὸ τοῦ ἄστεος, πέρην τῆς διὰ Κοίλης
καλεομένης ὁδοῦ, καταντίον δ᾽ αὐτοῦ αἱ ἵπποι τετάφαται αὗται αἱ τρεῖς Ὀλυμπιάδας ἀνελόμεναι. ἐποίη- 4
σαν δὲ καὶ ἄλλαι ἵπποι ἤδη τὠυτὸ τοῦτο Εὐαγόρεω
Λάκωνος, πλέω δὲ τούτων οὐδαμαί. Ὁ μὲν δὴ
πρεσβύτερος τῶν παίδων τῷ Κίμωνι Στησαγόρης ἦν
τηνικαῦτα παρὰ τῷ πάτρῳ Μιλτιάδῃ τρεφόμενος ἐν
τῇ Χερσονήσῳ, ὁ δὲ νεώτερος παρ᾽ αὐτῷ Κίμωνι ἐν
Ἀθήνῃσι, τοὔνομα ἔχων ἀπὸ τοῦ οἰκιστέω τῆς
Χερσονήσου Μιλτιάδεω Μιλτιάδης. CIV. Οὗτος 1
δὴ ὢν τότε ὁ Μιλτιάδης ἥκων ἐκ τῆς Χερσονήσου καὶ
ἐκπεφευγὼς διπλόον θάνατον ἐστρατήγεε Ἀθηναίων.
ἅμα μὲν γὰρ οἱ Φοίνικες αὐτὸν οἱ ἐπιδιώξαντες μέχρι
Ἴμβρου περὶ πολλοῦ ἐποιεῦντο λαβεῖν τε καὶ ἀνα-
γαγεῖν παρὰ βασιλέα, ἅμα δὲ ἐκφυγόντα τε τούτους 2
καὶ ἀπικόμενον ἐς τὴν ἑωυτοῦ, δοκέοντά τε εἶναι ἐν
σωτηρίῃ ἤδη, τὸ ἐνθεῦτέν μιν οἱ ἐχθροὶ ὑποδεξάμενοι
καὶ ὑπὸ δικαστήριον αὐτὸν ἀγαγόντες ἐδίωξαν τυραννίδος τῆς ἐν Χερσονήσῳ. ἀποφυγὼν δὲ καὶ τούτους

στρατηγὸς οὕτω Ἀθηναίων ἀπεδέχθη, αἱρεθεὶς ὑπὸ
τοῦ δήμου.

*Pheidippides sent to Sparta, who is met by the God Pan
on his road.*

CV. Καὶ πρῶτα μὲν ἐόντες ἔτι ἐν τῷ ἄστεϊ οἱ 1
στρατηγοὶ ἀποπέμπουσι ἐς Σπάρτην κήρυκα Φειδιππίδην, Ἀθηναῖον μὲν ἄνδρα, ἄλλως δὲ ἡμεροδρόμον
τε καὶ τοῦτο μελετῶντα, τῷ δή, ὡς αὐτός τε ἔλεγε
Φειδιππίδης καὶ Ἀθηναίοισι ἀπήγγελλε, περὶ τὸ
Παρθένιον οὖρος τὸ ὑπὲρ Τεγέης ὁ Πὰν περιπίπτει.
βώσαντα δὲ τὸ οὔνομα τοῦ Φειδιππίδεω τὸν Πᾶνα 2
Ἀθηναίοισι κελεῦσαι ἀπαγγεῖλαι, δι᾽ ὅ τι ἑωυτοῦ οὐδεμίαν ἐπιμέλειαν ποιεῦνται, ἐόντος εὐνόου Ἀθηναίοισι
καὶ πολλαχῇ γενομένου ἤδη σφι χρησίμου, τὰ δ᾽ ἔτι
καὶ ἐσομένου. καὶ ταῦτα μὲν Ἀθηναῖοι, καταστάντων 3
σφίσι εὖ ἤδη τῶν πρηγμάτων, πιστεύσαντες εἶναι
ἀληθέα ἱδρύσαντο ὑπὸ τῇ ἀκροπόλι Πανὸς ἱρόν, καὶ
αὐτὸν ἀπὸ ταύτης τῆς ἀγγελίης θυσίῃσι ἐπετέῃσι καὶ
λαμπάδι ἱλάσκονται.

The Spartans will come when it is full moon.

CVI. Τότε δὲ πεμφθεὶς ὑπὸ τῶν στρατηγῶν ὁ 1
Φειδιππίδης οὗτος, ὅτε πέρ οἱ ἔφη καὶ τὸν Πᾶνα
φανῆναι, δευτεραῖος ἐκ τοῦ Ἀθηναίων ἄστεος ἦν ἐν
Σπάρτῃ, ἀπικόμενος δὲ ἐπὶ τοὺς ἄρχοντας ἔλεγε· "Ὦ 2
"Λακεδαιμόνιοι, Ἀθηναῖοι ὑμέων δέονται σφίσι βοη-
"θῆσαι καὶ μὴ περιιδεῖν πόλιν ἀρχαιοτάτην ἐν τοῖσι
"Ἕλλησι δουλοσύνῃ περιπεσοῦσαν πρὸς ἀνδρῶν βαρ-
"βάρων· καὶ γὰρ νῦν Ἐρέτριά τε ἠνδραπόδισται καὶ
"πόλι λογίμῳ ἡ Ἑλλὰς γέγονε ἀσθενεστέρη." Ὁ μὲν 3

δή σφι τὰ ἐντεταλμένα ἀπήγγελλε, τοῖσι δὲ ἕαδε μὲν
βοηθέειν Ἀθηναίοισι, ἀδύνατα δέ σφι ἦν τὸ παραυτίκα ποιέειν ταῦτα οὐ βουλομένοισι λύειν τὸν νόμον·
ἦν γὰρ ἱσταμένου τοῦ μηνὸς εἰνάτη, εἰνάτῃ δὲ οὐκ
ἐξελεύσεσθαι ἔφασαν μὴ οὐ πλήρεος ἐόντος τοῦ
κύκλου.

Hippias' dream; and his lost tooth.

CVII. Οὗτοι μέν νυν τὴν πανσέληνον ἔμενον,   1
τοῖσι δὲ βαρβάροισι κατηγέετο Ἱππίης ὁ Πεισιστράτου ἐς τὸν Μαραθῶνα, τῆς παροιχομένης νυκτὸς
ὄψιν ἰδὼν ἐν τῷ ὕπνῳ τοιήνδε· ἐδόκεε ὁ Ἱππίης τῇ
μητρὶ τῇ ἑωυτοῦ συνευνηθῆναι. συνεβάλετο ὦν ἐκ   2
τοῦ ὀνείρου κατελθὼν ἐς τὰς Ἀθήνας καὶ ἀνασωσάμενος τὴν ἀρχὴν τελευτήσειν ἐν τῇ ἑωυτοῦ γηραιός.
ἐκ μὲν δὴ τῆς ὄψιος συνεβάλετο ταῦτα, τότε δὲ
κατηγεόμενος τοῦτο μὲν τὰ ἀνδράποδα τὰ ἐξ Ἐρετρίης ἀπέβησε ἐς τὴν νῆσον τὴν Στυρέων, καλεομένην
δὲ Αἰγίλειαν, τοῦτο δὲ καταγομένας ἐς τὸν Μαραθῶνα
τὰς νέας ὥρμιζε οὗτος, ἐκβάντας τε ἐς γῆν τοὺς
βαρβάρους διέτασσε. καὶ οἱ ταῦτα διέποντι ἐπῆλθε   3
πταρεῖν τε καὶ βῆξαι μεζόνως ἢ ὡς ἐώθεε, οἷα δέ οἱ
πρεσβυτέρῳ ἐόντι τῶν ὀδόντων οἱ πλεῦνες ἐσείοντο.
τούτων ὦν ἕνα τῶν ὀδόντων ἐκβάλλει ὑπὸ βίης
βήξας· ἐκπεσόντος δὲ ἐς τὴν ψάμμον αὐτοῦ ἐποιέετο
πολλὴν σπουδὴν ἐξευρεῖν. ὡς δὲ οὐκ ἐφαίνετό οἱ ὁ   4
ὀδὼν, ἀναστενάξας εἶπε πρὸς τοὺς παραστάτας· "Ἡ
"γῆ ἥδε οὐκ ἡμετέρη ἐστὶ οὐδέ μιν δυνησόμεθα ὑπο-
"χειρίην ποιήσασθαι· ὁκόσον δέ τί μοι μέρος μετῆν,
"ὁ ὀδὼν μετέχει."

The Athenians, drawn up in the sacred enclosure of Herakles, are joined by 1000 Plataeans.

CVIII. Ἱππίης μὲν δὴ ταύτῃ τὴν ὄψιν συνε- 1
βάλετο ἐξεληλυθέναι, Ἀθηναίοισι δὲ τεταγμένοισι ἐν
τεμένεϊ Ἡρακλέος ἐπῆλθον βοηθέοντες Πλαταιέες
πανδημεί· καὶ γὰρ καὶ ἐδεδώκεσαν σφέας αὐτοὺς
5 τοῖσι Ἀθηναίοισι οἱ Πλαταιέες, καὶ πόνους ὑπὲρ
αὐτῶν οἱ Ἀθηναῖοι συχνοὺς ἤδη ἀναιρέοντο· ἔδοσαν
δὲ ὧδε.

The origin of the connexion between Plataea and Athens.

Πιεζόμενοι ὑπὸ Θηβαίων οἱ Πλαταιέες ἐδίδοσαν 2
πρῶτα παρατυχοῦσι Κλεομένεΐ τε τῷ Ἀναξανδρίδεω
10 καὶ Λακεδαιμονίοισι σφέας αὐτούς, οἱ δὲ οὐ δεκόμενοι
ἔλεγόν σφι τάδε· "Ἡμεῖς μὲν ἑκαστέρω τε οἰκέομεν,
"καὶ ὑμῖν τοιήδε τις γίνοιτ' ἂν ἐπικουρίη ψυχρή·
"φθαίητε γὰρ ἂν πολλάκις ἐξανδραποδισθέντες ἤ τινα
"πυθέσθαι ἡμέων. συμβουλεύομεν δὲ ὑμῖν δοῦναι 3
15 "ὑμέας αὐτοὺς Ἀθηναίοισι, πλησιοχώροισί τε ἀνδράσι
"καὶ τιμωρέειν ἐοῦσι οὐ κακοῖσι." Ταῦτα συνεβούλευον
οἱ Λακεδαιμόνιοι, οὐ κατὰ εὐνοίην οὕτω τῶν Πλα-
ταιέων, ὡς βουλόμενοι τοὺς Ἀθηναίους ἔχειν πόνους
συνεστεῶτας Βοιωτοῖσι. Λακεδαιμόνιοι μέν νυν 4
20 Πλαταιεῦσι ταῦτα συνεβούλευον, οἱ δὲ οὐκ ἠπίσ-
τησαν, ἀλλ' Ἀθηναίων ἱρὰ ποιεύντων τοῖσι δυώδεκα
θεοῖσι ἱκέται ἱζόμενοι ἐπὶ τὸν βωμὸν ἐδίδοσαν σφέας
αὐτούς. Θηβαῖοι δὲ πυθόμενοι ταῦτα ἐστρατεύοντο
ἐπὶ τοὺς Πλαταιέας· Ἀθηναῖοι δέ σφι ἐβοήθεον.
25 μελλόντων δὲ συνάπτειν μάχην Κορίνθιοι οὐ περι- 5
εῖδον, παρατυχόντες δὲ καὶ καταλλάξαντες ἐπιτοε-

ψάντων ἀμφοτέρων, οὔρισαν τὴν χώρην ἐπὶ τοισίδε,
ἐὰν Θηβαίους Βοιωτῶν τοὺς μὴ βουλομένους ἐς
Βοιωτοὺς τελέειν. Κορίνθιοι μὲν δὴ ταῦτα γνόντες
ἀπαλλάσσοντο, 'Αθηναίοισι δὲ ἀπιοῦσι ἐπεθήκαντο
Βοιωτοί, ἐπιθέμενοι δὲ ἐσσώθησαν τῇ μάχῃ. ὑπερ- 6
βάντες δὲ οἱ 'Αθηναῖοι τοὺς οἱ Κορίνθιοι ἔθηκαν
Πλαταιεῦσι εἶναι οὔρους, τούτους ὑπερβάντες τὸν
'Ασωπὸν αὐτὸν ἐποιήσαντο οὖρον Θηβαίοισι πρὸς
Πλαταιέας εἶναι καὶ 'Υσιάς. ἔδοσαν μὲν δὴ οἱ
Πλαταιέες σφέας αὐτοὺς 'Αθηναίοισι τρόπῳ τῷ
εἰρημένῳ, ἧκον δὲ τότε ἐς Μαραθῶνα βοηθέοντες.

*The Athenian generals are divided in opinion. Some argue
against attack, others with Miltiades wish for an
immediate advance.*

CIX. Τοῖσι δὲ 'Αθηναίων στρατηγοῖσι ἐγίνοντο 1
δίχα αἱ γνῶμαι, τῶν μὲν οὐκ ἐώντων συμβάλλειν,
ὀλίγους γὰρ εἶναι στρατιῇ τῇ Μήδων συμβαλεῖν,
τῶν δὲ καὶ Μιλτιάδεω κελευόντων. ὡς δὲ δίχα τε 2
ἐγίνοντο καὶ ἐνίκα ἡ χείρων τῶν γνωμέων, ἐνθαῦτα
ἦν γὰρ ἐνδέκατος ψηφιδοφόρος ὁ τῷ κυάμῳ λαχὼν
'Αθηναίων πολεμαρχέειν, (τὸ παλαιὸν γὰρ 'Αθηναῖοι
ὁμόψηφον τὸν πολέμαρχον ἐποιεῦντο τοῖσι στρατηγοῖσι,) ἦν τε τότε πολέμαρχος Καλλίμαχος 'Αφιδναῖος,
πρὸς τοῦτον ἐλθὼν Μιλτιάδης ἔλεγε τάδε·

Speech of Miltiades.

" 'Εν σοὶ νῦν, Καλλίμαχε, ἐστὶ ἢ καταδουλῶσαι 3
"'Αθήνας, ἢ ἐλευθέρας ποιήσαντα μνημόσυνα λιπέσθαι
" ἐς τὸν ἅπαντα ἀνθρώπων βίον, οἷα οὐδὲ 'Αρμόδιός
" τε καὶ 'Αριστογείτων λείπουσι. νῦν γὰρ δή, ἐξ οὗ

" ἐγένοντο Ἀθηναῖοι, ἐς κίνδυνον ἥκουσι μέγιστον. καὶ
" ἢν μέν γε ὑποκύψωσι τοῖσι Μήδοισι, δέδοκται τὰ
" πείσονται παραδεδομένοι Ἱππίῃ, ἢν δὲ περιγένηται
" αὕτη ἡ πόλις, οἵη τέ ἐστι πρώτη τῶν Ἑλληνίδων
" πολίων γενέσθαι. κῶς ὦν δὴ ταῦτα οἷά τέ ἐστι   4
" γενέσθαι, καὶ κῶς ἐς σέ τοι τούτων ἀνήκει τῶν
" πρηγμάτων τὸ κῦρος ἔχειν, νῦν ἔρχομαι φράσων.
" ἡμέων τῶν στρατηγῶν ἐόντων δέκα δίχα γίνονται αἱ
" γνῶμαι, τῶν μὲν κελευόντων, τῶν δὲ οὐ συμβάλλειν.
" ἢν μέν νυν μὴ συμβάλωμεν, ἔλπομαί τινα στάσιν   5
" μεγάλην ἐμπεσοῦσαν διασείσειν τὰ Ἀθηναίων φρο-
" νήματα ὥστε μηδίσαι· ἢν δὲ συμβάλωμεν πρίν τι
" καὶ σαθρὸν Ἀθηναίων μετεξετέροισι ἐγγενέσθαι,
" θεῶν τὰ ἴσα νεμόντων οἷοί τέ εἰμεν περιγενέσθαι τῇ
" συμβολῇ. ταῦτα ὦν πάντα ἐς σὲ νῦν τείνει καὶ ἐκ   6
" σέο ἤρτηται· ἢν γὰρ σὺ γνώμῃ τῇ ἐμῇ προσθῇ, ἔστι
" τοι πατρίς τε ἐλευθέρη καὶ πόλις πρώτη τῶν ἐν τῇ
" Ἑλλάδι, ἢν δὲ τὴν τῶν ἀποσπευδόντων τὴν συμ-
" βολὴν ἕλῃ, ὑπάρξει τοι τῶν ἐγὼ κατέλεξα ἀγαθῶν
" τὰ ἐναντία."

*The Polemarch Kallimachos is convinced, and four of the
Strategi surrender their days of command to Miltiades.*

CX. Ταῦτα λέγων ὁ Μιλτιάδης προσκτᾶται τὸν
Καλλίμαχον. προσγενομένης δὲ τοῦ πολεμάρχου
τῆς γνώμης ἐκεκύρωτο συμβάλλειν. μετὰ δὲ οἱ
στρατηγοί, τῶν ἡ γνώμη ἔφερε συμβάλλειν, ὡς
ἑκάστου αὐτῶν ἐγίνετο πρυτανηίη τῆς ἡμέρης, Μιλτιάδῃ παρεδίδοσαν· ὁ δὲ δεκόμενος οὔτι κω συμβολὴν
ἐποιέετο, πρίν γε δὴ αὐτοῦ πρυτανηίη ἐγένετο.

Miltiades waits until his right day for command comes round, and then draws out the men for action.

CXI. Ὡς δὲ ἐς ἐκεῖνον περιῆλθε, ἐνθαῦτα δὴ **1**
ἐτάσσοντο ὧδε Ἀθηναῖοι ὡς συμβαλέοντες· τοῦ μὲν
δεξιοῦ κέρεος ἡγέετο ὁ πολέμαρχος Καλλίμαχος· ὁ
γὰρ νόμος τότε εἶχε οὕτω τοῖσι Ἀθηναίοισι, τὸν
πολέμαρχον ἔχειν κέρας τὸ δεξιόν. ἡγεομένου δὲ
τούτου ἐξεδέκοντο ὡς ἠριθμέοντο αἱ φυλαὶ, ἐχόμεναι
ἀλλήλων· τελευταῖοι δὲ ἐτάσσοντο, ἔχοντες τὸ
εὐώνυμον κέρας, Πλαταιέες. ἀπὸ ταύτης γάρ σφι **2**
τῆς μάχης Ἀθηναίων θυσίας ἀναγόντων ἐς τὰς πανηγύριας τὰς ἐν τῇσι πεντετηρίσι γινομένας κατεύ-
χεται ὁ κῆρυξ ὁ Ἀθηναῖος, ἅμα τε Ἀθηναίοισι λέγων
γίνεσθαι τὰ ἀγαθὰ καὶ Πλαταιεῦσι. τότε δὲ τασσα- **3**
μένων τῶν Ἀθηναίων ἐν τῷ Μαραθῶνι ἐγίνετο
τοιόνδε τι· τὸ στρατόπεδον ἐξισούμενον τῷ Μηδικῷ
στρατοπέδῳ, τὸ μὲν αὐτοῦ μέσον ἐγίνετο ἐπὶ τάξιας
ὀλίγας, καὶ ταύτῃ ἦν ἀσθενέστατον τὸ στρατόπεδον,
τὸ δὲ κέρας ἑκάτερον ἔρρωτο πλήθεῖ.

The charge.

CXII. Ὡς δέ σφι διετέτακτο καὶ τὰ σφάγια **1**
ἐγίνετο καλὰ, ἐνθαῦτα ὡς ἀπείθησαν οἱ Ἀθηναῖοι,
δρόμῳ ἵεντο ἐς τοὺς βαρβάρους. ἦσαν δὲ στάδιοι
οὐκ ἐλάσσονες τὸ μεταίχμιον αὐτῶν ἢ ὀκτώ. οἱ δὲ **2**
Πέρσαι ὁρέοντες δρόμῳ ἐπιόντας παρεσκευάζοντο ὡς
δεξόμενοι, μανίην τε τοῖσι Ἀθηναίοισι ἐπέφερον καὶ
πάγχυ ὀλεθρίην, ὁρέοντες αὐτοὺς ὀλίγους, καὶ τούτους
δρόμῳ ἐπειγομένους, οὔτε ἵππου ὑπαρχούσης σφι
οὔτε τοξευμάτων. ταῦτα μέν νυν οἱ βάρβαροι κατεί- **3**

καζον, Ἀθηναῖοι δὲ ἐπείτε ἀθρόοι προσέμιξαν τοῖσι
βαρβάροισι, ἐμάχοντο ἀξίως λόγου. πρῶτοι μὲν
γὰρ Ἑλλήνων πάντων τῶν ἡμεῖς ἴδμεν δρόμῳ ἐς
πολεμίους ἐχρήσαντο, πρῶτοι δὲ ἀνέσχοντο ἐσθῆτά
τε Μηδικὴν ὁρέοντες καὶ τοὺς ἄνδρας ταύτην ἐσθη-
μένους· τέως δὲ ἦν τοῖσι Ἕλλησι καὶ τὸ οὔνομα τὸ
Μήδων φόβος ἀκοῦσαι.

*The Athenian centre is repulsed; but their two wings turn
the enemy, and then close up and engage and beat the
forces that had repulsed their centre, and follow them
with slaughter to their ships.*

CXIII. Μαχομένων δὲ ἐν τῷ Μαραθῶνι χρόνος   1
ἐγίνετο πολλός. καὶ τὸ μὲν μέσον τοῦ στρατοπέδου
ἐνίκων οἱ βάρβαροι, τῇ Πέρσαι τε αὐτοὶ καὶ Σάκαι
ἐτετάχατο· κατὰ τοῦτο μὲν δὴ ἐνίκων οἱ βάρβαροι,
καὶ ῥήξαντες ἐδίωκον ἐς τὴν μεσόγαιαν, τὸ δὲ κέρας
ἑκάτερον ἐνίκων Ἀθηναῖοί τε καὶ Πλαταιέες. νικῶντες   2
δὲ τὸ μὲν τετραμμένον τῶν βαρβάρων φεύγειν ἔων,
τοῖσι δὲ τὸ μέσον ῥήξασι αὐτῶν συναγαγόντες τὰ
κέρεα ἀμφότερα ἐμάχοντο καὶ ἐνίκων Ἀθηναῖοι.
φεύγουσι δὲ τοῖσι Πέρσῃσι εἵποντο κόπτοντες, ἐς ὃ
ἐπὶ τὴν θάλασσαν ἀπικόμενοι πῦρ τε αἴτεον καὶ
ἐπελαμβάνοντο τῶν νεῶν.

*Kallimachos and Stesileos fall. Kynegeiros loses his right
hand in the struggle at the ships.*

CXIV. Καὶ τοῦτο μὲν ἐν τούτῳ τῷ πόνῳ ὁ
πολέμαρχος Καλλίμαχος διαφθείρεται, ἀνὴρ γενόμενος ἀγαθός, ἀπὸ δ' ἔθανε τῶν στρατηγῶν Στησίλεως
ὁ Θρασύλεω· τοῦτο δὲ Κυνέγειρος ὁ Εὐφορίωνος

ἐνθαῦτα ἐπιλαβόμενος τῶν ἀφλάστων νεὸς τὴν χεῖρα
ἀποκοπεὶς πελέκεϊ πίπτει, τοῦτο δὲ ἄλλοι Ἀθηναίων
πολλοί τε καὶ ὀνομαστοί.

Seven of the Persian ships are taken: the rest sail towards
Sunium. A treasonable signal.

CXV. Ἑπτὰ μὲν δὴ τῶν νεῶν ἐπεκράτησαν
τρόπῳ τοιούτῳ Ἀθηναῖοι, τῇσι δὲ λοιπῇσι οἱ βάρβαροι ἐξανακρουσάμενοι, καὶ ἀναλαβόντες ἐκ τῆς
νήσου, ἐν τῇ ἔλιπον, τὰ ἐξ Ἐρετρίης ἀνδράποδα,
περιέπλωον Σούνιον, βουλόμενοι φθῆναι τοὺς Ἀθηναίους ἀπικόμενοι ἐς τὸ ἄστυ. αἰτίη δὲ ἔσχε ἐν
Ἀθηναίοισι ἐξ Ἀλκμαιωνιδέων μηχανῆς αὐτοὺς ταῦτα
ἐπινοηθῆναι· τούτους γὰρ συνθεμένους τοῖσι Πέρσῃσι
ἀναδέξαι ἀσπίδα ἐοῦσι ἤδη ἐν τῇσι νηυσί.

The Athenian army returns to Athens in time to meet the
Persian fleet, which, after waiting a short time off
Phalerum, returned to Asia.

CXVI. Οὗτοι μὲν δὴ περιέπλωον Σούνιον· Ἀθηναῖοι δὲ, ὡς ποδῶν εἶχον, τάχιστα ἐβοήθευν ἐς τὸ
ἄστυ, καὶ ἔφθησάν τε ἀπικόμενοι πρὶν ἢ τοὺς βαρβάρους ἥκειν, καὶ ἐστρατοπεδεύσαντο ἀπιγμένοι ἐξ
Ἡρακλείου τοῦ ἐν Μαραθῶνι ἐν ἄλλῳ Ἡρακλείῳ τῷ
ἐν Κυνοσάργεϊ. οἱ δὲ βάρβαροι τῇσι νηυσὶ ὑπεραιωρηθέντες Φαλήρου (τοῦτο γὰρ ἦν ἐπίνειον τότε τῶν
Ἀθηναίων), ὑπὲρ τούτου ἀνακωχεύσαντες τὰς νέας
ἀπέπλωον ὀπίσω ἐς τὴν Ἀσίην.

Numbers of the slain, 6400 Persians, 192 Athenians.
How Epizelos lost his sight.

CXVII. Ἐν ταύτῃ τῇ ἐν Μαραθῶνι μάχῃ ἀπέθα-   1

νον τῶν βαρβάρων κατὰ ἑξακισχιλίους καὶ τετρακοσίους ἄνδρας, Ἀθηναίων δὲ ἑκατὸν ἐνενήκοντα καὶ
δύο· ἔπεσον μὲν ἀμφοτέρων τοσοῦτοι, συνήνεικε δὲ   2
αὐτόθι θῶυμα γενέσθαι τοιόνδε, Ἀθηναῖον ἄνδρα
Ἐπίζηλον τὸν Κουφαγόρεω ἐν τῇ συστάσι μαχόμενόν
τε καὶ ἄνδρα γινόμενον ἀγαθὸν τῶν ὀμμάτων στερηθῆναι, οὔτε πληγέντα οὐδὲν τοῦ σώματος οὔτε
βληθέντα, καὶ τὸ λοιπὸν τῆς ζόης διατελέειν ἀπὸ
τούτου τοῦ χρόνου ἐόντα τυφλόν. λέγειν δὲ αὐτὸν   3
ἤκουσα περὶ τοῦ πάθεος τοιόνδε τινὰ λόγον, ἄνδρα οἱ
δοκέειν ὁπλίτην ἀντιστῆναι μέγαν, τοῦ τὸ γένειον
τὴν ἀσπίδα πᾶσαν σκιάζειν· τὸ δὲ φάσμα τοῦτο
ἑωυτὸν μὲν παρεξελθεῖν, τὸν δὲ ἑωυτοῦ παραστάτην
ἀποκτεῖναι. ταῦτα μὲν δὴ Ἐπίζηλον ἐπυθόμην
λέγειν.

Warned in a dream Datis restores an image of Apollo.

CXVIII. Δᾶτις δὲ πορευόμενος ἅμα τῷ στρατῷ   1
ἐς τὴν Ἀσίην, ἐπεί τε ἐγένετο ἐν Μυκόνῳ, εἶδε ὄψιν
ἐν τῷ ὕπνῳ. καὶ ἥτις μὲν ἦν ἡ ὄψις, οὐ λέγεται, ὁ
δὲ, ὡς ἡμέρη τάχιστα ἐπέλαμψε, ζήτησιν ἐποιέετο
τῶν νεῶν, εὑρὼν δὲ ἐν Φοινίσσῃ νηὶ ἄγαλμα Ἀπόλλωνος κεχρυσωμένον ἐπυνθάνετο ὁκόθεν σεσυλημένον εἴη· πυθόμενος δὲ ἐξ οὗ ἦν ἱροῦ, ἔπλωε τῇ
ἑωυτοῦ νηὶ ἐς Δῆλον. καὶ ἀπίκατο γὰρ τηνικαῦτα οἱ   2
Δήλιοι ὀπίσω ἐς τὴν νῆσον, κατατίθεταί τε ἐς τὸ ἱρὸν
τὸ ἄγαλμα, καὶ ἐντέλλεται τοῖσι Δηλίοισι ἀπαγαγεῖν
τὸ ἄγαλμα ἐς Δήλιον τὸ Θηβαίων· τὸ δ' ἐστὶ ἐπὶ
θαλάσσῃ Χαλκίδος καταντίον. Δᾶτις μὲν δὴ ταῦτα   3
ἐντειλάμενος ἀπέπλεε, τὸν δὲ ἀνδριάντα τοῦτον
Δήλιοι οὐκ ἀπήγαγον, ἀλλά μιν δι' ἐτέων εἴκοσι

Θηβαῖοι αὐτοὶ ἐκ θεοπροπίου ἐκομίσαντο ἐπὶ Δήλιον.

*The captured Eretrians are treated kindly by Darius and
assigned lands in Kissia.*

CXIX. Τοὺς δὲ τῶν Ἐρετριέων ἠνδραποδισ- 1
μένους Δᾶτίς τε καὶ Ἀρταφέρνης, ὡς προσέσχον ἐς
τὴν Ἀσίην πλέοντες, ἀνήγαγον ἐς Σοῦσα. βασιλεὺς
δὲ Δαρεῖος πρὶν μὲν αἰχμαλώτους γενέσθαι τοὺς
Ἐρετριέας ἐνεῖχέ σφι δεινὸν χόλον οἷα ἀρξάντων
ἀδικίης προτέρων τῶν Ἐρετριέων, ἐπεῖτε δὲ εἶδέ 2
σφεας ἀπαχθέντας παρ' ἑωυτὸν καὶ ὑποχειρίους
ἑωυτῷ ἐόντας, ἐποίησε κακὸν ἄλλο οὐδέν, ἀλλά σφεας
τῆς Κισσίης χώρης κατοίκισε ἐν σταθμῷ ἑωυτοῦ, τῷ
οὔνομά ἐστι Ἀρδέρικκα, ἀπὸ μὲν Σούσων δέκα καὶ
διηκοσίους σταδίους ἀπέχοντι, τεσσεράκοντα δὲ ἀπὸ
τοῦ φρέατος, τὸ παρέχεται τριφασίας ἰδέας· καὶ γὰρ
ἄσφαλτον καὶ ἅλας καὶ ἔλαιον ἀρύσσονται ἐξ αὐτοῦ
τρόπῳ τοιῷδε· ἀντλέεται μὲν κηλωνηΐῳ, ἀντὶ δὲ 3
γαυλοῦ ἥμισυ ἀσκοῦ οἱ προσδέδεται· ὑποτύψας δὲ
τούτῳ ἀντλέει καὶ ἔπειτα ἐγχέει ἐς δεξαμενήν· ἐκ δὲ
ταύτης ἐς ἄλλο διαχεόμενον τράπεται τριφασίας
ὁδούς. καὶ ἡ μὲν ἄσφαλτος καὶ οἱ ἅλες πήγνυνται
παραυτίκα, τὸ δὲ ἔλαιον συνάγουσι ἐν ἀγγηΐοισι, τὸ
οἱ Πέρσαι καλέουσι ῥαδινάκην· ἔστι δὲ μέλαν καὶ
ὀδμὴν παρεχόμενον βαρέαν. ἐνθαῦτα τοὺς Ἐρετριέας 4
κατοίκισε βασιλεὺς Δαρεῖος, οἳ καὶ μέχρι ἐμέο εἶχον
τὴν χώρην ταύτην φυλάσσοντες τὴν ἀρχαίην γλῶσσαν. τὰ μὲν δὴ περὶ Ἐρετριέας ἔσχε οὕτω.

Three days after the full moon, 2000 Spartans arrive at Athens. Curiosity to see the slaughtered Medes induces them to march to Marathon.

CXX. Λακεδαιμονίων δὲ ἧκον ἐς τὰς Ἀθήνας δισχίλιοι μετὰ τὴν πανσέληνον, ἔχοντες σπουδὴν πολλὴν καταλαβεῖν οὕτω, ὥστε τριταῖοι ἐκ Σπάρτης ἐγένοντο ἐν τῇ Ἀττικῇ. ὕστεροι δὲ ἀπικόμενοι τῆς συμβολῆς ἱμείροντο ὅμως θηήσασθαι τοὺς Μήδους, ἐλθόντες δὲ ἐς τὸν Μαραθῶνα ἐθηήσαντο. μετὰ δὲ αἰνέοντες Ἀθηναίους καὶ τὸ ἔργον αὐτῶν ἀπαλλάσσοντο ὀπίσω.

Were the Alkmaeonidae guilty of the treasonable signal to the Persians? Their antecedents are against it.

CXXI. Θῶυμα δέ μοι, καὶ οὐκ ἐνδέκομαι τὸν 1 λόγον, Ἀλκμαιωνίδας ἄν κοτε ἀναδέξαι Πέρσῃσι ἐκ συνθήματος ἀσπίδα, βουλομένους ὑπὸ βαρβάροισί τε εἶναι Ἀθηναίους καὶ ὑπὸ Ἱππίῃ, οἵτινες μᾶλλον ἢ ὁμοίως Καλλίῃ τῷ Φαινίππου, Ἱππονίκου δὲ πατρὶ, φαίνονται μισοτύραννοι ἐόντες. Καλλίης τε γὰρ 2 μοῦνος Ἀθηναίων ἁπάντων ἐτόλμα, ὅκως Πεισίστρατος ἐκπέσοι ἐκ τῶν Ἀθηνέων, τὰ χρήματα αὐτοῦ κηρυσσόμενα ὑπὸ τοῦ δημοσίου ὠνέεσθαι, καὶ τὰ ἄλλα τὰ ἔχθιστα ἐς αὐτὸν πάντα ἐμηχανᾶτο.

[Account of Kallias.]

CXXII. [Καλλίεω δὲ τούτου ἄξιον πολλαχοῦ 1 μνήμην ἐστὶ πάντα τινὰ ἔχειν. τοῦτο μὲν γὰρ τὰ προλελεγμένα, ὡς ἀνὴρ ἄκρος ἐλευθερῶν τὴν πατρίδα, τοῦτο δὲ τὰ ἐν Ὀλυμπίῃ ἐποίησε, ἵππῳ νικήσας,

τεθρίππῳ δὲ δεύτερος γενόμενος, Πύθια δὲ πρότερον
ἀνελόμενός, ἐφανερώθη ἐς τοὺς Ἕλληνας πάντας
μεγίστῃσι δαπάνῃσι, τοῦτο δὲ κατὰ τὰς ἑωυτοῦ　　2
θυγατέρας ἐούσας τρεῖς οἷός τις ἀνὴρ ἐγένετο. ἐπειδὴ
γὰρ ἐγένοντο γάμου ὡραῖαι, ἔδωκέ σφι δωρεὴν μεγα-
λοπρεπεστάτην ἐκείνῃσί τε ἐχαρίσατο. ἐκ γὰρ πάντων τῶν Ἀθηναίων τὸν ἑκάστη ἐθέλοι ἄνδρα ἑωυτῇ
ἐκλέξασθαι, ἔδωκε τούτῳ τῷ ἀνδρί.]

*The Alkmaeonidae could have had no wish to enslave
Athens, and for my part I acquit them.*

CXXIII.　Καὶ οἱ Ἀλκμαιωνίδαι ὁμοίως ἢ οὐδὲν　　1
ἔσσον τούτου ἦσαν μισοτύραννοι. θῶυμα ὦν μοι,
καὶ οὐ προσίεμαι τὴν διαβολήν, τούτους γε ἀναδέξαι
ἀσπίδα, οἵτινες ἔφευγόν τε τὸν πάντα χρόνον τοὺς
τυράννους, ἐκ μηχανῆς τε τῆς τούτων ἐξέλιπον οἱ
Πεισιστρατίδαι τὴν τυραννίδα. καὶ οὕτω τὰς Ἀθήνας　　2
οὗτοι ἦσαν οἱ ἐλευθερώσαντες πολλῷ μᾶλλον ἤπερ
Ἁρμόδιός τε καὶ Ἀριστογείτων, ὡς ἐγὼ κρίνω. οἱ
μὲν γὰρ ἐξηγρίωσαν τοὺς ὑπολοίπους Πεισιστρατιδέων Ἵππαρχον ἀποκτείναντες, οὐδέ τι μᾶλλον
ἔπαυσαν τοὺς λοιποὺς τυραννεύοντας, Ἀλκμαιωνίδαι
δὲ ἐμφανέως ἠλευθέρωσαν, εἰ δὴ οὗτοί γε ἀληθέως
ἦσαν οἱ τὴν Πυθίην ἀναπείσαντες προσημαίνειν
Λακεδαιμονίοισι ἐλευθεροῦν τὰς Ἀθήνας, ὥς μοι
πρότερον δεδήλωται. CXXIV.　Ἀλλὰ γὰρ ἴσως τι　　1
ἐπιμεμφόμενοι Ἀθηναίων τῷ δήμῳ προεδίδοσαν τὴν
πατρίδα. οὐ μὲν ὦν ἦσάν σφεων ἄλλοι δοκιμώτεροι
ἔν γε Ἀθηναίοισι ἄνδρες, οὐδ' οἳ μᾶλλον ἐτετιμέατο.
οὕτω οὐδὲ λόγος αἱρέει ἀναδεχθῆναι ἔκ γε ἂν τούτων　　2
ἀσπίδα ἐπὶ τοιούτῳ λόγῳ. ἀνεδέχθη μὲν γὰρ ἀσπίς,

καὶ τοῦτο οὐκ ἔστι ἄλλως εἰπεῖν· ἐγένετο γάρ· ὃς
μέντοι ἦν ὁ ἀναδέξας, οὐκ ἔχω προσωτέρω εἰπεῖν
τούτων.

*Origin of the wealth of the Alkmaeonidae. Kroesos taken
at his word.*

CXXV. Οἱ δὲ Ἀλκμαιωνίδαι ἦσαν μὲν καὶ τὰ   1
ἀνέκαθεν λαμπροὶ ἐν τῇσι Ἀθήνῃσι, ἀπὸ δὲ Ἀλκμαίωνος καὶ αὖτις Μεγακλέος ἐγένοντο καὶ κάρτα λαμ-
προί. τοῦτο μὲν γὰρ Ἀλκμαίων ὁ Μεγακλέος τοῖσι   2
ἐκ Σαρδίων Λυδοῖσι παρὰ Κροίσου ἀπικνεομένοισι
ἐπὶ τὸ χρηστήριον τὸ ἐν Δελφοῖσι συμπρήκτωρ τε
ἐγίνετο καὶ συνελάμβανε προθύμως, καί μιν Κροῖσος
πυθόμενος τῶν Λυδῶν τῶν ἐς τὰ χρηστήρια φοι-
τεόντων ἑωυτὸν εὖ ποιέειν μεταπέμπεται ἐς Σάρδις,
ἀπικόμενον δὲ δωρέεται χρυσῷ, τὸν ἂν δύνηται τῷ
ἑωυτοῦ σώματι ἐξενείκασθαι ἐσάπαξ. ὁ δὲ Ἀλκμαίων   3
πρὸς τὴν δωρεὴν ἐοῦσαν τοιαύτην τοιάδε ἐπιτηδεύσας
προσέφερε· ἐνδὺς κιθῶνα μέγαν καὶ κόλπον πολλὸν
καταλιπόμενος τοῦ κιθῶνος, κοθόρνους τοὺς εὕρισκε
εὐρυτάτους ἐόντας ὑποδησάμενος ἤιε ἐς τὸν θησαυρὸν,
ἐς τὸν οἱ κατηγέοντο, ἐσπεσὼν δὲ ἐς σωρὸν ψήγματος,   4
πρῶτα μὲν παρέσαξε παρὰ τὰς κνήμας τοῦ χρυσοῦ
ὅσον ἐχώρεον οἱ κόθορνοι, μετὰ δὲ τὸν κόλπον πάντα
πλησάμενος χρυσοῦ καὶ ἐς τὰς τρίχας τῆς κεφαλῆς
διαπάσας τοῦ ψήγματος καὶ ἄλλο λαβὼν ἐς τὸ
στόμα ἐξήιε ἐκ τοῦ θησαυροῦ, ἕλκων μὲν μόγις τοὺς
κοθόρνους, παντὶ δέ τεῳ οἰκὼς μᾶλλον ἢ ἀνθρώπῳ,
τοῦ τό τε στόμα ἐβέβυστο καὶ πάντα ἐξώγκωτο.
ἰδόντα δὲ τὸν Κροῖσον γέλως ἐσῆλθε, καί οἱ πάντα   5
τε ἐκεῖνα διδοῖ καὶ πρὸς ἕτερα δωρέεται οὐκ ἐλάσσω

ἐκείνων. οὕτω μὲν ἐπλούτησε ἡ οἰκίη αὕτη μεγάλως,
καὶ ὁ Ἀλκμαίων οὗτος οὕτω τεθριπποτροφήσας
Ὀλυμπιάδα ἀναιρέεται.

*Kleisthenes, tyrant of Sikyon, invites candidates for the
hand of his daughter.*

CXXVI. Μετὰ δὲ, γενεῇ δευτέρῃ ὕστερον, Κλεισ-   1
θένης μιν ὁ Σικυῶνος τύραννος ἐξήειρε ὥστε πολλῷ
ὀνομαστοτέρην γενέσθαι ἐν τοῖσι Ἕλλησι, ἢ πρότερον ἦν. Κλεισθένεϊ γὰρ τῷ Ἀριστωνύμου τοῦ
Μύρωνος τοῦ Ἀνδρέω γίνεται θυγάτηρ, τῇ οὔνομα ἦν
Ἀγαρίστη. ταύτην ἠθέλησε Ἑλλήνων πάντων ἐξευ-
ρὼν τὸν ἄριστον τούτῳ γυναῖκα προσθεῖναι. Ὀλυμ-   2
πίων ὦν ἐόντων καὶ νικῶν ἐν αὐτοῖσι τεθρίππῳ ὁ
Κλεισθένης κήρυγμα ἐποιήσατο, ὅστις Ἑλλήνων
ἑωυτὸν ἀξιοῖ Κλεισθένεος γαμβρὸν γενέσθαι, ἥκειν ἐς
ἑξηκοστὴν ἡμέρην ἢ καὶ πρότερον ἐς Σικυῶνα ὡς
κυρώσοντος Κλεισθένεος τὸν γάμον ἐν ἐνιαυτῷ, ἀπὸ
τῆς ἑξηκοστῆς ἀρξαμένου ἡμέρης. ἐνθαῦτα Ἑλλή-   3
νων ὅσοι σφίσι τε αὐτοῖσι ἦσαν καὶ πάτρῃ ἐξωγκωμένοι, ἐφοίτεον μνηστῆρες, τοῖσι Κλεισθένης καὶ
δρόμον καὶ παλαίστρην ποιησάμενος ἐπ' αὐτῷ τούτῳ
εἶχε.

The suitors.

CXXVII. Ἀπὸ μὲν δὴ Ἰταλίης ἦλθε Σμιν-   1
δυρίδης ὁ Ἱπποκράτεος Συβαρίτης, ὃς ἐπὶ πλεῖστον
δὴ χλιδῆς εἰς ἀνὴρ ἀπίκετο (ἡ δὲ Σύβαρις ἤκμαζε
τοῦτον τὸν χρόνον μάλιστα), καὶ Σιρίτης Δάμασος
Ἀμύριος τοῦ σοφοῦ λεγομένου παῖς. οὗτοι μὲν ἀπὸ   2
Ἰταλίης ἦλθον, ἐκ δὲ τοῦ κόλπου τοῦ Ἰονίου Ἀμφί-

μνηστος Ἐπιστρόφου Ἐπιδάμνιος· οὗτος δὲ ἐκ τοῦ
Ἰονίου κόλπου. Αἰτωλὸς δὲ ἦλθε Τιτόρμου τοῦ
ὑπερφύντος τε Ἕλληνας ἰσχύϊ καὶ φυγόντος ἀνθρώπους ἐς τὰς ἐσχατιὰς τῆς Αἰτωλίδος χώρης, τούτου
τοῦ Τιτόρμου ἀδελφεὸς Μάλης. ἀπὸ δὲ Πελοπον- 3
νήσου Φείδωνος τοῦ Ἀργείων τυράννου παῖς Λεωκήδης, Φείδωνος δὲ τοῦ τὰ μέτρα ποιήσαντος Πελοποννησίοισι καὶ ὑβρίσαντος μέγιστα δὴ Ἑλλήνων
ἀπάντων, ὃς ἐξαναστήσας τοὺς Ἠλείων ἀγωνοθέτας
αὐτὸς τὸν ἐν Ὀλυμπίῃ ἀγῶνα ἔθηκε, τούτου τε δὴ
παῖς, καὶ Ἀμίαντος Λυκούργου Ἀρκὰς ἐκ Τραπεζοῦντος, καὶ Ἀζὴν ἐκ Παίου πόλιος Λαφάνης Εὐφορίωνος τοῦ δεξαμένου τε, ὡς λόγος ἐν Ἀρκαδίῃ
λέγεται, τοὺς Διοσκούρους οἰκίοισι καὶ ἀπὸ τούτου
ξεινοδοκέοντος πάντας ἀνθρώπους, καὶ Ἠλεῖος Ὀνο-
μαστὸς Ἀγαίου. οὗτοι μὲν δὴ ἐξ αὐτῆς Πελοπον- 4
νήσου ἦλθον, ἐκ δὲ Ἀθηνέων ἀπίκοντο Μεγακλέης τε
ὁ Ἀλκμαίωνος τούτου τοῦ παρὰ Κροῖσον ἀπικομένου,
καὶ ἄλλος Ἱπποκλείδης Τισάνδρου, πλούτῳ καὶ εἴδεϊ
προφέρων Ἀθηναίων. ἀπὸ δὲ Ἐρετρίης ἀνθεύσης
τοῦτον τὸν χρόνον Λυσανίης, οὗτος δὲ ἀπ᾽ Εὐβοίης
μοῦνος. ἐκ δὲ Θεσσαλίης ἦλθε τῶν Σκοπαδέων
Διακτορίδης Κραννώνιος, ἐκ δὲ Μολοσσῶν Ἄλκων.

He tests their courage and temper for a year.

CXXVIII. Τοσοῦτοι μὲν ἐγένοντο οἱ μνηστῆρες. 1
ἀπικομένων δὲ τούτων ἐς τὴν προειρημένην ἡμέρην
ὁ Κλεισθένης πρῶτα μὲν τὰς πάτρας τε αὐτῶν
ἀνεπύθετο καὶ γένος ἑκάστου, μετὰ δὲ κατέχων
ἐνιαυτὸν διεπειρᾶτο αὐτῶν τῆς τε ἀνδραγαθίης καὶ
τῆς ὀργῆς καὶ παιδεύσιός τε καὶ τρόπου, καὶ ἑνὶ

ἑκάστῳ ἰὼν ἐς συνουσίην καὶ συνάπασι, καὶ ἐς
γυμνάσιά τε ἐξαγινέων ὅσοι ἦσαν αὐτῶν νεώτεροι,
καὶ τό γε μέγιστον, ἐν τῇ συνιστίῃ διεπειρᾶτο· ὅσον
γὰρ κατεῖχε χρόνον αὐτούς, τοῦτον πάντα ἐποίεε καὶ
ἅμα ἐξείνιζε μεγαλοπρεπέως. καὶ δή κου μάλιστα 2
τῶν μνηστήρων ἠρέσκοντό οἱ οἱ ἀπ' Ἀθηνέων ἀπιγμένοι, καὶ τούτων μᾶλλον Ἱπποκλείδης ὁ Τισάνδρου
καὶ κατ' ἀνδραγαθίην ἐκρίνετο, καὶ ὅτι τὸ ἀνέκαθεν
τοῖσι ἐν Κορίνθῳ Κυψελίδῃσι ἦν προσήκων.

Hippokleides 'doesn't care'.

CXXIX. Ὡς δὲ ἡ κυρίη ἐγένετο τῶν ἡμερέων 1
τῆς τε κατακλίσιος τοῦ γάμου καὶ ἐκφάσιος αὐτοῦ
Κλεισθένεος, τὸν κρίνοι ἐκ πάντων, θύσας βοῦς
ἑκατὸν ὁ Κλεισθένης εὐώχεε αὐτούς τε τοὺς μνηστῆρας
καὶ τοὺς Σικυωνίους πάντας. ὡς δὲ ἀπὸ δείπνου 2
ἐγένοντο, οἱ μνηστῆρες ἔριν εἶχον ἀμφί τε μουσικῇ
καὶ τῷ λεγομένῳ ἐς τὸ μέσον. προϊούσης δὲ τῆς
πόσιος κατέχων πολλὸν τοὺς ἄλλους ὁ Ἱπποκλείδης
ἐκέλευσε τὸν αὐλητὴν αὐλῆσαί οἱ ἐμμέλειαν, πειθο-
μένου δὲ τοῦ αὐλητέω ὠρχήσατο. καί κως ἑωυτῷ
μὲν ἀρεστῶς ὠρχέετο, ὁ δὲ Κλεισθένης ὁρέων ὅλον τὸ
πρῆγμα ὑπώπτευε. μετὰ δὲ ἐπισχὼν ὁ Ἱπποκλείδης 3
χρόνον ἐκέλευσέ οἱ τινα τράπεζαν ἐσενεῖκαι, ἐσελ-
θούσης δὲ τῆς τραπέζης πρῶτα μὲν ἐπ' αὐτῆς ὠρχήσατο Λακωνικὰ σχημάτια, μετὰ δὲ ἄλλα Ἀττικά, τὸ
τρίτον δὲ τὴν κεφαλὴν ἐρείσας ἐπὶ τὴν τράπεζαν
τοῖσι σκέλεσι ἐχειρονόμησε. Κλεισθένης δὲ τὰ μὲν 4
πρῶτα καὶ τὰ δεύτερα ὀρχεομένου ἀποστυγέων γαμβρὸν ἄν οἱ ἔτι γενέσθαι Ἱπποκλείδην διὰ τήν τε ὄρχη-
σιν καὶ τὴν ἀναιδείην κατεῖχε ἑωυτόν, οὐ βουλόμενος

ἐκραγῆναι ἐς αὐτόν, ὡς δὲ εἶδε τοῖσι σκέλεσι χειρονο-
μήσαντα, οὐκέτι κατέχειν δυνάμενος εἶπε· "Ὦ παῖ
"Τισάνδρου, ἀπωρχήσαό γε μὴν τὸν γάμον." ὁ δὲ
Ἱπποκλείδης ὑπολαβὼν εἶπε· "Οὐ φροντὶς Ἱππο-
"κλείδῃ."

*Kleisthenes chooses Megakles as his daughter's husband,
and consoles the other suitors by a present of a talent.*

CXXX. Ἀπὸ τούτου μὲν τοῦτο ὀνομάζεται. Κλει-   1
σθένης δὲ σιγὴν ποιησάμενος ἔλεξε ἐς μέσον τάδε·
"Ἄνδρες παιδὸς τῆς ἐμῆς μνηστῆρες, ἐγὼ καὶ πάντας
"ὑμέας ἐπαινέω, καὶ πᾶσιν ὑμῖν, εἰ οἷόν τε εἴη, χαρι-
"ζοίμην ἄν, μήτ᾽ ἕνα ὑμέων ἐξαίρετον ἀποκρίνων μήτε
"τοὺς λοιποὺς ἀποδοκιμάζων· ἀλλ᾽ οὐ γὰρ οἷά τέ ἐστι   2
"μιῆς πέρι παρθένου βουλεύοντα πᾶσι κατὰ νόον
"ποιέειν, τοῖσι μὲν ὑμέων ἀπελαυνομένοισι τοῦδε τοῦ
"γάμου τάλαντον ἀργυρίου ἑκάστῳ δωρεὴν δίδωμι
"τῆς ἀξιώσιος εἵνεκεν τῆς ἐξ ἐμεῦ γῆμαι καὶ τῆς
"ἐξ οἴκου ἀποδημίης, τῷ δὲ Ἀλκμαίωνος Μεγακλέϊ
"ἐγγυῶ παῖδα τὴν ἐμὴν Ἀγαρίστην νόμοισι τοῖσι
"Ἀθηναίων." Φαμένου δὲ ἐγγυᾶσθαι Μεγακλέος
ἐκεκύρωτο ὁ γάμος Κλεισθένεϊ.

Kleisthenes the Reformer.

CXXXI. Ἀμφὶ μὲν κρίσιος τῶν μνηστήρων   1
τοσαῦτα ἐγένετο, καὶ οὕτω Ἀλκμαιωνίδαι ἐβώσθησαν
ἀνὰ τὴν Ἑλλάδα· τούτων δὲ συνοικησάντων γίνεται
Κλεισθένης τε ὁ τὰς φυλὰς καὶ τὴν δημοκρατίην
Ἀθηναίοισι καταστήσας, ἔχων τὸ οὔνομα ἀπὸ τοῦ
μητροπάτορος τοῦ Σικυωνίου· εὗτός τε δὴ γίνεται   2
Μεγακλέϊ καὶ Ἱπποκράτης, ἐκ δὲ Ἱπποκράτεος
Μεγακλέης τε ἄλλος καὶ Ἀγαρίστη ἄλλη, ἀπὸ τῆς

Κλεισθένεος Ἀγαρίστης ἔχουσα τὸ οὔνομα, ἣ συνοι-
κήσασά τε Ξανθίππῳ τῷ Ἀρίφρονος καὶ ἔγκυος
ἐοῦσα εἶδε ὄψιν ἐν τῷ ὕπνῳ, ἐδόκεε δὲ λέοντα τεκεῖν·
καὶ μετ' ὀλίγας ἡμέρας τίκτει Περικλέα Ξανθίππῳ.

The fall of Miltiades B.C. 489.   *He asks for 70 ships and
some soldiers.*

CXXXII. Μετὰ δὲ τὸ ἐν Μαραθῶνι τρῶμα
γενόμενον Μιλτιάδης, καὶ πρότερον εὐδοκιμέων παρὰ
Ἀθηναίοισι, τότε μᾶλλον αὔξετο. αἰτήσας δὲ νέας
ἑβδομήκοντα καὶ στρατιήν τε καὶ χρήματα Ἀθηναίους, οὐ φράσας σφι, ἐπ' ἣν ἐπιστρατεύσεται
χώρην, ἀλλὰ φὰς αὐτοὺς καταπλουτιεῖν, ἤν οἱ
ἔπωνται, ἐπὶ γὰρ χώρην τοιαύτην δή τινα ἄξειν, ὅθεν
χρυσὸν εὐπετέως ἄφθονον οἴσονται, λέγων τοιαῦτα
αἴτεε τὰς νέας. Ἀθηναῖοι δὲ τούτοισι ἐπαερθέντες
παρέδοσαν.

He sails to Paros.

CXXXIII. Παραλαβὼν δὲ ὁ Μιλτιάδης τὴν   1
στρατιὴν ἔπλεε ἐπὶ Πάρον, πρόφασιν ἔχων, ὡς οἱ
Πάριοι ὑπῆρξαν πρότεροι στρατευόμενοι τριήρεϊ ἐς
Μαραθῶνα ἅμα τῷ Πέρσῃ. τοῦτο μὲν δὴ πρόσχημα
λόγου ἦν, ἀτάρ τινα καὶ ἔγκοτον εἶχε τοῖσι Παρίοισι
διὰ Λυσαγόρην τὸν Τισίεω, ἐόντα γένος Πάριον,
διαβαλόντα μιν πρὸς Ὑδάρνεα τὸν Πέρσην. ἀπικό-   2
μενος δὲ ἐς τὴν ἔπλεε ὁ Μιλτιάδης τῇ στρατιῇ
ἐπολιόρκεε Παρίους κατειλημένους ἐντὸς τείχεος, καὶ
ἐσπέμπων κήρυκα αἴτεε ἑκατὸν τάλαντα, φὰς, ἢν μή
οἱ δῶσι, οὐκ ἀπαναστήσειν τὴν στρατιήν, πρὶν ἢ
ἐξέλῃ σφέας. οἱ δὲ Πάριοι, ὅκως μέν τι δώσουσι   3

Μιλτιάδη ἀργυρίου, οὐδὲ διενοεῦντο, οἱ δὲ, ὅκως
διαφυλάξουσι τὴν πόλιν, τοῦτο ἐμηχανῶντο, ἄλλα τε
ἐπιφραζόμενοι, καὶ τῇ μάλιστα ἔσκε ἑκάστοτε ἐπίμαχον τοῦ τείχεος, τοῦτο ἅμα νυκτὶ ἐξηείρετο
διπλήσιον τοῦ ἀρχαίου.

*The priestess Timo admits him to the temple of Demeter.
He is seized with a panic and in retreating injures his
thigh.*

CXXXIV. Ἐς μὲν δὴ τοσοῦτο τοῦ λόγου οἱ   1
πάντες Ἕλληνες λέγουσι, τὸ ἐνθεῦτεν δὲ αὐτοὶ
Πάριοι γενέσθαι ὧδε λέγουσι· Μιλτιάδη ἀπορέοντι
ἐλθεῖν ἐς λόγους αἰχμάλωτον γυναῖκα, ἐοῦσαν μὲν
Παρίην γένος, οὔνομα δέ οἱ εἶναι Τιμοῦν, εἶναι δὲ
ὑποζάκορον τῶν χθονίων θεῶν. ταύτην ἐλθοῦσαν
ἐς ὄψιν Μιλτιάδεω συμβουλεῦσαι, εἰ περὶ πολλοῦ
ποιέεται Πάρον ἑλεῖν, τὰ ἂν αὐτὴ ὑπόθηται, ταῦτα
ποιέειν. μετὰ δὲ τὴν μὲν ὑποθέσθαι, τὸν δὲ ἀπικό-   2
μενον ἐπὶ τὸν κολωνὸν τὸν πρὸ τῆς πόλιος ἐόντα τὸ
ἕρκος θεσμοφόρου Δήμητρος ὑπερθορεῖν, οὐ δυνάμενον
τὰς θύρας ἀνοῖξαι, ὑπερθορόντα δὲ ἰέναι ἐπὶ τὸ
μέγαρον ὅ τι δὴ ποιήσοντα ἐντός, εἴτε κινήσοντά τι
τῶν ἀκινήτων εἴτε ὅ τι δή κοτε πρήξοντα· πρὸς τῇσι
θύρῃσί τε γενέσθαι, καὶ πρόκατε φρίκης αὐτὸν
ὑπελθούσης ὀπίσω τὴν αὐτὴν ὁδὸν ἵεσθαι, καταθρώσκοντα δὲ τὴν αἱμασιὴν τὸν μηρὸν σπασθῆναι.
οἱ δὲ αὐτὸν τὸ γόνυ προσπταῖσαι λέγουσι.

The Oracle at Delos forbids the punishment of Timo.

CXXXV. Μιλτιάδης μέν νυν φλαύρως ἔχων   1
ἀπέπλεε ὀπίσω, οὔτε χρήματα Ἀθηναίοισι ἄγων

οὔτε Πάρον προσκτησάμενος, ἀλλὰ πολιορκήσας τε ἓξ καὶ εἴκοσι ἡμέρας καὶ δηιώσας τὴν νῆσον. Πάριοι δὲ πυθόμενοι, ὡς ἡ ὑποζάκορος τῶν θεῶν 2 Τιμὼ Μιλτιάδῃ κατηγήσατο, βουλόμενοί μιν ἀντὶ τούτων τιμωρήσασθαι, θεοπρόπους πέμπουσι ἐς Δελφούς, ὥς σφεας ἡσυχίη τῆς πολιορκίης ἔσχε, ἔπεμπον δὲ ἐπειρησομένους, εἰ καταχρήσονται τὴν ὑποζάκορον τῶν θεῶν ὡς ἐξηγησαμένην τοῖσι ἐχθροῖσι τῆς πατρίδος ἅλωσιν καὶ τὰ ἐς ἔρσενα γόνον ἄρρητα ἱρὰ ἐκφήνασαν Μιλτιάδῃ. ἡ δὲ Πυθίη οὐκ ἔα, φᾶσα 3 οὐ Τιμοῦν εἶναι τὴν αἰτίην τούτων, ἀλλὰ δέειν· γὰρ Μιλτιάδεα τελευτᾶν μὴ εὖ, φανῆναί οἱ τῶν κακῶν κατηγεμόνα.

Miltiades is impeached by Xanthippos. He is fined 50 talents, and soon afterwards dies of a mortification of his thigh. His son pays the fine.

CXXXVI. Παρίοισι μὲν δὴ ταῦτα ἡ Πυθίη 1 ἔχρησε. Ἀθηναῖοι δὲ ἐκ Πάρου Μιλτιάδεα ἀπονοστήσαντα ἔσχον ἐν στόμασι, οἵ τε ἄλλοι καὶ μάλιστα Ξάνθιππος ὁ Ἀρίφρονος, ὃς θανάτου ὑπαγαγὼν ὑπὸ τὸν δῆμον Μιλτιάδεα ἐδίωκε τῆς Ἀθηναίων ἀπάτης εἵνεκεν. Μιλτιάδης δὲ αὐτὸς μὲν παρεὼν 2 οὐκ ἀπελογέετο (ἦν γὰρ ἀδύνατος ὥστε σηπομένου τοῦ μηροῦ), προκειμένου δὲ αὐτοῦ ἐν κλίνῃ ὑπεραπελογέοντο οἱ φίλοι, τῆς μάχης τε τῆς ἐν Μαραθῶνι πολλὰ ἐπιμεμνημένοι καὶ τὴν Λήμνου αἵρεσιν, ὡς ἑλὼν Λῆμνόν τε καὶ τισάμενος τοὺς Πελασγοὺς παρέδωκε Ἀθηναίοισι. προσγενομένου δὲ τοῦ δήμου 3 αὐτῷ κατὰ τὴν ἀπόλυσιν τοῦ θανάτου, ζημιώσαντος δὲ κατὰ τὴν ἀδικίην πεντήκοντα ταλάντοισι, Μιλ-

τιάδης μὲν μετὰ ταῦτα σφακελίσαντός τε τοῦ μηροῦ
καὶ σαπέντος τελευτᾷ, τὰ δὲ πεντήκοντα τάλαντα
ἐξέτισε ὁ παῖς αὐτοῦ Κίμων.

How Miltiades took Lemnos.
The Pelasgic builders, driven out of Attica, settle in Lemnos and elsewhere.

CXXXVII. Λῆμνον δὲ Μιλτιάδης ὁ Κίμωνος 1
ὧδε ἔσχε· Πελασγοὶ ἐπεί τε ἐκ τῆς Ἀττικῆς ὑπὸ
Ἀθηναίων ἐξεβλήθησαν, εἴτε ὧν δὴ δικαίως εἴτε
ἀδίκως· τοῦτο γὰρ οὐκ ἔχω φράσαι, πλὴν τὰ
λεγόμενα, ὅτι Ἑκαταῖος μὲν ὁ Ἡγησάνδρου ἔφησε ἐν
τοῖσι λόγοισι λέγων ἀδίκως· ἐπείτε γὰρ ἰδεῖν τοὺς 2
Ἀθηναίους τὴν χώρην, τὴν σφίσι αὐτοῖσι ὑπὸ τὸν
Ὑμησσὸν ἐοῦσαν ἔδοσαν οἰκῆσαι μισθὸν τοῦ τείχεος
τοῦ περὶ τὴν ἀκρόπολίν κοτε ἐληλαμένου, ταύτην ὡς
ἰδεῖν τοὺς Ἀθηναίους ἐξεργασμένην εὖ, τὴν πρότερον
εἶναι κακήν τε καὶ τοῦ μηδενὸς ἀξίην, λαβεῖν φθόνον
τε καὶ ἵμερον τῆς γῆς, καὶ οὕτω ἐξελαύνειν αὐτοὺς
οὐδεμίαν ἄλλην πρόφασιν προϊσχομένους τοὺς Ἀθη-
ναίους· ὡς δὲ αὐτοὶ Ἀθηναῖοι λέγουσι, δικαίως
ἐξελάσαι. κατοικημένους γὰρ τοὺς Πελασγοὺς ὑπὸ 3
τῷ Ὑμησσῷ ἐνθεῦτεν ὁρμεομένους ἀδικέειν τάδε·
φοιτᾶν γὰρ αἰεὶ τὰς σφετέρας θυγατέρας τε καὶ τοὺς
παῖδας ἐπ᾽ ὕδωρ ἐπὶ τὴν Ἐννεάκρουνον (οὐ γὰρ εἶναι
τοῦτον τὸν χρόνον σφίσι κω οὐδὲ τοῖσι ἄλλοισι
Ἕλλησι οἰκέτας), ὅκως δὲ ἔλθοιεν αὗται, τοὺς Πελασγοὺς ὑπὸ ὕβριός τε καὶ ὀλιγωρίης βιᾶσθαί σφεας.
καὶ ταῦτα μέντοι σφι οὐκ ἀποχρᾶν ποιέειν, ἀλλὰ
τέλος καὶ ἐπιβουλεύοντας ἐπιχειρήσειν ἐπ᾽ αὐτοφώρῳ φανῆναι. ἑωυτοὺς δὲ γενέσθαι τοσούτῳ ἐκεί- 4

νων ἄνδρας ἀμείνονας, ὅσῳ παρεὸν αὐτοῖσι ἀποκτεῖναι
τοὺς Πελασγοὺς, ἐπεί σφεας ἔλαβον ἐπιβουλεύοντας,
οὐκ ἐθελῆσαι, ἀλλά σφι προειπεῖν ἐκ τῆς γῆς ἐξιέναι.
τοὺς δὲ οὕτω δὴ ἐκχωρήσαντας ἄλλα τε σχεῖν χωρία
καὶ δὴ καὶ Λῆμνον. ἐκεῖνα μὲν δὴ Ἑκαταῖος ἔλεξε,
ταῦτα δὲ Ἀθηναῖοι λέγουσι.

'The Lemnian deeds.' The Pelasgians carry off Attic
women to Lemnos, whose children giving them alarm
they kill both them and their mothers.

CXXXVIII. Οἱ δὲ Πελασγοὶ οὗτοι Λῆμνον 1
τότε νεμόμενοι καὶ βουλόμενοι τοὺς Ἀθηναίους
τιμωρήσασθαι, εὖ τε ἐξεπιστάμενοι τὰς Ἀθηναίων
ὁρτὰς, πεντηκοντέρους κτησάμενοι ἐλόχησαν Ἀρτέμιδι ἐν Βραυρῶνι ἀγούσας ὁρτὴν τὰς τῶν Ἀθηναίων
γυναῖκας, ἐνθεῦτεν δὲ ἁρπάσαντες τούτων πολλὰς
οἴχοντο ἀποπλέοντες, καί σφεας ἐς Λῆμνον ἀγαγόντες παλλακὰς εἶχον. ὡς δὲ τέκνων αὗται αἱ 2
γυναῖκες ὑπεπλήσθησαν, γλῶσσάν τε τὴν Ἀττικὴν
καὶ τρόπους τοὺς Ἀθηναίων ἐδίδασκον τοὺς παῖδας.
οἱ δὲ οὔτε συμμίσγεσθαι τοῖσι ἐκ τῶν Πελασγίδων
γυναικῶν παισὶ ἤθελον, εἴ τε τύπτοιτό τις αὐτῶν ὑπ'
ἐκείνων τινός, ἐβοήθεόν τε πάντες καὶ ἐτιμώρεον
ἀλλήλοισι· καὶ δὴ καὶ ἄρχειν τε τῶν παίδων οἱ
παῖδες ἐδικαίευν καὶ πολλὸν ἐπεκράτεον. μαθόντες 3
δὲ ταῦτα οἱ Πελασγοὶ ἑωυτοῖσι λόγους ἐδίδοσαν· καί
σφι βουλευομένοισι δεινόν τι ἐσέδυνε, εἰ δὴ διαγινώ-
σκοιεν σφίσι τε βοηθέειν οἱ παῖδες πρὸς τῶν κουριδιέων γυναικῶν τοὺς παῖδας καὶ τούτων αὐτίκα ἄρχειν
πειρῷατο, τί δὴ ἀνδρωθέντες δῆθεν ποιήσουσι. ἐνθαῦτα 4
ἔδοξέ σφι κτείνειν τοὺς παῖδας τοὺς ἐκ τῶν Ἀττικέων

γυναικῶν. ποιεῦσι δὴ ταῦτα, προσαπολλύουσι δέ
σφεων καὶ τὰς μητέρας. ἀπὸ τούτου δὲ τοῦ ἔργου
καὶ τοῦ προτέρου τούτων, τὸ ἐργάσαντο αἱ γυναῖκες
τοὺς ἅμα Θόαντι ἄνδρας σφετέρους ἀποκτείνασαι,
νενόμισται ἀνὰ τὴν Ἑλλάδα τὰ σχέτλια ἔργα πάντα
Λήμνια καλέεσθαι.

This crime was followed by a dearth; and the Delphic
Oracle orders the Pelasgians to give the Athenians
satisfaction. The Pelasgians will only comply under
impossible conditions.

CXXXIX. Ἀποκτείνασι δὲ τοῖσι Πελασγοῖσι   1
τοὺς σφετέρους παῖδάς τε καὶ γυναῖκας οὔτε γῆ
καρπὸν ἔφερε οὔτε γυναῖκές τε καὶ ποῖμναι ὁμοίως
ἔτικτον καὶ πρὸ τοῦ. πιεζόμενοι δὲ λιμῷ τε καὶ
ἀπαιδίη ἐς Δελφοὺς ἔπεμπον, λύσιν τινὰ αἰτησόμενοι
τῶν παρεόντων κακῶν. ἡ δὲ Πυθίη σφέας ἐκέλευε   2
Ἀθηναίοισι δίκας διδόναι ταύτας, τὰς ἂν αὐτοὶ
Ἀθηναῖοι δικάσωσι. ἦλθόν τε δὴ ἐς τὰς Ἀθήνας οἱ
Πελασγοί, καὶ δίκας ἐπηγγέλλοντο βουλόμενοι
διδόναι παντὸς τοῦ ἀδικήματος. Ἀθηναῖοι δὲ ἐν τῷ   3
πρυτανηΐῳ κλίνην στρώσαντες ὡς εἶχον κάλλιστα
καὶ τράπεζαν ἐπιπλέην ἀγαθῶν πάντων παραθέντες
ἐκέλευον τοὺς Πελασγοὺς τὴν χώρην σφίσι παραδιδόναι οὕτω ἔχουσαν. οἱ δὲ Πελασγοὶ ὑπολαβόντες   4
εἶπαν· "Ἐπεὰν βορέῃ ἀνέμῳ αὐτημερὸν νηῦς ἐξανύσῃ
"ἐκ τῆς ὑμετέρης ἐς τὴν ἡμετέρην, τότε παραδώσο-
"μεν." Τοῦτο εἶπαν ἐπιστάμενοι τοῦτο εἶναι ἀδύνατον
γενέσθαι· ἡ γὰρ Ἀττικὴ πρὸς νότον κέεται πολλὸν
τῆς Λήμνου.

The impossible made possible by Miltiades.

CXL. Τότε μὲν τοσαῦτα· ἔτεσι δὲ κάρτα πολ- 1
λοῖσι ὕστερον τούτων, ὡς ἡ Χερσόνησος ἡ ἐν Ἑλλησ-
πόντῳ ἐγένετο ὑπ᾽ Ἀθηναίοισι, Μιλτιάδης ὁ Κίμωνος
ἐτησίων ἀνέμων κατεστηκότων νηῒ κατανύσας ἐξ
Ἐλαιοῦντος τοῦ ἐν Χερσονήσῳ ἐς τὴν Λῆμνον
προηγόρευε ἐξιέναι ἐκ τῆς νήσου τοῖσι Πελασγοῖσι,
ἀναμιμνήσκων σφέας τὸ χρηστήριον, τὸ οὐδαμὰ
ἤλπισαν σφίσι οἱ Πελασγοὶ ἐπιτελέεσθαι. Ἡφαι- 2
στιέες μέν νυν ἐπείθοντο, Μυριναῖοι δὲ οὐ συγγινω-
σκόμενοι εἶναι τὴν Χερσόνησον Ἀττικὴν ἐπολιορ-
κέοντο, ἐς ὃ καὶ αὐτοὶ παρέστησαν. οὕτω δὴ τὴν
Λῆμνον ἔσχον Ἀθηναῖοί τε καὶ Μιλτιάδης.

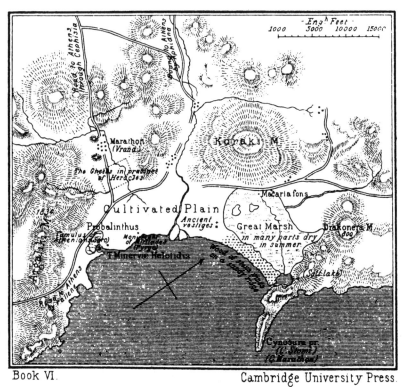

Book VI.   Cambridge University Press.

SITE OF THE BATTLE OF MARATHON

Commentary

1.1 Ἀρισταγόρης: Aristagoras, the son-in-law of Histiaeus the tyrant of Miletus, had taken over the rule of the city when the King's suspicions had detained Histiaeus at the royal court in Susa (5.30.2-3). He took the lead in instigating the Ionian Revolt in 500/499 but, when things took a turn for the worse, he withdrew to a fortress he had prepared for himself at Myrcinus in Thrace, where he subsequently met his death at the hands of the Thracians (5.124-6). This is dated by Thucydides (4.102.2) 59 years before the foundation of Amphipolis in 437/6 (Diodorus 12.32.3) and so must have taken place in 496/5.

ἀποστήσας: participle of the transitive first aorist of ἀφίστημι 'I cause to revolt'. ἔστησα, the first aorist of ἵστημι is transitive in meaning, as opposed to the second aorist ἔστην and to the perfect ἕστηκα which are both intransitive.

μεμετιμένος: Ionic perf. part. pass. of μεθίημι 'I release' (Attic μεθειμένος). Histiaeus had long been seeking to return to Miletus: according to Herodotus (5.35.4) he had even sought to bring on the revolt of Ionia for this very purpose.

Ἀρταφέρνης ὁ Σαρδίων ὕπαρχος: Artaphernes was the brother of Darius and satrap of Lydia with his seat at Sardis in the valley of the Hermus some 50 miles inland from the Aegean coast (5.25.1). The word ὕπαρχος, denoting 'sub-ruler' or 'deputy', is used in Greek with a wide range of meanings covering rulers or governors of varying degrees of rank and authority. The meaning in the present passage is clearly 'satrap', and justifiable inasmuch as the satrap is in a sense the King's deputy. The word σατράπης is the hellenised form of the Persian *xshachapava* (literally 'kingdom protector') but does not occur before the time of Xenophon, though Herodotus does use the derived noun σατραπηίη ('satrapy') at 1.192.2 and 3.89.1. Since the word is in both passages stated to be the Persian equivalent of the Greek ἀρχή it had not yet acquired in Herodotus' day the familiarity which it enjoyed in the vocabulary of Greeks of the fourth century.

κατὰ κοῖόν τι δοκέοι Ἴωνας ἀπεστάναι: 'on what ground he thought that the Ionians had revolted', where ἀπεστάναι is the second perf. inf. active of ἀφίστημι with intransitive meaning.

ὁ δὲ οὔτε εἰδέναι ἔφη: 'he not only said that he didn't know', 'he not only denied that he knew'. οὔτε...τε means 'both...and', 'not only...but also'. With the verb φημί, the negative οὐ adheres so closely to its verb (what grammarians call 'adherescent') that in indirect speech οὐ is usually attached to φημί even when it belongs in sense to the following infinitive. In other words in

85

a negative indirect statement introduced by φημί, οὐ is removed from its infinitive and precedes φημί in the main clause. Cf. 50.2, 52.4, 61.4, 99.2.

ὡς οὐδὲν δῆθεν τῶν παρεόντων πρηγμάτων ἐπιστάμενος: 'as though in fact he knew nothing about present matters'. The use of the particle δῆθεν implies that the statement is mistaken or untrue. It is used with ὡς in a participial phrase in four other passages of Herodotus (1.73.5, 3.74.4, 6.39.1, 8.5.1).

1.2 τοι: 'I would have you know', 'mark my words', used to direct the attention of the addressee to the remarks of the speaker.

ὑπόδημα: 'shoes' or 'sandals', literally 'something tied on beneath' (ὑπό). The related verb ὑποδέω means 'I put footwear on someone's feet', and in the middle 'I put my shoes on'.

2.1 ταῦτα: 'these things', used with reference to what precedes, as opposed to τάδε, which refers to what follows.

ἐς τὴν ἀπόστασιν ἔχοντα: 'referring to revolt'. ἔχω is used intransitively with the preposition in the sense of 'to be directed towards', 'to pertain to', 'to concern'. Cf. note on 19.1 below.

συνιέντα: acc. sing. masc. pres. part. act., from συνίημι, 'I understand'.

ὑπὸ τὴν πρώτην ἐπελθοῦσαν νύκτα: 'at the time of/under cover of the next night'. ὑπό is used with the acc. in the temporal meaning of 'during', 'in the course of'. Cf. 9.51.4, 9.58.2.

Σαρδὼ νῆσον τὴν μεγίστην: cf. 5. 106.6, where the same claim is made. Σαρδώ is the Greek name of Sardinia. At c.9187 sq. miles, it is in fact smaller than Sicily (area 9860 sq. miles), though, since it was less familiar than Sicily to the Greeks of Herodotus' day, its size was doubtless exaggerated. The earliest writer who seems to be aware of the true facts is Strabo (2.15.9). The fertility of its southern portion and great mineral wealth would have made it a highly desirable acquisition from the Persian point of view. It had already attracted the attention not only of the sage Bias of Priene, who had vainly proposed to the Ionians that they migrate there at the time of the Persian conquest of Ionia (1.170.2), but also of Aristagoras himself, who had considered Sardinia as a possible refuge before selecting Myrcinus (5.124.2).

ὑποδεξάμενος κατεργάσεσθαι: 'had promised to subdue'. This, the reading of the *OCT* and of some Herodotean manuscripts, gives the normal Greek construction of the accusative and future infinitive following a verb of hoping, promising, threatening or swearing when the reference is to future time. The majority of mss have the aorist infinitive κατεργάσασθαι, which is no less acceptable by the rules of Greek grammar. These allow the alternative construction of a prolative infinitive, especially when there is no change of subject (Goodwin 1286), just as in English one can say 'I promise to come' as an alternative to 'I promise that I shall come'.

ὑπέδυνε τῶν Ἰώνων τὴν ἡγεμονίην: 'he attempted to worm his way into the leadership of the Ionians', the incohative use of the imperfect conveying the implication that the attempt was unsuccessful. Cf. note on 5.1 below, and cf. 16.2 and 108.2).

2.2 διαβὰς: 'having crossed', aor. part. of διαβαίνω.

ἐδέθη ὑπὸ Χίων: 'he was put in fetters by the Chians', who had been freed from the tyranny of Strattis at the outbreak of the revolt.

καταγνωσθεὶς πρὸς αὐτῶν νεώτερα πρήσσειν πρήγματα...ἐκ Δαρείου: 'having been condemned for planning untoward actions against them at the instigation of Darius'. νεώτερα πράττω and the cognate verb νεωτεροποιέω, meaning 'make innovations', 'change the *status quo*', is particularly common in political contexts, where it signfies 'to introduce revolutionary political change'. In the present context, the more general meaning is more likely.

3 ἐπέστειλε τῷ 'Αρισταγόρῃ: for the meaning of ἀφίστημι: see note on 1.1 above. The events in question are narrated at 5.35.

εἴη...ἐξεργασμένος: periphrastic perf. opt. of ἐξεργάζομαι. In this clause Herodotus has changed the mood of the direct question into the corresponding tense of the optative, even though in the previous clause he retained the indicative ἐπέστειλε. Both constructions are possible in secondary sequence (Goodwin 1481), and to use both within one sentence is not uncommon, especially when the verb in the optative is in some sense a consequence of the verb in the indicative. Cf. Xenophon, *Anab.* 2.1.3, οὗτοι ἔλεγον ὅτι Κῦρος τέθνηκεν, 'Αριαῖος δὲ πεφευγὼς...εἴη), where Ariaeus' flight is intimately bound up with and a result of the death of Cyrus, the main subject of the report. However the distinction is not always evident, and at times the two constructions are employed merely for the sake of variety.

τὴν...γενομένην αὐτοῖσι αἰτίην οὐ...ἐξέφαινε: 'he did not at all (μάλα) refer to (literally 'allow to appear') the real cause that affected them', where αὐτοῖσι belongs grammatically to both αἰτίην and ἐξέφαινε. The aor. part. γενομένην ('having come into being') does duty for the non-existent past participle of εἶναι.

ἐξαναστήσας: transitive first aor. part. of ἐξανίστημι 'I uproot'. Histiaeus' tale of the proposed population exchange between Ionia and Phoenicia would have seemed all the more credible when the Ionians recalled Darius' transplantation of Paeonians to Phrygia in 510 (5.15.3, 17.1, 23.1, 98.1), where they remained until the outbreak of the Ionian Revolt gave them the opportunity to return to their homeland (5.98.1). They may also have remembered the transportation of the people of Barce in North Africa to Bactria in c.511 (4.204.2). The transplanting of trouble makers continued to be part of official Persian policy with the removal of Milesians to Ampe on the Persian Gulf in 494 (see ch. 20 below), and of Eretrians to Ardericca in Susiana in 491 (see 6.119 and *Anth.* Pal. 7.259). Ionian reluctance to move was responsible for their rejection of Bias' plan to migrate to Sardinia in 545 (1.170) and of the Spartan attempt to relocate them in 479 to the lands of the medising mainland Greeks (9.106; Diod. 11.37.1-3).

ἐδειμάτου τοὺς Ἴωνας: 'he was seeking to scare the Ionians', imperf. of δειματόω with conative meaning.

4.1 μετὰ δὲ: and 'afterwards', 'thereafter', where μετά is used adverbially rather than as a preposition. So 1.88.2, 1.128.2, 1.150.1, and cf. 38.1, 62.2, 97.2, 103.2, 110, 120, 125.4, 129.3 and 134.2 below.

δι' ἀγγέλου ποιεύμενος: 'communicating through the agency of a messenger'. Cf. 8.134.2, διὰ χρηστηρίων ποιεύμενος.

'Αταρνείτεω: a man from Atarneus, a Greek city in western Asia Minor opposite Mytilene on the island of Lesbos.

βιβλία: 'in letters', the plural of βίβλιον, meaning literally 'a strip of papyrus' (βίβλος) and used of anything made up from papyrus strips, such as letters, books or documents.

προλελεσχηνευμένων: gen. pl. of the perf. part. of προλεσχηνεύομαι 'I converse beforehand', a verb used only here, though the verbal adj. περιλεσχήνευτος appears at 2.135, and the simple verb λεσχηνεύομαι occurs in other writers of Ionic prose.

ἀποστάσιος πέρι: 'concerning a revolt'. The accent on a preposition which follows rather than precedes the noun which it governs (a 'post-positive preposition') is placed on the first rather than on the final syllable. Cf. 57.4 and 101.2 below.

4.2 τὰ ἀμοιβαῖα: 'the answers', where βίβλια is to be understood. The word and its related verb are in this sense essentially poetic.

5.1 κατῆγον: 'attempted to restore him', a conative imperfect (Goodwin 1255), with the implication that the attempt was a failure. Cf. ὑπέδυνε at 2.1 above and ἐδίδοσαν at 108.2 below. κατάγω in a political context regularly means 'reinstate', 'bring back from exile'.

οἷα ἐλευθερίης γευσάμενοι: 'inasmuch as they had tasted freedom', the causal use of the participle, when it is frequently preceded by οἷα or ἅτε (Goodwin 1575).

5.2 ἐπειρᾶτο κατιών: 'endeavoured to return'. In Attic this verb is normally construed with the infinitive, while Herodotus prefers the participle. The Attic construction is not unknown to Herodotus (e.g. at 5.71.1 and at 138.3 below), and indeed the participial construction is occasionally found in Attic (e.g. at Plato, *Theaetetus* 190e).

τιτρώσκεται τὸν μηρὸν: 'is wounded in the thigh', an accusative of respect (Goodwin 1058).

τευ: Ionic gen. sing. of the indef. pron. τις (Attic τινος or του).

ἀπωστὸς τῆς ἑωυτοῦ γίνεται: 'is driven out of his own city'. ἀπωστὸς is the verbal adj. from ἀπωθέω 'I thrust away', used with γίνεται as a periphrasis for the simple verb ἀπωθέεται. With τῆς ἑωυτοῦ, the noun πόλεως (or rather the Ionic form πόλιος) is to be understood.

δοῦναί οἱ νέας: 'to give him ships', where οἱ is the dat. sing. of the third person pronoun used here, as in Attic, as an indirect reflexive referring to the subject of the principal verb (Goodwin 987). In Herodotus this pronoun may also occur as a direct reflexive (Goodwin 988).

5.3 ἔπλωον...ἐλάμβανον: imperf. denoting a customary or repeated action (Goodwin 1253.2).

τὰς ἐκ τοῦ Πόντου ἐκπλωούσας τῶν νεῶν: 'those of the ships which were sailing from the Pontus', with reference to the merchant ships bringing grain from the Black Sea area to Miletus.

πλὴν ἢ ὅσοι...ἔφασαν ἑτοῖμοι εἶναι: 'except those who said they were willing'. When πλὴν is used as a conjunction, it is often followed by a tautological ἤ as at 2.111.3. The use of the masc. ὅσοι and ἑτοῖμοι to agree with a preceding fem. noun is a *constructio ad sensum*, where Herodotus is thinking not so much of the ships as of the crew who manned them. Cf. ch. 8.2 below.

6 συστραφέντες: nom. pl. of the second aor. pass. of συστρέφω 'I collect'.

περὶ ἐλάσσονος ποιησάμενοι: 'having paid less attention to', 'regarding as of lesser importance', the opposite of the more common phrase περὶ πολλοῦ (πλείονος) ποιέομαι, 'I value highly/more highly'.

Κύπριοι νεωστὶ κατεστραμμένοι: 'the Cypriots who had only recently been subdued', where κατεστραμμένοι is perf. part. pass. of καταστρέφω. Cyprus had been in revolt for little more than a year in 498/7. For the suppression of the revolt, see 5.116.

7 προβούλους: 'representatives', the official name of the delegates from the various cities which administered the Panionium.

Πανιώνιον: the meeting place of the federation of Ionian communities situated at the foot of the northern slopes of Mt. Mycale, and site of the sanctuary and sacred grove of Poseidon Heliconius. This federation, known as the Ionian League, had been formed initially to conduct the cult and celebrate the festival of the god, but in the course of time, it came to acquire political as well as religious functions (see, e.g. 1.141 and 1.170). For a list of the member states, see 1.142.

ἀντίξοον: 'contrary to', 'opposed to', a peculiarly Ionic word equivalent to the Attic ἐναντίον, which is quite common in Herodotus, e.g. 4.129.1, 6.50.2, 7.218.2, 8.119.

ῥύεσθαι: 'to protect', another Ionic word which in Attic is restricted for the most part to poetry.

τὴν ταχίστην: 'with all speed', 'as quickly as possible', an adverbial accusative. The full phrase τὴν ταχίστην ὁδόν occurs in Xenophon (*Anab.* 1.2.20), and accounts for the feminine gender.

προναυμαχήσοντας: 'in order to fight on behalf of', where the fut. participle expresses purpose (Goodwin 1563.4).

8.1 πεπληρωμένῃσι τῇσι νηυσὶ: 'with their ships manned', a dative of accompaniment. This construction is particularly common in Attic with reference to military and naval forces (Goodwin 1189-90).

σὺν δέ σφι: 'and with them'. σφι is the Ionic form of the dat. sing. of the third person pronoun ἕ, which in Attic serves as an indirect reflexive only. Here it is used as an ordinary third person pronoun, equivalent to the Attic αὐτοῖς.

Πριηνέες: the inhabitants of Priene, a city on the north shore of the Gulf of Latmus near the mouth of the Maeander, which included in its territory the promontory of Mycale and the site of the Panionium (see ch. 7 above).

Μυούσιοι: the citizens of Myus, a city to the north east of Miletus. In ancient times it was situated on the Gulf of Latmus, but the site is now some 15 km. inland. Though originally a place of some importance, the silting up of its harbour had by the 5th. century greatly diminished its significance.

Μυουσίων δὲ Τήϊοι εἴχοντο: 'the Teians came next to the Myians'. For this use of the middle of ἔχω, cf. note on 111.1 below. Teos was a city on the southern shore of the Promontory of Erythrae, lying opposite the north coast of the island of Samos.

8.2 Ἐρυθραῖοί τε: the inhabitants of Erythrae, situated on the gulf of the same name on the west coast of the Mimas peninsula opposite the island of Chios.

Φωκαιέες: the people of Phocaea on the north coast of the Gulf of Smyrna opposite the northern tip of the Mimas peninsula. Herodotus' list of participants shows that, though members of the Panionium, Ephesus, Colophon, Lebedos and Clazomenae played no part in the Lade campaign. Of these, Clazomenae had already been regained by the Persians (5.123), while Colophon, which lay several miles inland and could not be supplied directly by sea, probably came to terms with Artaphernes. The other two non-combatants may also have submitted or been recaptured. For a discussion of the size, population and economy of the participants in the revolt, see C. Roebuck, *Ionian Trade and Colonization*, New York, 1959, pp. 22-3.

9.1 τῶν δὲ βαρβάρων...ἦσαν ἑξακόσιαι: 600 is the conventional number for the size of the Persian fleet (e.g. during the Scythian expedition, 4.87.1; in the Marathon campaign, 95.2 below) and is doubtless an exaggeration, but the Persians certainly did have in operation a fleet of considerable size, comprising contingents from all the traditional maritime nations of the empire.

ἀπίκατο: 'arrived'. The ending -ατο represents the Ionic form of the 3rd. pers. pluperf. pass. of verbs with a consonantal stem in the perfect tenses, resulting from a peculiarly Ionic treatment of the sonant n, i.e. of the Indo-European ending -νται/-ντο. In such cases, Attic resorts to the periphrastic form ἀφιγμένοι εἰσί/ἦσαν, though Ionicisms such as ἐτετάχατο (and the corresponding perfect forms in -αται) occasionally occur in Thucydides (3.13.3, 5.6.5). Cf. τετάφαται at 103.3 and ἐτετάχατο at 113.1 below.

οἱ Περσέων στρατηγοί: Herodotus curiously fails to name the Persian commander. It is possible that he was Datis, who subsequently commanded in the Marathon campaign. See Burn, *PG*, pp. 210-11 and 218, who argues from a passage in the Lindos Temple Chronicle that some of the entries referring to Datis and Mardonius belong to 494 rather than to 490.

καταρρώδησαν, μὴ οὐ δυνατοὶ γένωνται ὑπερβαλέσθαι: 'were afraid that they would be unable to prevail', where the more vivid subjunctive is retained in preference to the optative after a verb of fearing in historic sequence (Goodwin 1378). ὑπερβάλλω in the active means 'surpass', 'exceed', and in the middle has the significance of 'conquer', both transitive and intransitive.

καὶ οὕτω: 'and in this event'.

οὔτε τὴν Μίλητον οἷοί τε ἔωσι ἐξελεῖν...πρός τε Δαρείου κινδυνεύσωσι... λαβεῖν: 'not only would they be unable to destroy Miletus but...were in fact in danger of suffering harm at the hands of Darius'. πρός with the gen. is used (as an alternative to ἐκ and ὑπό) in Ionic Greek to express the agent.

μὴ οὐκ ἐόντες: 'unless they were'. μὴ οὐ is used with the part. to indicate an exception to a preceding negative statement (Goodwin 1617b). Cf. note on 106.3 below.

9.2 τῶν Ἰώνων τοὺς τυράννους: these included Oliatus of Mylasa, Histiaeus of Termera and Aristagoras of Cyme, whose depositions, along with that of Coes of Mytilene, Herodotus records at 5.37. Other tyrants deposed in 499 included Aeaces of Samos (ch. 13.2 below) and presumably Strattis of Chios, tyrant in 513 and restored to power by 480 (4.138, 8.132). The deposition of the tyrants is narrated at 5.37, though none of the names given in that passage are those of ethnic Ionians.

9.3 εὖ ποιήσας φανήτω: 'let himself show himself as benefactor'. Persian kings kept a list of benefactors (in Persian *orosangai*). See 3.140.1, 8.85.3; Thucydides 1.129.3 and 1.137.4. φανήτω is the 3rd. person sing. 2nd. imperative pass. (with middle/reflexive force) of φαίνω.

πειράσθω ἀποσχίζων: 'let him try to detach'. For the construction, see note on 5.2.above.

9.4 εἰ δὲ ταῦτα μὲν οὐ ποιήσουσι: 'but if they do not do this', where the fut. indic. is used in place of ἄν with the subj. to denote a strong threat or warning (Goodwin 1405). Though the negative in conditional clauses is normally μή, οὐ is used here because the negative goes closely with its verb, so closely in fact that the two words practically form one compound word (οὐ ποιεῖν as a phrase is equivalent to the English 'fail to do', 'refuse to 'do'. Cf. Thuc. 3.55.3 εἰ δ' ἀποστῆναι Ἀθηναίων οὐκ ἠθελήσαμεν, 'if we refused to revolt from the Athenians').

ἐπηρεάζοντες: 'making threats', an Ionic usage. In Attic, this verb is commonly employed in the sense of 'insult', 'address with abusive language', 'treat shamefully'.

τά πέρ σφεας κατέξει: 'which will indeed actually befall them', a parenthetical expression not intended to form part of the message the Persians wish to be passed on to the Ionians.

ἐκτομίας: 'eunuch', a noun formed from the verb ἐκτέμνω, 'castrate'.

Βάκτρα: also known to the Greeks as Zariaspa, the capital of the satrapy of Bactria, modern Balkh in Afghanistan.

10 ἀγνωμοσύνῃ τε διεχρέοντο: 'continued to behave stubbornly', 'went on displaying obstinacy'. ἀγνωμοσύνη, literally 'lack of sensitivity', covers a wide range of meanings from 'folly' to 'inability to show consideration'. In the sense of 'arrogance', 'perverse obduracy', the word is a favourite of Herodotus (2.172.2, 4.93, 5.83.1, 9.3.1). The compound verb διαχράομαι is frequently followed in Herodotus by an abstract noun (often denoting a mental condition) in the dative where Attic prefers the simple χράομαι, and may correspond to the English verb 'experience'. Cf. 7.210.1 and 11.2 below.

οὐ προσίεντο τὴν προδοσίην: 'refused to entertain the idea of treachery'. προσίεντο is 3rd. pers. plur. of the imperf. middle of προσίημι, meaning 'admit', 'accept', 'submit to'.

ἰθέως ἀπικομένων...τῶν Περσέων: 'immediately after the arrival of the Persians', 'as soon as the Persians arrived'. Adverbs such as ἅμα, αὐτίκα, εὐθύς are frequently used with the participle as substitutes for a temporal clause (Goodwin 1572).

11.1 ἠγορεύοντο: from ἀγορεύομαι, 'address the assembly', an epic verb which occurs elsewhere only in Homer, Theognis and Sophocles. The very form of the verb is Homeric (e.g. *Iliad* 4.1), and is used here to invest the debate with an epic dignity.

ἐν δὲ δή: 'and among them', where ἐν is used adverbially. Cf. 50.2, 70.3 and 86.4 below.

11.2 Ἐπὶ ξυροῦ γὰρ ἀκμῆς ἔχεται ἡμῖν τὰ πρήγματα: 'since our fortunes are on a razor's edge', another epic usage (cf. *Iliad* 10.173), indicating a situation which is evenly balanced between success and failure. The particle γάρ is here used in an anticipatory sense, looking forward to the explanation given in the following sentence (see Denniston, *GP*, pp. 69-70, and cf. 130.2 below). This sentence is cited by [Longinus], *On the Sublime* 22.1-2 as an example of the rhetorical figure *hyperbaton*, a dislocation of the usual word order for special effect. He rewrites the sentence using the normal word order as follows: 'Men of Ionia, now is the time to face hardship: for our affairs are on a razor's edge', and maintains that Herodotus has the speaker invert the thought sequence both by postponing the name of the addressees and by giving the reason for the exhortation (introduced by γάρ) before the explanation itself in his haste to make his point. 'Longinus' then goes on with some justification to argue that the sentence is constructed in such a way in the interest of apparent spontaneity, as if the words were forced on the speaker by the situation.

εἰ δὲ μαλακίη τε καὶ ἀταξίη διαχρήσεσθε: 'but if you continue to behave in a weak and undisciplined manner'. Conditional clauses referring to the future which contain a threat or warning regularly take the fut. indic. for vividness (Goodwin 1405). The contrast with the less vivid ἢν μὲν βούλησθε ταλαιπωρίας ἐνδέκεσθαι which precedes could not be expressed more clearly.

οὐδεμίαν...ἔχω ἐλπίδα μὴ οὐ δώσειν ὑμέας δίκην: 'I have no hope that you will not pay the penalty'. For the construction after verbs of hoping, see note on 2.1 above. Though οὐ is the regular negative in indirect statement, μή is normal when the principal verb is one of hoping, threatening, promising or swearing (Goodwin 1496). The double negative μή οὐ is regularly found with an infinitive that itself depends on a negative verb (Goodwin 1616).

11.3 θεῶν τὰ ἴσα νεμόντων: 'if the gods grant both sides equal treatment', where the part. is conditional. The notion that the gods give both sets of combatants equality of opportunity is characteristic of Herodotus. Cf. 109.5 below, where the same statement is put into the mouth of Miltiades at Marathon. In his own person the historian refers to the role of divine providence in upholding a balance both at 3.108.2, where he contrasts relatively infertile carnivores with their more prolific prey, and at 8.13 where he detects the hand of god in the destruction of a large number of Persian ships, with the design of equalising the strengths of the Greek and Persian fleets.

ἐπιτράπουσι σφέας αὐτοὺς τῷ Διονυσίῳ: 'they entrusted themselves to Dionysius', i.e. they appointed Dionysius commander of the Ionian fleet. One suspects that he owed his appointment less to his ability than to his birthplace: in the interest of maintaining some degree of Ionian unity, a commander from a minor city was less contentious and more likely to win general acceptance than one from Miletus or Samos, which were traditional enemies. Unfortunately, as events were to prove, the insignificance of his city undermined his influence when decisions had to be made.

12.1 ἀνάγων...ἐπὶ κέρας τὰς νέας: 'leading the ships out to sea in column'. ἀνάγω, literally 'lead up', comes to mean 'take out to sea', since, from the viewpoint of someone standing on the shore, the sea can be seen as being in a sense at a higher level. κέρας, literally 'horn', is used with reference to anything similar in shape: in military terminology, it comes to mean 'column'. In the phrase ἐπὶ κέρως, this meaning is found in both Thucydides (2.90.4, 6.32.2) and Xenophon (*Cyr.* 6.3.34).

ὅκως τοῖσι ἐρέτῃσι χρήσαιτο: 'as often as he made use of the rowers'. The temporal use of the conjunction ὅκως occurs in Homer and Tragedy as well as in Herodotus, who is particularly fond of using it with the opt. (e.g. 1.17.1, 1.100.2, 1.186.1), where it indicates repetition (Goodwin 1431.2).

διέκπλοον ποιεύμενος: 'carrying out the manoeuvre known as the breakthrough', literally 'a sailing through and out'. In naval engagements the ships of the rival fleets were normally drawn up in a long line facing the enemy. The *diekplous* was a tactic whereby individual ships, or, according to some scholars, a squadron of ships belonging to one of the sides made a sudden charge at speed, forced their way through gaps between the enemy vessels, turned round and attempted to ram and disable their unprotected sterns or flanks. See esp. J.S. Morrison and R. Williams, *Greek Oared Ships*, Cambridge, 1968, pp. 137-9 and J. Lazenby, "*The Diekplous*", *Greece and Rome* 34, 1987, pp. 169-77. This is the earliest known occasion on which this tactic, later to be perfected by the Athenians, was employed.

93

τοὺς ἐπιβάτας ὁπλίσειε: 'armed the marines'. The *epibatai* were hoplite fighting men in full armour who formed part of the crew of a trireme and fought from the deck in naval engagements when the occasion required. For the number of marines on board a trireme, see note on 15.2 below.

ἔχεσκε: 'continued to keep'. The endings -σκον and -σκομην are attached in Ionic to the imperf. and 2nd. aor. (in Homer also to the 1st. aor.) with iterative force.

δι' ἡμέρης: 'throughout the day', 'all day long'. Temporal διά with the gen. expresses duration of time in both Herodotus and Attic.

12.2 τετρυμένοι τε ταλαιπωρίησί τε καὶ ἡλίῳ: 'worn out with hardship and the sun'. ἡλίῳ is particularly applicable to the marines, who were stationed on deck, while ταλαιπωρίησι refers equally to the efforts of the oarsmen and to the weight of the equipment borne by the marines.

ἔλεξαν πρὸς ἑωυτοὺς τάδε: 'they spoke to one another as follows', where the reflexive pron. is equivalent to the reciprocal (Goodwin 996). Cf. 42.1 and 138.3 below.

12.3 παραβάντες: 2nd. aor. part. of παραβαίνω, 'transgress', 'sin against'.

ἀναπίμπλαμεν: literally 'we fill up', here used metaphorically, as elsewhere in Herodotus (e.g. 5.4.2, 9.87.1) to mean 'fill up the full measure of', i.e. 'endure'.

ἐκπλώσαντες ἐκ τοῦ νόου: literally 'having sailed out of their minds', a particularly apt metaphor in the context. The phrase also appears at 3.155.3

ἀλαζόνι: 'braggart', 'loudmouth'.

ἐπιτρέψαντες ἡμέας αὐτοὺς ἔχομεν: 'we have entrusted ourselves'. The use of the aor. part. with ἔχω as equivalent to a perf. tense is common in Herodotus and Tragedy. It differs from the perf. only in laying greater emphasis on the permanent state resulting from the action in question (Goodwin 1262).

ἐπίδοξοι τὠυτὸ τοῦτο πείσεσθαι: 'likely to have the very same experience', where πείσεσθαι is the fut. inf. of πάσχω.

καὶ ὁτιῶν ἄλλο: 'anything else at all', 'anything else whatsoever'.

καὶ τὴν μέλλουσαν δουληίην...ἤ τις ἔσται: 'even this future slavery, whatever it may be'.

φέρετε...μὴ πειθώμεθα αὐτοῦ: 'come then, let us not obey him'. The imper. and subj. are often preceded in exhortations by words such as φέρε (φέρετε), ἄγε (ἄγετε) and ἴθι (Goodwin 1345).

12.4 οἷα στρατιὴ: 'like an army', 'just as if they were an army'.

ἐσκιητροφέοντο: 'they kept themselves in the shade', from σκιά (σκιή), 'shadow'. At 3.12.4 Herodotus uses the word intransitively in the active in a context where the Persians are said to keep off the sun by wearing caps on their heads.

οὐκ ἐθέλεσκον: on the iterative termination -σκον, see note on ἔχεσκε at 12.1 above.

ἀναπειρᾶσθαι: 'to exercise', a verb used with particular reference to the navy in Thucydides (7.7.4, 7.12.5, 7.51.2).

13.1 μαθόντες δὲ ταῦτα γινόμενα ἐκ τῶν Ἰώνων: 'learning that this was being done by the Ionians'. For the acc. and part. following a verb of perception, see Goodwin 1588. For ἐκ used to express the agent after a passive verb, see note on 9.1 above, and cf. 22.1, 42.1, 61.4, 78.2, 97.2, 124.2 below.

οἱ στρατηγοὶ τῶν Σαμίων...ἐκείνους...λόγους: this phrase possesses both subject and object but lacks a verb, which has to be supplied from ἐδέκοντο τοὺς λόγους in the subsequent clause.

Αἰάκης: the former tyrant of Samos from c.514, (he was already in power at the time of Darius' Scythian expedition, 4.138.2) deposed in 499 along with the other Ionian tyrants. His father Syloson was the brother of the sixth century tyrant Polycrates, and ruled briefly himself from c.517.

τὰ βασιλέος πρήγματα ὑπερβαλέσθαι: 'to overcome the power of the king'.

ὑπερβαλοίατο: 3rd.pers. plur. aor. opt. middle of ὑπερβάλλω, where Attic has the ending -οιντο. Ionic regularly has -ατο when the stem ends in -ε, -αι, -ει, -οι or a consonant. Cf. ἠπιστέατο at 44.3.

πενταπλήσιον: literally 'five times as great', here used hyperbolically to mean little more than 'even larger', 'much greater'.

13.2 προφάσιος...ἐπιλαβόμενοι: 'having seized upon an excuse'. Verbs denoting 'touch' (ἅπτομαι, θιγγάνω) or 'laying hold of' (ἔχομαι) are regularly followed by the gen. (Goodwin 1099).

εἶδον τοὺς Ἴωνας οὐ βουλομένους εἶναι χρηστούς: literally 'they saw that the Ionians were refusing to be good', i.e. 'were refusing to do their duty'. For the construction, see note on 13.1 above. Herodotus goes out of his way both here and earlier in the chapter, when he refers to Ionian lack of discipline, to convey to the reader the Samian viewpoint, at least in part because he obtained much of his information from Samian sources when he was living there in exile. More realistic explanations for the Samian behaviour would have been the desire to emerge on the winning side and reluctance to play a full role in a campaign initiated by their enemies the Milesians.

ἐν κέρδεϊ ἐποιεῦντο: 'they regarded it as gain', literally 'in the category of gain'. Cf. 1.131.1. ἐν νόμῳ ποιευμένους, 'reckoning it as lawful', 9.42.2 ἐν ἀδείῃ οὐ ποιεύμενοι, 'not considering it safe'.

ἀπεστέρητο τὴν ἀρχὴν: 'he had been deprived of his rule'. When a verb that takes two accusatives in the active is used in the passive, one of them (usually the one denoting a person) serves as the subject while the other is retained as object (Goodwin 1239).

14.1 ὦν: resumptive particle serving to link this passage to the last mention of the Phoenicians in chapter 6.

ἀντανῆγον...τὰς νέας ἐπὶ κέρας: 'put to sea against in column'. See note on 12.1 above.

14.2 κατὰ τὰ συγκείμενα πρὸς τὸν Αἰάκεα: 'in accordance with their understanding with Aeaces'. Reluctance to participate in a revolt instigated by their hated rival the Milesians was also a factor.

ἀνηκουστήσαντες τοῖσι στρατηγοῖσι: 'having disobeyed the generals'. Presumably they were political opponents of the former tyrant and men of property (cf. 22.1 below).

14.3 τὸ κοινὸν τῶν Σαμίων: 'the Samian state', 'the Samian government'.

ἔδωκε...ἀναγραφῆναι: 'gave them the privilege of being inscribed', where ἀναγραφῆναι is aor. inf. pass. of ἀναγράφω, 'engrave'. Presumably the privilege was awarded soon after the fall of the tyranny in 479.

πατρόθεν: literally 'from one's father', used here to mean that these Samians were permitted to add the name of their father beside their own on the inscription. Cf. 8.90.4, where Xerxes has recorded the patronymics of the trierarchs who distinguished themselves at Salamis.

τοὺς προσεχέας: 'those placed next them', 'those adjacent'. For the disposition of the Ionians, see ch. 8.2 above.

ὡς δὲ: 'and in like manner'. Accented ὥς is a demonstrative adverb of manner.
15.1 περιέφθησαν τρηχύτατα: 'were handled very roughly'. περιέφθησαν is the aor. pass. of περιέπω, 'treat', 'deal with'. The phrase also occurs at 1.73.4 and 1.114.3.

οὐκ ἐθελοκακέοντες: literally 'not willing themselves to play the coward', i.e. 'not fighting to the best of their ability', 'fighting only halfheartedly'. This verb appears several times in Herodotus. See, e.g. 1.127.3, 5.78, 9.67.

ὥσπερ καὶ πρότερον εἰρέθη: see 8.1.above. εἰρέθην regularly occurs in Herodotus (e.g. 4.77.2, 4.156.3) as the Ionic equivalent of the Attic ἐρρήθην.
15.2 τεσσεράκοντα...ἐπιβατεύοντας: 'forty men serving as marines'. For the marines, see note on 12.1 above. The number of marines on board a ship varied from city to city according to fighting tactics and the size of deck. The figure of 40 is the largest recorded, except perhaps for Xerxes' marines at Salamis, when his ships each carried 30 prominent Persians or Medes (to guarantee loyalty on the part of the others?) on deck in addition to an unspecified number of native fighters (7.184.2). The regular number of marines on board Athenian ships was ten (see L. Casson, *Ships and Seamanship in the Ancient World*, Baltimore and London, 1971, p. 304 and note 21; J.S. Morrison and J.A. Coates, *The Athenian Trireme*, Cambridge, 1986, pp. 108-11).

οὐκ ἐδικαίευν γενέσθαι τοῖσι κακοῖσι αὐτῶν ὅμοιοι: literally 'nor did they think it right that they should be like their cowards', i.e. 'they resolved not to resemble the cowards who were on their own side'. For δικαιόω with the inf., see also 86.1 and 138.2 below.

διεκπλώοντες: 'attempting to implement the *diekplous*'. For this manoeuvre, see note on 12.1 above.
16.1 οὗτοι δὲ: the particle δέ is here otiose, but commonly occurs in conjunction with a demonstrative pronoun especially when that pronoun answers

a preceding relative (here ὅσοισι) that is itself accompanied by δέ. See Denniston *GP*, p. 184.

Μυκάλην: see chs 7 and 8.1 above. Mycale was the scene of the culminating battle of the Persian invasion of Greece, where in 479 the Greek fleet under Leotychidas and Xanthippus destroyed what remained of Xerxes' fleet.

16.2 θεσμοφορίων: the Thesmophoria was a festival of Demeter, who was often worshipped with the cult title Thesmophoros ('the Bringer of Justice') and celebrated over much of the Greek world, often open only to women.

οὔτε προακηκοότες: 'not having heard in advance', perf. part. act. of προακούω.

ἰδόντες τε: the τε picks up οὔτε προακηκοότες in the previous clause. For οὔτε...τε, see note on 1.1.

πάγχυ...καταδόξαντες: 'having come to the certain conclusion that'.

ἰέναι ἐπὶ τὰς γυναῖκας: 'were going after the women'.

ἔκτεινον: 'they proceeded to kill', an incohative imperf. See note on 2.1 above, and cf. 5.1, 107.2, 108.4 and 133.1.

17 Διονύσιος δὲ ὁ Φωκαιεὺς: see note on 12.1.

ἔμαθε...τὰ πρήγματα διεφθαρμένα: 'he saw that the cause was lost', acc. and part. after a verb of perceiving (see note on 13.1). διεφθαρμένα is perf. part pass. of διαφθείρω.

σὺν τῇ ἄλλῃ 'Ιωνίῃ: 'along with the rest of Ionia'.

ἰθέως ὡς εἶχε: 'just as he was'. ἔχω is commonly used intransitively with an adverb as a synonym for the verb εἰμί with the corresponding adjective. Cf. 49.2, 139.3.

γαύλους...καταδύσας: 'having sunk the vessels'. καταδύνω, 'I sink' has two aorists, a 1st. aor. κατέδυσα which is transitive, 'I caused to sink', and an intrans. 2nd. aor. κατέδυν. The word γαῦλος, (literally 'pail', 'tub)', is used metaphorically of things shaped like a tub. Here the reference is to Phoenician merchant ships. See L. Casson, *Ships and Seamanship in the Ancient World*, p. 66.

Καρχηδονίων δὲ καὶ Τυρσηνῶν: 'Carthaginians and Etruscans', the two great powers of the western Mediterranean in the 6th century who, sometimes acting in concert, served as a break on Greek expansion in the region.

18 ὑπορύσσοντες τὰ τείχεα: 'undermining the walls', from ὀρύσσω, 'dig'.

κατ' ἄκρης: literally 'from the highest point', here meaning 'utterly', 'completely'.

ἕκτῳ ἔτεϊ: 'in the sixth year'. Since the revolt broke out in 500/499, Herodotus dates the event somewhere in the summer of 494.

19.1 Χρεωμένοισι γὰρ 'Αργείοισι περὶ...σωτηρίης τῆς πόλιος: 'when the Argives were consulting the oracle about the salvation of their city', a reference to the war fought with Sparta in 494, which culminated in the Argive defeat at Sepeia (chs 71-81 below; 7.48; [Plut.], *Moralia* 245c-e; Pausanias 3.4.1). As this oracular consultation is omitted from Herodotus' narrative of the war in question, it is unclear whether it took place at the start of the campaign or after the defeat at Sepeia.

ἐπίκοινον χρηστήριον: 'a joint oracle'. Such a double oracle is without parallel in the Delphic tradition. See PW, Vol. 1, pp. 158-60; Fontenrose, *DO*, pp. 70-1, 168-9.

τὸ μέν νυν ἐς αὐτοὺς 'Αργείους ἔχον: 'the oracle pertaining to the Argives'. See note on 2.1.above.

ἐπεὰν κατὰ τοῦτο γένωμαι τοῦ λόγου: 'when I reach this point in my narrative'. The part of the oracle referring to the Argives is cited in ch. 77.

19.2 οὐ παρεοῦσι: the delivery of an oracle to a questioner who was not physically present is unprecedented. If Herodotus' story is accepted, it would be natural to suppose, (with How and Wells, Vol. 2, p. 70), that the Milesians had previously asked the Argives to enquire on their behalf, but Milesians normally consulted Didyma, not Delphi, and Fontenrose points out that Herodotus is our sole authority for the double oracle: Pausanias (2.20.10) and the Suda (s.v. Telesilla) mention only the Argive part, and Tzetzes (*Chil.* 8.3.6-9) knows only the Milesian.

Καὶ τότε δὴ...: the oracle is no. 83 in PW's list of responses (Vol. 2, p. 37) and Q134 in Fontenrose *DO*. PW (Vol. 1, pp. 159-60) believe it to be genuine and date the response to a time when Miletus was already under siege; Fontenrose *DO* (p. 169) lists it among the quasi-historical responses and thinks it originated in a collection of non-Delphic prophecies such as that ascribed to Bacis.

κακῶν ἐπιμήχανε ἔργων: 'deviser of wicked deeds'. If authentically Delphic, this oracle would certainly be in accord with Apollo's pro-Persian stance at this time.

πόδας νίψουσι: 'will wash the feet', i.e. when they have been reduced to slavery after the fall of the city.

κομήταις: 'to those with long hair', a Greek view of a Persian characteristic also in evidence in the epithet βαθυχαιτήεις in the epitaph allegedly composed for his own tomb by Aeschylus.

νηοῦ δ' ἡμετέρου...ἄλλοισι μελήσει: 'our temple will be an object of care to others'. The impersonal verb μέλει, 'it concerns', is followed by the dat. of the person who is concerned and the gen. of the object of concern.

Διδύμοις: the site of the most famous oracle of Apollo in Ionia, situated some 10 miles to the south of Miletus and controlled, until the time of the Ionian Revolt, by a clan of priests known as the Branchidae, who claimed descent from Apollo's son Branchus.

19.3 ἐν ἀνδραπόδων λόγῳ ἐγίνοντο: 'were ranked in the category of slaves'. Cf. 23.6 below and 3.120.3, σὺ γὰρ ἐν ἀνδρῶν λόγῳ, 'for you count as a man'.

ὁ νηός...ἐνεπίμπρατο: 'the temple was set alight', a statement that is at variance with Callisthenes (Frag. 14J), who attributes the sacrilege to the Branchidae themselves, acting in 479 in collusion with Xerxes, who subsequently moved them, at their own request, to Sogdiana, where their descendants were encountered by Alexander the Great (cf. Curtius 7.5.28-35). Parke (*The Oracles of Apollo in Asia Minor*, London, 1985, pp. 39-41) argues in favour of the version of Herodotus and believes Callisthenes' account to have originated with the Milesians in Alexander's army who sought to blacken the Branchidae lest Alexander restore them to their former position of authority at Didyma. See also Fontenrose, *Didyma: Apollo's Oracle, Cult and Companions*, Berkeley, Los Angeles and London, 1985, pp. 122-3 with note 20, who also accepts Herodotus' version, while denying that the Branchidae survived as a distinct clan as late as the reign of Alexander.

πολλάκις μνήμην...ἐποιησάμην: 'I have frequently made mention of'; 'frequently' is something of an exaggeration, since there are only two other references to Didyma (1.92.2 and 5.36.3, both in connection with dedications of Croesus).

20 ἐπὶ τῇ Ἐρυθρῇ καλεομένῃ θαλάσσῃ: 'near what is known as the Red Sea'. From other mentions of the 'Red Sea' in Herodotus (e.g. 1.180.1, 1.189.1), the term is used of the Persian Gulf, and at times (e.g. 3.30.3, 4.37, 4.39.1, 4.41), even of the Indian Ocean. Herodotus' term for what we know as the Red Sea is 'Arabian Gulf' (2.102.1; 2.158.3, 4.39.1). Though Greeks of the classical period tended to ascribe the name of the sea to the colour of its water (so Ctesias, Frag. 66J), from the time of Alexander onwards, the prevalent view was to connect it with a King Erythras (Strabo 16.3.5, 16.4.20; Curtius 8.9.14, 10.1.13; Pliny, *NH* 6.13.2, 19.1.2; Arrian, *Ind.* 37.3). This version seems to have originated with Mithropastes, son of Arsites, Darius III's satrap of Hellespontine Phrygia, an exiled Persian aristocrat who met Alexander's admiral Nearchus in the course of the latter's voyage from the mouth of the Indus to the Persian Gulf in 325/4 at an entertainment provided by the Persian governor Mazenes on the island of Oaracte (Qeshm). According to Mithropastes, Erythras was a local king who had been buried on the (imaginary?) island of Ogyris and subsequently became the recipient of a heroic cult after his death.

αὐτοὶ μὲν οἱ Πέρσαι εἶχον τὰ περὶ τὴν πόλιν: if the deportation of the Milesians was as thorough as Herodotus states, why were there still Milesians in the area in 479, when they were ordered by the Persians to guard the passes to Mt. Mycale (9.99.3, 9.104.1)? Presumably the historian is guilty of some exaggeration, and only the more nationalistic Milesians were in fact deported.

Καροὶ Πηδασεῦσι: the Carians of Pedasa. There were several places of this name in Asia Minor, of which the most important lay some 5 km. north of Halicarnassus at the site of the modern Gökceler (mentioned at 1.175 and 8.104; Strabo 13.1.59; Pliny, *NH* 5.29.107). However the Pedasa of the present passage must be placed somewhere in the area of Miletus. It should probably be identified with the place of this name from which Philip V was required to remove his garrison by the terms of the treaty imposed by the Romans in 196 (Polybius 18.44.4; Livy 33.30.3), and which subsequently entered into a sympolity with Miletus (A. Rehm, *Inschriften Delphinion*, in G. Kawerau and A. Rehm, *Das Delphinion in Milet* (Th. Wiegand (ed.), *Milet: Ergebnisse der Ausgrabungen und Untersuchungen seit dem Jahre 1899*, Vol. 1, fasc. 3, Berlin, 1914), no. 149, and may be the Pedasa which in Strabo's day was included in the territory of the Hellenistic foundation of Stratonicea (Strab. 13.1.59).

21.1 οὐκ ἀπέδοσαν τὴν ὁμοίην: sc. χάριν: 'they did not pay back the same kindness', 'they did not return the favour'.

Συβαρῖται: the people of Sybaris, Miletus' sister city and trading partner at the head of the Tarentine Gulf in the south of Italy, at at the mouth of the rivers Sybaris and Crathis, founded by Achaeans in 720 (trad.). It owed its reputation for great wealth and luxury to its commanding position in a large and extremely fertile plain as well as to its location on the trade route from Ionia to Etruria.

Λᾶόν τε καὶ Σκίδρον: colonies of Sybaris on the west coast of Italy. Laus (the Lavinium of the Romans) was founded at the mouth of the river of the same name and was an important stage in the transportation of goods from Miletus to Etruria: these were unloaded at Sybaris, conveyed by land across the isthmus to Laus and thence again by sea to their Etruscan destinations. The site of Scidrus is still unknown. For a plausible identificaion of the site, see T.J. Dunbabin *The Western Greeks*, Oxford, 1948, p. 204.

Συβάριος...ἁλούσης ὑπὸ Κροτωνιητέων: the destruction of Sybaris by her great rival Croton took place in 510. See also 5.44.5. After the destruction, the survivors retreated to the colonies of Laus and Scidrus.

ἡβηδὸν: adverb meaning 'from youth upwards'.

ἀπεκείραντο τὰς κεφαλὰς: 'they had their heads shaved', as a sign of mourning (cf. 9.24). The form ἀπεκείραντο is from the verb κείρω, 'shave'.

προσεθήκαντο: 'they imposed upon themselves', 'they assumed', aor. middle of προστίθημι.

πόλιες γὰρ αὗται...τῶν ἡμεῖς ἴδμεν: for τούτων τὰς ἡμεῖς ἴδμεν. In Greek a relative pronoun in the acc. case is frequently attracted to the gen. or dat. case of its antecedent, even where, as here, the antecedent is not expressed. See Goodwin 1301-2 and cf. 86.δ2, 87 and 112.3 below.

ἀλλήλῃσι ἐξεινώθησαν: 'were closely linked to one another in ties of friendship and hospitality'. So Athenaeus 12.519B. The links in this case were mainly commercial.

21.2 τῇ τε ἄλλῃ πολλαχῇ, καὶ δὴ καὶ ποιήσαντι: 'in many other ways and above all when he created', a dat. of time (Goodwin 1192) or of advantage (Goodwin 1165-6).

Φρυνίχῳ: son of Polyphradmon, the greatest tragic poet of the day, active from 511 until at least 476.

δρᾶμα Μιλήτου ἅλωσιν: the choice of a contemporary non-mythological subject was a radical innovation. The *Capture of Miletus* may or may not have been the play's title (some scholars identify this play with Phrynichus' *Phoenissae*).

διδάξαντι: 'having produced/put on the stage', literally 'taught', from the role of the dramatist in training the chorus of the play.

ἐζημίωσάν...χιλίῃσι δραχμῇσι: 'they fined him 1000 drachmas', a dat. of price, an extension of the dat. of means/manner.

ὡς ἀναμνήσαντα οἰκήϊα κακά: 'on the ground that he had reminded them of misfortunes that were their own'. Despite what Herodotus says, moving an audience to tears and thus arousing the pity and fear that Aristotle regards as the proper function of tragedy was not an offence under Athenian law and so can hardly have constituted the formal charge. The charge brought against Phrynichus may have been one of impiety (so Burn, *PG*, pp. 223-4) or a prosecution brought by the magistrates known as the *agoranomoi* against the individual responsible for the breakdown of law and order in a place under their jurisdiction (so R.A. Bauman, *Political Trials in Ancient Greece*, London and New York, 1990, pp. 12-16). In any event, the motive for the prosecution was undoubtedly political. As with the motive, the identity of the prosecutors is a matter for conjecture. If the aim was to illustrate Persian brutality and depravity, the prosecutors will have belonged to the anti-Persian camp; if to illustrate the folly of resistance, Persia's friends will have been responsible.

22.1 Μιλησίων ἠρήμωτο: 'had been emptied of Milesians', plup. pass. of ἐρημόω, 'I make desolate', indicating a state in the past arising from some even earlier activity, with the gen. of separation (Goodwin 1117). This statement is much exaggerated (see note on 20 above).

τοῖσί τι ἔχουσι: literally 'those who have something', i.e. the propertied classes, the rich.

τὸ...ἐς τοὺς Μήδους ἐκ τῶν στρατηγῶν...ποιηθέν: 'what had been done by the generals with respect to the Persians', with reference to the defection recorded in ch. 13 above. The preposition ἐς here means 'in regard to' (cf. note on 2.1 above). For the use of ἐκ with the gen. to express the agent, see note on 13.1 above, and cf. 42.1, 66.4, 78.2, 124-1.

πρὶν ἤ...ἀπικέσθαι τὸν τύραννον: 'before the tyrant arrived', since they rightly feared that the Persians would restore Aeaces. The temporal conjunction πρίν is normally construed with the inf. when the principal clause is positive and by a finite verb when the principal clause is negative (Goodwin 1470). In Herodotus πρίν is often followed by the adverb ἤ (see, e.g. 1.78.2, 2.2.1, and ch. 116 and 133.2 below), since it is equivalent syntactically to a comparative adverb, and indeed in both Herodotus and Thucydides the same construction is used after the comparative πρότερον with the same meaning (Goodwin 1474).

ἐδόκεε βουλευομένοισι...μένοντας: 'they resolved in deliberating to remain'. The impers. verb δοκεῖ, 'it seems good', takes the dat. (hence βουλευομένοισι), but the historian changes the construction before the end of the sentence and writes μένοντας rather than μένουσι under the influence of the following inf. δουλεύειν, a mild and understandable anacolouthon.

Ζαγκλαῖοι: the inhabitants of Zancle, a city on the eastern coast of Sicily directly opposite Rhegium in the toe of Italy, which subsequently changed its name to Messene. According to Herodotus, the change was made by Cadmus of Cos when he acquired the place c.490, while Thucydides (6.4.5) and Pausanias (4.23.9) ascribe it to Anaxilas of Rhegium. The inconsistency is not great since Anaxilas was originally Cadmus' overlord.

22.2 ἐπεκαλέοντο τοὺς Ἴωνας: presumably because a large part of its population consisted of Ionians from Euboea (Thuc. 6.4.5), though as Zancle was under the control of the Dorian Hippocrates of Gela at the time, the ethnicity of the settlers perhaps mattered less than their availability, if indeed Hippocrates himself was in any way involved in the enterprise.

Καλὴν ἀκτὴν: the 'Fair Coast', also written as one word, Caleacte, a new foundation on the northern coast of Sicily, which was otherwise empty of Greek settlement, between Himera in the west and Mylai in the east. The site was comparatively unattractive apart from its proximity to forest land capable of producing good quality timber, and possessing neither rich agricultural land nor a decent harbour. It would have made a suitable base of operations against the northern Sicels, and may even have been conceived as such by Hippocrates, but in fact the city never attained any position of significance in Sicily.

Σικελῶν: the Greek name for the native inhabitants of Sicily, as opposed to the Sicilian Greeks.

πρὸς...Τυρσηνίην τετραμμένη: 'turned towards Etruria', 'facing Etruria', perf. part. pass of τρέπω, 'turn'. The phrase may be a hint that at least some of the settlers earned a living through piracy, with Etruscan shipping as their prey, doubtless using ships constructed from the abundant timber of the area.

ἐστάλησαν: 'they set out', aor. pass. of στέλλω, 'send'. The middle and pass. of the verb regularly have this sense, as indeed does the act. voice when used intransitively.

23.1 τοιόνδε δή τι συνήνεικε γενέσθαι: 'the following took place', where συνήνεικε is the Ionic aor. of συμφέρω (Attic συνήνεγκε) used impersonally in the sense of 'happen', 'occur'. Cf. 117.2 below.

Λοκροῖσι τοῖσι Ἐπιζεφυρίοισι: 'the Epizephyrian Locrians', i.e. the inhabitants of Locri on the east coast of Italy, so called to distinguish them from the Locrians of the Greek mainland, whose colonists they were. Even in Greece, three groups of Locrians were distinguished, the Ozolian Locrians who lived on the north coast of the Corinthian Gulf, and the eastern Locrians on the south coast of the Malian Gulf and on the Euripus opposite Euboea, themselves often split in two by Phocian territory to form the Epicnemidian and Opuntian Locrians.

βασιλεὺς: here, as often elsewhere in Herodotus, the meaning is 'sole ruler', without any implication that the office was hereditary. Scythes could just as well, and with greater accuracy, be called a tyrant, and the use of βασιλεύς may simply reflect the favourable attitude to Scythes of Herodotus' informant.

περικατέατο: 'was sitting round about', i.e. 'was besieging', Ionic imperf. of περικάθημαι.

23.2 Ἀναξίλεως: tyrant of Rhegium from 494 until 476 (Diodorus 11.48.2).

ἐὼν διάφορος τοῖσι Ζαγκλαίοισι: 'being at variance with the Zanclaeans'. Given the proximity of the two cities with only the Straits of Messana lying between, this mutual animosity is not unexpected.

συμμίξας τοῖσι Σαμίοισι: 'having communicated with the Samians', aor. part. of συμμείγνυμι, 'mix together', and used in the middle and pass., as well as intransitively in the act., in the meaning 'have dealings with', 'make overtures to'.

ἐᾶν χαίρειν: literally 'allow to rejoice', used idiomatically with the meaning 'leave alone', 'let go of', 'drop all notions of', 'forget about'.

23.3 ὡς ἐπύθοντο ἐχομένην τὴν πόλιν: 'when they learned that the city was now being occupied'. For the acc. and part. construction, see note on 13.1 above. ὡς is here temporal, as at 69.1 below.

Ἱπποκράτεα: tyrant of Gela, a Greek city on the south coast of Sicily, from 498 until 491, who in the course of his short reign was able to exercise control over a fair part of the island at the expense of both Greek and Sicel communities.

23.4 ὡς ἀποβαλόντα τὴν πόλιν: causal, 'as having lost', 'on the grounds that he had lost'. As Hippocrates could hardly have punished Scythes for carelessly losing his own city, he must have done so because his own interests had been affected as a result of Scythes' incompetence. The phrase suggests that Scythes was himself subordinate to Hippocrates, and may have owed his own office to him. In this event Herodotus' description of the latter as Scythes' 'ally' is somewhat misleading, where 'suzerain' or 'overlord' would be more appropriate.

Ἴνυκον: Inyx (the *OCT* reads Ἴνυκα) was an obscure town of uncertain location somewhere within Hippocrates' territory. It is perhaps to be identified with Inycus, a petty township visited later by the sophist Hippias of Elis (Plato, *Hipp. Major* 282E).

κοινολογησάμενος: 'having entered into negotiations with'.

23.5 εἰρημένος: perf. part. pass. of λέγω, here meaning 'fixed', 'agreed upon'.

τῶν ἐπίπλων: 'moveable property', as opposed to fixtures, from ἔπιπλον, a noun used only in the plural both in this sense and also more generally with the meaning 'implements', 'furniture'.

ἀνδραπόδων τὰ ἡμίσεα: 'half the slaves'. The adj. ἥμισυς, 'half', can be used in the neut. with the article followed by the partitive gen. (τὸ ἥμισυ τῶν νηῶν) or alternatively it may derive its number and gender from the noun which it qualifies, as in the phrase αἱ ἡμίσεαι τῶν νηῶν.

23.6 ἐν ἀνδραπόδων λόγῳ εἶχε: literally 'he kept them in the category of slaves', i.e. 'as slaves'. For this use of λόγος, see note on 19.3 above.

εἶχε δήσας: 'he put them in chains and kept them confined'. See note on 12.3 above.

τοὺς δὲ κορυφαίους: 'the leading men', 'the chiefs', from κορυφή, 'head', 'top', 'peak'. Cf. the use of the word at 98.2 with the meaning 'the leading states'.

κατασφάξαι: inf. of purpose, common after verbs of giving, choosing and appointing (Goodwin 1532).

οὐ...οἵ γε Σάμιοι ἐποίησαν ταῦτα: if there is any truth in the version of Pausanias which substitutes Messenians for Herodotus' Samians and dates the episode to the 7th century (4.23.9), the two peoples will have henceforth held the city in common.

24.1 Ἱμέρην: a city on the north coast of Sicily, a colony of Zancle (Thuc. 6.5.1) founded in 649 (trad.) (Diod. 13.62.4).

δικαιότατον: Herodotus probably intends a contrast with the court physician Democedes of Croton (3.132-7) or with Histiaeus of Miletus (5.24.35, 106-7), who both schemed during an enforced residence at court to obtain their release and subsequently broke a pledge they had made to Darius.

24.2 παραιτησάμενος βασιλέα: 'having entreated the King' and so obtained permission. The verb παραιτέομαι means 'ask for', 'appeal to', 'intercede'.

ἀπονητὶ: 'without effort', 'without a struggle'.

περιεβεβλέατο: 3rd. pers. plur. pluperf. pass. of περιβάλλω, in the sense of 'come into possession of'. For the ending -έατο, see note on 13.1, and cf. κεκοσμέαται (41.4), ἐπικτέαται (58.1).

25.1 κατῆγον: 'proceeded to restore'. For this verb, see note on 5.1 above.

25.2 διὰ τὴν ἔκλειψιν τῶν νεῶν: 'because of the defection of the ships', with reference to the incident narrated at 14.2 above.

ἔσχον: 'took possession of', aor. of ἔχω. The aor. of most verbs denoting a state or condition is used to indicate the entry into that state (ingressive aor.). See Goodwin 1260, and cf. 36.1, 83.1, 115, 137.1, 140.2, and ἐπλούτησε at 125.5.

ἐθελοντὴν...ὑποκυψάσας: 'submitting voluntarily'. ὑποκύπτω, literally 'stoop', is used metaphorically of bending beneath foreign yoke, and ἐθελοντήν is an adverb meaning 'of one's own free will'.

ἀνάγκῃ προσηγάγοντο: 'they brought over by force'. Since this clause is parallel to τὰς μὲν...ὑποκυψάσας , which is in the acc. in apposition to Καρίην, we might naturally expect the part. προσαχθείσης, but Herodotus abandons the sentence structure at this point and embarks on a fresh clause. For an earlier example of such anacolouthon, see note on 21.1.

26.1 ὁλκάδας: 'merchant ships'.

τὰ...περὶ Ἑλλήσποντον ἔχοντα πρήγματα: 'his business interests in the Hellespont'.

οὐ προσιεμένη μιν: 'because it refused to admit him'. προσίημι, or more frequently the middle προσίεμαι, is used with the meaning 'admit', 'accept', 'allow'.

27.1 Φιλέει δὲ κως προσημαίνειν: sc. ὁ θεός, 'the god is somehow prone to warn in advance'. φιλέω with the inf. means 'tend to', 'be in the habit of'.

εὖτ' ἂν μέλλῃ μεγάλα κακὰ...ἔσεσθαι: 'when great misfortunes are about to befall'. Temporal conjunctions are followed by ἄν with the subj. to denote general or repeated statements (Goodwin 1393.1). μέλλω, 'intend to', 'be about to' is regularly followed by either the pres. or fut. inf. (Goodwin 1254).

27.2 τοῦτο μὲν: followed by τοῦτο δέ, 'in the first place...in the second place'. Cf. 44.1, 69.3, 101.3, 107.2, 114 below.

πέμψασι: dat. pl. aor. part. of πέμπω, in agreement with σφι, a sort of dat. of advantage in a statement of time (Goodwin 1165), used with reference to the person interested in the actions of the subject.

χορὸν νεηνιέων: 'a chorus of youths', presumably participants in the Pythian Games of 494.

ἀπήνεικε: Ionic aor. of ἀποφέρω. Cf. 129.3.

τὸν αὐτὸν τοῦτον χρόνον: 'at this very same time', a rare use of the acc. of time instead of the dat. to denote the time at which an action occurs, by analogy with expressions such as τὸ νῦν, 'now' and πρῶτον, 'in the first place'.

παισὶ γράμματα διδασκομένοισι: 'as the boys were learning their letters', another 'temporal' dat. of advantage.

ὥστε...εἷς μοῦνος ἀπέφυγε: 'with the result that one single boy escaped'. Consecutive clauses take the inf. when the result is one that the action of the leading verb tends to produce, and the indic., as here, when the emphasis is placed on the actual result produced (Goodwin 1450).

27.3 προέδεξε: Ionic aor. of προδείκνυμι, 'signify in advance'.

ὑπολαβοῦσα ἐς γόνυ τὴν πόλιν ἔβαλε: 'catching the city, it brought it to its knees', a metaphor from the sport of wrestling.

ἐπὶ δὲ τῇ ναυμαχίῃ: 'on top of the sea fight'.

καταστροφὴν εὐπετέως αὐτῶν ἐποιήσατο: 'he easily subdued them'. The middle of ποιέω with a noun is frequently used as a periphrastic alternative to the verb from which the noun is derived. Cf. 61.1, 78.2, 101.2.

28.1 Θάσον: an island in the north Aegean off the Thracian coast, which controlled territory on the adjacent mainland (peraea). There were mines on both island and mainland dependencies which produced silver and gold (see ch. 47 below), and it was these that attracted the attention of Histiaeus.

Φοίνικες: a reference to Darius' Phoenician fleet.

28.2 λιμαινούσης: a rare verb, from the noun λῖμος, meaning 'starve', 'suffer from hunger', also used at 7.25.1.

Ἀταρνέος: a Greek city on the mainland of Asia Minor, directly opposite the island of Lesbos and currently controlled by Chios (see 1.160.4).

ὡς ἀμήσων: 'in order to harvest', where the fut. part. is used to express purpose (Goodwin 1563.4). Cf. 33.2, 34.1, 35.3, 81, 111.1. 134.2, 139.1.

ἐκ Καΐκου πεδίου: the valley of the river Caicus, which flows into the Gulf of Elea in Aeolis, formed a fertile area which could serve as a useful source of supplies for Histiaeus.

Μυσῶν: the inhabitants of Mysia, a district in the north west of Asia Minor to the north of Lydia.

Ἅρπαγος: otherwise unknown. The name is Median, the most famous bearer being the Mede who betrayed Astyages to Cyrus and was subsequently employed by the latter to subdue the Greeks of Asia Minor in 545 (1.108ff, 162ff).

ἀποβάντι: 'having disembarked', aor. part. of ἀποβαίνω.

29.1 συνέστασαν: 'held out', 'stood their ground', intrans. pluperf. of συνίστημι.

ἡ...ἵππος: 'the cavalry', collective noun by synecdoche for οἱ ἱππέες. In a non-collective sense, ἡ ἵππος means 'mare'.

τὸ τε δὴ ἔργον τῆς ἵππου τοῦτο ἐγένετο: literally 'and so the act of the cavalry was this', i.e. 'it was this action of the cavalry which proved decisive'. For this use of ἔργον, cf. 8.102.2, 9.102.2.

τετραμμένων: perf. part. pass. of τρέπω, 'rout', 'put to flight'.

ἐλπίζων οὐκ ἀπολέεσθαι ὑπὸ βασιλέος: 'hoping not to perish at the hands of the King'. For the construction with verbs of hoping, see Goodwin 1286 and note on 2.1.above. When the subject of the inf. is the same as that of the principal verb, it is generally left unexpressed, or, when specified, is in the nom. (Goodwin 895, 927). ἀπολέεσθαι is the Ionic fut. inf. middle of ἀπόλλυμι, used here as the equivalent of a pass. with the meaning 'be put to death'.

ἁμαρτάδα: Ionic form of the Attic ἁμαρτία, ἁμάρτημα, 'fault', 'mistake'.

φιλοψυχίην...ἀναιρέεται: literally 'love of life', especially in the sense of 'love of continuing to live', and so equivalent to 'cowardice', 'faintheartedness'. ἀναιρέω, 'I take up', is used in the middle to mean 'entertain', 'assume'.

29.2 συγκεντηθήσεσθαι: fut. inf. pass. of συγκεντέω, 'stab', 'pierce'. For the fut. inf. with see μέλλω note on 27.1 above.

30.1 εἰ μέν...ἀνήχθη...παρὰ βασιλέα...ὁ δὲ οὔτ' ἂν ἔπαθε κακὸν οὐδὲν: 'had he been taken up country to the King, not only would he have suffered any harm'. ἀνήχθη is an emendation for the tautological ἄχθη ἀχθόμενος of the manuscripts. In past unreal conditions, the verb in the protasis is in the aor. indic., while the apodosis has the aor. indic. with ἄν (Goodwin 1397). For the use of the particle δέ in the apodosis, see Denniston *GP*, p. 180. Where apodotic δέ occurs in Herodotus, the apodosis normally begins with a pronoun and there are usually two alternative hypotheses in the sentence. For οὔτε...τε, see note on 1.1 above.

δοκέειν ἐμοί: 'as it seems to me', an absolute inf. (Goodwin 1534), found more commonly with ὡς or ὅσον (cf. ὡς ἀπεικάσαι 'to hazard a guess' and ὅσον ἐμέ γ᾽ εἰδέναι, 'to the best of my knowledge').

ἀπῆκέ τ᾽ ἂν αὐτῷ: 'but he would have let him off', where the unexpressed subject is Darius. ἀπῆκε is Ionic aor. of ἀφίημι.

ἀνεσταύρωσαν: 'they impaled him', from σταυρός, 'stake'. It was only in Roman times that the noun came to mean 'cross' and the corresponding verb σταυρόω, 'crucify'. Impalement was a common form of punishment in Achaemenid Persia. See 3.159.1 for the Babylonian rebels, and 7.238.1 for Leonidas' head. Cf. also the Behistun Inscription (R. Kent, *Old Persian*, American Oriental Series, no. 33, ed. 2, New Haven, 1953, DB III; Rüdiger Schmitt, *The Bisitun Inscriptions of Darius the Great: Old Persian Text*, Corpus Inscriptionum Iranicarum, Part i, Vol. I, London, 1991) col. 2.76 (the Mede Phraortes), col. 2.91 (the rebel Tritantaichmes), col. 3.92 (Arakha the Armenian).

ταριχεύσαντες: 'having preserved'. ταριχεύω is the verb used to denote the pickling and preserving of fish or meat in salt. It can also be used of human bodies in the sense of 'mummify'. The noun τάριχος can mean both 'piece of salted fish' and 'mummy'.

ἐπαιτιησάμενος: 'having blamed', 'having found fault with'.

περιστείλαντας: 'having wrapped', from περιστέλλω, 'place round about', 'wrap all over'.

ὡς ἀνδρὸς μεγάλως ἑωυτῷ τε καὶ Πέρσῃσι εὐεργέτεω: 'as being a man who had been a great benefactor to himself and to the Persians'. εὐργετής, 'benefactor', is properly speaking a noun, but is here followed by the dat. as if it were equivalent to the participle εὐεργετέων. The service rendered was presumably his role in preserving the bridges over the Danube during Darius' Scythian expedition (4.187). Darius may also be referring to the official list of Royal Benefactors (*orosangai*) maintained by the Persian kings (3.140.1, 3.160.2, 8.85.3; Thuc. 1.129.3; Arrian, *Anab.* 3.27.4).

31.1 τῷ δευτέρῳ ἔτεϊ: 'next year', literally 'in the second year', i.e. in 493.

ὅκως...λάβοι: 'whenever it took', temporal, as elsewhere in Herodotus (e.g. 61.3, 75.1, 77.3, 121.2, 137.3, below). Indefinite temporal and conditional clauses referring to the future are followed by ἄν with the subj. in primary sequence, and by the opt. without ἄν in historic sequence (Goodwin 1431.2).

ἐσαγήνευον: 'they netted', from σαγήνη, 'fish net'.

31.2 σαγηνεύουσι...τόνδε τὸν τρόπον: so Plato, *Menexenus* 240C, *Laws* 698D, where the procedure is said to have been implemented at Eretria in 490, though in fact it can have been practised only on small islands with comparatively flat terrain. Larger islands like Lesbos and Chios can hardly have been netted in the way Herodotus describes.

ἀνὴρ ἀνδρὸς ἀψάμενος τῆς χειρός: verbs of touching (ἅπτομαι, ψαύω, θιγγάνω) and laying hold of (λαμβάνομαι and its compounds) take the gen.

of the person or thing touched (Goodwin 1099). The double gen. found here is unusual: χειρός is probably the object of ἀψάμενος with ἀνδρός as the possessive gen. ('touching the hand of each man'), though it would also be possible to explain the double gen. along the lines of μου λαβόμενος τῆς χειρός (Plato, *Charmides* 153B) 'touching me and touching my hand', i.e. 'touching me by the hand'.

κατὰ ταὐτά: 'in the very same way'.

32 ἐνθαῦτα: 'in these circumstances'. Cf. 99.2 and 138.4 below.

οὐκ ἐψεύσαντο τὰς ἀπειλάς: 'they did not belie the threats'. ψεύδομαι with the acc. can mean either 'deceive', 'be mistaken in', or, as here, 'prove something false'.

ἐξέταμνον: 'they proceeded to castrate', from τάμνω, the Ionic form of τέμνω, 'cut'.

ἀντὶ τοῦ εἶναι ἐνόρχιας: 'instead of being testicled', i.e. 'instead of still retaining their testicles'. *OCT* here reads ἀντὶ εἶναι ἐνορχέας and in Herodotus, the prep. ἀντί is occasionally construed with the simple inf. where Attic would require an inf. preceded by the gen. of the def. art. Cf. 1.210.2, ἀντὶ ἄρχεσθαι ὑπ' ἄλλων ἄρχειν ἁπάντων, 'to rule everyone instead of being ruled by others', 7.170.2, ἀντὶ μὲν Κρητῶν γενέσθαι Ἰήπυγας Μεσσαπίους, ἀντὶ δ' εἶναι νησιώτας ἠπειρώτας, 'to become Messapian Iapygians instead of Cretans and mainlanders instead of islanders'. The correct Ionic form of the adj. ἐνορχής is uncertain. A 6th century BC inscription from Miletus offers ἐνορχής (3rd declension), whereas the mss. of Herodotus are divided (here they vary between ἐνόρχιας and ἐνόρχας, and at 8.105.2 they have ἐνορχέων or ἐνορχίων for the gen. pl.).

αὐτοῖσι τοῖς ἱροῖσι: 'temples and all', a dat. of accompaniment, where the pronoun αὐτός is used in such expressions as αὐτοῖς ἀνδράσι, 'men and all' (Thuc. 2.90.6, 4.14.1), αὐτῇσι ῥίζῃσι, 'roots and all' (*Iliad* 9.542), αὐτοῖς στεφάνοις, 'crowns and all' (Xen. *Cyr.* 3.3.40). See Goodwin 1191, and cf. note on 8.1 above. Since the Ionians were able to furnish Xerxes with 100 ships only 13 years later (7.94), the destruction descibed here must be exaggerated to at least some extent.

τὸ τρίτον: 'for the third time'. Here Herodotus must be thinking of the Ionians of the mainland only, as the islanders had never been subject to Lydia.

πρῶτον μὲν ὑπὸ Λυδῶν: by Croesus (1.26-8), though in fact two earlier Lydian rulers, Gyges and Ardys, had captured Colophon and Priene respectively (1.15).

δὶς...ὑπὸ Περσέων: the first occasion was the subjugation by Harpagus in c.545 (1.16-7), the second refers to the present situation, at the end of the Ionian Revolt.

33.1 τὰ ἐπ' ἀριστερὰ ἐσπλώοντι: 'those on the left (as they appear) to one sailing in', i.e. 'on the left, as one sails in', a dat. of relation with τινι to be understood as the subject of the part. (Goodwin 1172). The cities the historian has in mind are the Greek states on the European shore of the Hellespont, which are named individually in the next sentence.

τὰ...ἐπὶ δεξιὰ: the cities on the opposite coast in Asia Minor.

Χερσόνησός: the Thracian Chersonese, now called the Gallipoli peninsula, at the time ruled as the personal possession of the Athenian Miltiades (see ch. 35 ff. below).

πόλιες συχναὶ: B. Isaac, *The Greek Settlements in Thrace until the Macedonian Conquest*, Leiden, 1986, pp. 187-97 lists no fewer than 20 communities, but not all of these were fully fledged cities in their own right. Cardia, Crithote, Sestos and Elaeus were the most significant.

Πέρινθος: the modern Eregli, derived from its alternative name of Heraclea, a Megarian colony on the northern shore of the Propontis (Sea of Marmora), about half way between the Chersonese and Byzantium.

τὰ τείχεα τὰ ἐπὶ Θρηΐκης: 'the forts on the Thracian coast'. A τεῖχος, literally 'wall', was a fortified and so defensible place of habitation lacking the size, importance and civic institutions which would have made it worthy of the rank of *polis*. Four such places in existence in the fifth century are known by name (Tyrodiza, Serioteichos, Didymoteichos and Daunioteichos).

Σηλυβρίη: Selymbria, now Silivri, another Megarian colony on the north coast of the Propontis, situated between Perinthus and Byzantium.

Βυζάντιον: like Perinthus and Selymbria, a colony of Megara.

33.2 οἱ πέρηθε Καλχηδόνιοι: 'the Chalcedonians who are beyond them', i.e. 'on the further side of'. Chalcedon was yet another Megarian colony but situated on the Asian shore of the Bosporus directly opposite Byzantium.

Εὔξεινον: the Black Sea, the later and more euphemistic name for what was originally the Pontos Axeinos ('the Inhospitable Sea').

Μεσαμβρίην: the modern Nesebur, a foundation on a site previously inhabited by Thracians, located on a small peninsula to the north of what is now the Gulf of Burgos on the Bulgarian Black Sea coast. Strabo (7.6.1) calls the city a Megarian colony, but he may be using the term loosely of settlers who themselves came from other Megarian colonies. Pseudo-Scymnus (737-42) agrees with Herodotus about the identity of the settlers, but connects them with Darius' Scythian expedition some 20 years earlier. Moreover since Herodotus' own narrative at 4.93 indicates the existence of Mesembia at this time, it may be that the new settlers of 493 reinforced a pre-existing city.

οἴκησαν: 'came to live in', ingressive aor. (see note on 25.2).

καταλεχθείσας: 'the aforementioned', aor. pass of καταλέγω.

Προκόννησον: literally 'Roe Deer Island', a Milesian settlement on the island of the same name situated in the western half of the Propontis, about equidistant between the north and south coasts.

Ἀρτάκην: a city on the south coast of the island of Arctonnesus ('Bear Island') in the Propontis, to the west of Cyzicus, to which it served as a harbour.

ἐξαιρήσοντες: 'in order to destroy', 'with the intention of destroying', a fut. part. of purpose (see note on 28.2, and cf. 34.1, 35.3, 81, 134.2, 139.1).

προσσχόντες: aor. part. of προσέχω, used intransitively to mean 'put in at', where the object (νέας) is to be understood. Cf. 1.2.1, 3.48.2.

33.3 Κύζικον: an important Milesian colony on the south coast of Arctonnesus, separated from the Asiatic shore by a narrow channel which could be opened up or blocked off at will. Due to its strategic position, it was a port of call for most of the shipping that passed through the Propontis.

οὐδὲ ἔπλωσαν ἀρχήν: 'they didn't sail at all'. ἀρχήν is properly the acc. of the noun ἀρχή, 'beginning', used adverbially in the sense of 'at first' (Goodwin 1060) and, more idiomatically, with negatives to mean 'not at all', (cf. 86.β2 below; 1.193.3, 3.39.4, 7.26.2).

τῷ ἐν Δασκυλείῳ ὑπάρχῳ: 'the satrap based at Dascyleum. ὕπαρχος is the regular word in Herodotus to denote a satrap (see note on 1.1 above). Dascyleum was a town on the south coast of the Propontis well to the east of Cyzicus, where the satrap of the province known to the Greeks as Hellespontine Phrygia had his residence.

Καρδίης: a city on the west coast of the Chersonese built at the narrowest part of the isthmus connecting the peninsula to the mainland. A joint colony of Miletus and Clazomenae (Strabo 14.1.6), it was strengthened with a new intake of settlers organised by Miltiades (Pseudo-Scymnus 699 ff.). The Persian failure to reduce Cardia is surprising if they were intent on a thorough subjugation of the peninsula. Since we are not even told that they attempted to do so, the Cardians may already have come to terms.

34.1 Μιλτιάδης ὁ Κίμωνος: the younger Miltiades, the future victor at Marathon in 490. For his career, and that of his father and grandfather, see J.K. Davies, *APF*, no. 8429.

Μιλτιάδεω τοῦ Κυψέλου: the elder Miltiades, founder of the Philaid mini-empire in the Chersonese; half-brother to the elder Cimon and uncle to Miltiades the younger. See ch. 38 and 39 below. His father Cypselus, archon in 597/6, was named for the Corinthian tyrant of the same name, probably to advertise a marriage link between the tyrant's daughter and Cypselus' father Agamestor.

πρότερον: 'in the past'. The exact date is disputed, and could fall any time within the years 560-46, when the reigns of Peisistratus (35.1) and Croesus (37.1) overlapped.

Δόλογκοι: an obscure Thracian tribe (mentioned also by Pliny *NH* 4.11.41, Solinus 68.3 and Stephanus of Byzantium) whose territory lay within the Chersonese, and who subsequently shared its lands with the new Greek settlers.

Ἀψινθίων: a better known Thracian tribe (cf. 9.119-20, where they sacrificed the Persian Oeobazus while he was attempting to pass through their lands) who inhabited the Aegean coast from the Chersonese in the east to the region around Aenus in the west. (See Isaac, *op. cit.*, pp. 146-7.)

τοὺς βασιλέας: an interesting parallel to the Spartan dyarchy.

χρησομένους: 'to consult the oracle about the war', fut. part. expressing purpose. (See 28.2. note and cf. 33.2, 34.1, 35.3, 81, 111.1, 134.2, 139.1.)

34.2 ἀνεῖλε...ἐπάγεσθαι: 'she replied that they should invite'.

ὃς ἄν...πρῶτος ἐπὶ ξείνια καλέσῃ: 'whoever should be the first to invite them to hospitality', an indefinite relative clause with ἄν and the subj. referring to the future (Goodwin 1403, 1434). On this oracular response, see the discussion in PW, I p. 148 and Fontenrose *DO*, Q109. The motif 'the first you meet' is a common one in Delphic lore, and should be compared with similar responses such as PW no. 20 (= *DO* L2), where Manto daughter of Teiresias is advised to marry the first man she meets on leaving the temple; PW no. 23 (= *DO* Q73) in which the Sicyonians are warned that a tyranny will be established by the first citizen to whom a son will be born on his return home; PW no. 78 (= *DO* Q129) where Phormio of Croton is told that his wound will be cured by the first person to invite him to dinner upon leaving the temple; PW no. 190 (= *DO* L28) in which Xuthus is given as his son the first boy he encounters on leaving the temple; PW no. 313 (= *DO* L79) where Melanthus of Messenia is instructed to live where he is first honoured by hosts who set feet and a head before him at dinner; PW no. 322 (= *DO* L82) in which Cephalus is advised to lie with the first woman he meets if he wants a child; PW no. 381 (= *DO* L166), where Magnesian colonists are given as their guide the first man they meet on leaving the temple; PW no. 532 (= *DO* L128) in which the king of Haliartus is instructed to relieve a drought by killing the first person who meets him on his return home.

τὴν ἱρὴν ὁδόν: 'the Sacred Way', the route from Delphi east through Phocis, Chaeronea and Thebes to Eleusis, where it joined the more famous Sacred Way leading to Athens. It was sacred in the sense that all pilgrims to Delphi were under Apollo's protection and was the route taken by processions to Delphi by land approaching from the west.

ἐκτράπονται ἐπ' Ἀθηνέων: 'they turned off towards Athens', a historic pres. (Goodwin 1252). Since the direct route from Delphi to Thrace would have led the envoys north into Thessaly and not south into Attica, their diversion was a major one which is left entirely unmotivated.

35.1 τηνικαῦτα: 'at that time'. For the date, see note on 34.1 above.

ἐδυνάστευε: 'was influential', 'was of importance', as the head of a prominent Athenian family.

οἰκίης τεθριπποτρόφου: 'a house that raced four-horse chariots', for participation in the equestrian events at the major pan-Hellenic games. Only wealthy families could afford such extravagances (see, e.g. Aristophanes, *Clouds* 12-24), but the renown brought by such a victory to the winning family and city made horse-rearing a worthwhile investment politically (Isocrates 16.32-4; Plut. *Alc.* 11).

ἀπ' Αἰακοῦ τε καὶ Αἰγίνης: Aeacus was son of Zeus by the nymph Aegina and father of Telamon, himself the father of Ajax.

Φιλαίου τοῦ Αἴαντος: Philaeus is variously described as son of Ajax (e.g. Plut. *Solon* 10) and as son of Eurysaces son of Ajax, as in Pausanias (1.35.2).

γενομένου πρώτου τῆς οἰκίης ταύτης ᾿Αθηναίου: 'being the first of his house to become an Athenian'. Belief in the family's link with Athens seems to originate with the passage in the Catalogue of Ships where Ajax is said to have stationed his twelve Salaminian ships alongside those of the Athenians (*Iliad* 2.557-8). According to Plut. (*loc. cit.*), Eurysaces and Philaeus handed Salamis over to Athens in exchange for Athenian citizenship, and their descendants came to be known as the Philaidae.

35.2 ἐν τοῖσι προθύροισι: 'in his porch', literally the area in front of the door, the recess outside the front door similar to that in the house of Callias described in Plato's *Protagoras* (314C-D), where Socrates and Hippocrates have a conversation before they are admitted within by the porter. The word is also used of the front door itself, as at 91.2 below. Herodotus does not specify the location of Miltiades' house, but it was probably in Laciadae just to the west of Athens, where the family was resident when Cleisthenes reformed the tribal system.

ἔχοντας...αἰχμὰς: 'carrying spears', a barbarian practice according to Thuc. (1.5.3-6.2). The more civilised Greeks, apart from those of the north west, such as the Ozolian Locrians, Aetolians and Acarnanians, had given up the habit in everyday life, as indeed had some of the more advanced non-Greek peoples.

προσεβώσατο: 'he shouted out to them', the Ionic form of the Attic προσεβοήσατο.

ἐδέοντο αὐτοῦ τῷ θεῷ μιν πείθεσθαι: 'they asked him to obey the god'. Literally the phrase means 'they asked him that he should obey the god', a tautology caused by the conflation of two distinct constructions, the simple (prolative) inf. of indirect command and the acc. and inf. of indirect statement. Both αὐτοῦ and μιν refer to Miltiades, the former being in the gen. after ἐδέοντο, the latter the subject of πείθεσθαι.

35.3 οἷα ἀχθόμενόν: the part. with οἷον, οἷα or ἅτε expresses cause (see note on 5.1 above). Like most aristocrats, Miltiades was opposed to the rule of a tyrant which denied him the scope for exercising meaningful political leadership in Athens in his own person.

ἐκποδών: an adverb meaning 'out of the way', derived from πούς, 'foot'. Cf. ἐμποδών, 'in the way'.

ἐπειρησόμενος...εἰ ποιέῃ: 'to ask if he should do', where the fut. part. expresses purpose (see note on 28.2). The mss. read ποιοῖ or ποιοίη: the emendation ποιέῃ makes Herodotus retain the subj. of the direct deliberative question ('Am I to do what the Dolonci ask?') See Goodwin 1490-1. Herodotus is at pains to show that Miltiades embarked on his undertaking only with the backing of Apollo: it is probable that the story is derived from the defence offered by the younger Miltiades at his trial in 492 (see 104.2

below), when he was anxious to justify his uncle's exercise of a tyranny as the fulfilment of a divine mandate.

36.1 Ὀλύμπια ἀναραιρηκώς: 'having won an Olympic victory'. ἀναραιρηκώς is the Ionic perf. part. act. of ἀναιρέω (Attic ἀνῃρηκώς). Verbs of winning (νικάω, ἀναιρέω) are often followed by an acc. indicating the victory (νικᾶν νίκην), a cognate or adverbial acc. (Goodwin 1051-2). This construction is extended to the kind of victory won (e.g. ναυμαχίαν, Παναθήναια). Cf. Πύθια ἀνελόμενος at 122.1 below.

παραλαβὼν Ἀθηναίων πάντα τὸν βουλόμενον: 'taking with him any Athenian who wished'. Herodotus fails to explain the episode from the Peisistratid standpoint: since Athens was under a tyranny at the time, the project can have gone ahead only if it enjoyed Peisistratid support. It is likely that Peisistratus was as keen to get rid of Miltiades as Miltiades was to get away from him.

ἔσχε τὴν χώρην: 'he took possession of the land'. ἔσχε is an ingressive aor. (see note on 25.2 above).

36.2 ἀπετείχισε: 'he walled off', the first of several attempts to exclude marauding Thracians from the Chersonese. The fortifications, which were built across the isthmus at its narrowest point (the modern Bulair Peninsula), were later rebuilt by Pericles when an additional thousand settlers were dispatched in c.447 (Plut. *Per.* 19.1), and again by Dercyllidas in 398 in response to appeals from the inhabitants (Xen. *Hell.* 3.2.8-10; Diod. 14.38.7). He too sent fresh settlers to make good the depletion of the population caused by Lysander's expulsion of Athenians in 403 (Xen. *Hell.* 2.2.2). Further strengthening of the fortifications had to be undertaken later by Justinian (Procopius, *De Aed.* 4.10.5).

ἐκ Καρδίης...ἐς Πακτύην: for Cardia, see note on 33.3 above. Pactye was situated on the east coast of the Chersonese at a site as yet unidentified.

ἵνα μὴ ἔχοιέν σφεας...δηλέεσθαι: 'so that they would be unable to injure them', a final opt. in historic sequence (Goodwin 1365). δηλέομαι is largely confined to epic and to Ionic prose.

στάδιοι ἕξ τε καὶ τριήκοντα: 'the isthmus is 36 stades in length'. Xenophon (*Hell.* 3.2.10) gives 37, and PseudoScylax (670) the round number of 40. The stade was equivalent to 600 Greek feet, but feet of different lengths were employed in different states, the Attic foot of some 295 km. and the Olympic foot of c.320 km. being the most common. If Herodotus is measuring in Attic stades, the length of the wall would be about 6·3 km. or just under 4 miles; if in the Olympic stade, the length would be roughly 7 km. or 4⅓ miles.

σταδίων εἴκοσι καὶ τετρακοσίων τὸ μῆκος: μῆκος is acc. of respect (Goodwin 1058). The modern equivalent would be some 74 km. or 46 miles (Attic) or (Olympic) c.81 km. (just over 50 miles).

37.1 ὠσάμενος: 'having thrust back', aor. part. middle of ὠθέω, 'push', in the sense of pushing back from oneself or to one's own benefit.

Λαμψακηνοὶ: the citizens of Lampsacus, a Phocaean colony with an excellent harbour on the Asiatic shore of the Hellespont which guarded the eastern entrance to this strategic sea route. The war reveals the extent of Miltiades' ambition to exercise some degree of control over the Asian shore opposite his existing territory. The Lampsacenes in their turn can hardly have relished the growth of such a powerful state and potential rival just across the strait from their city.

ἦν δὲ ὁ Μιλτιάδης Κροίσῳ...ἐν γνώμῃ γεγονώς: literally 'Miltiades was in Croesus' thoughts', i.e. 'was well known to Croesus'. Croesus' intervention on Miltiades' behalf should indicate that Miltiades was not only well known to Croesus but was a political ally. At the time when Croesus was looking for support in the Aegean against the potential threat from Persia, an alliance with the ruler of the state occupying such a strategic position would have been highly desirable, and, had he been in any way opposed to Miltiades, he would have been only too happy to let him languish in captivity.

πίτυος τρόπον: 'in the manner of a pine'. τρόπον, like its synonym δίκην, behaves much in the manner of a preposition governing the gen. The usage is mainly poetic, but occurs elsewhere in Herodotus (e.g. at 2.57.2, 3.98.4). The expression 'like a pine' subsequently became proverbial to denote utter destruction (Aelian, *VH* 6.13, Suda). Croesus' phrase was particularly apt in that the site of Lampsacus had been previously known as Pityoessa, 'abounding in pine trees' (Charon of Lampsacus, Frag. 7, cited by Plut., *Mor.* 255B).

37.2 πλανωμένων...ἐν τοῖσι λόγοισι: 'being at a loss in their reasoning'. The verb means literally 'wander' and is here used metaphorically with regard to indecision over the meaning of the phrase. Cf. πλανωμένου ἐν τῷ λόγῳ at 2.115.3, where the expression means something like 'be inconsistent in what one says'.

μόγις κοτὲ μαθών: 'having at last understood, and only with difficulty'.

πίτυς μούνη δενδρέων πάντων ἐκκοπεῖσα βλαστὸν οὐδένα μετίει: 'the pine alone among trees does not put forth shoots once cut down'. μετίει is from μεθίημι, 'send forth'. According to Theophrastus (*HP* 3.9.5, it is the πεύκη, usually identified with the black pine (*pinus nigra*) which behaves in this way, not the πίτυς, (the Aleppo pine, *pinus halepensis*). Cf. Pliny, *NH* 16-19.46 (derived from Theophrastus' account) which has the *picea* (= Gk. πίτυς) put forth new shoots after burning, but contrasts the *picea* with the larch (*larix*), which does not. Modern opinion is that while most conifers may survive a superficial burning, only the yew would renew itself after a fire on the scale envisaged by Croesus. See Suzanne Amigues' translation and comments in the Budé edition of Theophrastus (*Théophraste, Recherches sur les Plantes*, Tome II, Paris, 1989, pp. 151-3).

πανώλεθρος: 'utterly destroyed', an essentially poetic adj. used here in a passive sense which, though somewhat tautological, seeks to emphasise the totality and irreversibility of the destruction. At 85.2 below, the word is used in the active sense of 'all-destroying'.

38.1 μετὰ δὲ: 'and afterwards', an adverbial use of the preposition. See note on 4.1 above and cf. 62.2, 97.2, 103.2, 110, 120, 125.2, 129.3, 134.2 below.

Στησαγόρη: nothing is known about Stesagoras apart from what we are told in this passage and at 103.2-4, where he is described as the elder son of Cimon and already in the Chersonese when his father was killed by the Peisistratids.

ἀδελφεοῦ...ὁμομητρίου: 'his brother on the mother's side', 'his maternal half-brother'. Nothing is known of the lady who was the mother of the elder Cimon and Miltiades by different husbands. Her first marriage was to Cypselus the father of Cimon and archon in 597/6 (see note on 34.1 above), her second to the totally obscure Stesagoras. Since the elder Miltiades died childless, his branch of the Philaidae died out with him, but his heirs Stesagoras and Miltiades the younger and their descendants are regarded as Philaids in the later tradition. This suggests either that he formally adopted his nephews or that the elder Stesagoras was himself a Philaid: in the latter event the mother of the elder Miltiades and Cimon was married to two men who were themselves related by blood (cousins, or even brothers?). The family tree is as follows:

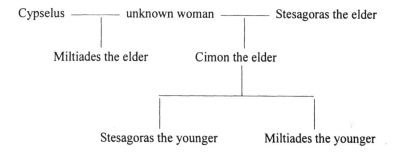

τελευτήσαντι: probably in 516 or 515 (see note on 40.1 below).

θύουσι, ὡς νόμος οἰκιστῇ: the founder of a city was regarded as more than mortal and, as the city's greatest benefactor, received heroic honours after death. Contrary to normal practice, a founder was normally buried within the city walls, usually in the *agora*, where he was accorded a conspicuous tomb which became the centre of his posthumous cult. On the anniversary of his death, there would be a public sacrifice at the tomb, a feast and the celebration of musical or athletic contests in his honour. See I. Malkin, *Religion and Colonization in Ancient Greece*, Leiden, 1987, pp. 189-203. The verb θύω is normally used of sacrifices to gods, and ἐναγίζομαι to heroes (see 2.44.5), but this distinction is not always observed (θύω is used of sacrifices to the heroes Onesilus at 5.114 2 and Artachaites at 7.117.2; cf. Plut. *Arat.* 53.4. Note also the use of the noun θυσία in connection with the heroic honours paid to Brasidas at Thuc. 5.11.1 and Arist. *Nic. Eth.* 1134b27, as well as to Aratus at Polyb. 8.12.8).

οὐδενὶ ἐγγίνεται ἀγωνίζεσθαι: 'it is not permitted to any to compete'. The 3rd. pers. sing. of the verb ἐγγίγνομαι is used impersonally in both Ionic and Attic in the sense of 'it is possible', 'it is permitted'.

38.2 κατέλαβε ἀποθανεῖν: 'it happened to him that he died', i.e. 'it was his fate to die'. The impersonal use of καταλαμβάνει with the acc. and inf. is common in Herodotus (see e.g. 2.152.2, 3.65.1, 3.118.1, 4.105.1).

πληγέντα τὴν κεφαλήν: 'struck on the head'. πληγέντα is 2nd. aor. part. pass. of πλήσσω (Attic πλήττω), 'I strike', and is an acc. of respect (Goodwin 1058).

ἐν τῷ πρυτανηΐῳ: 'in the prytaneum', a public building central to the political and religious life of the Greek city, in which the eternal flame of the sacred hearth was maintained. Uses to which the building was put would vary, but might include service as a court of law, as a meeting place for officials or priests, as a sanctuary for fugitives, as a dining place for state magistrates and their official guests, or as a storeroom for state archives. See S.G. Miller, *The Prytaneum; its Function and Architectural Form*, Berkeley, Los Angeles and London, 1978, pp. 4-24.

αὐτομόλου...τῷ λόγῳ, πολεμίου...τῷ ἔργῳ: a 'seeming deserter, but in actual fact an enemy'. τῷ λόγῳ, 'in appearance', 'in theory' is often contrasted with τῷ ἔργῳ or τῷ ὄντι, 'in reality'.

ὑποθερμοτέρου: 'somewhat inclined to passion'. The adj. θερμός, 'hot', 'passionate' is here doubly qualified, first by the prefix ὑπο- (cf. ὑπόλευκος, 'whitish', ὑπόψυχρος, 'coldish'), and then by the use of the comparative degree (cf. ἀμελέστερος, 'rather careless'). For the combination of the two, cf. ὑπομαργότερος 'inclined to madness' at 3.29.1 (of Cambyses), 3.145.1 (of Charilaus), and at ch. 75.1. below (of Cleomenes).

39.1 Μιλτιάδεα τὸν Κίμωνος: the younger Miltiades (see notes on 34.1 and 38.1 above).

καταλαμψόμενον τὰ πρήγματα: 'to take control of affairs', fut. part. expressing purpose (see note on ch. 7 above). λάμψομαι is the Ionic equivalent of the Attic λήψομαι, the fut. of λαμβάνω.

οἱ Πεισιστρατίδαι: the sons of the tyrant Peisistratus included Hippias, who inherited the tyranny on his father's death in 528/7, Hipparchus, who supervised cultural affairs for his brother ([Aristotle], *Ath. Pol.* 18.1) and Thessalus, who remained a private citizen (Thuc. 1.20.2, 6.55.1; Diod. 10.17.1). The term may also include Hippias' half brothers Iophon and Hegesistratus, the former ruler of Sigeum (Hdt. 5.94.1).

οἵ μιν...ἐποίευν εὖ: 'who treated him well'. In particular Hippias selected him to hold the eponympous archonship for 524/3 (ML, 6C; C.W. Fornara, *Translated Documents of Greece and Rome*, ed. 2, vol. 1, Cambridge, 1982, 23C; R. Develin, *AO*, p. 47).

ὡς οὐ συνειδότες δῆθεν τοῦ πατρὸς...τὸν θάνατον: 'just as though they were not involved in his father's death', where the particle δῆθεν adds a touch of irony (see note on 1.1 above). σύνοιδα is regularly used to mean 'have knowledge of something along with someone else', 'be privy to', 'be implicated in'.

ἐν ἄλλῳ λόγῳ σημανέω: 'I shall show in another part of my work'. λόγος and the plur. λόγοι are commonly used in Herodotus to refer to his work as a whole (e.g. 2.123.1, 6.19.2, 7.93, 7.152.3), as well as to particular section of it (e.g. 1.106.2, 1.184, 2.38.2, 2.99.1, 2.161.3, 5.22.1, 7.213.3). σημανέω is the Ionic fut. of σημαίνω, from an original σημανέσω which, with the loss of inter-vocalic sigma, appears in Attic in the contracted form σημανῶ. The story of the murder of the elder Cimon is told in ch. 103 below.

39.2 εἶχε κατ' οἴκους: 'he kept himself indoors', an intransitive use of ἔχω (cf. 2.91.4, 3.128.2). At 3.79.3 (κατ' οἴκους ἑωυτοὺς οἱ μάγοι ἔχουσι), the historian uses the verb transitively with the same meaning.

δηλαδὴ: 'ostensibly to show him honour'. δηλαδὴ is used both in the literal sense of 'clearly', 'manifestly' and ironically with the implication 'or so at least was his claim', as here and at 4.135.2. ἐπιτιμέω, if the text is sound, must here be equivalent to the simple τιμέω, 'honour', 'show respect for' rather than the usual 'criticise', 'find fault with' or, as at 4.43.6, 'impose a penalty on'. However the verb is unattested in this sense elsewhere in classical Greek and the text may be corrupt. (ἔτι τιμέων, 'still showing respect for' has been suggested as a possible emendation.)

ὡς συλλυπηθησόμενοι: 'in order to share his grief', a fut. part. expressing purpose (see note on ch. 7).

ἐδέθησαν: 'they were put in fetters', from δέω, 'tie', 'bind'. The verb δέω, 'need', 'implore' has ἐδεήθην as its aor. pass.

πεντακοσίους βόσκων ἐπικούρους: 'maintaining 500 mercenaries'. βόσκω, literally meaning 'feed', 'tend animals', can also be used in the more general sense of 'keep'. ἐπίκουρος, derived from the verb ἐπικουρέω, 'help', originally meant 'helper', 'ally', but came also to mean 'mercenary soldier', as opposed to a citizen soldier.

γαμέει Ὀλόρου...θυγατέρα Ἡγησιπύλην: Miltiades had been married previously to an Athenian wife who was the mother of his eldest son Metiochus (see ch. 41 below). His second marriage to a foreign wife was not all that rare for aristocratic Athenians prior to 451, when Pericles' citizenship law allowed marriage only to women born to two Athenian parents. By this second marriage, Miltiades became the father of Cimon. It is uncertain whether Miltiades' daughter Elpinice was born to Hegesipyle or to the anonymous first wife. Since the name Olorus was also borne by the father of Thucydides the historian, who admits to possessing some influence in Thrace (4.105.1), and whose monument was subsequently erected among those of the Philaid family, there was clearly some kind of link between the two men, though the precise nature of the connection is obscure.

40.1 νεωστὶ μὲν ἐληλύθεε ἐς τὴν Χερσόνησον: 'he had recently come to the Chersonese', where ἐληλύθεε is the plup. of ἔρχομαι, 'come'. The chronology is somewhat vague, and the only fixed point is the flight to Athens, securely dated to 493. His earlier flight from, and return to, the Chersonese, which happened two years earlier, must therefore be placed in 495, and cannot reasonably be dated 'not long after his arrival in the Chersonese', which took place at least 15 years previously, before the expulsion of Hippias in 510. Herodotus seems to be reckoning not from Miltiades' first arrival sanctioned by Hippias, but from his second, when restored by the Dolonci, though the illogical mention of his (second) return before the historian narrates the flight and exile which preceded this return has unnecessarily obscured the meaning. For a good analysis of the problem, see Burn, *PG*, pp. 218-20.

κατελάμβανε δέ μιν ἐλθόντα ἄλλα τῶν κατεχόντων πρηγμάτων χαλεπώτερα: 'there befell him on his arrival other troubles that were more severe than those currently besetting him'. The plur. of πρᾶγμα often means 'trouble', 'annoyance', esp. in the phrases πρήγματα ἔχειν ('have trouble', as at 7.147.1) and πρήγματα παρέχειν ('cause trouble', as at 1.155.1). By 'the troubles in which he was currently involved', Herodotus means the Scythian invasion, while 'the more severe troubles which befell him' refers to the arrival of the Phoenician fleet, the immediate occasion of his flight. Herodotus here anticipates his account at 41.1 below.

τρίτῳ ἔτεϊ: literally 'in the third year of these events'. Since τούτων must refer to the approach of the Phoenician fleet and Miltiades' subsequent flight in 493 (cf. τρίτῳ ἔτεϊ in the last sentence of section 2 below), the meaning here must be 'in the third year before these events' (i.e. in 495). Doubts about the syntax of this phrase have led some scholars to emend the text to read τρίτῳ...ἔτεϊ <πρὸ> τούτων.

Σκύθαι...οἱ νομάδες: 'the wandering Scythians'. For these nomadic Scythians, see 4.11.1.

ἐρεθισθέντες ὑπὸ...Δαρείου: 'provoked by Darius'. The reference is to Darius' Scythian expedition of 513, but if these irritations were not translated into action for some eighteen years, the Scythians showed remarkable restraint. It is possible that they may have seen Persian preoccupation with the Ionian Revolt as a good opportunity for retaliation, but even so they will have wasted some four years after its outbreak before taking action. It is possible that Herodotus has confused the Scythians with the Thracians, not all of whom will have been mollified by Miltiades' marriage to Hegesipyle. Some scholars, accepting Nepos' statement (*Milt.* 3.6) that Miltiades' flight was precipitated not by the Scythians but by the Persians, who believed the story of his disloyalty at the time the Scythian expedition, are of the opinion that he stayed away from the Chersonese until the outbreak of the Ionian Revolt (see H.T. Wade-Gery, *Essays in Greek History*, Oxford, 1958, p. 158 ff.). However the distinctly muddled account of Nepos has no greater (and probably much less) claim to reliability than the words of Herodotus in the present passage.

40.2 ἀπηλλάχθησαν: aor. pass. of ἀπαλλάσσω, here meaning 'depart'.

κατήγαγον ὀπίσω: 'reinstated him', 'brought him back from exile', the usual meaning of this compound of ἄγω.

τῶν τότε μιν κατεχόντων: 'those events in which they were at that time involved', with reference to his flight of 495.

41.1 Τενέδῳ: a small island off the coast of Asia Minor, some 12 miles south of the entrance to the Hellespont.

ἀπέπλωε ἐς τὰς ᾿Αθήνας: the flight is left unmotivated by the historian. If Wade-Gery is correct in his assumption that Miltiades was absent from the Chersonese from 513 until 499 (see note on 40.1 above), he will have returned in order to bring his principality into the revolt on the rebel side, and fled when its collapse appeared to be imminent. Alternatively he may have feared that Darius would lend some credibility to the slanders spread by Lysagoras of Paros (see 132.1 below) or might be antagonised by his annexation of Lemnos and Imbros (see 136.2, 140.2; Nepos, *Milt.* 1.4), on the grounds that it was undertaken more for the benefit of Athens than of Persia.

τοῦ Μέλανος κόλπου: the Black Gulf was the name given to the sea which separates the western coast of the Chersonese from the adjacent parts of Thrace.

παραμείβετό: 'was passing by', i.e. 'proceeded along'.

41.2 ἐς ῎Ιμβρον: an island some 15 miles west of the southern part of the Chersonese.

41.3 ἀνήγαγον παρὰ βασιλέα: 'they took him up country to the King'.

χάριτα μεγάλην καταθήσεσθαι: 'that they would win great favour'. καταθήσεσθαι is fut. inf. middle of κατατίθημι in the sense of 'lay up a store of', as with κλέος 'glory' at 7.220.4 and 9.78.2.

ὅτι δὴ...ἀπεδέξατο: 'because, as they believed', 'on the grounds that', introducing the reasoning of the Phoenicians, not that of the historian, with a hint that he himself believes it to be false. See Denniston, *GP*, p. 231.

πείθεσθαι κελεύων τοῖσι Σκύθησι: the reference is to 4.136-7, where Miltiades supports the Scythians in their vain attempt to persuade the Greek guardians of the bridge across the Danube to cut off the Persians on the other side of the river.

λύσαντας τὴν σχεδίην: 'having broken the pontoon bridge'. σχεδίη means 'raft' or 'float', here with reference to the bridge of boats constructed by Darius to enable his troops to cross the Danube.

41.4 ἐποίησε κακόν...οὐδὲν Μητίοχον: 'he did Metiochus no harm', an instance of the use of an external and internal acc. with the same verb. The construction is particularly common in phrases denoting doing something to or saying something about a person (ἀγαθά/κακά ποιεῖν/λέγειν). See Goodwin 1073, and cf. ch. 102 below.

τὰ ἐς Πέρσας κεκοσμέαται: 'who are regarded as Persians'. κεκοσμέαται is 3rd. pers. perf. plur. of κοσμέω, where the Attic form would be κεκοσμήνται.

In Ionic, the ending is -αται, before which the long vowel is shortened to ε (Goodwin 778.3 and cf. notes on 13.1 and 44.3). Neut. pl. subjects are often followed, as here, by a plur. rather than a sing. verb when they refer to persons (Goodwin 899.2). κοσμέω, literally 'adorn', 'equip', can also have, in the pass., and followed by the preposition εἰς, the meaning of 'be assigned to', 'be regarded as' (cf. the use of τελέων ἐς at 53.1 and 108.5 below). Metiochus is not known ever to have returned to Athens, but one suspects that Xerxes would have had a use for him had his invasion of 480 been successful.

42.1 κατὰ τὸ ἔτος τοῦτο: 'in this year', i.e. in 493.

ἐς νεῖκος φέρον Ἴωσι: literally 'that contributed to strife with the Ionians', i.e. 'was prejudicial to', 'was hostile to', where φέρω is used intransitively. Cf. its use at 1.10.3 and 4.90.1 in the sense of 'be conducive to', and at ch. 110 below, where it means 'incline'.

Ἀρταφέρνης ὁ Σαρδίων ὕπαρχος: see note on 1.1 above.

σφίσι αὐτοῖσι: see note on 12.2 above, and cf. 138.3.

ἵνα δωσίδικοι εἶεν: 'in order that they might refer these disputes to judgment', a rare adj. found only in this passage in classical Greek. For the opt. in historic sequence in final clauses, see Goodwin 1365. The passage strikingly illustrates the Persian concern for good government.

καὶ μὴ ἀλλήλους φέροιέν τε καὶ ἄγοιεν: 'and in order not to pillage and plunder one another', for the more usual ἄγειν καὶ φέρειν. The phrase is common in Herodotus (e.g. 1.88.3, 3.39.3, 9.31.5 and ch. 90 below), and is parallel to the Latin *ferre et agere*. Of the two verbs, φέρω refers to loot that is portable, ἄγω to animals.

42.2 καὶ τὰς χώρας...μετρήσας: the phrase explains the second benefit that Persian rule brought to Ionia, following on from τάδε μὲν χρήσιμα... ἐγένετο in 42.1.

μετρήσας κατὰ παρασάγγας: 'measuring it out in parasangs'. A *parasang* was a Persian measure of length (modern Persian *farsang*), originally a variable unit indicating the distance a beast of burden could walk in an hour, but adopted by the Greeks as the equivalent of 30 stades or 18,000 Greek feet. On the stade and Greek foot, see note on 36.2.above. As a Greek unit of length, the parasang would be roughly equivalent to $30^{1}/_{3}$ miles.

ἑκάστοισι: 'for each'. Presumably tribute was to be paid not only by Ionians but by all the other peoples who had participated in the revolt.

κατὰ χώρην: 'territory by territory', where κατά is used in a distributive sense. Cf. 5.15.3 κατ' ἐωυτοὺς ἕκαστοι ἐτράποντο','they went to their several houses'.

οἳ...διατελέουσι ἔχοντες...καὶ ἐς ἐμὲ: literally 'which continue to be from that time till my day', i.e. 'which remain unchanged from that time up to my own'. If by 'up till my day' Herodotus means 'up to the time I am writing this sentence', we are faced with the uncomfortable prospect of having to believe that, after joining the Delian League, the Ionians paid tribute to both

120

Persia and Athens. This is a situation that some scholars are willing to accept, despite the absence of any evidence for Ionian complaints about the unfairness of having to pay two suzerains simultaneously. It is possible, even likely, that at the time the Ionians allied with Athens, the Athenians used Artaphernes' work as the basis of their own tribute assessments, with the result that Artaphernes' scheme in a sense still remained in use even in Herodotus' day. Yet while Artaphernes' figures were based purely on agricultural production, it is clear from Plut. *Arist.* 24 that the Athenians took account of both agricultural and other Ionian resources, and some modification of Artaphernes' calculations was inevitable. More probably Herodotus is using 'up to my day' more loosely to mean something like 'up to a time that I myself can recall', as a vague equivalent for 'up to the time the Ionians defected from Persia and joined the Delian League', a continuing process not finally completed until the 460s, when the historian was in his teens.

43.1 ταῦτα μὲν εἰρηναῖα ἦν: 'these were matters conducive to peace'.

ἅμα δὲ τῷ ἔαρι: 'at the beginning of spring', i.e. the spring of 492.

Μαρδόνιος ὁ Γωβρύεω: Mardonius' father Gobryas was an Achaemenid who had helped to put Darius on the throne in 522 and subsequently became one of his most trusted advisors. The two men were doubly related by marriage, Darius having married Gobryas' daughter (7.2.2) and Gobryas being the husband of Darius' sister (7.5.1). See J.M. Balcer, *A Prosopographical Study of the Ancient Persians Royal and Noble c. 550-450 BC*, Lewiston, Queenston and Lampeter, 1993, no. 41.

νεωστὶ γεγαμηκώς: the marriage had in fact taken place at least five years previously, since a Persepolis tablet of 498 refers to Mardonius' wife as daughter of the King.

τοῖσι μὴ ἀποδεκομένοισι: 'to those who do not believe'.

τοῖσι ἑπτά: the seven conspirators who overthrew the Magi and established Darius on the throne (3.70.2-3).

ὡς χρεὸν εἴη δημοκρατέεσθαι Πέρσας: 'that the Persians should have a democratic form of government'. χρεόν is the Ionic form of the Attic χρεών, 'necessity'. For the use of the opt. in historic sequence in indirect statement, see Goodwin 1481. The reference is to the debate on constitutions at 3.80. Both here and in that passage Herodotus insists on the accuracy of his claim, in the face of the incredulity of Greeks who were aware that democracy, or indeed any other from of constitution apart from absolute autocracy, was alien to the Persian tradition. Such criticism was doubtless made during the public recitations at which Herodotus read from his work in progress.

δημοκρατίας κατίστα: 'he proceeded to set up democracies', where κατίστα is 3rd. pers. sing. imperf. of καθίστημι (Attic καθίστη). Herodotus here seems to assume that what was acceptable to Greeks must be no less so to Persians, and fails to consider that the democracies may have been instituted to dispel some of the odium incurred under the previous system of rule by

Persian-backed tyrannies.

43.4 χρῆμα πολλὸν νεῶν: 'a large number of ships'. χρῆμα, literally 'thing', is frequently used by Herodotus to indicate anything unusually large or extraordinary, as at 1.36.1, ὑὸς χρῆμα μέγα, literally 'a huge thing of a boar', and, more particularly, to indicate a large number or quantity (e.g. πολλὸν χρῆμα τῶν τέκνων, 3.109.3; πολλὸν χρῆμα χρυσοῦ, 3.130.5; χρῆμα πολλὸν ἀρδίων,'a large number of arrowheads', 4.81.6).

ἐπί τε Ἐρέτριαν καὶ Ἀθήνας: the ostensible objectives of the expedition, since these cities were the ones which had actively participated in the Ionian Revolt (5.99).

44.1 πρόσχημα: 'the ostensible objective'. πρόσχημα is often used, as here and at 7.157.1, of an alleged reason or pretext as opposed to the true or underlying one. Cf. the use of πρόφασις at 94.1 below. The phrase πρόσχημα τοῦ λόγου occurs at 4.167.3 and at ch. 133.1 below.

ὅσας ἂν πλείστας δύναιντο καταστρέφεσθαι: 'to subdue as many as they could', where the superl. adj. forming the antecedent is incorporated into the relative clause (see Goodwin 1037).

τοῦτο μὲν...τοῦτο δὲ: 'on the one hand...on the other', 'in the first place... in the second place', 'not only...but also', 'both...and'. Cf. 27.1 above and 69.3, 101.3 and 114 below.

οὐδὲ χεῖρας ἀνταειραμένους: 'who did not even lift a hand against them'. For this phrase, cf. 3.144.1.

Μακεδόνας: the Macedonians, under their current king Amyntas I, had already accepted Persian suzerainty in 512, at the time of Megabazus' conquest of Thrace (5.17.1, 7.108.1), but their submission was purely formal, and no Persian army had entered the country at the time.

πρὸς τοῖσι ὑπάρχουσι: 'in addition to those who already existed'. ὑπάρχω, 'begin', 'be from the beginning', not infrequently serves as a synonym for the verb 'be'.

τὰ...ἐντὸς Μακεδόνων ἔθνεα: 'the tribes on this side of Macedonia', i.e. 'to the east of Macedonia', where Herodotus is writing from the viewpoint of the Persians, not of the Greeks.

44.2 διαβαλόντες: aor. part. of διαβάλλω, used intransitively with the meaning of 'cross over'.

πέρην: Ionic form of πέραν, 'across', which may be used adverbially, as here, or as a preposition with the gen.

ὑπὸ τὴν ἤπειρον: 'keeping close to the mainland', i.e. 'along the coastline', 'hugging the coast of the mainland'.

Ἀκάνθου: a city on the east coast of Chalcidice, guarding the approach to Acte, the most easterly of the three peninsulas which form its southern part.

τὸν Ἄθων περιέβαλλον: 'they attempted to round Athos', a conative imperf. (see note on 5.1 above and Goodwin 1255). Athos is properly the mountain at the southern tip of Acte, but is also used to denote the whole peninsula. A good description is given at 7.22.

σφι περιπλώουσι: literally 'to them as they were sailing round', aor. part. of περιπλέω.

ἄπορος: regularly used to denote anything difficult or impossible to handle or deal with.

κάρτα τρηχέως περίεσπε: 'handled them very roughly', aor. part. of περιέπω, 'treat'.

ἐκβάλλων πρὸς τὸν ῎Αθων: 'dashing them ashore on Athos'.

44.3 κατὰ τριηκοσίας...τὰς διαφθαρείσας: 'those destroyed amounted to some three hundred'. διαφθαρείσας is acc. pl. fem. aor. part. of διαφθείρω. κατά with the acc. is regularly used by Herodotus to indicate an approximate number, 'about', 'around' (cf. 79.1 and 117.1 below), where Attic prefers περί, ὡς, εἰς or μάλιστα.

ὑπὲρ δὲ δύο μυριάδας ἀνθρώπων: 'more than 20,000 men', with διαφθαρῆναι to be understood from διαφθαρείσας. It was to avoid a similar disaster that Xerxes had a canal cut through Athos as a preliminary to his invasion of 480 (see 7.22-4).

ὥστε...θηριωδεστάτης ἐούσης τῆς θαλάσσης: 'for inasmuch as the sea is full of monsters', a causal use of the participle in a situation where Attic favours ἅτε, οἷον or οἷα (Goodwin 1575). For this use of ὥστε, cf. 52.3, 94.1 and 136.2 below.

ὑπὸ τῶν θηρίων: since θηρίον normally refers to mammals as opposed to birds and fish, it is possible that Herodotus is thinking of the mauling of the men washed ashore by wild beasts. However the use of the adj. θηριώδης of sea creatures earlier in the sentence makes it more likely that he has in mind sea-monsters of some sort. Though the Greek for any kind of marine monster is usually κῆτος, there are examples of the application of θηρίον to sea creatures such as eels and fish (Antiphanes, Frag. 147.7; Aristotle, *Historia Animalium* 598B1). David Greene and Robin Waterfield both translate the word as 'shark', for which the usual word is καρχαρίας (or ῥίνη) perhaps because these were highly regarded as a source of food, and in all likelihood abundant, in the city of Torone and the adjacent peninsula of Sithonia (Athenaeus 163D, 310C).

νέειν οὐκ ἠπιστέατο: 'they didn't know how to swim', where ἠπιστέατο is 3rd. pers. plur. imperf. of ἐπίσταμαι (Attic ἐπίσταντο), with -ατο for Attic -ντο and epsilon in place of the preceding alpha (cf. ἐδυνέατο for Attic ἐδύναντο at 4.110.1.

κατὰ τοῦτο: 'for this reason'.

45.1 Βρύγοι: a tribe who lived originally in Macedonia and whose name is cognate with that of the Phrygians, who crossed from Europe to Asia Minor and settled there c.800 (7.73). Some of the Brygi inhabited in the classical period an area in Illyria near the border with Epirus (Strabo 7.7.8), but the

Brygi who attacked Mardonius in 492 are clearly a distinct branch of this people, who inhabited an area in the vicinity of Chalcidice adjacent to the Pierians (7.185.2), who at 7.112 are themselves located east of the Strymon between Mt. Pangaeum and the Aegean.

ἀπανέστη: 'he departed', intrans. second aor. of ἀπανίστημι, 'cause to depart'.

πρὶν ἤ σφεας ὑποχειρίους ἐποιήσατο: 'before reducing them to subjection', 'until he conquered them'. The temporal conjunction πρίν is normally followed by the inf. in affirmative sentences, but when, as here, the verb in the principal clause is negative, πρίν takes a finite mood of the verb (Goodwin 1469-71). In Herodotus, πρὶν ἤ and πρότερον ἤ are construed in exactly the same way, with no change of meaning (see 22.1 above and Goodwin 1474).

45.2 ἅτε...προσπταίσας: 'inasmuch as he had suffered a reverse'. See note on 44.3 above.

αἰσχρῶς ἀγωνισάμενος: 'having fought ignominiously', something of an exaggeration in that Mardonius can hardly be blamed for the storm. However, if he were really aiming at the subjugation of Athens and Eretria in the course of this expedition, as we are told at 43.4 above, Herodotus' comment is understandable in the light of his failure to do so.

ἀπηλλάχθη: 'departed', aor. pass. of ἀπαλλάσσω, 'remove'.

46.1 δευτέρῳ δὲ ἔτεϊ τούτων: literally 'in the second year of these things', i.e.' in the following year' (491).

διαβληθέντας...ὡς ἀπόστασιν μηχανῶατο: 'slandered on the grounds that they were plotting a revolt' μηχανῶατο is the Ionic form of the 3rd. pers. plur. opt. of μηχανάομαι, with the expected -ατο where Attic has -ντο. The mood here is the opt. of indirect speech, since the charge of plotting was one alleged by Thasos' enemies, not stated as an unquestioned fact by the historian (in which case the mood would have been ind.); see Goodwin 1506.

ὑπὸ τῶν ἀστυγειτόνων: the identity of these neighbours can only be a matter for conjecture. The context and the geography of the area suggests that Abdera, her main rival for Thracian trade, was one of the culprits, but there are other possibilities, such as the people of the colony of Neapolis, certainly hostile to their mother city in 409-7 (ML 89; Fornara 156).

Ἄβδηρα: a Greek city on the Aegean coast, in a fertile district east of the Nestus, founded originally from Clazomenae and resettled from Teos (1.168; Strabo 14.1.30).

46.2 οἷα ὑπὸ Ἱστιαίου...πολιορκηθέντες: on the syntax, see note on 44.3 above. Histiaeus' siege of Thasos is narrated in ch. 28 above.

προσόδων ἐουσέων μεγάλων: apart from the revenues derived from the mines described below, Thasos' sources of wealth were its timber, wine and marble industries.

ναυπηγεύμενοι: 'having ships constructed'. The act. of this verb is used of the activities of shipwrights, the middle of those who commission them (Goodwin 1242.2).

περιβαλλόμενοι: 'surrounding themselves with'.

ἐκ τε τῆς ἠπείρου: Thasos had a *peraea* on the adjacent mainland, the coastal strip between Mt. Symbolon and the Aegean, stretching roughly from the Strymon to the Nestus, which included the cities of Galepsus, Oisyme, Antisara, Neapolis, Pistyrus and Stryme. Possession of these places gave Thasos access to the interior and in particular to the silver and gold of Mt. Pangaeum.

ἡ πρόσοδος: for a general discussion of the mineral resources of Thasos in antiquity, see M.I. Finley, *Trade and Politics in the Ancient World*, Aix-en-Provence, 1965, pp. 28-32; R. Osborne, *Classical Landscape with Figures: the Ancient Greek City and its Countryside*, London, 1987, pp. 76 and 79; L. Nixon and S. Price, in O. Murray and S. Price (eds), *The Greek City from Homer to Aristotle*, Oxford, 1990, pp. 152-3.

ἀπὸ τῶν μετάλλων: the mines on Thasos were situated for the most part in the eastern coastal area, with some smaller mining districts opened up later in the western part of the island. The principal metal mined was silver, with smaller amounts of gold, copper and lead.

46.3 Σκαπτησύλης: a small settlement on an unidentified site opposite the island of Thasos which, if a Greek name in origin, would mean 'Dug-out Forest', but it may be just the hellenised version of a Thracian name.

τὸ ἐπίπαν: 'in general', 'for the most part', 'as a general rule'.

συχνὰ δὲ οὕτω, ὥστε...προσήϊε: 'but so great that there came in', a consecutive clause with the indic., emphasising the attainment of the result rather than the general tendency (Goodwin 1450).

Θασίοισι ἐοῦσι καρπῶν ἀτελέσι: 'those of the Thasians who were exempt from paying tax on their agricultural produce'. The Thasian mines were state-controlled and produced revenue for the city sufficient to free the Thasians from the usual tax burdens that were necessary to defray the costs of government. In the 5th century Thasos was still sufficiently prosperous to afford (along with Aegina) the highest tribute assessment (30 tal. per year) imposed on any member of the Delian League.

ἔτεος ἑκάστου: 'every year', a gen. of time (Goodwin 1136).

47.1 οἱ μετὰ Θάσου κτίσαντες τὴν νῆσον: 'those who settled in the island along with Thasus'. Greek tradition has the Phoenicians establish settlements in various parts of the northern Aegean, including the Thracian mainland (Hegesippus, *FGH* 391J, Frag. 3), Pangaeum (Clem. Alex., *Strom.* 1.75.8), the isthmus of Pallene (Conon, *FGH* 26J, Frag. 1), Euboea (Strabo 10.1.8), Samothrace and Rhodes (Diod. 5.58), as well as in Thasos. Greek mythology connects these settlements, as well as the alleged colonies on Thera (4.147.4), Melos (Callimachus Frag. 582; Steph. Byz. s.v. Melos) and Anaphe (Steph. Byz. s.v. Anaphe), with Phoenician Cadmus as he wandered about the area in search of his sister Europa who had been abducted by Zeus. Like Membliaros the founder of Anaphe and Mimallis who founded Melos, the eponymous Thasus was represented as a son of Agenor and brother of Cadmus (Euripides, *Phrixus*, Frag. 819 Nauck). For Herodotus, evidence for the Phoenician connection was strengthened by the existence in Tyre of a temple of Heracles Thasius (2.44.3). Archaeological evidence for a series of Phoenician settlements throughout the north Aegean is non-existent, and the first undoubtedly historical colony on Thasos was that established by the Parians at the end of the 8th or early 7th century.

Θάσου τούτου τοῦ Φοίνικος: the Greek is ambiguous and can mean either 'Thasus the Phoenician' or 'Thasus son of Phoenix'. Since Euripides makes Thasus the brother, not the son of Phoenix, the former translation is more likely to be correct.

τὸ οὔνομα ἔσχε: 'it acquired its name', an ingressive aor. (see note on 25.2 above. Earlier names of Thasos are said to have been Aeria (Steph. Byz. s.v. Thasos) and Odonis (Hesychius).

ἀντίον...Σαμοθρηΐκης: i.e. in the eastern coastal region. The island of Samothrace lies some 50 miles to the south east of Thasos.

47.2 ἀνεστραμμένον ἐν τῇ ζητήσι: 'overturned in the course of the search' (i.e. for precious metals). ἀναστραμμένον is perf. part. pass. of ἀναστρέφω.

48.1 ἀπεπειρᾶτο...τῶν Ἑλλήνων, ὅ τι ἐν νόῳ ἔχοιεν: literally 'made trial of what the Greeks had in their minds', i.e. 'attempted to test Greek intentions'. For the use of the opt. in indirect questions, see Goodwin 1481.

48.2 διέπεμπε...κήρυκας ἄλλους ἄλλῃ: 'he proceeded to send heralds in different directions, some in one direction, others in another'. ἄλλος and its adverbial derivatives such as ἄλλῃ, ἄλλοθι, ἄλλοσε, ἄλλοθεν, ἄλλοτε, are frequently used in pairs to indicate division, as in the phrase ἄλλοι ἄλλα λέγουσι, 'one person says one thing, another something else', 'different people say different things', 'there are as many sayings as there are speakers'. Here the sense of difference is reinforced by the δι- prefix of the verb διέπεμπε and the use of ἄλλους ἄλλῃ is somewhat tautological.

δασμοφόρους πόλιας τὰς παραθαλασσίους: 'the tribute paying cities along the sea coast', i.e. the cities on the Aegean seaboard of Asia Minor. δασμός, (literally 'division', from δατέομαι, 'divide') acquires the meaning 'tribute', and is used as a synonym of the more common φόρος.

49.1 πολλοὶ μὲν ἠπειρωτέων: including presumably those who subsequently supported Xerxes, such as the Macedonians, Thessalians and Boeotians.

ἔδοσαν τὰ προΐσχετο αἰτέων: 'they gave what he put forward as a demand'.

αἰτήσοντες: 'to make the demand', fut. part. of purpose (see note on ch. 7 above).

πάντες νησιῶται: something of an exaggeration, since Naxos was still independent (see ch. 95 below), as were Carystus and Eretria in Euboea (see chs 98 and 99).

49.2 οἵ τε δὴ ἄλλοι νησιῶται διδοῦσι γῆν τε καὶ ὕδωρ...καὶ δὴ καὶ Αἰγινῆται: 'other islands gave earth and water, and the Aeginetans in particular', 'among the islanders who gave earth and water were the Aeginetans'. See notes on 21.2 above, and cf. 73.2 and 137.4 below.

Ἀθηναῖοι ἐπεκέατο: 'the Athenians attacked them'. ἐπεκέατο is the Ionic equivalent of the Attic ἐπεκεῖντο; see note on 44.3 above.

ἐπὶ σφίσι ἔχοντας: literally 'being against them', i.e. 'being hostile to them', 'being ill-disposed towards them', where ἔχω is used intransitively as a virtual synonym of the verb 'to be' with a prepositional phrase (ἐπὶ σφίσι) that is equivalent to an adverb such as κακῶς, ἐναντίως or δυσμενῶς which would more commonly be found in this construction (see note on 17.1 above and cf. 139.3 below). σφίσι is the dat. plur. of the 3rd. pers. reflexive pron., used indirectly as in Attic, with reference to the subject of the principal verb (Goodwin 987). Athens and Aegina had been at war ever since Aeginetan involvement in Athens' war with the Boeotians which followed Cleomenes' triple invasion of Attica c.506 (see Book 5. 81.3).

φοιτέοντές...ἐς τὴν Σπάρτην: since Sparta could hardly have been responsible for Aeginetan medism, the Athenian action makes sense only if they were seeking Sparta's intervention in her capacity as hegemon of the Peloponnesian League. On the question of Aeginetan membership of the League, opinion is divided. See D.M. Leahy, 'Aegina and the Peloponnesian League', *CP* 49, 1954, pp. 232-43; D.M. MacDowell, 'Aegina and the Delian League', *JHS* 80, 1960, pp. 118-21; G.E.M. de Ste-Croix, *The Origins of the Peloponnesian War*, London, 1972, pp. 333-5.

κατηγόρεον...τὰ πεποιήκοιεν: 'they charged them with what they had done', where the opt. of indirect speech is used in place of the indic. to indicate that the Athenian accusation is subjective rather than objective, or in other words, that the charge, whether true or false, is one alleged by the Athenians, not one accepted as valid by the historian (see Goodwin 1502.4).

50.1 Κλεομένης: Agiad king of Sparta from c.520 until 490/89, whose earlier career is given in Book 5, chs 39-54, 64-76 and 90.

διέβη ἐς Αἴγιναν: in view of his earlier treatment at the hands of the Athenians, Cleomenes can hardly have intervened merely to please Athens. Alarm at the growth of medism in the Peloponnese and adjacent territories, which had already induced him to take action against Argos in 494 (see ch. 76-83 below), is a far more credible motive.

50.2 ἐπειρᾶτο συλλαμβάνων: 'he attempted to arrest'. For the use of the part. with πειράομαι, see note on 5.2 above.

ἀντίξοοι: 'opponents'. See note on ch. 7 above.

ἐν δὲ: 'and included among them', where ἐν is used adverbially. Cf. 11.1 above and 70.3 and 86.4 below.

ὃς οὐκ ἔφη αὐτὸν οὐδένα ἄξειν χαίροντα: 'who said that he would not get away with taking anybody away'. For οὐ φημί, 'I say that...not', see note on 1.1 above, and cf. 52.4 and 99.2 below. A compound negative (such as οὐδένα) following a simple negative has the effect, contrary to English usage, of strengthening the neg. (Goodwin 1619). The part. χαίρων (literally 'rejoicing') is often found idiomatically in the sense of 'with impunity', 'scot free'. Cf. the similar use of κλαίων, literally 'weeping', to mean 'to one's sorrow' (Goodwin 1564).

ἄνευ...Σπαρτιητέων τοῦ κοινοῦ: 'without the authorisation of the Spartan government'. For the use of κοινόν, see note on 14.3 above. Crius' argument will probably have been that Cleomenes' intervention in the internal affairs of an ally was a foreign policy change and as such required the approval of the Spartan assembly.

ἀναγνωσθέντα χρήμασι: 'induced by money', 'bribed'. ἀναγιγνώσκω in Attic usually means 'read', and the meaning 'persuade', is peculiarly Ionic. Cf. ch. 75.3 and 83.2 below, and, in Attic, Antiphon 2.2.7. The charge is likely to have gained some degree of plausibility in the light of earlier incidents from Cleomenes' career: in 499, the intervention of his young daughter Gorgo was needed to avert his corruption at the hands of Aristagoras (5.51.2-3), and in 494, he was accused of accepting bribes from the Argives (see ch. 82.1 below).

ἅμα...ἄν μιν τῷ ἑτέρῳ βασιλέϊ: 'he would have come together with the other king to arrest him'. The pres. inf. with ἄν is used in indirect speech to represent what in direct speech would have been ἄν with the imperf. indicating unreality in present time ('you would have come and would now be doing the arresting'). See Goodwin 1397. Crius' claim is the first appearance in Spartan history of the argument that the two kings, when acting in concert, had absolute power in the state, or at least had greater constitutional power than one king acting alone. The claim resurfaces in chs 73 and 86 below, and, at a later date, in 243, when Agis IV and Cleombrotus II, acting as a team, revived it in justification of their defiance of the ephors (Plut. *Agis* 12.1), and yet again in 228, when Cleomenes III sought the restoration of his Eurypontid opposite number Archidamus V, in order to strengthen him in his imminent conflict with the ephors (Plut. *Cleom.* 5.2). How valid the claim really was is uncertain, and it seems for the most part to be little more than a product of royal propaganda to be dragged out of the cupboard whenever the ephorate and the dyarchy came into conflict.

50.3 Δημαρήτου: Cleomenes' royal colleague, Eurypontid king from c.515 until 491.

εἴρετο τὸν Κρῖον ὅ τι οἱ εἴη τὸ οὔνομα: 'he asked Crius what his name was', where the opt. εἴη represents the pres. ind. in an indirect question in historic sequence (Goodwin 1481).

οἱ τὸ ἐὸν ἔφρασε: 'he told him what it really was', 'he told him the exact truth'. Since the literal meaning of κριός is 'ram', Cleomenes is enabled to make a punning reference to this in his retort. For a similar pun on the name Crius, see Simonides Frag. 507 (in D. Campbell, *Greek Lyric* Vol. 3, Loeb Classical Library, Cambridge Mass. and London, 1991, p. 371).

καταχαλκοῦ...τὰ κέρεα: 'cover your horns with bronze'. κέρας in Attic has two stems, κερατ- and κερα- (Ionic κερε-): in the meaning 'horn', the plur. is more commonly κέρατα, in the sense of 'wing of an army', it is κέρα. In Herodotus, the stem is regulaly κερε-.

ὡς συνοισόμενος μεγάλῳ κακῷ: 'since you are about to meet with a great misfortune'. Cleomenes' departure from Aegina with his objective unfulfilled does not necessarily imply his acceptance of the validity of Crius' argument: lack of the means to counter it at a time when no opposition was expected gave him little option. His bitter parting shot and his intolerance of opposition would have ensured that he would sooner or later be back, and back with a vengeance.

51 διέβαλλε: a durative or conative imperf. See notes on 2.1 and 5.1 above.

οἰκίης...τῆς ὑποδεεστέρης: 'of the inferior house'. Though in fact the powers of the two houses were equal, the Agiad family did enjoy a greater measure of respect than the Eurypontids. The Spartans themselves accounted for this by tracing the Agiad family to Eurysthenes, the elder of the Heraclid twin brothers who acquired the sovereignty of Laconia at the time of the Dorian conquest of the Peloponnese, while the Eurypontids were believed to descend from Procles, the younger twin (4.147; Pausanias 3.1.6-7). Modern scholarship, while rejecting the story of the twins, is on the whole willing to accept the superiority of the Agiad pedigree, on the ground that, while the names of the early Agiad kings from the eponymous Agis I downwards look authentic, the same cannot be said for the early part of the Eurypontid pedigree which includes bogus names such as Sous, Prytanis and Eunomus, which were probably added to the authentic list in order to obtain a family tree that was equal in length to that of the Agiads. It is generally accepted that the authentic Eurypontid pedigree was shorter than that of the Agiads, and that the first Eurypontid king was created to share power with an Agiad whose family was already well established as rulers of Sparta. Because of Cleomenes' remarks to the priestess of Athena at Athens that he was not a Dorian but an Achaean (5.72.3), some scholars are of the opinion that the Agiads were descended from the old Mycenaean kings of Laconia, but were subsequently obliged to share power with the rulers of a tribe of later arrivals. However the extreme weakness and poverty of the Mycenaean remnant in Laconia at the time of the Dorian conquest scarcely suggests a group able to treat with the Dorians on anything like equal terms, still less to secure recognition for its ruling family. In any case Cleomenes may have merely been upholding the view that the Heraclids were Achaeans rather than Dorians, in the sense that they merely led the Dorians into the Peloponnese without themselves being of Dorian blood. It is also possible that he was referring to his Achaean descent through his mother, a relative of the ephor Chilon and of probable pre-Dorian descent (5.41.3; Paus. 3.3.9; G.L. Huxley, *Early Sparta*, London, 1962, pp. 68-71). It is much more likely that the

Eurypontid kings were created either to act as a check on the existing Agiads or at the time when the village of Mesoa, with which the Eurypontids had close links (Paus. 3.12.8) was merged with Pitana, the ancestral village of the Agiads (Paus. 3.14.2).

κατ' ἄλλο μὲν οὐδὲν ὑποδεεστέρης: 'in other respects in no way inferior'. For the acc. of respect, see Goodwin 1058.

ἀπὸ γὰρ τοῦ αὐτοῦ γεγόνασι: 'they were born of the same ancestry'. The reference is to Aristodemus, the father of Eurysthenes and Procles, to Aristodemus' great-great-grandfather Heracles (see ch. 52.1 below), and, indirectly, to Heracles' father Zeus.

52.1 ὁμολογέοντες οὐδενὶ ποιητῇ: 'agreeing with no poet'. The identity of the poet who wrote on the return of the Heracleidae is unknown. Some mention of it seems to have been made in the Hesiodic Eoiae (Frag. 233), and in the Spartan poet Cinaethon (Schol. on Apollonius Rhod. 1.1356-7), but details are lacking.

λέγουσι αὐτὸν Ἀριστόδημον: Herodotus here cites the Spartan tradition, as contrasted with the story as told by the unnamed poets. It seems to be the version of the poets that is adopted by Apollodorus (2.8.2) and Pausanias (3.1.6), according to whom Aristodemus died at Delphi or Naupactus before the expedition set out, either struck by lightning or shot down by the arrows of Apollo in anger at his consultation of Heracles in preference to the Delphic oracle, or, alternatively, killed by Medon and Strophius, the sons of Pylades and Electra, who wished to help their cousin Tisamenus, the target of the projected expedition.

Ὕλλου: son of Heracles and Deianeira, who had led an earlier unsuccessful expedition aimed at the conquest of the Peloponnese.

ἐκτέαται: Ionic 3rd. pers. perf. of κτάομαι. See note on κεκοσαμέαται at 41.4 above.

52.2 Ἀργείην: despite her name, this lady was of Theban origin, and was the sister of Theras, the eponymous founder of the colony on the island of Thera (4.147.1).

Πολυνείκεος: son of Oedipus, killed in the course of an attempt to wrest the Theban throne from his brother Eteocles with the backing of his father-in-law Adrastus king of Argos in the expedition of the 'Seven Against Thebes'.

νούσῳ τελευτᾶν: 'died of disease', i.e. 'died a natural death' as opposed to death by violence or in battle.

52.3 κατὰ νόμον: 'according to law' or 'according to custom'.

ὥστε καὶ ὁμοίων καὶ ἴσων ἐόντων: 'inasmuch as they were alike and equal'. For causal ὥστε, see note on 44.3 above and cf. 94.1 and 136.2 below.

ἢ καὶ πρὸ τούτου: 'or even before this', i.e. 'even before they tried to find out for themselves'.

52.4 τὴν δὲ οὐδὲ αὐτὴν φάναι διαγινώσκειν: 'and she said that even she could not tell them apart'. τὴν δέ, 'and she', is a relic of the original use of what became the article as a pers. pronoun, found also in Attic with δέ in situations where the subject changes at the beginning of a sentence (Goodwin 983). For οὐδὲ...φάναι, 'deny', 'say that...not', see note on 1.1 above, and cf. 50.2, 61.4, 99.2.

εἰδυῖαν...καὶ τὸ κάρτα: 'though she knew it perfectly well'. εἰδυῖα is fem. part. of οἶδα, here used in a concessive sense.

βουλομένην...εἴ κως ἀμφότεροι γενοίατο βασιλέες: 'since she wished, if it were at all possible, that both should become kings'. For γενοίατο, see note on 13.1 above.

ἐάν πως with the subj. (in primary sequence) and εἴ πως with the opt. (in historic) are used to mean 'if perchance', 'in the hope that', like Latin si *forte* with the subj. Herodotus uses the construction after a verb of wishing both here and in Book 9.14.

ὅ τι χρήσωνται τῷ πρήγματι: 'how they were to handle the matter'.
52.5 τιμᾶν δὲ μᾶλλον τὸν γεραίτερον: 'but to pay more honour to the elder', with a pun on the two meanings of γεραίτερος ('elder' and 'more honourable'). This oracle appears as no. 157 in PW and L160 in Fontenrose *DO*.

τοῖσι...Λακεδαιμονίοισι ἀπορέουσι...ὑποθέσθαι ἄνδρα Μεσσήνιον: 'a Messenian man made the suggestion to the Spartans in their perplexity'. ὑποθέσθαι is the aor. inf. middle of ὑποτίθημι, 'suggest'.

τῷ οὔνομα εἶναι Πανίτην: 'whose name was Panites'. εἶναι here replaces the expected indic. by way of assimilation to the inf. ὑποθέσθαι. Relative and temporal clauses dependent on an inf. of indirect speech may themselves have a verb in the inf. by way of assimilation to the mood of the verb in the clause on which they depend (Goodwin 1524). Other examples of such assimilation in Herodotus may be found at 1.94.3, 5.84.1, 8.111.3, 8.118.4 and at 137.2 below.
52.6 τὴν γειναμένην: 'the mother'. ἐγεινάμην is a causative aor. from the verb γίνομαι (Attic γίγνομαι) meaning 'I give birth to', which is mainly Ionic and poetic. Attic prefers to use γεννάω in this sense.

ἤν...φαίνηται αἰεὶ ποιεῦσα: 'if she clearly always does the same', the usual meaning of φαίνομαι with the part. With the inf., the meaning is 'seem to', 'appear to' (see Goodwin 1592).

ἤν δὲ πλανᾶται: literally 'if she wanders', used of random or irregular action, and so equivalent to 'if she varies the order'.

ἐναλλάξ: an adv. meaning 'alternately', 'now in one way, now in another'.

τραπέσθαι: 2nd. aor. middle of τρέπω, 'turn', with intrans. meaning ('turn to', have recourse to'), as opposed to the trans. 1st. aorists ἔτρεψα and ἐτρεψάμην.
52.7 πρὸς τῆς γειναμένης: 'by its mother', 'at the hands of its mother'. For πρός with the gen. in this sense, see note on 9.1 above.

ἐν τῷ δημοσίῳ: 'at public expense'. A less probable translation would be 'in a public building', with an anachronistic reference to a *syssition* or mess hall, in which Spartan boys of the classical period lived and were educated, but if so, Herodotus appears unaware that the king's eldest son was exempted from such training (Plut. *Agesilaus* 1.2).

52.8 τοὺς ἀπὸ τούτων...ὡσαύτως διατελέειν: 'those descended from them continued in the same way'. Though several instances of such animosity are known later than the time of Herodotus (Agis II and Pausanias; Pausanias and Agesilaus; Leonidas II and Agis IV), the clash between Cleomenes I and Demaratus is the only example known earlier than or contemporary with Herodotus' work.

53.1 ταῦτα...τάδε: 'what precedes', 'what I have indicated'...'what follows', 'the following'.

κατὰ τὰ λεγόμενα ὑπ' Ἑλλήνων: 'in accordance with what is said by the Greeks in general', as opposed to a purely Spartan tradition.

ἐς Ἕλληνας οὗτοι ἐτέλεον: 'these were reckoned as Greeks'. τελέω, in the sense of 'pay taxes', is used with the prep. εἰς to mean literally 'be enrolled as a taxpayer in a particular group', and metaphorically 'be reckoned as belonging to', 'be classified as'. Cf. ἐς Βοιωτοὺς τελέειν at ch. 108.5 below.

μέχρι Περσέος: 'going back as far as Perseus'. Perseus was the father of Alcaeus father of Amphitryon, the reputed father of Heracles, as well as of Electryon, father of Heracles' mother Alcmene. The genealogy is as follows:

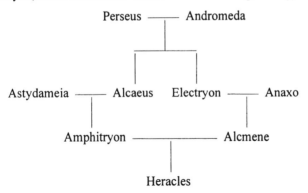

53.2 ἀνέκαθεν: an adv. meaning literally 'from above', whether of place or of time, used here in the sense of 'further up the family tree'.

ὀρθῷ λόγῳ χρεομένῳ: 'making use of true reasoning'.

εἴρηταί μοι: 'has been said by me'. The dat. of the agent (for ὑπό μου) is found in Herodotus, as in Attic, regularly with the verbal adj., and not uncommonly with the perf. and pluperf. pass. (Goodwin 1186-8). Cf. 82.2, 123.2 and 130.2 below.

Δανάης τῆς Ἀκρισίου: the mother of Perseus, imprisoned by her father to ensure that she would never give birth to the son destined to slay his grandfather, but impregnated by Zeus in the form of a shower of gold.

φαινοίατο: Ionic form of the Attic φαινοίντο (see note on ὑπερβαλοίατο at 1.3 above).

Αἰγύπτιοι ἰθαγενέες: 'genuine Egyptians'. The word is rare. Herodotus seems to have in mind its use at *Odyssey* 14.203, where the disguised Odysseus tells the swineherd Eumaeus that, though born to a concubine, he was treated as the equal of his legitimate brothers. Herodotus also uses the word at 2.17.6 of the mouths of the Nile that were natural, as opposed to the artificial constructions dug out by human labour. In mythology Danae's father Acrisius was a descendant of Io, the mother by Zeus of Epaphus, who was born in Egypt and married Memphis, daughter of the Nile God. Their progeny resided in Egypt until the flight to Greece of Danaus with his fifty daughters in an attempt to save them from marriage to their fifty cousins, the sons of Danaus' brother Aegyptus. The family tree is as follows:

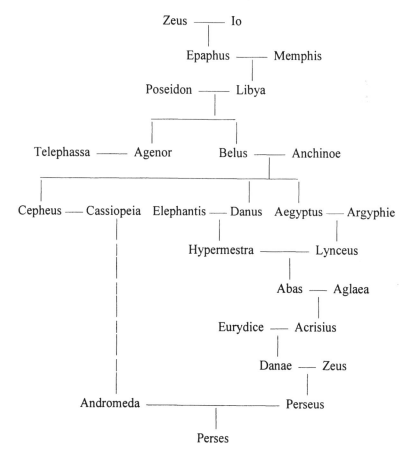

Herodotus' attribution of Egyptian descent to Heracles aroused the ire of Plutarch, who uses the present passage as proof of the historian's alleged philobarbarism (*Moralia* 857F), but since Herodotus accepts Io's Greek descent at 1.1.4, her descendants too must surely have been conceived by him as partially Greek, and the use of the word may well be ironic.

54 ἐὼν Ἀσσύριος ἐγένετο ῞Ελλην: 'though he was a native of Assyria, he became a Greek'. This alleged Persian version inverts the Greek myth, according to which Perseus was an ethnic Greek who developed an Assyrian link by virtue of his marriage to Andromeda daughter of king Cepheus. Though usually located in Ethiopia (Euripides, *Andromeda*; Eratosthenes, *Catasterismi* 15; Apollodorus 2.4.3), Cepheus is associated in some versions of the myth with territories in Asia. The common confusion between Syria and Assyria in ancient writers (cf. Hdt.7.63) makes it unclear whether Cepheus' ties are with the former or with the latter: the Syrian connection makes him king of Joppa in Palestine (Strabo 11.2.35, 16.2.28; Josephus, *Bell. Jud.* 3.9.3; Pliny *NH* 5.14.69; 5.34.128) while his uncle Agenor ruled Tyre and Sidon, and Pliny (*NH* 6.35.182) is able to make use of the Andromeda story as proof that Ethiopian kings once ruled in Palestine. Hellanicus on the other hand (Frag. 59J) has Cepheus ruling the Cephenes in Babylonia, while Herodous himself connects Cepheus with Persia (7.61.3, cf. 7.150.2). The first of the two Herodotean passages attests his familiarity with the tradition recorded by Hellanicus and ascribes Persian assumption of their current name to the desire to honour Perseus' son Perses. According to the scholiast on Dionysius Periegetes 1053, Cepheus was expelled from his kingdom in Mesopotamia by the Chaldaeans, and sought refuge with his grandson Perses among the Artaeans, while Arrian (*Bithynica* Frag. 53, Roos) repeats the tradition that the Persians were formerly known as the Cephians at the time when Babylon served as their capital city. All these passages provide some evidence of an Assyrian connection for Cepheus' descendants.

τοὺς...Ἀκρισίου γε πατέρας: see note on 53.2 above.

55 ταῦτα...περὶ τούτων εἰρήσθω: 'let this be sufficient on the topic', 'enough said on this subject'. εἰρήσθω is 3rd. pers. perf. imper. pass. of λέγω, meaning literally 'let it have been said', used to express a command that is intended to be valid once and for all (Goodwin 1274).

ὅ τι δὲ ἐόντες Αἰγύπτιοι καὶ ὅ τι ἀποδεξάμενοι ἔλαβον τὰς Δωριέων βασιληΐας: 'how it came about that though they were Egyptians and in return for what services they obtained the kingship of the Dorians'. ἀποδεξάμενοι is aor. part. middle of ἀποδείκνυμι, meaning 'perform' or 'display'. 'Kingship of the Dorians' refers not just to the two Spartan royal families but to the Temenid rulers of Argos and to the Cresphontids of Messenia, who were all believed to have come to power following the Dorian conquest of the Peloponnese.

ἄλλοισι...εἴρηται: 'it has been told by others', another dat. of the agent (see note on 53.2 above). Herodotus omits details of the actual conquest of the Peloponnese on the grounds that he has nothing to add to existing accounts. He will have had in mind both epic poems (for pseudo-Hesiod and Cinaethon, see note on 52.1 above) and prose narratives (Pherecydes the genealogist and the earlier logographers such as Hecataeus or Charon of Lampsacus). However he does make incidental allusions to these events at 9.26.2-4 and 9.27.2-3.

56.1 γέρεά...τάδε: Herodotus' list of the privileges of Spartan kings, which is the most complete that we possess, goes back to a reliable Spartan source. He divides his list into religious, military and civil, with the religious privileges split between the present passage and 57.2-3.

ἱρωσύνας δύο: religious conservatism will have ensured the retention of priesthoods by the kings long after the curtailment of their secular powers, since the kings were seen as intermediaries between the gods and mankind. This link between king and god was felt in other states even after the abolition of the monarchy, and helps to explain the retention of the royal title for magistrates whose functions were partially religious, like the *archon basileus* and the *phylobasileis* at Athens, the *rex sacrorum* at Rome, and the *basileis* in archaic Chios (ML 8); and at Megara (IG VII 1-15).

Διός τε Λακεδαίμονος: 'Zeus Lacedaemon'. It is uncertain whether Lacedaemon is to be taken adjectivally in the sense of 'Lacedaemonian Zeus', i.e. Zeus in his capacity as guardian of the Spartan state, or as a noun in apposition to 'Zeus', in the sense of 'Zeus Lacedaemon', where Lacedaemon is to be understood as a cult title originating in the fusion of Zeus with the eponymous hero Lacedaemon, in mythology a son of Zeus and the nymph Taygete and husband of Sparte daughter of the river god Eurotas (Paus. 3.1.2). The former interpretation would have as parallels cult titles such as Zeus Hellenios (9.7.2) and Ithomatas (Paus. 3.26.6), Aphrodite Cnidia (Paus. 1.1.3), Apollo Amyclaeus (Paus. 3.10.8), and Artemis Brauronia (Paus. 1.23.7), while for the latter there are similar syncretisms such as Poseidon Erechtheus (Apollodorus 3.15.1), Zeus Agamemnon (Lycophron, *Alexandra* 1124) and Artemis Dictynna (Paus. 3.24.9).

Διὸς οὐρανίου: 'heavenly Zeus', a common cult title of the god, which he shares with his daughter Aphrodite, and one of more universal application than the cult of the parochial Zeus Lacedaemon. It was in their role as priests of Zeus that the kings conducted state sacrifices, as well as those performed at the beginning of military expeditions and at the frontier when leaving Spartan territory (Xenophon, *Lac. Pol.* 13.2, 15.2).

πόλεμόν γε ἐκφέρειν ἐπ' ἣν ἂν βούλωνται χώρην: 'to wage war against whatever country they wish', a generic relative clause (Goodwin 1431). In early times the kings certainly exercised this right, which is last attested in 506, when Cleomenes launched his abortive invasion of Attica (5.74.1). In the classical period, war was declared by the popular assembly confirmed by a vote of the Peloponnesian League, and the mobilisation was carried out by the ephors: the assembly also designated one of the two kings to command the army (see 5.75.2; A.H.M. Jones, *Sparta*, p. 15; G.E.M. de Ste. Croix, *The Origins of the Peloponnesian War*, London, 1972, pp. 96-151). If the right of the kings to declare war was ever formally abolished, Herodotus was supplied with information that must have been out of date by half a century, but their right may merely have been left in abeyance rather than abrogated.

ἐν τῷ ἄγεϊ ἐνέχεσθαι: 'was liable to incur pollution', 'was subject to a curse', in the sense that the penalty for conviction was outlawry. In fact no example is known, and Aristocles and Hipponoides, found guilty of insubordination against Agis II, were merely exiled (Thuc. 5.72.1).

ἑκατὸν δὲ ἄνδρας...φυλάσσειν αὐτούς: the Royal Bodyguard consisted of 300 *hippeis* selected in the classical period by three officers known as *hippagretai*, who were themselves chosen by the ephors, probably one from each tribe (Xen. *Lac. Pol.* 4.3); in Herodotus' day it was the kings who made the selection (7.205.2). The historian's figure of 100 is inaccurate. He may be thinking of the strength of the contingent supplied by each of the three tribes rather than the overall total, since he does give the correct figure elsewhere (see 7.205.2 and 8.124.3). The context makes it clear that in Herodotus' day at least they were young men who, despite their name, were an entirely separate unit from the regular cavalry, which was established as late as 425/4 (Thuc. 4.55.2). The *hippeis* presumably fought on horseback at an earlier period and are likely to have constituted the cavalry that Pausanias records as participants in the First Messenian War (4.7.5, 4.8.12), though in the classical period they normally fought on foot (Thuc. 5.72.4; Strabo 10.4.18). They are also mentioned at 1.67.5, where the five senior members of those serving in their last year of duty in the unit, named *agathoergoi* ('benefactors'), acted as troubleshooters and undertook specific missions authorised by the state, as well as at 7.205.2, where they accompany Leonidas to Thermopylae, and at 8.124.3, where all 300 serve as a guard of honour to Themistocles during his visit to Sparta in 480. See also J.F. Lazenby, *The Spartan Army*, Warminster, 1985, pp. 10-12; I.G. Spence, *The Cavalry of Ancient Greece*, Oxford, 1993, pp. 2-4; L.J. Worley, *Hippeis: the Cavalry of Classical Greece*, Boulder, San Francisco and Oxford, 1994, pp. 23-6.

προβάτοισι: animals for sacrificing either at the start of a military expedition (Xen. *Hell.* 3.4.3, *Lac. Pol.* 13.2) or at the crossing of a frontier (*diabateria*, Thuc. 5.54.2, 5.55.3, 5.116.1; Xen. *Hell.* 3.4.3, 3.5.7, 4.7.2, 5.1.33, 5.3.14, 5.4.37, 5.4.47, 6.5.12), or as a preliminary to joining battle (*sphagia*, Hdt. 9.33.1, 9.36, 9.61.3; Xen. *Hell.* 3.1.17, 4.2.20, *Lac. Pol.* 13.8; Plut. *Lyc.* 22.2, *Arist.* 17.6 and 18.2). Sacrificial animals regularly accompanied Spartan armies (Xen. *Lac. Pol.* 13.3, cf. ch. 76.1 below). The word πρόβατον covers all domesticated ruminants, though in Attic prose it is almost entirely restricted to sheep. In the case of the *diabateria*, a goat was the usual victim. For further information on Spartan sacrifice, see W.K. Pritchett, *The Greek State at War*, Vol. 3, Berkeley, Los Angeles and London, 1979, pp. 67-90.

ὁκόσοισι ἂν ἐθέλωσι: ὁκόσοισι is assimilated to the case of its antecedent προβάτοισι (see note on 21.1 above and Goodwin 1031). For the use of ἂν with the subj. in indefinite and generic relative clauses, see note on 34.2 above and Goodwin 1431.

57.1 ἢν θυσίη τις δημοτελὴς ποιέηται: 'if (i.e. 'whenever') a sacrifice is made at public expense'. Here ἤν with the subj. denotes a general condition representing a customary or repeated action (Goodwin 1393). The law requiring a king to officiate at public sacrifices is ascribed by Xenophon (*Lac. Pol.* 15.1.2) to Lycurgus.

πρώτους...ἵζειν: 'they sit first', either with reference to the place of honour or in the temporal meaning that they are the first to take their seats.

ἄρχεσθαι: the subject of this inf. is not the kings, as the strict rules of grammar would require, but the servants and waiters who set the food before the diners and who are the subject of νέμοντας.

διπλήσια νέμοντας ἑκατέρῳ τὰ πάντα ἢ τοῖσι ἄλλοισι: 'distributing twice as much of everything to each king as to the others'. Cf. 3.74.2 τὰ πάντα μυρία, 'everything beyond measure; 9.81.2 πάντα δέκα, 'ten of everything', and Xen. *Lac. Pol.* 15.4, where the kings are said to receive a double portion of food at public meals.

σπονδαρχίας: 'the privilege of pouring the first libation', a word occurring only here.

τῶν τυθέντων τὰ δέρματα: 'the skins of the animals sacrificed', where τυθέντων is aor. pass. part. of θύω. Cf. Xen. *Lac. Pol.* 15.5, where Lycurgus is said to have given the kings a pig from each litter produced and the right to portions of the victims slaughtered at state sacrifices.

57.2 νεομηνίας δὲ ἀνὰ πάσας: 'on the occasion of every new moon'. Since Greek calendars were lunar and months determined by the phases of the moon, νεομηνία came to mean 'the first day of the month'. If the manuscript reading νεομηνίας δὲ πάσας (as in *OCT*) is retained, the acc. will denote a point of time in place of the much more usual dat. Cf. note on τὸν αὐτὸν τοῦτον χρόνον at 27.2. Some editors, unhappy with this abnormality, would amend the text to read νεομηνίας ἀνὰ πάσας, with ἀνά used distributively in the sense of 'on the first day of every month'; this is the text printed here.

ἑβδόμας ἱσταμένου τοῦ μηνός: 'the seventh day of the month'. In the calendar of most Greek states (with significant exceptions such as Mytilene which used the ordinal numbers to indicate the count of days just like modern calendars), the month was divided into three parts for the purpose of reckoning dates. Exact names varied from city to city, but for the first third of the month, days were generally reckoned as rising, (ἱσταμένου), for the second third as 'being in their middle' (μεσοῦντος), or else 'after the ten' (ἐπὶ δέκα), and in the last third as 'declining' or 'departing' (φθίνοντος, λήγοντος, ἀπίοντας, ἀνομένου). Hence ἑβδόμας ἱσταμένου means literally 'on the 7th day of the rising part of the month'. The word νουμηνία and the use of the ordinal with ἱσταμένου are both attested epigraphically for Laconia (A.E. Samuel, *Greek and Roman Chronology*, Munich, 1972, p. 94).

137

ἐκ τοῦ δημοσίου: literally 'from the public treasury', here equivalent to 'at public expense'.

ἐς 'Απόλλωνος: 'for Apollo's sanctuary', where a noun like ἱερόν, νηόν or τέμενος is to be understood. Since the seventh day of the month was regarded as the day of the god's birth (Hesiod, *Works and Days* 770-1) and, as such, sacred to him, his festivals tended to be celebrated on the 7th (e.g. at Athens the Thargelia, the Pyanopsia and the Boedromia on the 7th day of the months to which they gave their names.

μέδιμνον...Λακωνικήν: it is clear from a comparison of Plut. *Lyc.* 12.2 with Athenaeus 141C that the Laconian *medimnus* was half as much again as its Attic equivalent, and if the Attic measure is taken as amounting roughly to 52 litres, a Laconian *medimnus* would approximate to some 78 litres.

τετάρτην Λακωνικήν: 'a Laconian quart'. The name of the measure of which the τετάρτη is a fourth part is unknown. Since the *medimnus* of grain which formed the kings' monthly allowance corresponded exactly to the amount contributed each month by Spartan *homoioi* to their *syssition* (Plut. and Athenaeus, locc. citt.), one might similarly expect the royal monthly wine allowance to be the same as the monthly Spartan wine contribution to the *syssition* of 8 Attic *choes*, and if so, with a *chous* approximating to $3^1/_4$ litres (see W.F. Richardson, *Numbering and Measuring in the Classical World*, Auckland, 1985, p. 38; O.W. Dilke, *Mathematics and Measurement*, London, 1987, p. 26) the Laconian quart may correspond to about 26 litres.

προεδρίας ἐξαιρέτους: 'select places of honour', usually in the front row. *Proedria* was one of the privileges commonly awarded by Greek states in honorific decrees.

προξείνους ἀποδεικνύναι τούτοισι προσκεῖσθαι: 'it falls to them to designate *proxenoi*'. A *proxenos* was a prominent citizen and resident of state A who served in his own city as an official representative of state B in any negotiations or other business involving the two states. His duties would include the provision of hospitality for visiting official delegations of state B when they were transacting business in state A, and, more generally, the rendering of assistance to individuals from state B, e.g. in judicial proceedings, when they had occasion to visit state A. He would also be regarded in state A as something of an expert on the foreign and domestic policy of state B, whose knowledge and expertise could win him considerable influence in his own state. On the institution of *proxenia*, see F. Adcock and D.J. Mosley, *Diplomacy in Ancient Greece*, London, 1975, pp. 160-5. Herodotus' statement that the kings appointed *proxenoi* is ambiguous in its failure to make clear whether the kings selected Spartans to be the *proxenoi* at Sparta of other states, or whether they appointed foreigners to represent Spartan interests in their own states. On the former interpretation (which is strongly supported by Herodotus' use of the words τοὺς...τῶν ἀστῶν), he would be thinking of the kings' appointment of Spartan citizens, (presumably to look after the interests of other states at Sparta), but if so, this alleged power of the kings violates the almost universal Greek practice whereby *proxenoi* were appointed by the state whose interests they were being asked to represent. Mosely may be correct in suggesting ('Spartan Kings and Proxeny', *Athenaeum* 49, 1971, pp. 433-5) that the kings were involved only when the foreign state failed to appoint one in the first place. Certainly we do not hear of other states retaliating by denying Sparta the right to appoint her own *proxenoi* in their cities, and it was the Athenians and not a Spartan king who in 368/7 appointed Coroebus as the Athenian *proxenos* at Sparta (Tod *GHI* 135). For these reasons modern scholars are inclined to doubt Herodotus' statement.

Πυθίους: in a democratic city like Athens, state envoys sent to consult Delphi (in Attic termed *theopropoi*) were appointed by the assembly, but it is fully in accord with Spartan thinking that this should be a prerogative of the kings. Presumably all four *Pythioi* went to consult Apollo and had joint charge of the god's written oracular response, so that any attempt to tamper with the response would be unlikely to succeed, unless with the collusion of all four. Hence Cleomenes in 491 and Pleistoanax in 426 both found it impossssible to obtain the response they wished in any other way than by resorting to bribery of the Pythia (see ch. 66 below and Thuc. 5.16.2). Apart from the present passage, *Pythioi* are mentioned only by Xenophon (*Lac. Pol.* 15.5) and by Cicero (*De Divinatione* 1.43.95, *augur*).

σιτεόμενοι μετὰ τῶν βασιλέων τὰ δημόσια: 'taking their meals along with the kings at public expense'. Cf. Xen. *Lac. Pol.* 15.5, ἔδωκε (sc. Lycurgus) καὶ συσκήνους δύο ἑκατέρῳ προσελέσθαι οἳ δὴ καὶ Πύθιοι καλοῦνται. Unlike all other Spartiates, who were required to pay fees for the privilege of belonging to a *syssition*, the kings, along with their *Pythioi*, shared one single *syssition*, to which they not only made no contribution, but themselves received double rations, at state expense.

57.3 μὴ ἐλθοῦσι...τοῖσι βασιλεῦσι: 'if the kings do not come', where the negative μὴ is used with the part. because the phrase is equivalent to a conditional clause (Goodwin 1612).

δύο χοίνικας: at Athens a *choinix* was one forty-eighth of a *medimnos* and so equivalent to little more than a litre, but on the assumption that there were 48 *choinikes* also in a Laconian *medimnos*, which was presumably the same as the Aeginetan *medimnos* (Pheidonian standard), and so about $1\frac{1}{2}$ times the amount of an Athenian *medimnos* (cf. the figures cited for *syssition* contributions by Plut, *Lyc.* 12.2, using the Attic standard and Dicaearchus as quoted by Athenaeus 4.141C, using the Aeginetan), 2 Laconian *choinikes* would amount to roughly 3 litres.

οἴνου κοτύλην: an Attic *kotyle* was one quarter of a *choinix*; if this is true for the Laconian (= Aeginetan/Pheidonian) *kotyle* as well, the Laconian *kotyle* would correspond to $\frac{3}{8}$ litre approximately.

διπλήσια πάντα: see note on 57.1 above.

τὠυτὸ δὲ τοῦτο: 'in the same way', 'on the same basis', an adverbial acc. (Goodwin 1060).

πρὸς ἰδιωτέων: see note on 9.1 above. Cf. πρὸς ἀνδρῶν βαρβάρων at 106.2 below.

57.4 πατρούχου τε παρθένου πέρι: 'concerning a girl who is an heiress'. For postpositive περί, see note on at 4.1 above, and cf. 101.2 below. πατροῦχος is the Spartan equivalent of the Athenian ἐπίκληρος, a daughter who has no brothers and who is consequently heir to her father's estate. Under Athenian law, a girl in this position would have been claimed in marriage by her nearest paternal male relative, and obligated to marry him to ensure that her father's property remained within the family. At Sparta it looks as if there was no such requirement, and that selection of her prospective husband was entrusted to the king, unless of course his role amounted to little more than determining which male relative had the best claim to her hand (a role determined at Athens by the legal process of *diadikasia*). On the *patrouchos*, see D.M. Macdowell, *Spartan Law*, Edinburgh, 1986, pp. 95-7.

ἐς τὸν ἱκνέεται ἔχειν: 'as to who is the one appropriate to have her'. ἱκνέομαι, 'arrive', is used in Ionic impersonally in the 3rd. pers. sing. of the pres. and imperf. in the sense of 'it is/was appropriate' (cf. 2.36.1, 9.26.6 and ch. 84.3 below). The part ἱκνεύμενα in the sense of 'fitting' occurs at 86.3 below and the corresponding adverb ἱκνευμένως at ch. 65.4.

ἢν μή περ ὁ πατὴρ αὐτὴν ἐγγυήσῃ: 'if her father has not betrothed her'. For the syntax, see note on 57.1 above.

θετὸν παῖδα ποιέεσθαι: 'to adopt a child'. θετός is the verbal adj. from the middle of τίθημι, in the sense of 'adopt', as opposed to γένει or γόνῳ υἱός ('son by birth'). The role of the Spartan king was filled at Athens by the *phrateres* and demesmen, to whom the adopting parent would present the adoptee, and who would subsequently serve as witnesses that the adoption had taken place. See L. Rubinstein, *Adoption in Fourth Century Athens*, Copenhagen, 1993, pp. 36-45.

57.5 παρίζειν βουλεύουσι τοῖσι γέρουσι: 'they sit alongside the Elders when they deliberate'. The *gerontes* (literally 'old men') were the members of the *gerousia*, the Spartan Council, which was originally the advisory body to the kings, but which in the classical period served as the principal day to day organ of administration. Among its functions were the preparation of the agenda for meetings of the assembly, the judging of serious criminal cases such as murder and treason, a general oversight of the administration, and the right to assist and advise the kings in the conduct of foreign policy. Membership of the *gerousia* was to all intents and purposes restricted to a select group of families, and members were chosen for life by the assembly from suitable candidates over the age of sixty. Herodotus' use of παρίζειν suggests that the kings were not themselves technically Elders in the proper sense of the word, in that the age limit did not apply to them and they were members *ex officio*, not elected by the assembly.

ἐοῦσι δυῶν δέουσι τριήκοντα: 'who were 28 in number'. The phrase means literally 'being thirty lacking two', where δέουσι is dat. plur. of the part. of δέω governing the gen. In Ionic, where the dual had gone out of use before the classical period, the gen. and dat. of δύο have plur. endings (δυῶν, δυοῖσι). The regular Greek forms for 18 and 19 are ὀκτωκαίδεκα and ἐννεακαίδεκα, but expressions like ἑνὸς (δυοῖν) δέοντες εἴκοσι (τριάκοντα etc.) are just as common (Goodwin 382.3). Cf. Latin *duodeviginti, undeviginti*.

ἢν δὲ μὴ ἔλθωσι: 'if ever (i.e. 'whenever') they don't come'. See note on 57.1 above.

τοὺς μάλιστά σφι...προσήκοντας: 'those most nearly related to them', 'those closest in kinship'.

δύο ψήφους τιθεμένους, τρίτην δὲ τὴν ἑωυτῶν: 'casting two votes, and a third, namely their own'. Herodotus' language is ambiguous: does he mean that the two kinsmen most closely related to the kings individually cast three votes, two for the king they are representing and then their own, or that the proxies between them, i.e. collectively, cast the two royal votes and then their own? On the former interpretation, he will have believed that the kings had two votes each, but on the latter, that they had only one. Thucydides (1.20) certainly understands Herodotus' text to mean that each king has two votes, and proceeds on the strength of this belief to castigate popular mistaken beliefs about Spartan institutions. It is true that he does not name Herodotus as the culprit, but the second example which he cites (the non-existent Pitanate *lochos*) is undoubtedly intended as the refutation of a specific statement made by Herodotus at 9.53.2. However given the ambiguity of Herodotus' Greek he should perhaps be given the benefit of the doubt.

58.1 τοῦ κοινοῦ: see notes on 14.3 and 50.2 above.

ἐπεὰν ὦν τοῦτο γένηται: 'whenever this happens', a temporal clause denoting repetition (Goodwin 1431.1).

καταμιαίνεσθαι: 'to defile oneself', by tearing one's hair or clothes or throwing dust on the head as a token of mourning.

μὴ ποιήσασι ὦν τοῦτο: the part. is used with μή in a conditional sense. See note on 57.3 above and Goodwin 1612.

ἐπικέαται: 'are imposed', Ionic 3rd. pers. perf. of ἐπίκειμαι, where Attic would have ἐπίκεινται. See notes on περιβεβλέατο at 24.2, κεκοσμέαται at 41.4 and ἠπιστέατο at 44.3 above.

58.2 τοῖσι Λακεδαιμονίοισι: this term covers not just Spartiates but all free born inhabitants of Spartan territory.

ἐπέαν...ἀποθάνῃ: see note on 58.1 above.

χωρὶς Σπαρτιητέων: 'in addition to the Spartiates', 'as well as the Spartiates'.

ἀριθμῷ: 'in certain numbers', 'in a fixed number'.

τῶν περιοίκων: literally 'dwellers around'. The *perioikoi* were the free born inhabitants who lived in the various townships of Laconia (and some in Messenia), who enjoyed full autonomy in local affairs but lacked Spartan citizenship. Like Spartiates, but unlike helots, they were required to perform military service in the Spartan army and could earn their own living by cultivating the land or by engaging in trade, industry or manufacturing, three activities denied to Spartiates by law.

ἐς τὸ κῆδος ἰέναι: 'to go to the funeral'. κῆδος, meaning literally 'grief', came to be used in the more specific sense of 'mourning for the dead', 'funerary rites'.

58.3 τῶν εἱλωτέων: the helots were state-owned serfs attached to the plots of the individual Spartiates which they were required to cultivate in return for the right to retain a proportion of its produce for their own sustenance. Because they greatly outnumbered the Spartiates, they were seen as a threat to the safety of the state and rigorously suppressed to discourage revolt.

σύμμιγα τῆσι γυναιξί: 'intermingled with the women'. With the exception of great state and family occasions such as weddings, funerals or festivals, the women in most Greek states did not intermingle freely with males.

κόπτονταί: 'they strike (their foreheads)', middle voice since it is their own heads that they strike, as opposed to the act. which would be used of striking the heads of others.

φάμενοι: the pres. part. of φημί, whether act. or middle in form, is rare in Attic, which prefers φάσκων. In Herodotus, both φάς and φάμενος are used freely, with no difference in meaning.

τὸν ὕστατον...ἀπογενόμενον τῶν βασιλέων: 'the last king who has just died'. ἀπογίγνομαι in Attic usually means 'be absent', though as a euphemism for 'die' the word is common in Herodotus (2.85.1, 2.136.2, 3.111.3, 5.4.1) and not unknown to Thucydides (2.34.2, 2.51.5).

εἴδωλον: an image or statue, necessary in the case of Leonidas, whose corpse was decapitated by Xerxes at Thermopylae (7.238.2, 9.78.3). We have no evidence for this practice in the cases of Cleombrotus I killed at Leuctra in 371, Agis III killed at Megalopolis in 331 or Areus I killed at Corinth in 264, but certainly the bodies of both Agesipolis I, who died in Chalcidice in 380 and Agesilaus, who died in Egypt in 360, were embalmed in honey or wax and brought back to Sparts for burial (Xen. *Hell.* 5.3.19; Diod. 15.93.6, Plut. *Ages.* 40.3, Nepos *Ages.* 8.7).

ἐν κλίνῃ εὖ ἐστρωμένῃ: 'on a well dressed bier', where ἐστρωμένῃ is perf. part. pass. of στορέννυμι or στόρνυμι, 'spread', 'strew' 'make smooth'.

ἀγορὴ: 'trading', or, more generally, 'public business' of any kind, such as would be transacted in the *agora*.

δέκα ἡμερέων: 'for ten days', 'within a period of ten days', a gen. of time denoting the period within which business is suspended (Goodwin 1136).

οὐδ' ἀρχαιρεσίη συνίζει: 'nor are electoral meetings constituted'.

59 τῷ δημοσίῳ: 'the state treasury', as at 57.2 above.

προοφειλόμενον: literally 'previously owed', i.e. 'arrears of tribute'. Cf. 3.67.3, where the accession of Smerdis is marked by the remission of military service for the subject peoples and a three year exemption from tribute.

60 οἱ κήρυκες: the heralds at Sparta formed a guild called the Talthybiadae, named for Talthybius, Agamemnon's herald at Troy, who subsequently had a shrine at Sparta (7.134.1).

αὐληταὶ: these are mentioned as members of the king's staff by Xenophon (*Lac. Pol.* 13.7). Their duties included the provision of a marching rhythm for the army in the field (Thuc. 5.70; Cicero *Tusc. Disp.* 2.16.37; Val. Max. 2.6.2; Plut. *Lyc.* 21.3) and accompanying the slaughter of a goat at pre-battle sacrifices (Xen. *Lac. Pol.*13.8).

μάγειροι: those employed in slaughtering animals and more generally catering for the army and for the mess halls, who were regarded as sufficiently important to have their own patron heroes Matton ('Kneader') and Keraon ('Mixer'). These heroes had statues erected in a public place in the community (Athenaeus 39E).

οὐ κατὰ λαμπροφωνίην ἐπιτιθέμενοι ἄλλοι σφέας παρακληΐουσι: 'nor do others apply themselves to the herald's profession or exclude them (i.e. members of the families of hereditary heralds) because of the loudness of their voice'.

61.1 κοινὰ τῇ Ἑλλάδι ἀγαθὰ προεργαζόμενον: literally 'working common good things for Greece', i.e. 'working for the common good of Greece'. The significance of the προ- in the compound verb is that Cleomenes was doing the spadework for the Greek cause which would later eliminate Persian influence in Greece.

οὐκ Αἰγινητέων οὕτω κηδόμενος, ὡς φθόνῳ καὶ ἄγῃ χρεόμενος: 'not so much out of concern for the Aeginetans as influenced by envy and malice'. The only known earlier attempt by Demaratus to obstruct Cleomenes was in 506, when he thwarted Cleomenes' invasion of Attica (see 5.75). There may have been policy differences between the two kings (Demaratus' subsequent behaviour suggests that he may have believed cooperation with Persia to be in Sparta's best interests and regarded Cleomenes' activities as likely to ruin any chances of securing such cooperation), though a personality clash may also have been a factor. Cleomenes was not only the Agiad king and, as such, belonged to the more respected house (see ch. 51 above), but enjoyed greater influence by virtue of having been on the throne for a longer period (Plut. *Mor.* 218A implies a time when Demaratus' father Ariston was Cleomenes' colleague), while his abrasive and overbearing personality undoubtedly alienated many of his contemporaries. He was so much the more influential of the two that Demaratus may well have come to resent him and to feel on the present occasion that, if the coercion of Aegina was successful, it would merely strengthen the hand of his colleague to an even greater degree.

διὰ πρῆγμα τοιόνδε: 'thanks to some such circumstance as the following'.

ἐπίβασιν ἐς αὐτὸν ποιεύμενος: 'making an attack upon him', a paraphrase for the simple verb ἐπιβαίνω. See note on 27.3 above, and cf. 78.1 below.

'Αρίστωνι: father of Demaratus and Eurypontid king of Sparta, overlapping the latter years of the reign of Anaxandridas and the first part of that of Cleomenes.

61.2 τῷ προσεκέετο...μάλιστα: 'to whom he was most of all attached'.

61.3 ἐοῦσαν γάρ μιν τὸ εἶδος φλαύρην: the construction is unclear, and there is an element of anacoluthon in the sentence. Probably the clause is to be taken with ὁρῶσα, as the first of the two observations of the nurse, and the clause beginning with οἷα should be regarded as interrupting the sentence structure. Alternatively the clause might be the object of ἐφόρεε, the first word in the next sentence: on this interpretation Herodotus may have felt that the parenthetical clauses which lie between interrupt the sentence structure to such an extent that in the interests of clarity, it was desirable to insert a new object αὐτήν for the verb ἐφόρεε.

οἷα ἀνθρώπων...ὀλβίων θυγατέρα...ἐοῦσαν: causal, 'inasmuch as she was the daughter of wealthy parents', with the noun in the same case as the part. of the preceding clause.

πρὸς δὲ: 'and furthermore', 'and in addition', with πρός used adverbially, as at 95.2 and 125.5 below.

συμφορὴν τὸ εἶδος αὐτῆς ποιευμένους: 'regarding her appearance as a disaster/misfortune'. On this use of ποιέομαι, see note on 13.2 above.

τὸ τῆς Ἑλένης ἱρόν: a shrine jointly dedicated to Helen and Menelaus, more commonly referred to as the Menelaum.

ἐν τῇ Θεράπνῃ: Therapne lay outside the confines of the city of Sparta, on the other bank of the Eurotas, some two miles to the south of the city, on the site of a Mycenaean settlement. See also Isocrates, *Helen* 63, Paus. 3.19.9. The site also had close associations with Helen's brothers Castor and Polydeuces, in that it was believed to be their earthly place of burial (Pindar, *Pyth.* 11.65, *Nem.* 10.56-7.

ὕπερθε τοῦ Φοιβηΐου ἱροῦ: the shrine of Apollo, which lay on the western bank of the Eurotas, was the scene of the annual fights between two groups of youths (Cicero, *Tusc. Disp.* 5.27.77, Paus. 3.14.9-10, Lucian, *Anacharsis* 38).

ὅκως δὲ ἐνείκειε: 'whenever she brought her', where ὅκως is used as a temporal conjunction with the opt. to denote repetition in historic sequence (see note on 31.2 above and cf. 75.1, 77.3, 121.2, 137.3 and 138.2 below).

ἐπιφανῆναι: 2nd. aor. inf. pass. of ἐπιφαίνω, used intransitively with the meaning 'appear'. φαίνω and its compounds have two aor. pass. forms, a 1st. aor. ἐφάνθην, used in the true passive sense of 'be shown', and a 2nd. aor. ἐφάνην, used as an intransitive middle meaning 'appear'.

61.4 δέξαι: Ionic aor. inf. from δείκνυμι, 'show'.

τὴν δὲ οὐ φάναι: 'and she said no', 'and she refused'. For τὴν δέ, see note on 52.4 above, and for οὐ φάναι, see notes on 1.1, 50.2 and 52.4 above. Cf. 99.2 below.

ἀπειρῆσθαι γάρ οἱ ἐκ τῶν γειναμένων μηδενὶ ἐπιδεικνύναι: 'for it had been forbidden to her by her parents to show her to anyone'. ἀπειρῆσθαι is perf. inf. pass. of ἀπαγορεύω, 'I forbid'. Verbs of preventing, forbidding and others of a similar negative meaning are followed by the inf. (Goodwin 1519) or by the inf. with μή (Goodwin 1615). For ἐκ with the gen. to denote the agent after a verb in the pass., see note on 13.1 above, and cf. 22.1, 42.1, 78.2 and 124.2.

πάντως ἑωυτῇ κελεύειν ἐπιδέξαι: 'order her to show her in spite of everything/notwithstanding'.

61.5 περὶ πολλοῦ ποιευμένην ἰδέσθαι: 'put a great deal of emphasis on seeing her'. For this phrase, see note on ch. 6 above, and cf. 104.1 and 134.1 below. The middle of ὁράω, with act. meaning, as here, is essentially poetic and Ionic.

εἶπαι: the 1st. aor. εἶπα is essentially Ionic (cf. 82.1, 100.1, 139.4), though certain forms (notably εἶπας, εἴπατε, εἰπάτω) are preferred in Attic to the corresponding forms of the 2nd. aor. εἶπον.

οὗτος δὴ ὁ τοῦ ᾿Αρίστωνος φίλος: in Herodotus the particle δή is frequently used with the pronoun οὗτος to indicate that the individual in question has already been mentioned in the narrative. Here it is used to affirm the identity of this friend of Ariston with the friend referred to in section 2 above. See Denniston *GP*, p. 209 and 63.1 below.

62.1 ἔκνιζε: 'was chafing'; literally 'was scratching'. This verb is also used metaphorically at 7.10. and 7.12.1.

ὑποδέκεται...δώσειν: 'he promised to give'. For the fut. inf. with verbs of hoping, promising etc., see note on 2.1 above and Goodwin 1286.

οὐδὲν φοβηθεὶς ἀμφὶ τῇ γυναικὶ: 'in no way afraid for his wife'. The prep. ἀμφί is rare in Attic prose and, where it occurs, normally takes the acc. With the dat., the prep. is essentially poetic, though there are other instances in Herodotus (1.140.3, 3.32.1, 5.19.2, 5.52.1 and ch. 129.2 below). In Attic, 'fear for' is usually expressed by ὑπέρ with the gen. or περί with the dat.

ἐπὶ τούτοισι: 'on these conditions'.

ὅρκους ἐπήλασαν: (sc. ἀλλήλοισι) 'they imposed oaths on one another'. For this use of ἐπελαύνω, cf. 1.146.3, σφίσι αὐτῇσι ὅρκους ἐπήλασαν.

62.2 μετὰ δέ: 'and afterwards', where μετά is used adverbially. See note on 4.1, and cf. 38.1, 97.2 and 103.2.

ὅ τι δὴ ἦν: 'whatever it was'. The indef. pron. ὅστις is made even vaguer by the addition of particles like δή, ποτε and δήποτε. See also 134.2 below.

ἀναγκαζόμενος...τῷ τε ὅρκῳ: though Cicero, echoing the tenets of Hellenistic philosophy, is willing to admit that there are circumstances in which promises made under oath may be broken (*De Officiis* 3.24.92-3.32.115), such a view would have been seen as impious in a conservative society such as Sparta, and, for an honourable and deeply religious man of the old school like Agetus, there could have been no alternative to honouring his pledge.

τῆς ἀπάτης τῇ παραγωγῇ: literally 'by the seduction of the deceit', i.e. the deception practised on him as a result of Ariston's trick.

63.1 τὴν τρίτην...γυναῖκα: since it was the son of this third marriage who succeeded Ariston on the throne, lack of a male heir must surely have played a large part in his decision to marry for a third time, and if the ephors were as concerned for the survival of the Eurypontid house as they were for the Agiad (see 5.39.2), they are likely to have put pressure on him to take action.

τοῦτον δὴ τόν Δημάρητον: following his father's example, he in turn was to acquire a wife by unconventional means (see 65.2 below). For οὗτος δή, see note on 61.5 above.

63.2 ἐν θώκῳ κατημένῳ: (from καθῆμαι) literally 'as he was sitting in his chair', where θῶκος is the Ionic form (cf. 1.181.4, 9.94.1) of θᾶκος, 'seat', 'chair', a rare and less prosaic synonym of ἕδρα. Like ἕδρα, θᾶκος comes to denote the official sitting or deliberation of magistrates and legislative bodies, and is here best translated as 'sitting of the Council'. Cf. Paus. 3.7.7, who writes μετὰ τῶν ἐφόρων καθημένῳ ἐν βουλῇ. The passage provides evidence for consultation between kings and ephors on matters of policy, presumably on a regular basis.

γέγονε: perf. of γίγνομαι, 'am born'.

ἠγάγετο τὴν γυναῖκα: 'he married the woman'. The middle of ἄγω (cf. Latin *duco*) is used as a synonym for γαμέω.

ἐπὶ δακτύλων συμβαλλόμενος: 'calculating them on his fingers'. Cf. the use of πεμπάζω, 'count on the five fingers' as a general word for 'calculate'.

ἀπομόσας: 'deny on oath', as at 2.179.1 and ch. 65.3 below.

οὐκ ἂν ἐμὸς εἴη: 'he cannot be mine', a potential opt. with ἄν (Goodwin 1327-31). Here the construction has the force of a strong assertion.

πρῆγμα...οὐδὲν ἐποιήσαντο: 'they paid no attention to it', 'they gave no thought to it', an expression equivalent to the commoner οὐδένα λόγον ποιεῖσθαι τινος, or ἐν οὐδενὶ λόγῳ ποιεῖσθαι τι. The expression also occurs at 7.150.3.

τῷ Ἀρίστωνι τὸ εἰρημένον μετέμελε: 'Ariston repented of what had been said'. μεταμέλει is normally used as an impersonal verb with the dat. of the person and a participial phrase in agreement indicating the activity of which one repents, as, e.g. μετεμέλησέ σφι ταῦτα ποιήσασι at 1.130.2. Here the verb is used personally in the sense of 'cause repentance', with τὸ εἰρημένον as subject: 'what had been said caused Ariston to repent'. This construction is also used at 9.1.1, τοῖσι ἡγεομένοισι τὰ πρὸ τοῦ πεπρηγμένα μετέμελε.

παῖδα...ἐς τὰ μάλιστα οἱ ἐνόμισε εἶναι: 'he believed he really was his son'.

ἀνδρὶ εὐδοκιμέοντι διὰ πάντων δὴ τῶν βασιλέων: something of an exaggeration, in that Ariston is little more than a name to us, being eclipsed by his colleague Anaxandridas (cf. Jacoby, *FGrH* 105 Frag. 1 and Plut. *Mor.* 216F-217A, 218A, where Anaxandridas is credited with six apophthegms as against Ariston's three, of which the third is clearly anachronistic).

ἀρὴν ἐποιήσαντο: 'they prayed', periphrastically for ἠράσαντο. Both ἀρά in the sense of 'prayer' and its related verb are essentially poetic (in prose, the usual meaning is 'curse'), but the word is used here in preference to the normal εὐχή to bring out the significance of Demaratus' name.

64 Δημάρητος δὲ ἔσχε τὴν βασιληΐην: 'Demaratus succeeded to the throne', where ἔσχε is ingressive (see note on 25.2 above).

ἔδεε...ἀνάπυστα γενόμενα ταῦτα καταπαῦσαι Δημάρητον τῆς βασιληΐης: 'it was fated that these things should become known and put an end to Demaratus' kingship'. The impers. δεῖ usually means 'it is necessary', but in Herodotus commomly has the meaning 'it is destined that'. Cf. 2.161.3, 5.33.2, 8.53.1, 9.109.2 and ch. 135.3 below. ἀνάπυστος is the verbal adj. from ἀναπυνθάνομαι, 'find out', 'ascertain'. Cf. 9.109.1 and ch. 66.3 below.

δι' ἃ Κλεομένεϊ διεβλήθη: the text at this point is corrupt. The mss. read διὰ τό or διὰ τά. The text printed, δι' ἅ, 'wherefore', does not give good sense. διότι, 'because', is to be preferred as a stopgap. The phrase Κλεομένεϊ διεβλήθη should mean 'he was on bad terms with Cleomenes'. The act. voice of this verb means 'slander', while διαβάλλω τινα τινι can also mean 'I set someone at variance with another', as at Thuc. 8.88. The passive of this construction, διαβάλλομαι with the dat., is common in Herodotus in the sense of 'be on bad terms with', 'be alienated from', 'incur the ill will of', as at 1.118.2, 5.35.1, 8.22.3, 9.116.2.

πρότερόν: in 506, when Cleomenes was seeking to undo Cleisthenes' new constitution at Athens (see 5.75).

τότε ἐπ' Αἰγινητέων τοὺς μηδίσαντας διαβάντος Κλεομένεος: see chs 49-51 above. μηδίζω means 'be pro-Persian', 'act in the interests of Persia', 'be in sympathy with the Persians', where the Medes serve as a substitute for their Persian kinsmen. The verb περσίζω is found in classical authors only in the sense of 'speak Persian' (Xen. *Anab.* 4.5 34).

65.1 Ὁρμηθεὶς...ἀποτίνυσθαι: literally 'rushing to avenge himself', i.e. 'being eager for revenge'.

τοῦ Ἄγιος: at 8.131.2, where Herodotus is reproducing the official Eurypontid pedigree, the name of Leotychidas' grandfather is given as Agesilaus.

οἰκίης τῆς αὐτῆς Δημαρήτῳ: i.e. he was a Eurypontid. The exact relationship between Demaratus and Leotychidas is uncertain. If the Herodotean manuscripts are correct at 8.131.3, where it is stated that all of Leotychidas' ancestors but the last two were kings of Sparta, the two men had a common great-grandfather in king Hippocratidas. However in order to reconcile Herodotus' pedigree (Theopompus...Anaxandridas...Archidamus...Anaxilaus... Leotychidas [I]...Hippocratidas...Agesilaus...Menares...Leotychidas [II] with the family tree of Demaratus given by Paus. 3.7.6 (Theopompus... Archidamus [I]...Zeuxidamus...Anaxidamus...Archidamus [II]...Agesicles

...Ariston...Demaratus), some editors amend the text of Hdt. 8.131.3 to read 'all of Leotychidas' ancestors but the last seven were kings of Sparta', thus giving the two men a common ancestor in Theopompus, king during the late 8th and early 7th century. However it is difficult to believe that in this situation there were no living Eurypontids more closely related to Demaratus than was Leotychidas, whose accession to the throne appears to have been uncontested. Moreover the earlier Leotychidas [I] on Herodotus' list, who is absent from that of Pausanias, is mentioned as king by the contemporary or near-contemporary Alcman (Frag. 5, Page = Pap. Ox. 2390 Frag. 2, col. ii) as well as by Plutarch (*Lyc.* 13.5, *Mor.* 224D). Herodotus' pedigree thus has a better claim to authenticity than that recorded by Pausanias, and emendation of Hdt. 8.131.3 is unnecessary. Of the two most recent translators of Herodotus, David Grene (p. 605) accepts the emendation, while the Penguin version (p. 569 in the older edition, p. 493 with note on p. 597 in the new edition of Marincola) rejects it.

ἐπ' ᾧ τε, ἢν αὐτὸν καταστήσῃ βασιλέα.. ἕψεταί οἱ ἐπ' Αἰγινήτας: 'on condition that, if he made him king, he would follow his lead against the Aeginetans'. ἐφ' ᾧ and ἐφ' ᾧτε, 'provided that', 'on condition that', are construed either with the inf. (as at 1.22.4, 3.83.2, 7.154.3) or, as here and at 7.158.5, with the fut. indic. (Goodwin 1460). Conditional clauses referring to the future take ἄν with the subj. (Goodwin 1403): in indirect speech, the subj. with ἄν may be retained, as in the present passage, or be changed to the opt. with loss of ἄν (Goodwin 1497.2).

65.2 ἁρμοσαμένου...Πέρκαλον: 'had betrothed Percalus to himself'. ἁρμόζω, meaning literally 'fit', 'adapt', 'accomodate', acquires the subsidiary meaning of 'betroth': in the middle, the meaning is that it is the prospective groom himself, rather than his father, who arranges the betrothal.

τὴν Χίλωνος: the rarity of this name makes it almost certain that Percalus' father is a descendant of the famous ephor of the name who held the office in 556/5 and won a place among the Seven Sages of Greece (1.59.2; 7.235.2; P. Poralla, *PL*, no. 760). Presumably it was as much the political influence and prestige of his family as the beauty of his daughter that attracted both Leotychidas and Demaratus. By this marriage, Demaratus also obtained a link with the Agiad family, since Cleomenes' mother (name unknown) was the daughter of Prinetadas, who, as the son of a Demarmenus (5.41.3), was presumably the younger Chilon's brother. Full details of the pedigree are lacking, but since Demarmenus named one of his sons for the famous ephor, he is likely to have been a relative, and on chronological grounds should belong to the same generation (perhaps a brother). The pedigree may be set out as follows:

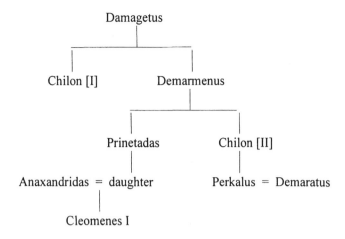

φθάσας αὐτὸς...ἁρπάσας: 'getting in first and seizing'. φθάνω, 'antici-pate' is used idiomatically with the pres. or aor. part. In this construction, the aor. part. is aspectual rather than temporal, i.e. it does not indicate time prior to that of the principal verb. See Goodwin 1586.

ἁρπάσας καὶ σχὼν γυναῖκα: 'having snatched her and obtained her as his wife'. Bride snatching was a well established custom at Sparta (Plut. *Lyc.* 15.4-9, Athenaeus 555 BC), but the near universal practice elsewhere in the Greek world whereby the bride's father arranged the marriage also existed at Sparta (see 57.4 above and 71.2 below), and bride snatching may have been in most cases little more than a symbolic nuptial ritual (see Paul Cartledge, 'Spartan Wives: Liberation or License?', *CQ* 31, 1981, pp. 99-100; D.M. MacDowell, *Spartan Law*, Edinburgh, 1986, pp. 77-81). Demaratus at least seems to have taken the wife snatching ceremony quite literally, and presum-ably pressurised Chilon into accepting the legitimacy of his action: perhaps the prospect of becoming a king's father-in-law and so equalling his brother's status made the situation tolerable, if not highly desirable.

65.3 κατόμνυται Δημαρήτου: 'took an oath against Demaratus', i.e. 'lodged a complaint against Demaratus under oath'.

φὰς αὐτὸν οὐκ ἱκνεομένως βασιλεύειν: 'saying that he was not right-fully king'. For φάς, see note on 58.3 above. ἱκνεομένως is the adverbial form derived from the neut. part. of ἱκνέομαι, used in Ionic in the sense of 'fitting', 'proper' (see note on 57.4 above). ἱκνέεται is itself used imperson-ally to mean 'it is right that'. In negative sentences with φημί in the sense 'I say that...not', the negative is regularly removed from the noun clause and taken closely with φημί (see notes on 1.1 and 50.2 above), but here the negative is semantically linked so closely with ἱκνεομένως that the two words are treated as being virtually one. Cf. 66.2 below.

ἐδίωκε: literally 'pursued', here used in the legal sense of 'prosecute'. Herodotus does not specify the composition of the court, but it was probably a joint session of *gerontes* and ephors, the body which normally sat in judgment on kings (Paus. 3.5.2).

ἀνασώζων: literally 'preserving', here 'preserving in the mind', i.e. 'recalling'.

συμβαλόμενος τοὺς μῆνας: the reference is to Ariston's words at 63.2 above.

65.4 ἐπιβατεύων: the verb from ἐπιβάτης, literally 'one who goes on to something', usually with reference to ships ('marine') or chariots ('fighter from a chariot'). Here the verb is used metaphorically with the meaning 'take one's stand on', as at 3.63.3 and 9.95.

ἱκνεομένως: see notes on 57.4 and 65.3 above.

66.1 ἀνοίστου δὲ γενομένου...ἐς τὴν Πυθίην: 'the matter having been referred to the Delphic priestess'. ἄνοιστος is the verbal adj. of ἀναφέρω. The verbal adjs. of φέρω are οἰστός ('bearable,) and οἰστέος ('that must be borne'), derived from the fut. stem οἴσ-.

66.2 προσποιέεται Κλεομένης Κόβωνα: 'Cleomenes won the support of Cobon'. In the act. the verb means 'attach something to something else', and in the middle 'procure for oneself', 'attach to oneself', 'win over', as well as 'lay claim to', 'pretend'. Cobon, otherwise unknown, was probably one of Cleomenes' prominent guest friends. For the institution of *xenia* and the mutual obligations incurred by the establishment of this link, see G. Herman, *Ritualised Friendship and the Greek City*, Cambridge, 1987.

πρόμαντιν: the Delphic priestess (Pythia) who served as the medium through whom Apollo was believed to communicate his oracles. Bribery of the oracle was a risky, indeed sacrilegious matter, but since Demaratus' two *Pythioi* will have accompanied those in the service of Cleomenes on the mission, tampering with the written response was out of the question, and Cleomenes needed a clear and unequivocal oracle that Demaratus' *Pythioi* would be unable to challenge.

ὑστέρῳ: since Demaratus is unlikely to have prejudiced his chances of restoration had he been aware of Cleomenes' corruption of the Pythia, the truth can only have been discovered after he had burnt his boats by fleeing to Persia (67.1 and 70.2 below). This is likely to have happened no earlier than the greater part of a year later (see note on 67.2 below).

67.1 ἐκ τοιοῦδε ὀνείδεος: 'as a result of the following insult'.

ἦρχε αἱρεθεὶς ἀρχήν: 'he held a magistracy to which he had been elected'. It is unfortunate that the historian neglects to identify the magistracy in question. It was surely sufficiently important to be deemed worthy compensation for the loss of the kingship, but if Demaratus was elected to the ephorate, as some have supposed, this magistracy was well enough known to Herodotus' audience to deserve a mention. More probably Demaratus' presence at the *gymnopaedia* was required by the nature of his substitute office, and, if so, he may have served as one of the five *bidaeoi*, the magistrates who were charged with the supervision of the boys' and young men's exercises (Paus. 3.11.2).

γυμνοπαιδίαι: a festival in honour of Apollo, one of the three most important in Sparta, at which choruses of boys and older men competed in singing, dancing and gymnastics (Paus. 3.11.9). It was celebrated in the heat of summer, about the end of July (Plato, *Laws* 633c. Cf. Thuc.5. 82.2 and Xen. *Hell*. 6.4.16). As not enough remained of the year 491 to accomodate both Demaratus' election to a magistracy and the celebration of the *gymnopaidia*i, the festival in question is best dated to 490.

ἐπὶ γέλωτί τε καὶ λάσθη: 'by way of mockery and insult'. The latter noun is rare, occurring in Greek literature before the Roman period only here and in an epigram of the Hellenistic poet Aeschrion (D.L. Page, *Epigrammata Graeca*, Oxford, 1975, lines 657-665).

67.3 ἄρξειν: here the verb is used in the sense of 'begin'.

μυρίης: μυρίοι, meaning 'countless', came to be used as an equivalent of the numeral 10,000, in which sense it is written μύριοι, with change of accent. Because of its meaning, it is normally used only in the plural, though the sing. is found with collective nouns (e.g. ἵππον μυρίην, 1.27.3; ὄψιν μυρίην, 2.136.1; ἵππος μυρίη, 7.41.2, and cf. χιλίην ἵππον, 5.63.3; ἵππος ἄλλη χιλίη, 7.41.1; τὴν ἵππον τὴν χιλίην, 8.113.2).

εἴπας: see note on εἶπαι at 61.5 above.

κατακαλυψάμενος: 'having covered his head (with his cloak)' as a mark of shame or dejection (cf. Homer, *Od*. 8.92, 10.53; Euripides, *Hippolytus* 243).

68.1 ἐσθεὶς ἐς τὰς χεῖράς οἱ τῶν σπλάγχνων: 'putting into her hands a portion of the entrails'. By making her a participant in the sacrifice, Demaratus' intention was to lay his mother open to a curse if she forswore herself, and so to ensure that she answered truthfully. His action has a parallel at Lycurgus, *In Leocratem* 20, where the orator calls upon witnesses to swear an oath of disclaimer (ἐξομόσασθαι λαβόντας τὰ ἱερά). ἐσθεὶς is aor. part. of εἰστίθημι, and σπλάγχνων is a partitive gen., used where the verb affects its object only in part (some of the entrails as opposed to all of them). See Goodwin 1097.

καταπτόμενος: literally 'touching', 'laying hold of'. The verb might be used in its literal sense here if an image of Zeus were actually present: more probably we should understand the word in its metaphorical sense of 'appeal to', as at 8.65.6 Δημαρήτου τε καὶ ἄλλων μαρτύρων καταπτόμενος.

τοῦ ἑρκείου Διὸς: Herkeios was an epithet of Zeus in his capacity as god of the family or household, derived from ἕρκος, ('enclosure' 'courtyard'), where an altar of the god would be found.

ὀρθῷ λόγῳ: 'in very truth'.

68.2 ματαιότερον: 'more irreverent'.

ὀνοφορβόν: 'ass keeper', 'muleteer','stableman'.

68.3 μετέρχομαι: here used in the sense of 'implore'. Cf. 4.7.1 τὸν χρυσὸν τὸν ἱρόν...θυσίῃσι...ἱλασκόμενοι μετέρχονται ἀνὰ πᾶν ἔτος, and 69.1 below.

τεκεῖν γὰρ ἄν οἱ καὶ τὰς προτέρας γυναῖκας: 'for his previous wives would have borne him children', the apodosis of a past unreal condition (Goodwin 1397), where we must supply a protasis such as 'if he had not been impotent'.

69.1 κατειρήσεται: fut. pass. of καταλέγω, from the perf. stem seen in εἴρημαι, more common than the alternative form ῥηθήσομαι.

ὥς με ἠγάγετο 'Αρίστων: 'when Ariston took me', where ὥς is temporal. Cf. 23.3 above and 69.2 below.

εἰδόμενον 'Αρίστωνι: 'in the likeness of Ariston'. The middle part. of ὁράω is used with the dat. in poetry and in Hdt. in the sense of 'like', 'resembling'. Cf. 7.56.2 Ζεὺς ἀνδρὶ εἰδόμενος Πέρσῃ.

69.2 οἰχώκεε: 'he departed', pluperf. of οἴχομαι. In Attic prose, the only tenses in use are the pres., fut. and imperf., but Hdt. makes free use also of the perf. and plup. (cf. 1.189.1; 4.136.3; 8.108.1; 9.98.1).

οὐκ ὑπεδέκετο: 'he refused to admit it', i.e. 'he kept on denying it'. Cf. 3.130.1.

κατωμνύμην: 'I swore it under oath'.

φαμένη αὐτὸν οὐ καλῶς ποιέειν ἀπαρνεύμενον: 'saying that he was not doing right in denying it'. The neg. οὐ goes more closely with καλῶς (οὐ καλῶς = αἰσχρῶς) than with φαμένη and is thus placed next to the adverb (see note on 65.3 above).

69.3 τοῦτο μέν...τοῦτο δὲ: see notes on 27.2 and 44.1 above, and cf. chs 101.3 and 114 below.

'Αστραβάκου: a Spartan hero (who for Daniel Ogden, *The Crooked Kings of Ancient Greece*, London, 1997, pp. 111-15, was less of a hero and more of a grotesque, ithyphallic demon with apotropaic and protective powers), reputed to be the great-great-grandson of Agis the eponymous ancestor of the Agiad family. Given the animosity between Agiads and Eurypontids (see note on 52.8), it is perhaps not inappropriate that it should have been an Agiad who made a cuckold of a Eurypontid king. According to the tale, he and his brother Alopecus were both driven mad when they unearthed the image of Artemis which Orestes and Iphigeneia had brought back from the Crimea (Paus. 3.16.6 and 9). His name, thought to be connected with the word ἀστράβη, 'pack saddle', suggests that he was the patron hero of mule-drivers, and seems to lie behind the story that Demaratus' mother slept with a muleteer. Ogden, who also maintains (*Greek Bastardy*, Oxford, 1996, pp. 234 and 257) that the explanation given by Demaratus' mother implies a joint insemination by Ariston and Astrabacus, traces this belief to a kind of marriage ritual (cf. W. Burkert, 'Demaratus, Astrabakos und Herakles: Konigsmythos und Politik zur Zeit der Perserkriege (Herodot 6.67-9)', *Museum Helveticum* 22, 1965, pp. 166-77; A. Seeberg, 'Astrabika (Herodotus 6.68-9)', *Symbolae Osloenses*

41, 1966, pp. 48-75) in which the husband is thought to embody a god during the act of intercourse.

ἀναίρεον: in the context of oracles and prophecies, the verb means 'proclaim', 'decree', 'ordain', give an oracular response'. Cf. 1.13.1.

69.4 ἐν γάρ σε τῇ νυκτὶ ταύτῃ ἀναιρέομαι: 'for it was on this night that I conceived you', an example of the rhetorical figure hyperbaton, in which the prepositional phrase ἐν τῇ νυκτί is broken up by the insertion of the pronoun σε, which would more naturally be placed closer to its verb. The disruption of the natural order is perhaps intended to indicate the emotional turmoil affecting Demaratus' mother as she tells her tale.

οὐ φήσειέ σε ἑωυτοῦ εἶναι: 'he said you weren't his'. For οὐ φημί, see note on 1.1, and cf. 50.2 and 52.4 above.

ἀπέρριψε τὸ ἔπος: 'uttered the remark'. ἀπορίπτω usually has this sense in contexts where disparagement or insult is intended on the part of the speaker. Cf. 1.153.2, 4.142, 8.92.2.

69.5 ἐννεάμηνα καὶ ἑπτάμηνα: eight month pregnancies are perhaps omitted because of a belief that eight month children tended to be still-born. See the Hippocratic treatise traditionally (e.g. in the Littré edition, vol. 7) known as *Peri Heptamenou* (= *De Septimestri Partu*), but in B. Joly's more recent Budé translation combined with and printed under the title of the *Peri Octamenou* (*De Octimestri Partu*) (Hippocrate, Tome XI, Paris, 1970, pp. 149-81), 2.1, 2.2, 5.1. Cf. 4.1, φήσουσι (sc. γυναῖκες) τίκτειν καὶ ἑπτάμηνα καὶ ὀκτάμηνα καὶ ἐννεάμηνα καὶ δεκάμηνα καὶ ἑνδεκάμηνα, καὶ τούτων τὰ ὀκτάμηνα οὐ περιγίνεσθαι, τὰ δ' ἄλλα περιγίνεσθαι. Other medical writers who mention the non-viability of the eight month child include the Pythagoreans (Diog. Laert. 8.29, cf. Censorinus, *De Die Natali* 9.33, 11.2-10), Empedocles (H. Diels and W. Kranz, *Die Fragmente der Vorsokratiker*, ed. 10, Berlin, 1952, 31 B69) and Aelius Quintilianus 3.23. Even Aristotle (*Genertation of Animals* 772b) states that 'the eight month child will live, but less often'. On the other hand Damastes (*On the Care of Pregnant Women and Infants* 2) is prepared to accept the viability of eight month children. The idea that the eight month child is unlucky, even doomed, depends on the view that children are born an exact number of days after the date of conception, and is based less on sound medical gounds than on Pythagorean theories on the harmoniousness or otherwise of the sequence of numbers determined from calculations of the lengths of the early stages of foetal devevlopment. See A.E. Hanson, 'The Eight Month's Child and the Etiquette of Birth', *Bulletin of the History of Medicine* 61, 1987, pp. 589-602; H.N. Parker, 'Greek Embryological Calendars and a Fragment from the Lost Work of Damastes, On the Care of Pregnant Women and of Infants', *CQ* 49, 1999, pp. 515-34.

λόγους...ἄλλους: here equivalent to 'other tales', 'other stories'.

ἀκήκοας: 2nd. pers. sing. perf. of ἀκούω.

70.1 ἐπόδια: Attic ἐφόδια, 'provisions for a journey', including food and money.

τῷ λόγῳ φάς: 'saying by way of pretext', 'in pretence', giving the ostensible objective of his trip, where λόγῳ is used as the opposite of ἔργῳ or τῷ ὄντι. See note on 38.2 above.

70.2 ἔφθη ἐς Ζάκυνθον διαβάς: 'having crossed from Zacynthos before they got there'. For φθάνω, see note on 65.2 above. Zacynthos is an island in the Ionian Sea due west of the Peloponnesian state of Elis.

ἐπιδιαβάντες: 'having crossed over in pursuit of him'. Cf. 4.122.3.

μετὰ δὲ: 'and afterwards'. See note on 4.1 above.

γῆν τε καὶ πόλις: in Asia Minor, including Pergamum, Halisarna and Teuthrania (Xen. *Hell.* 3.1.6), which were inherited by his descendants. It was traditional for Persian rulers to receive prominent Greek exiles, to whom they assigned territories which would provide them with revenues for their maintenance. So Histiaeus (Hdt. 5.11.2), Metiochus (ch. 41.4 above), Gongylus of Eretria (Xen. *Hell.* 3.1.6) and Themistocles (Thuc. 1.138.5; Plut. *Them.* 29.7). Demaratus subsequently accompanied Xerxes on his invasion of Greece as one of his respected advisors on Greek affairs (Hdt.7.3.2, 7.101.1, 7.234, 7.237), though Plut. (*Them.* 29.5-6) has a less favourable account of Demaratus' later career.

70.3 Λακεδαιμονίοισι...ἀπολαμπρυνθείς: 'he became renowned in the eyes of the Spartans', a claim that is somewhat exaggerated in that he had to play second fiddle to Cleomenes throughout his reign, and emerged as something of a defeatist who was for the most part content to react to rather than to mould foreign policy. Even Plutarch was able to discover only three apophthegms to ascribe to his reign (*Mor.* 220A-B): the remaining five in his collection all belong to Demaratus' life in exile.

ἐν δὲ δή: 'and among them', adverbial, as at 11.1 and 50.2 above and at 86.4 below.

Ὀλυμπιάδα σφι ἀνελόμενος τεθρίππῳ προσέβαλε: 'he assigned to them an Olympic victory which he had won in the four-horse chariot race', where with the adj. Ὀλυμπιάδα the noun νικήν is to be understood, and taken as the object of both ἀνελόμενος and προσέβαλε. Victories in the Panhellenic games were proclaimed in the name of the winner, with the addition of the name of his city. In equestrian events, it was the name of the owner of the victorious team which was announced, and in suppressing his own name in favour of that of his city, Demaratus will have sought to confer additional glory on his fellow citizens by implying that the team was owned by the state rather than by himself, thereby taking the opportunity for once to upstage Cleomenes.

πάντων δὴ τῶν γενομένων βασιλέων: 'of all the kings who ever existed at Sparta'. His victory was subsequently equalled by that of Cynisca, sister of king Agesilaus (Xen. *Ages.* 9.6; Paus. 3.8.1 and 3.15.1. Cf. Plut. *Ages.* 20.1).

71.1 Κύνισκον: a diminutive of κύων, meaning literally 'puppy' (Attic uses κυνάριον and κυνίδιον). Cf. the name Cynisca ('Little Bitch') given to Zeuxidamus' grand-daughter, Agesilaus' sister (Poralla *PL* no. 459).

μετεξέτεροι: 'some', an Ionic pronoun equivalent to the Attic ἔνιοι or τινες. Cf. 1.63.1, 1.95.1, 1.199.5.

οὐκ ἐβασίλευσε: 'did not become king', ingressive aor. See note on at 25.2 above.

Εὐρυδάμην: Poralla *PL* no. 319. Nothing more is known about this lady or her family.

ἔρσεν: neut. of ἐρσήν, the Ionic form of ἀρσήν or ἀρρήν, 'male', 'masculine'.

Λαμπιτώ: Poralla *PL* no. 474. Her name is given as Lampido by [Plato], *Alc.* I 124a and Plut. *Ages* 1.1.

Ἀρχίδημος...γαμέει: marriage between nephew and aunt, though less common than between uncle and niece, was not unknown in the Greek world. Marriage to a relative (endogamy) was favoured as a means of keeping property within the family, and seems to have been particularly common in both royal families. Cf. in the Agiad line, the uncle-niece marriages of Anaxandridas (5.39.1) and of Leonidas and Gorgo (7.239.4). The Agiad Cleombrotus II (Plut. *Agis* 11.5) and the Eurypontids Eudamidas II (Plut. *loc. cit.*) and Archidamus V (Polybius 4.35.13) were all married to relatives.

72.1 τίσιν τοιήνδε...ἐξέτισε: 'he paid the following penalty', a cognate or internal acc. (Goodwin 1051).

ἐστρατήγησε...ἐς Θεσσαλίην: according to Pausanias (3.7.9), the expedition was directed against the Aleuadae, the leading family in Thessaly and their power base Larissa, probably as part of a campaign to overthrow medising regimes which had encouraged and supported Xerxes' invasion. The Aleuadae, headed by the three brothers Thorax, Eurypylus and Thrasydaeus (9.58.1), were notorious for their devotion to Persia (9.1). This campaign is probably to be identified with that mentioned by Plutarch (*Mor.* 859D), where Leotychidas is credited with the overthrow of two Thessalian dynasts, Aristomedes and another, whose name has been corrupted in the mss. tradition, but which may be restored as Agelaus. The expedition is to be dated not long after the Persian withdrawal in 479, and perhaps in 476 if Diodorus (11.48.2) has confused the date of Leotychidas' deposition with that of his death (which belongs to 469, on the assumption that the length of his reign is correctly given as 22 years in the same passage. See note on 72.2 below).

παρεὸν δέ οἱ ὑποχείρια πάντα ποιήσασθαι: 'though it was in his power to subdue everything'. παρεόν is the part. of the impers. πάρεστι, 'it is possible', used in the acc. absolute construction, normal with impersonal verbs (Goodwin 1569). Since Leotychidas' campaign did meet with some success (see previous note), a more charitable explanation for his failure at Larissa might be simply that the Aleuadae were too strong to dislodge.

ἐδωροδόκησε ἀργύριον πολλόν: 'he took a large sum of money as a bribe'. δωροδοκέω is usually used absolutely with the meaning 'accept bribes', as in ch. 82 below, but here it appears to be transitive, as in Plato, *Rep.* 590a, unless ἀργύριον is to be construed as another internal acc.

72.2 ἐπ' αὐτοφώρῳ δὲ ἁλούς: 'having been caught in the act', where ἁλούς is the aor. participle from ἁλίσκομαι, which serves as the pass. of αἱρέω, 'take'. The true pass. of this verb (ᾑρέθην) usually means 'was chosen', thus serving as pass. of the middle αἱρέομαι, 'choose'.

αὐτοῦ: 'there', adverbial.

ἐπικατήμενος χειρίδι: 'sitting on his sleeve', used to cover the hand and lower arm in cold weather, and on the present occasion presumably hanging loose from his garment.

ἔφυγε: 'he was banished', used, as at 123.1 below, in the legal and judicial sense as pass. to ἐκβάλλω or ἐξελαύνω.

ὑπὸ δικαστήριον ὑπαχθείς: 'having been brought before a law court', i.e.'having been put on trial'. The court which sat in judgment on a king was composed of the *gerontes* and ephors sitting jointly (Paus. 3.5.2).

τὰ οἰκία οἱ κατεσκάφη: 'his house was demolished', aor. pass. of κατασκάπτω. For the demolition of a king's house as a judicial penalty, see also Thuc. 5.63.2, who records the imposition of the same punishment on Agis II in 418.

ἔφυγε δὲ ἐς Τεγέην: to the sanctuary of the temple precinct of Athena Alea (Paus. 3.7.10), where king Pausanias subsequently sought refuge in 394 (Paus. 3.5.6). For other instances, see Hdt. 9.37.4 (Hegesistratus) and Paus. 3.5.6 (Chrysis). King Pleistoanax on the other hand fled to the Lycaeum when exiled in 446 (Thuc. 5.16.3).

ἐτελεύτησε ἐν ταύτῃ: if Diodorus correctly gives the length of Leoty-chidas' reign as 22 years (11.48.2), his death must have occurred in 469/8 rather than in 476/5 as stated in the same passage, since he came to the throne in 491. The date of 469/8 also suits the figure of 42 years ascribed by Diodorus to his grandson and successor Archidamus, who is last mentioned alive in 428 (Thuc. 3.1.1; Diod. 12.52.1) and was dead by 426 (Thuc. 3.89.1). If so, the date of 476/5 given by Diodorus for Leotychidas' death will be that of his trial and condemnation, and the years of exile reckoned as part of his reign, as in the parallel case of Pleistoanax who was king from 458/7 to 446/5 and again from 426 until 408/7, but is credited by Diodorus (13.75.1) with a reign of fifty years.

73.1 τότε: 'at this time', i.e. 'at the time of which I am speaking', with refer-ence to the time of Leotychidas' accession to the throne, as opposed to that of his death. The narrative resumes from ch. 50, following the lengthy digres-sion on Spartan customs and the circumstances of Leotychidas' accession.

ὡς τῷ Κλεομένεϊ ὡδώθη τὸ ἐς τὸν Δημάρητον πρῆγμα: 'when his plot against Demaratus had gone well for Cleomenes', or, with preservation of Herodotus' metaphor, 'when the road which Cleomenes had taken against Demaratus had brought him success'. ὁδόω, derived from ὁδός, 'road', means literally 'lead along the correct way', 'direct', 'guide', and is used metaphorically both here and at 4.139.2, τὰ ἀπ᾽ ὑμέων χρηστῶς ὁδοῦται, 'the road along which you guide us is good'.

ἐδικαίευν: see note on 15.2 above.

73.2 ἔτι ἀντιβαίνειν: 'to resist any more', a favourite word of the historian. Cf. 3.72.5; 5.40.1; 8.3.1.

ἦγον: 'proceeded to take away'. See note on 5.1 above.

καὶ δὴ καὶ Κρῖόν: on καὶ δὴ καί, see notes on 21.2 and 49.1 above, and cf. 137.4 below. Crius was a prominent 'nationalist' at Aegina, who had previously obstructed Cleomenes' attempt to arrest Aeginetan medisers (see ch. 50 above). He later fought bravely against Xerxes at Salamis (8.92.1).

τοὺς ἐχθίστους Αἰγινήτῃσι Ἀθηναίους: it was the Athenians who had instigated Cleomenes' intervention in the first place (see ch. 49.2 above). This mutual antagonism had come to a head soon after 506, when Aegina became involved in the war between Athens and Boeotia (see Hdt. 5.81-6), but geographical proximity and trade rivalry had poisoned relations between the two states for most of the preceding century.

74.1 ἐπάϊστον γενόμενον κακοτεχνήσαντα ἐς Δημάρητον: literally 'having been detected in his plots against Demaratus', i.e. 'when reports of his machinations against Demaratus became known'. ἐπάϊστον is the verbal adj. from ἐπαΐω, 'perceive', 'have knowledge of', commonly used in Hdt, as here, with the part. (cf. 2.119.3; 3.15.4; 7.146.1; 8.128.2).

ὑπεξέσχε: 'he withdrew secretly', used intransitively, as at 5.72.1 and 8.132.2. The secrecy was necessary if he was to to avoid a prosecution for treason and/or impiety.

ἐς Θεσσαλίην: the choice of pro-Persian Thessaly as a refuge by such a staunch anti-Persian is at first sight surprising, in fact so surprising that scholars have sought to emend the text to read Σελλασίην, a place in Spartan territory to the north of Sparta (see D. Hereward in *Classical Review* 1, 1951, p. 146, who asks, 'Why should Cleomenes want to go to Thessaly? If his plan was to return to Sparta with the help of the Arcadians, why didn't he go to Arcadia first?' Cf. A. Griffiths, 'Was Kleomenes Mad?', in A. Powell (ed.), *Classical Sparta: Techniques behind her Success*, London, 1989, p. 74, note 22). However, though Sellasia was not within the polis territory of Sparta, it did lie in perioecic lands, and Cleomenes would there have been at the mercy of the Spartan authorities, should they wish to arrest him. Thessaly on the other hand was at this time the strongest power in the north of Greece and no friend of the Spartan government: what Cleomenes needed in the first instance was an assurance of safety, and his choice of the one Greek state sufficiently strong and antagonistic to defy any demand for his extradition was sensible in the circumstances. It was only when it became clear that the Spartan authorities had no intention of applying for his extradition and that his Thessalian hosts were unwilling to take any active steps to promote his restoration that he moved to Arcadia.

νεώτερα ἔπρησσε πρήγματα: 'he sought to initiate a revolutionary move-ment'. The phrase is suggestive of the verb νεωτερίζω and its related noun νεωτεροποιΐα, which are used of political movements designed to change the *status quo*, in this instance to overturn the existing alliance of the Arcadian communities with Sparta, and eventually the decision of the Spartan authori-ties to banish him.

συνιστὰς τοὺς Ἀρκάδας ἐπὶ τῇ Σπάρτῃ: 'uniting the Arcadians against Sparta'. The Arcadians had a long history of disunity, and were riven by petty animosities, above all between Mantinea in the north and Tegea in the south. Though the Arcadians had been enrolled piecemeal in the Peloponnesian League, there was a good deal of internal dissension which Cleomenes hoped to turn to his own advantage. Numismatic evidence indicates the existence of a sort of unified Arcadian League in the early fifth century (see W.H. Wallace, 'Kleomenes, Marathon, the Helots and Arkadia', *JHS* 74, 1954, pp. 32-5; R.T. Williams, *The Confederate Coinage of the Arcadians in the Fifth Century BC*, New York, 1965), but it is doubtful whether this League had anything to do with Cleomenes' activities in the area. It is more likely to have been a later development.

ὅρκους προσάγων σφι ἦ μὲν ἕψεσθαί σφεας αὐτῷ τῇ ἂν ἐξηγῆται: 'putting oaths to them to follow him wherever he led them'. The particles ἦ μέν (poetic and Ionic) and ἦ μήν (Attic) are used with the inf. after ὄμνυμι, 'swear' and other verbs and phrases of similar meaning. In τῇ ἂν ἐξηγῆται, the more vivid subj. with ἄν is here used in preference to the opt. without ἄν in an indefinite relative clause (Goodwin 1431b).

Νώνακριν: an Arcadian town in the territory of Pheneus in the north of the country close to the border with Achaea, reputedly named form the wife of Lycaon, the Arcadian king who was either blasted by lightning or trans-formed into a wolf for serving human flesh to Zeus (Paus. 8.2.3, 8.17.6).

τῶν Ἀρκάδων τοὺς προεστεῶτας ἀγινέων: 'bringing the leading men of the Arcadians'. προεστεῶτας is the second perf. of προΐστημι, 'put in charge', with intransitive meaning. ἀγινέω is the Ionic form corresponding to the Attic ἄγω.

ἐξορκοῦν τὸ Στυγὸς ὕδωρ: 'to administer an oath by the waters of Styx', where the person or object by which the oath is sworn is put in the acc. (Goodwin 1049). Oaths sworn by the Styx were regarded as particularly solemn by gods and men (*Iliad* 2.755, 14.271, 15.37; Hesiod, *Theogony* 775, 805-6; Vergil, *Aeneid* 12.816). This oath was particularly appropriate for Arcadians, who gave the name of the river of the underworld to a stream near Nonacris which in falling over rocks into the river Crathis formed the highest waterfall in Greece. Because of its exceptional coldness, this water was believed in antiquity to be deadly to humans and corrosive to metals: only the hoof of a horse was thought to be proof against corrosion, and Alexander the Great was rumoured to have been killed by drinking from water smuggled into camp in this way (Paus. 8.17.6-18.6; Plut. *Alex.* 77.2; Arrian, *Anab.* 7.27.2; Justin 12.14.7).

74.2 στάζει ἐς ἄγκος: 'drips into a hollow'.

αἱμασιῆς τις περιθέει κύκλος: 'a circular wall (literally 'the circle of a wall') runs round it'. The word αἱμασία refers to a wall made of dry stones, and occurs elsewhere in Hdt. (e.g. 1.180.2, 1.191.5, 2.69.3, 2.138.3).

75.1 Μαθόντες...Κλεομένεα...ταῦτα πρήσσοντα: 'learning that Cleomenes was doing these things', acc. and part. instead of acc. and inf. after a verb of perception (Goodwin 1588). See note on 13.1 above.

κατῆγον αὐτὸν: see notes on 5.1 and 40.2 above.

ἐπὶ τοῖσι αὐτοῖσι...τοῖσι καὶ πρότερον ἦρχε: 'on the very same conditions as those under which he had ruled in the past', i.e. he was restored to the throne which he had vacated on fleeing the country, and granted immunity from prosecution for his corruption of the Pythia.

αὐτίκα ὑπέλαβε μανιὰς νοῦσος: 'a manic disease immediately seized him'.

ἐόντα καὶ πρότερον ὑπομαργότερον: 'being somewhat inclined to madness even before'. The adj. doubly tones down the extent of the madness (cf. the note on ὑποθερμοτέρου at 38.2 above) and may have been used by the historian's Spartan informants to explain the improbability of why someone who had browbeaten the authorities into granting his every wish should have suddenly been seized by madness. Cf. the use of the phrase οὐ φρενήρης, ἀκρομανής τε at 5.42.1. Pausanias' paraphrase of Hdt. at 3.4.1, ἐξώρμει τὰ πολλὰ ἐκ τοῦ νοῦ is also somewhat guarded, in that the prepositional phrase is qualified and the use of the imperf. tense is suggestive of a slow decline rather than of a sudden stroke. In fact his policies show little sign of an irrational mind, and stories of his madness are generally dismissed as inventions of his enemies such as the supporters of Demaratus or his own alienated half-brother Dorieus. However a few modern scholars who have submitted him to psychoanalysis have detected some of the symptoms of a manic depressive, a schizophrenic or at least a maladjusted personality. See esp. the discussion by Alan Griffiths, 'Was Kleomenes Mad?' in A. Powell (ed.), *Classical Sparta*, pp. 51-78. Certainly Cleomenes' penchant for abusing religion and perpetrating sacrilegious acts will have been seen by the superstitious Spartans as abnormal, if not evidence of mental derangement, and will have helped to make such charges credible.

ὅκως γάρ τεῳ ἐντύχοι Σπαρτιητέων: 'whenever he encountered a Spartiate', an indefinite/frequentative temporal clause. See notes on 31.1 and 61.3 above, and cf. also 77.3, 121.2, and 137.3 below.

ἐνέχραυε ἐς τὸ πρόσωπον τὸ σκῆπτρον: 'he would thrust his staff into his face'.

75.2 ἔδησαν οἱ προσήκοντες ἐν ξύλῳ: 'his relatives confined him in a pillory'. ξύλον, literally 'wood', is here used by metonymy for a wooden contraption in which one's feet are confined while the hands are left free, as they are not in the stocks, the mediaeval equivalent. In the laws of most Greek states, including presumably Sparta, an insane individual would be entrusted to the care of a guardian (ἐπιτρόπος, ἐπιμελητής , cf. Latin *curator*), who would normally be the closest agnate. In Cleomenes' case these would be his two surviving half-brothers Leonidas and Cleombrotus, of whom the former will have ruled Sparta during Cleomenes' period of exile, and may have been reluctant to relinquish power after Cleomenes' return. The complicity of Leonidas and Cleombrotus in Cleomenes' demise cannot be proved, but they had both motive and opportunity. At very least, they could be considered negligent in discharging the duties of guardianship.

φύλακον: the regular Ionic word for 'guard', equivalent to the Attic φύλαξ. Cf. 1.84.2, 1.89.3, 2.113.3.

ἠπείλεε τά μιν λυθεὶς ποιήσει: 'he proceeded to threaten him with what he would do to him if he secured his release', where λυθείς is temporal or conditional.

ἦν γὰρ τῶν τις εἱλωτέων: 'for he was one of the Helots'. For the Helots, see note on 58.3 above. Having no rights, the Helot guard would have been totally at the mercy of any Spartiate, and much more so when that Spartiate was a king.

ἤρχετο ἐκ τῶν κνημέων ἑωυτὸν λωβώμενος: 'he began mutilating himself from the shins upwards'. κνήμη denotes the part of the leg between the ankle and knee, as opposed to μῆρος, the part of the leg from the knee upwards. Cf. the story of Hegelochus (9.37), who obtained a knife in similar circumstances and cut off his foot in order to escape from the pillory. Cleomenes' death is far more horrific in that the self-mutilation apparently lacked purpose. Whether he really did kill himself in this way, or whether he was 'killed trying to escape', and the whole story of his madness and suicide fabricated by the authorities, remains a moot point.

75.3 κατὰ μῆκος: 'lengthwise', i.e. in vertical strips.

καταχορδεύων: literally 'making mincemeat of', i.e. 'turning into meat for the manufacture of sausages', from χορδή, 'guts', 'sausage'.

τὴν Πυθίην ἀνέγνωσε: 'he persuaded the Pythia'. For this meaning of ἀναγιγνώσκω, see note on 50.2 above.

ἐς Ἐλευσῖνα ἐσβαλὼν: in 506, at the time of the triple invasion of Attica by the Peloponnesians, Boeotians and Chalcidians. See Book 5.74.

ἔκειρε τὸ τέμενος τῶν θεῶν: 'he ravaged the precinct of the goddesses', i.e. Demeter and Core, the two goddesses worshipped at Eleusis. κείρω means literally 'crop', 'shear', 'fleece', 'cut one's hair', 'strip the foliage from'. From this last sense comes the meaning 'cut down fruit trees', and so, more generally, 'ravage'.

ἐξ ἱροῦ αὐτῶν τοῦ Ἄργου: 'from the holy ground of Argus', i.e. from ground consecrated to the hero Argus, which included a sacred grove (Paus.

2.20.8). This Argus was son of Zeus and Niobe (Paus. 3.4.1), who originally gave his name to the entire Peloponnese, though only the city of Argos chose to perpetuate it after the arrival in Greece of Pelops from Lydia.

τοὺς καταφυγόντας ἐκ τῆς μάχης: 'the fugitives from the battle'. The reference is to the battle of Sepeia in 494, where Cleomenes defeated the Argives, many of whom sought refuge in the sacred grove after the engagement. See chapters 78-80 below.

ἐν ἀλογίη ἔχων: 'holding it in little regard', 'holding it as of no account', a meaning of ἀλογία that is peculiarly Ionic (cf. 2.141.1, 4.150.4, 7.208.3, 7.226.2). In Attic, the word means 'lack of reasoning', 'absurdity', 'irrationality'.

76.1 μαντευομένῳ: 'as he was consulting the oracle', a not unusual preliminary to a campaign abroad. Argos was not only Sparta's traditional enemy but was showing an increasingly pro-Persian attitude in matters of foreign policy, which will have worried the Spartan authorities. For this oracle, see PW no. 86, Fontenrose *DO*, Q136.

Ἐρασῖνον: the modern Kephalari, a river in Argive territory which emerges from a limestone cliff at the foot of Mt. Chaon (modern Megalovouni) and flows into the sea north of Lerna, to the south of Argos (Paus. 2.36.6).

ἐκ τῆς Στυμφηλίδος λίμνης: a body of water by the city of Stymphalus in the north east of Arcadia, in modern times considerably larger than it was when seen by Pausanias (8.22.3). It was the breeding ground in Greek mythology of the monstrous flesh-eating birds which were cleared from the area by Heracles.

ἀναφαίνεσθαι ἐν Ἄργεϊ: for the tradition that the waters of Stymphalus ran underground only to reappear as the Erasinus, see Strabo 8.6.8, 8.8.4 and Pausanias 2.24.6, 8.22.3. Though the distance between the cave at Stymphalus and the source of the Erasinus is some 30 miles, this story is still believed by the locals, and indeed widely accepted by scholars (e.g. W.K. Pritchett, *Studies in Greek Topography*, Vol. I, Berkeley and Los Angeles, 1965, pp. 122-3). More probably the river is fed by rains falling over a considerable area of eastern Arcadia.

ἐσφαγιάζετο αὐτῷ: 'he sacrificed to it', i.e. to the river god. The reference is probably to *diabateria*, offerings made to mark the crossing of a frontier (see note on ch. 56 above), and indeed the historian himself implies this in the next sentence. However the Erasinus can hardly have formed the frontier between Argive territory and the Spartan controlled Thyreatis, which lay much further to the south. Either Cleomenes sacrificed to the Erasinus purely as a river god (and if he was looking for an excuse to abandon a direct land assault on Argos in the face of the strong Argive resistance, this is possible, even probable), or the Erasinus marked the border not between Laconia and Argolis but between the city of Argos and its subject perioecic territory. In this event, Cleomenes' action may be understood as a piece of propaganda designed to show that Sparta henceforth recognised the Erasinus as marking the frontier of the Argive state, or, in other words, that the perioecic territories to the south of the river were now to be freed from Argive control and given their autonomy. Certainly some Argive subjects *were* liberated as a result of this campaign (for Mycenae and Tiryns as Spartan allies at the time of Xerxes' invasion, see 7.202, 9.28.4; Diod. 11.65.2; Paus. 5.23.2); and for later Argive attempts to regain these lost territories, see Diod. *loc. cit.*; Paus. 5.23.3, 7.25.5 and esp. 8.27.1, where Tiryns, Hysiae, Orneae, Mycenae and Midea are named. For Lerna, which was undoubtedly to the south of the Erasinus frontier (Paus. 2.36.6), there is unfortunately no evidence. A.R. Burn (*PG*, pp. 228-9) offers yet another solution to the problem in identifying the Erasinus not with the Kephalari but with the modern Xabrio, which, since it debouches into the sea further south than the Kephalari, may possibly have marked the Spartan/Argive frontier in 494.

οὐ γὰρ ἐκαλλιέρεε...διαβαίνειν: 'for omens favourable to his crossing were not obtained'. καλλιερέω or καλλιερέομαι can be used with a personal subject in the sense of 'obtain a favourable omen', as at ch. 82.2 below and at 7.113.2. In the present passage, as at 7.134.2, 9.19.2 and 9.38.2, the verb is used either impersonally or with the offering (τὰ ἱρά) to be understood as subject.

Ἀργείους μέντοι οὐδ' ὣς χαιρήσειν: literally 'but not even so would the Argives rejoice'. χαίρω is often used idiomatically in the sense of 'get away with', 'escape punishment'.

Θυρέην: a city due south of Argos and east of Tegea, in the valley of the Tanaus, which gave its name to the adjacent territory of the Thyreatis (see Thuc. 2.27.2 and Paus. 2.38.5). It had formerly belonged to Argos, but had been seized by the Spartans by the time of Croesus' war with Cyrus, perhaps as a result of the Spartan victory over the Argives at Parparus ('The Battle of the Champions') in 547 or 546 (Hdt. 1.82.2). Since the Argives never recognised its loss, control of this border land continued to poison relations between the two states throughout the classical period and beyond. By entering the Thyreatis, Cleomenes was retreating to the south.

σφαγιασάμενος δὲ τῇ θαλάσσῃ ταῦρον: a similar sacrifice is made to Poseidon at *Odyssey* 3.5-6.

πλοίοισι...ἤγαγε ἔς τε τὴν Τιρυνθίην χώρην καὶ Ναυπλίην: Cleomenes embarked his army on boats and sailed north east across the Thyrean Gulf. Tiryns and Nauplia both lay to the east of Argos, the latter on the coast at a place which provided a good site to disembark. If the Argive army was blocking all approaches to the city by land, Cleomenes had little option but to go by sea, and, though the Spartans may have considered this to be untraditional, even undignified, Cleomenes' change of tactic certainly caught the Argives by surprise, and obliged them to abandon their chosen positions in order to return to protect their city. In chapter 92.1-2 we are informed that Cleomenes commandeered the boats from Aegina and Sicyon. Unless he had been planning a naval expedition all along, a considerable delay is likely to have occurred while he procured them. Scholars who believe that he had the vessels already prepared maintain that the unfavourable omens at the Erasinus were faked to forestall any objections to his plan.

77.1 τῷ κέεται Ἡσίπεια οὔνομα: 'to which the name of Hesepeia is given'. κεῖμαι, 'lie', is also used as the pass. of τίθημι. The place name is variously given in the manuscripts as Hesepeia, Sippeia and Sipeia, but is otherwise unattested (apart from a possible Arcadian analogue at Paus. 8.16.2, where the manuscripts read Sepia): modern scholars generally prefer to read Sepeia. Whatever the correct form of the name, the reference is to a place some two miles south east of Tiryns.

μεταίχμιον: literally 'between spears', i.e. the space between two armies, as at ch. 112.1 below. The word is also used (e.g. at 8.140β3) of a sort of no man's land, the ownership of which is disputed between two neighbouring states.

μὴ δόλῳ αἱρεθέωσι: 'lest they be caught by guile'. For the syntax of verbs of fearing, see Goodwin 1378: here the subj. of primary sequence is retained in secondary sequence in place of the opt. The aor. pass. of αἱρέω is used here, as elsewhere in Hdt., in the sense of 'be taken', whereas in Attic the meaning is regularly 'be chosen'. See note on 72.2 above.

77.2 τὸ ἐπίκοινα ἔχρησε ἡ Πυθίη: 'the Pythia declared an oracle to them in common', where ἐπίκοινα is adverbial acc. (Goodwin 1060). For the Milesian part of the oracle, see ch. 19.2 above. The oracle appears as PW no. 84 and Fontenrose *DO*, Q134.

ἀλλ᾽ ὅταν ἡ θήλεια τὸν ἄρσενα...ἐξελάσῃ: 'but when the female drives out the male'. For temporal ὅταν with the subj. referring to the future, see Goodwin 1434. It is possible that the oracle should be interpreted as little more that a figurative *adynaton*, in that chauvinistic Greeks would have had about as much belief in the ability of women to drive out men as we have in the ability of pigs to fly. More prosaically, the oracle would be predicting an Argive victory, in that only when pigs fly would the Argive women have cause to mourn. However, to safeguard Apollo's reputation in the event of a Spartan victory, the oracle would have been constructed in such a way as to allow for an alternative interpretation. Since the noun 'Sparta' is in Greek feminine and the city of Argos, though in fact neuter, could be represented by its eponymous hero Argus (masculine), the oracle could also be open to interpretation as the prediction of a Spartan victory over Argos. However some ancient writers, rejecting both explanations in favour of a more literal interpretation, saw fulfilment of the prophecy in the story of the Argive poetess Telesilla, whose patriotic verses encouraging Argive resistance could be said to have driven out the Spartans despite their victory in the field. This tale, told originally by the Argive local historian Socrates, is preserved by Plutarch (*Mor.* 223B-C, 245C-E) and Pausanias (2.20.8-10), but Herodotus' silence guarantees its falsity. Socrates' somewhat sensational account contained fabrications such as the forced entry of Demaratus into the city and his capture of the Pamphyliacum, which cannot possibly be true, not only because his role is othewise unattested, but because the reform of 506 (Hdt. 5.75.2) would have made it illegal for him to campaign alongside his colleague Cleomenes outside Spartan territory.

πολλὰς Ἀργείων ἀμφιδρυφέας...θήσει: 'will make many of the Argive women tear their cheeks', as a sign of mourning. The rare adj. ἀμφιδρυφής is derived from the verb δρύπτω, 'tear one's cheek': the intensive prefix ἀμφι- should refer to the laceration of both cheeks.

δεινὸς ὄφις τριέλικτος: 'a terrible snake of triple coils'. Since the snake was a Spartan emblem, this is perhaps another attempt to suggest an Argive victory. There may well be a reference to the story of the Heraclid conquest of the Peloponnese, in which the three victorious brothers cast lots to determine which portions of territory each should rule. According to Apollodorus (2.8.5), they found signs lying on the sacrificial altar: Temenus, who obtained Argos, found a toad, Cresphontes who drew Messenia, a fox, and Aristodemus, or his twin sons Eurysthenes and Procles, a serpent. According to Pausanias (10.26.3), Polygnotus the sculptor depicted Menelaus, in the statue erected at Delphi, with the device of a serpent on his shield, thus lending some support to the origin of the story as far back as the classical period.

77.3 ταῦτα δὴ πάντα συνελθόντα: 'all these things having coincided'.

δόξαν...ἐποίευν τοιόνδε: 'they proceeded to the following decision'.

ὅκως...προσημαίνοι...ἐποίευν...τὠυτὸ τοῦτο: 'whenever he gave a signal, they proceeded to do the very same'. For temporal ὅπως and its syntax, see note on 31.1 above, and cf. 61.3, 75.1, 121.2, and 137.3.

78.1 μαθὼν δέ...ποιεῦντας τοὺς Ἀργείους ὁκοῖόν τι ὁ σφέτερος κῆρυξ σημήνειε: 'on learning that the Argive women were doing whatever their (i.e. the Spartans') herald was signalling'. For the acc. and part. in indirect statement after a verb of perceiving, see Goodwin 1494 and 1588, and for the opt. in indefinite relative clauses, see Goodwin 1431.2.

ὅταν σημήνῃ ὁ κῆρυξ ποιέεσθαι ἄριστον: 'when the herald gave the signal to take breakfast'. For the retention in the historic sequence of indirect speech of ἄν with the subj in place of the opt. in temporal clauses with future reference, see Goodwin 1461.2. For the periphrasis ποιέεσθαι ἄριστον instead of the verb ἀριστάω or ἀριστοποιέομαι, see note on 27.3 above and cf. 61.1.

78.2 ταῦτα καὶ ἐγένετο ἐπιτελέα ἐκ τῶν Λακεδαιμονίων: 'this was accomplished successfully by the Spartans'. For the use of ἐκ to indicate the agent, see note on 13.1 above, and cf. 22.1, 42.1, 61.4 and 124.2. For the phrase ἐπιτελὴς γίνομαι, cf. 1.124.1 ταῦτά τε δὴ ὦν ἐπιτελέα ἐγίνετο.

ἐκ τοῦ κηρύγματος: 'in accordance with the proclamation', to be taken with ἄριστον ποιευμένοισι.

ἐπεκέατο: Ionic 3rd. plur. pluperf. of ἐπίκειμαι, 'attack'. See note on 44.3

above and cf. 49.2. Herodotus (with Polyaenus 1.14) is our only source for this particular story. Pausanias' brief version (2.20.8, 3.4.1) has nothing about deception or treachery, though Plutarch (*Mor.* 223B; cf. Cicero, *De Officiis* 1.10.33, where Cleomenes is unnamed) does narrate a tale of perfidy, even perjury on Cleomenes' part, whereby he makes a truce with the Argives for seven days, only to attack in the course of the third night, with the pretext that the truce covered only days, not nights. This version may reflect the official Argive account of the battle, and explain its alternative name which we find in our non-Herodotean sources. See Aristotle, *Politics* 1303a 7, who refers mysteriously to Cleomenes' slaughter of Argives ἐν τῇ ἑβδόμῃ (sc. ἡμέρᾳ) and Plutarch *Mor.* 245E (τὴν μάχην οἱ μὲν ἑβδόμῃ λέγουσιν ἱσταμένου μηνός).

πολλοὺς μὲν ἐφόνευσαν: 6000, according to Hdt. 7.148.2, though this figure gives the totality of Argive casualties suffered both in the battle and in the subsequent massacre in the grove. Plut. (*Mor.* 245E) rejects a tradition that the casualties amounted to 7777, while Pausanias (3.4.1) has 5000 killed in the grove alone, thus making the massacre more disastrous than the losses in battle.

τὸ ἄλσος τοῦ Ἄργου: the grove sacred to the hero Argus (the gen. of Argos the city would be Ἄργους). On the hero of this name, see note on 75.3 above.

ἐφύλασσον: 'they proceeded to keep a close watch on', to ensure that escape was impossible.

79.1 φὰς αὐτῶν ἔχειν τὰ ἄποινα: 'saying that he had their ransom'. For the form φάς, see note on 58.3 above. ἄποινα, 'ransom', is essentially a poetic word found in prose also at 9.120.3 and Plato, *Laws* 862c. The usual prose word for 'ransom' is τὰ λύτρα.

ἄποινα δέ ἐστι Πελοποννησίοισι δύο μνέαι τεταγμέναι κατ' ἄνδρα αἰχμάλωτον ἐκτίνειν: 'among the Peloponnesians two minae is the regular sum fixed as ransom for each prisoner'. τεταγμέναι is perf. part. pass. from τάσσω/τάττω. A payment of 2 minae (= 200 drachmae) per head as ransom appears also at 5.77.3, where the Athenians charge this amount to free the Boeotian and Chalcidian prisoners captured in 506. The norm appears to have been 100 drachmas (Androtion Frag. 44J; Aristotle, *Eth. Nic.* 1134B; Diodorus 14.102.2, 14.111.4), though even higher rates are attested ($2^1/_2$ minae, Plut. *Fab.* 7.4; 3 minae, Demosthenes 19.169, Aristotle, *Oec.* 1349b; 5 minae, Dem. 19.169, Livy 34.50.6, Plut. *Flam.* 13.5; still higher rates are not unknown ([Dem.] 12.3; Polyb. 21.26.8; Diod. 20.84.6). Ransom was normally arranged and paid by the family and friends of the captive, who raised the money as best they could. It was rare, but not entirely unknown, for the state to assume responsibility (in Hdt., the only recorded cases occur at 5.77.3 and 9.99.2). For ransoming in general, see W.K. Pritchett, *The Greek State at War*, Vol. 5, Berkeley, Los Angeles and Oxford, 1991, pp. 245-91.

κατὰ πεντήκοντα: 'about 50', where κατά is used to express a round number. See note on 44.3 above and cf. ch. 117 below.

ὅ τι ἔπρησσον: 'what they were doing', 'how they were faring', 'what was happening to them'.

πρίν γε δὴ αὐτῶν τις...κατεῖδε: 'until at length one of them looked down'. For the construction with πρίν, see note on 22.1 above.

80 πάντα τινὰ τῶν εἱλωτέων: 'every single one of the helots', not only because the collection and piling up of wood was a menial occupation, but because the helots, not being legally part of the state, technically freed the state from any taint of the sacrilege which the burning of a sacred grove would constitute. So too the claim of Cleomenes by a piece of sophistry that he ordered only the burning of firewood, not of the grove.

Ἄργου: for the hero Argus, see note on 75.3 above.

φάμενος: see note on 58.3 above.

συμβάλλομαι δ᾽ ἐξήκειν μοι τὸ χρηστήριον: 'I conjecture that the oracle has been fulfilled for me'.

81 ἤϊε ἐς τὸ Ἡραῖον θύσων: 'he proceeded to the Heraeum to sacrifice'. ἤϊε is the Ionic imperf. of εἶμι, 'go', where Attic has ᾔει. For the use of the fut. part. to express purpose, see note on 28.2, and cf. 33.2, 34.1, 35.3. The Heraeum was the sanctuary of Hera, the tutelary deity of Argos, constructed in the 8th century BC some 5 miles to the north east of the city. Since this was not on the direct route of Cleomenes' way back to Sparta, his detour was presumably made as an act of political propaganda under the cloak of religion to emphasise both Argive powerlessness and the long arm of a Spartan king.

ὁ ἱρεὺς ἀπηγόρευε: cf. the story of Cleomenes' forcible entry into the shrine of Athena on the Athenian Acropolis over the objections of the priestess (5.72.3). Both incidents demonstrate his willingness, even eagerness to indulge in sacrilege if it helped to humiliate a defeated people and emphasise the omnipotence of both Sparta and himself, provided of course that he could avoid incrimination on technical grounds.

ἐκέλευε τοὺς εἵλωτας: for much the same reason as in the case of the sacred grove.

82.1 ὑπῆγον οἱ ἐχθροὶ ὑπὸ τοὺς ἐφόρους: 'his enemies brought him before the ephors'. The identity of these enemies is unfortunately not specified, but his despotic and abrasive character ensured that there plenty of them around. One might be tempted to include the supporters of his colleague Demaratus, with whom he had clashed in 506 (5.75), to say nothing of his surviving half-brothers, who may well have shared the opinion of Dorieus (5.42). The ephors were presumably the proper authorities to approach with a view to the institution of legal proceedings, but the actual trial of a king would also have involved the *gerousia* (see note on 72.2 above).

φάμενοί: see note on 58.3 above.

παρεὸν εὐπετέως μιν ἑλεῖν: 'it being possible for him to capture it easily', acc. absolute from an impers. verb. See note on 72.1 above.

εἶπαι: see note on 61.5 above and cf. ἀπείπαντο at 100.1 below.

ἐξεληλυθέναι: perf. inf. of 'come out', used in the sense of 'be fulfilled', 'come true'.

πρίν γε δὴ ἱροῖσι χρήσηται καὶ μάθῃ: 'until such time as he made use of sacrifice and learned'. In sentences with a negative principal verb, πρίν referring to the future is normally followed by ἄν with the subj., or, in historic sequence by the opt. without ἄν. The use of πρίν and the subj. without ἄν is rare in prose outside Hdt. (it is found, e.g. at 1.32.5, 1.136.2 and 4.157.2), but common in Homer and tragedy. See Goodwin 1471-3.

82.2 καλλιερευμένῳ: 'while he was sacrificing', i.e. while he was attempting by means of sacrifice to obtain favourable omens. On this verb, see note on 76.1 above.

ὅτι οὐκ αἱρέει τὸ Ἄργος: 'that he would not capture Argos', where the pres. is used as a substitute for the fut. in the interests of vividness. Cf. the use of ποιέετε for ποιήσετε at 86.1 below.

αἱρέειν ἂν κατ' ἄκρης τὴν πόλιν: 'he would have made every effort to capture the city completely', where ἄν with the pres. inf. does duty for the nonexistent imperf. inf. to represent what in direct speech would have been an imperf. indic. denoting the action of an unreal condition represented as going on for some time in the past (Goodwin 1285 and 1397). For the phrase κατ' ἄκρης, see note on ch. 18 above.

πᾶν οἱ πεποιῆσθαι: 'everything had been done by him', where οἱ is dat. of the agent after a pass. See note on 53.2 above, and cf. 123.2 and 130.2 below.

οἰκότα: 'what is probable', Ionic perf. part. of εἴκω, where Attic uses ἐοικότα.

διέφυγε πολλὸν τοὺς διώκοντας: literally 'he escaped his prosecutors by much', i.e. 'he avoided condemnation at the hands of the prosecution by a large number of votes', where φεύγω and διώκω are both used in a legal sense. The mss. are divided between διαφεύγω and ἀποφεύγω. Both compounds occur in Hdt., but ἀποφεύγω (in *OCT*) is normal, at least in Attic, in the legal sense. πολλόν is an adverbial acc. (Goodwin 1060).

83.1 οἱ δοῦλοι...ἔσχον...τὰ πρήγματα: 'the slaves took over control of affairs', where ἔσχον is an ingressive aor. (see note on 25.2). The enormous losses sustained at Sepeia certainly will have made it impossible for the state to function effectively without some extension of the franchise, but the identity of these 'slaves' is problematic. They may have been, as Hdt. implies, the serfs or *gymnetes* (the 'Naked' or 'Unarmed'), who had toiled on the citizens' land, the Argive equivalent of the Spartan helots (Pollux 3.83; cf. Diod. 10.26 *oiketai*; and R.F. Willets, 'The Servile Interregnum at Argos', *Hermes* 87, 1959, pp. 495-506), but it is difficult to believe that the Argives took such a desperate step even in this emergency when there were more worthy and less politically sensitive candidates for citizenship available. Plut. (*Mor.* 245F) seeks to correct Herodotus by claiming that the new citizens were not serfs but *perioici*, the inhabitants of the various communities subordinate to the

Argive state, such as Tiryns and Orneae. He seems to have taken this statement from Aristotle, *Politics* 1303a, but it is by no means certain that Plutarch's interpretation of the Aristotle passage is correct. He clearly believes Aristotle to be using the word *perioici* as a term with the meaning it bore at Sparta, though in fact at *Politics* 1272a Aristotle uses the term of individuals who are the Cretan equivalent of the Spartan helots. If Aristotle uses the word in this latter sense at 1303a, he would be in agreement with Herodotus' interpretation. For a discussion of the problem, see W.G. Forrest, 'Themistocles and Argos', *CQ* 10, 1960, pp. 221-41, who makes a good case for believing that Hdt. has misunderstood the term *douloi*, which his Argive informants were using as a pejorative term for their *perioici*. R.A. Tomlinson (*Argos and the Argolid*, London, 1972, pp. 96-100) maintains that the difference between *douloi* and *perioici* was more apparent than real and that the political status of the Argive subject communities was no different from that of their serfs. See also E.W. Robinson, 'The First Democracies: Early Popular Government outside Athens', *Historia Einzelschrift* 107, Stuttgart, 1997, pp. 82-8.

ἐς ὃ ἐπήβησαν οἱ τῶν ἀπολομένων παῖδες: 'until the time that the sons of those killed attained maturity', where ἐπήβησαν is the Ionic form of the aor. of the verb equivalent to the Attic ἐφηβάω, from ἥβη, 'youth', 'maturity'. For the restoration of the former regime, which could conceivably have happened at any time in the 480s, 470s or indeed in the early 460s, Hdt. provides no date.

83.2 ἔσχον Τίρυνθα: ingressive aor. (seenote on 25.2). Tiryns was a township some $4^1/_2$ miles to the south east of Argos, and less than 1 mile from the sea. A place of importance in the Bronze Age, it was at this time but a shadow of its glorious past, and the ability of the expelled 'slaves' to occupy and retain it lends some support to the view that they originated in the subject communities. Tiryns was still independent of Argos at the time of Xerxes' invasion (see note on 76.1 above). It may possibly have been liberated by Cleomenes after Sepeia and still not formally reintegrated into the Argive state when occupied by the 'slaves'. Forrest (*op. cit.*) plausibly suggests that the expulsion of the 'slaves' from Argos is reflected in the change of attitude of the Argives towards the Arcadian revolt from Sparta c.470: in the first campaign which culminated in a battle in the vicinity of Tegea (Paus. 3.11.7), the Argive government which assisted the Arcadians would still have been in the hands of the 'slaves', while the failure to continue that support into the Dipaea campaign of the following year (Paus. 3.11.7, 8.8.6) suggests both a reversal of policy and a change of regime.

83.2 σφι ἦν ἄρθμια ἐς ἀλλήλους: literally 'there were friendly relations with one another', i.e. 'relations between the two factions were amicable'. The adj. ἄρθμιος, which means literally 'united' (cf. ἄρθρον, 'joint'), is used by Hdt. with the meaning 'on good terms' (cf. 7.101.2, 9.9.2).

Φιγαλεύς: an inhabitant of Phigaleia, a city in the south west of Arcadia near the river Neda and close to the frontier with Messenia and Triphylia.

ἀνέγνωσε: 'he induced'. See note on 50.2 above.

οἱ Ἀργεῖοι ἐπεκράτησαν: Tiryns was destroyed by the Argives following its recapture (Paus. 2.17.5, 2.25.8, 5.23.3), and if Forrest is correct in dating its recovery from the 'slaves' to 468, Herodotus' belief in a previous period of peaceful coexistence between the two regimes is likely to be correct.

84.1 ἀκρητοπότην: 'a drinker of unmixed wine', from κεράννυμι, 'mix'. Greeks regularly adulterated their wine with water before drinking, in the case of symposia in proportions fixed by the symposiarch or master of ceremonies (see J. Davidson, *Courtesans and Fishcakes*, London, 1997, pp. 46-8). To drink unmixed wine was the mark of the barbarian, above all of the Scythian (Plato, *Laws* 637e).

84.2 ἐπείτε σφι Δαρεῖον ἐσβαλεῖν ἐς τὴν χώρην: Darius' Scythian campaign, which took place somewhere in the years 514-512, is described in Book 4.

μεμονέναι: 'eager to punish him'. μεμονέναι is the inf. of μέμονα, an essentially poetic perf. tense with no pres. in regular use.

πέμψαντας δὲ ἐς Σπάρτην: the story of the Scythian embassy, though not impossible, is generally discounted on the grounds that there was no unified Scythian state, and that these nomads were too unsophisticated politically to be capable of diplomacy as Greeks understood it. If the story is a fabrication, it may have been invented by the Spartans to explain how Cleomenes acquired his taste for unmixed wine.

παρὰ Φᾶσιν ποταμόν: 'along the river Phasis', a river flowing into eastern shore of the Black Sea, in the country known in the ancient world as Colchis, covering much the same area as the modern state of Georgia. The plan appears to envisage a Scythian invasion of the Persian Empire from the north, through the Caucasus, Armenia and Media, where they would link up with the Spartans marching inland from the Aegean coast along the Royal Road as far as Mesopotamia, whence they were to turn north into Media.

ἀναβαίνειν: 'to march up country', i.e. away from the sea.

ἐς τὠυτὸ ἀπαντᾶν: 'to meet at the same place'.

84.3 μᾶλλον τοῦ ἰκνεομένου: 'more than was fitting'. See note on 57.4 above.

ἔκ τε τοῦ: 'ever since then', an emendation of the text, where the mss. have ἐκ τόσου or ἐκ τοσούτου, where τοῦ is to be explained as a relic of the archaic use of what was to become the definite article as a demonstrative pron. The expression is found at *Iliad* 8.296, and is parallel to the much commoner πρὸ τοῦ, 'formerly'. The normal Attic phrase is ἐκ τούτου (e.g. Xen. *Anab.* 5.8.15), and in Hdt. ἐκ τόσου (e.g. 5.88.3), which is retained here by *OCT*.

ἐπεὰν ζωρότερον βούλωνται πιεῖν: 'whenever they want a stronger drink than usual', a frequentative temporal clause with ἄν and the subj. (Goodwin 1431b). ζωρός is a synonym for ἄκρατος, with reference to wine unadulterated with water.

ἐπισκύθισον λέγουσι: 'they say "Pour out in Scythian fashion"', where ἐπισκύθισον is 2nd. pers. sing. aor. imper. of ἐπισκυθίζω. Cf. Anacreon Frag. 300B (Page) (= 356 Campbell):

> ἄγε δεῦτε
> Σκυθικὴν πόσιν παρ' οἴνῳ
> μελετῶμεν.

85.1 τελευτήσαντος δὲ Κλεομένεος: Hdt.'s narrative clearly places the death of Cleomenes prior both to the abortive democratic coup in Aegina in 491 or 490 (chs 88-9 below) and to the Marathon campaign, certainly of 490. If this chronology is to be accepted, we must pack into this one extremely eventful year the flight of Demaratus (see note on 67.2), the visit of Cleomenes and Leotychidas to Aegina, Cleomenes' flight to Thessaly and subsequent activities in Arcadia, his reinstatement, madness and death, the attempted coup in Aegina and the Marathon campaign. This is just possible (see N.G.L. Hammond, 'Studies in Greek Chronology of the Sixth and Fifth Centuries BC', *Historia* 4, 1955, pp. 406ff.), but the degree of compression required by this scheme makes it difficult to accept. It is more likely that Hdt.'s chronology needs revision, and that the trouble stirred up by Cleomenes in Arcadia was one of the reasons for the halfheartedness of the Spartans in coming to the support of Athens at Marathon (see note on 106.3 below). The strain on the chronology is somewhat lessened if Cleomenes' death is dated after rather than before the Marathon campaign, and so to the end of 490 or in 489. See T.J. Figueira, 'The Chronology of the Conflict between Athens and Aegina in Herodotus Book 6', *Quaderni Urbinati di Cultura Classica* 28, 1988, pp. 48-89 (reproduced in *Excursions in Epichoric History: Aiginetan Essays*, Lanham, 1993, pp. 113-49), who makes a good case for dating Cleomenes' death to the winter of 490/89 at the earliest. If this is the case, Aeginetan behaviour as described by Hdt. in this chapter will have been motivated by news not of Cleomenes' death but of his condemnation and exile.

καταβωσομένους: 'to inveigh against', 'to raise an outcry against', fut. part. expressing purpose (see note on ch. 7 above).

περὶ τῶν ἐν Ἀθήνῃσι ὁμήρων: see ch. 73 above.

περιυβρίσθαι: perf. inf. pass.

85.2 Θεασίδης: Poralla no. 356. Nothing is known of him outside this passage.

ὅκως...μή...ἐσβάλωσι: 'see to it that they do not bring'. ὅπως and ὅπως μή are commonly used with the fut. indic. to express a command or prohibition: the subj. also occurs less commonly (only here in Hdt.), but only with ὅπως μή. The construction is usually explained as an ellipse of a verb of taking care in the imper., such as ὁράω, εὐλαβέομαι, φυλάσσομαι, σκοπέω or ἐπιμελέομαι. See Goodwin 1352-4.

85.3 ἔσχοντο τῆς ἀρωγῆς: 'they refrained from carrying him off'. ἔσχοντο is aor. middle of ἔχω. ἔχομαι with the gen. usually means 'hold fast to', 'adhere to', as at 94.1 below. The meaning here, 'abstain from', is essentially poetic, though it also occurs at 7.169.2 and 7.237.3.

ἐπισπόμενον: aor. of ἕπομαι, 'follow', indicating voluntary rather than enforced accompaniment.

86.1 ἀπαίτεε τὴν παραθήκην: 'he demanded back the deposit', i.e. the hostages deposited at Athens by Cleomenes and Leotychidas (see 73.2 above).

προφάσιας εἶλκον: 'they proceeded to trot out all manner of excuses'. Cf. Aristophanes, *Lysistrata* 726-7:

πάσας τε προφάσιας ὥστ᾽ ἀπελθεῖν οἴκαδε
ἕλκουσιν.

φάντες δύο...βασιλέας παραθέσθαι καὶ οὐ δικαιοῦν τῷ ἑτέρῳ ἄνευ τοῦ ἑτέρου ἀποδιδόναι: 'saying that two kings had deposited them and that they did not think it right to hand them over to one king without the other'. The Athenians thus neatly turn back on the Spartans the words of Demaratus (see 50.2 and 73.1 above). For δικαιόω with the inf., see note on 15.2 above and cf. 138.2 below.

ποιέετε ὅσια: 'you will be acting rightly', where the pres. replaces the fut. in the interests of vividness. Cf. note on 82.2 above.

86.2 κατὰ τρίτην γενεὴν τὴν ἀπ᾽ ἐμέο: 'about the time of the third generation before me'. Since Hdt. normally reckons three generations to a century (see 2.142.2), the date should be somewhere about 550.

Γλαῦκον Ἐπικύδεος: Poralla, *PL*, no. 188. This man is not known outside the context of this story, which is also told by Plut. *Mor.* 556D and Pausanias 8.17.8. (Cf. Juvenal 13.199-203). The story is regarded as fictional by Fontenrose (p. 118).

περιήκειν τὰ πρῶτα: 'had attained the first position', 'was preeminent'.

ἀκούειν ἄριστα: 'be well spoken of', 'have the best reputation'. Cf. 9.79.1. ἀκούω is frequently used idiomatically as the pass. of λέγω, especially in the phrases εὖ and κακῶς ἀκούω, 'be well (badly) spoken of'. See Goodwin 1241.

δικαιοσύνης πέρι: 'concerning justice'. See note on 4.1 above.

86.3 συνενειχθῆναι δέ οἱ...τάδε λέγομεν: 'we say that the following befell him', where συνενειχθῆναι is the aor. inf. of συμφέρομαι with the dat. οἱ in the sense of 'happen to'.

ἐν χρόνῳ ἱκνεομένῳ: 'at the appointed time', 'in due time'.

βούλεσθαί οἱ ἐλθεῖν ἐς λόγους: 'wanted to have a conversation with him', 'wanted to speak with him'.

προϊσχόμενον τοιάδε: 'making the following proposition'.

86.4 ἐν δὲ: 'and within it', with the prep. ἐν used adverbially. See note on 11.1 above.

ἐμεωυτῷ λόγους ἐδίδουν: 'I began to take thought with myself', i.e. 'to reflect in my own mind'.

ἐπικίνδυνός ἐστι αἰεί...Ἰωνίη: presumably the historian is thinking of the many wars fought by the Ionians among themselves in the archaic period (see G.L. Huxley, *The Early Ionians*, London, 1966, chapter 5, pp. 47-54) and of the unrest brought about subsequently by their incorporation into first the Lydian and then the Persian Empires in the 6th century.

ἡ δὲ Πελοπόννησος ἀσφαλέως ἱδρυμένη: 'the Peloponnese being stable in security', a distinctly optimistic statement, given the war between Sicyon and Pellene (Aelian, *Var. Hist.* 6.1), the unrest at Corinth culminating in the overthrow of the Cypselids (Aristotle, *Pol.* 1315b26; Nicolaus of Damascus, Frag. 60), the war between Sparta and Tegea (Hdt. 1.65-8), and the war between Sparta and Argos c.547 ending with the Battle of the Champions (Hdt. 1.82), if indeed the two last wars antedate the Glaucus affair. The Milesian may have had in mind the relative stability effected by the Spartans with the conclusion of a series of alliances with Peloponnesian states that became the nucleus of what was to become the Peloponnesian League.

διότι χρήματα οὐδαμὰ τοὺς αὐτοὺς ἔστι ὁρᾶν ἔχοντας: 'because it is not possible to see the same people continue in possession of any property', where accented ἔστι is used in the sense of 'be possible'.

86.5 ἐξαργυρώσαντα: 'having converted it into silver'.

σύμβολα: tokens or tallies such as the two pieces of a divided coin, each of which was retained by one of the partners to the agreement, and brought together by the partners or their representatives as proof of identification when the money was reclaimed.

ἀποδοῦναι: 2nd. aor. inf. of ἀποδίδωμι, used as the equivalent of the imper. (Goodwin 1536). This use of the inf. is common where, as here, it is joined with another verb or verbs in the imper. (cf. 3.134.5, 3.155.5, 5.23.3), without being restricted to this situation (cf. 1.32.7).

86.β1 ἐπὶ τῷ εἰρημένῳ λόγῳ: 'on the terms stated', where εἰρημένῳ is perf. pass. of λέγω.

86.β2 διωθέετο: 'he attempted to spurn them', 'he kept trying to put them off'.

οὔτε με περιφέρει οὐδὲν εἰδέναι τούτων τῶν ὑμεῖς λέγετε: 'neither does it occur to me to know anything of what you say', where περιφέρει is used in the sense of 'put something back in one's memory', with a vague subject such as ἃ λέγετε to be supplied from the phrase that follows. τούτων τῶν λέγετε is used in place of τούτων ἃ λέγετε, with attraction of the rel. pron. to the case of its antecedent. See Goodwin 1031-2 and note on 21.1 above. Cf. ch. 87 and 112.3 below.

εἴ γε ἀρχὴν μὴ ἔλαβον: 'if I didn't receive it at all'. For ἀρχήν, see note on 33.3 above.

νόμοισι τοῖσι Ἑλλήνων χρήσομαι ἐς ὑμέας: literally 'I shall use Greek practices against you', i.e. 'I shall deal with you in accordance with Greek custom'.

ταῦτα...ἀναβάλλομαι κυρώσειν: 'I postpone fulfilment of these things'. The fut. inf. is normally used only to represent a fut. indic. in indirect statement. Otherwise this construction occurs mainly after μέλλω, 'intend

172

to', 'be about to'. However it may also be used in place of a pres. inf. when emphasis is placed on the notion of futurity (Goodwin 1277). Here Hdt. wishes to stress Glaucus' procrastination. Cf. 5.49.9 ἀναβάλλομαι ἐς τρίτην ἡμέρην ἀποκρινέεσθαι.

86γ συμφορὴν ποιεύμενοι: see note on 61.3 above.

χρησόμενος τῷ χρηστηρίῳ: 'in order to consult the oracle'. See note on ch. 7 above.

εἰ...τὰ χρήματα ληΐσηται: 'if he should plunder', the indirect quotation of the deliberative question 'Am I to plunder?', with retention of the subj. of the direct speech. For deliberative questions, see Goodwin 1358 (in direct speech) and 1490 (in indirect speech). Glaucus' question is intended to remind the reader or listener of Hesiod, *Works and Days* 320 ff., with the verb ληΐσηται borrowed from line 322.

μετέρχεται: 'rebuked him', historic pres.

τοισίδε τοῖσι ἔπεσι: PW no. 35, Fontenrose *DO*, Q92. PW (Vol. I, p. 381) argue for the authenticity of the oracle, while Fontenrose *DO* (pp. 118-19) regards it as a palpable fiction. In favour of the latter view is the similarity of the story to tales told by Conon 38 and Stobaeus, *Flor.* 3.28.21. The response itself is largely manufactured from various Hesiodic phrases.

86.γ2 κέρδιον: (sc. ἐστι) 'it is better', 'it is more profitable'. κέρδιον is a compar. adj. with no positive form in use, based on the noun κέρδος, 'advantage', 'gain', and serving as one of the comparatives of ἀγαθός.

Ὅρκου πάϊς: the personification of ὅρκος is borrowed from Hesiod, *Works and Days* 219 and 804, *Theogony* 231.

οὐδ' ἔπι χεῖρες, οὐδὲ πόδες: 'he has neither hands nor feet', where ἔπι with accent on the first syllable stands for ἔπεστι, 'there are on him'.

γενεὴν καὶ οἶκον ἅπαντα: the extirpation of the perjurer's family is taken over from Hesiod, *Works and Days* 282-5:

ὃς δέ κε...ἐπίορκον ὀμόσσας

ψεύσεται, ἐν δὲ δίκην βλάψας νηκέστου ἀασθῇ

τοῦ δὲ τ' ἀμαυροτέρη γενεὴ μετόπισθε λέλειπται.

ἀνδρὸς δ' εὐόρκου: this entire line is borrowed unchanged from Hesiod, *Works and Days* 285.

συγγνώμην τὸν θεὸν παραιτέετο...τῶν ῥηθέντων: 'he proceeded to ask forgiveness from the god for what had been said'. Verbs of asking (and also of teaching and concealing) are often followed by two accusatives, one of the person and the other of the thing requested (Goodwin 1069).

ἔφη τὸ πειρηθῆναι τοῦ θεοῦ καὶ τὸ ποιῆσαι ἴσον δύνασθαι: literally 'said that to put the god to the test and to commit the deed were of equal validity', i.e. 'were one and the same', 'were equally wicked'.

86.δ ὡρμήθη λέγεσθαι: 'began to be told', i.e. 'was mentioned in the first place'. Cf. 4.16.1 ὅδε ὁ λόγος ὅρμηται λέγεσθαι. The mss. are divided between ὁρμήθη and ὡρμήθη, the usual Attic form. Since the temporal augment is not

173

infrequently omitted in Hdt., the augmented form may be due to copyists familiar with Attic usage.

οὔτ' ἱστίη οὐδεμία νομιζομένη εἶναι Γλαύκου: 'nor is there any hearth acknowledged as belonging to Glaucus'. ἱστίη is the Ionic equivalent of Attic ἑστία, 'hearth', used by extension (the figure of speech called *synecdoche*) to mean 'house' (cf. 5.40.2 διξὰς ἱστίας οἴκεε), 'household', 'family', as at 1.176.3 οἱ πολλοὶ, πλὴν ὀγδώκοντα ἱστιέων.

ἐκτέτριπταί τε πρόρριζος: 'has been wiped out from the foundation', 'obliterated root and branch'. ἐκτέτριπται is perf. pass. of ἐκτρίβω, 'rub out'.

μηδὲ διανοέεσθαι περὶ παρακαταθήκης ἄλλο γε ἢ ἀποδιδόναι: 'not having any thought about a deposit other than to give it back'.

εἴπας: see note on 61.5 above.

87 πρὶν...δοῦναι δίκας: see note on 45.1.

τῶν ἐς Ἀθηναίους ὕβρισαν: attraction of the acc. case of the rel. pron. to the case of its antecedent (ἀδικημάτων). See note on 21.1. Cf. 86β2 above and 112.3 below.

Θηβαίοισι χαριζόμενοι: see 5.79-81, where Hdt. describes how the Thebans obtained Aeginetan help against Athens after the latter's defeat of Thebes in 506.

ὡς τιμωρησόμενοι...παρεσκευάζοντο: 'they began to make preparations with a view to punishing them'.

πεντετηρὶς: literally, 'period of five years', used above all in connection with quinquennial events such as festivals, and hence, by inclusive reckoning, equivalent to 'festival celebrated every four years', 'quadrennial festival'.

ἐπὶ Σουνίῳ: 'off Sunium', the cape at the south eastern tip of Attica, on which was built the famous temple of Poseidon. The festival in question was in all probability in honour of the sea god and included the boat race mentioned by Lysias (21.5).

τὴν θεωρίδα νέα: the ship which conveyed the *theoroi* or sacred delegates, the state appointed dignitaries who sailed from Athens to celebrate the festival.

88 οὐκέτι ἀνεβάλλοντο μὴ οὐ τὸ πᾶν μηχανήσασθαι: 'they no longer hesitated to devise everything possible'. Verbs denoting a negative idea such as preventing, refusing, hesitating or forbidding may be followed by μή with the inf.: when they are themselves negative, the inf. which follows may be preceded by μὴ οὐ (Goodwin 1550 and 1616).

Νικόδρομος: nothing is known of him apart from what we are told in the present passage and 91.1 below. The words ἀνὴρ δόκιμος suggest that he came from the same background as the governing oligarchy and was probably a disgruntled noble (see T.J. Figueira, *Aegina: Society and Politics*, New York, 1981, pp. 306-10).

μεμφόμενος μὲν τοῖσι Αἰγινήτησι προτέρην ἑωυτοῦ ἐξέλασιν: 'having a grudge against the Aeginetans for their earlier banishment of him'. μέμφομαι is followed by the dat. of the person who is blamed and the acc. of the ground of complaint.

ἀναρτημένους: 'were ready to', part. of an Ionic verb ἀνήρτημαι, used only in the perf. and followed by the inf., with the meaning 'be prepared to'. Cf. 1.90.1, 7.8.γ1.

συντίθεται ᾿Αθηναίοισι προδοσίην Αἰγίνης: 'he arranged a betrayal of Aegina to the Athenians'. His reliance on Athenian aid suggests that he was far from confident of his chances of staging a successful coup on his own and that the amount of domestic support he enjoyed was not particularly great. Nicodromus' compact with Athens was motivated less by his democratic sympathies than by the wish to profit from the interest the Athenians were showing in the island, which was soon to manifest itself in their dedication in 487 of a precinct in Attica to Aeacus, the ruler of Aegina in mythological times (Hdt. 5.89.2).

89 κατὰ συνεθήκατο ᾿Αθηναίοισι: 'according as he agreed with the Athenians', i.e. 'in accordance with his agreement with the Athenians', where κατά is equivalent to καθ᾽ ἅ.

ἐς δέον: 'at the right time', 'when needed'. δέον is neut. part. of the impers. verb δεῖ, 'it is necessary', 'it is fitting', used as a noun.

τῇσι Αἰγινητέων συμβαλεῖν: 'with which to engage in combat with the Aeginetans'. The disparity in naval strength between the two states is clear, and Athens at this time gave no indication of being the naval power she was to become within the next decade.

Κορινθίων ἐδέοντο χρῆσαί σφι νέας: 'they asked the Corinthians to lend them ships', where χρῆσαι is aor. of. κίχρημι, 'provide', 'lend'.

ἦσαν γὰρ σφίοι...φίλοι ἐς τὰ μάλιστα: this statement is supported by the Corinthian role in undermining the Spartan decision to restore Hippias to Athens c.504 (Hdt. 5.92-3), and came about in good part because the two cities had a common enemy in Megara; Corinth is also likely to have looked favourably on any diminution of the power of her trade rival Aegina. The friendship between the two states did not survive the creation of the new Athenian navy in 482-0.

πενταδράχμους ἀποδόμενοι: 'selling them for 50 drachmas each'. The verb for 'sell' has its various tenses supplied by three different verbs (pres. πωλέω, ἀποδίδομαι; fut. πωλήσω, ἀποδώσομαι; aor. ἀπεδόμην, perf. πέπρακα). It is possible that a few of these ships may have been been triremes, of which Corinth by now possessed a considerable number, and if so, they are likely to have exercised a significant influence on the outcome of a battle in which most of the Aeginetan and Athenian ships were penteconters (Thuc. 1.13.2, 14.1; H.T. Wallinga, *Ships and Sea Power before the Great Persian War*, Leiden, 1993, pp. 7, 140-2). For Athenian triremes at this date, see ch. 39.1 above.

δωρεὴν: *OCT* reads δωτίνην, an Ionic and poetic word for 'gift' (cf. 1.61.3), for which Attic prefers δωρεά.

ἑβδομήκοντα νέας τὰς ἁπάσας: 'seventy ships in all'. πᾶς and ἅπας accompanied by the article are used with numerals in the sense of 'in all'.

Cf. 1.214.3 βασιλεύσας τὰ πάντα ἑνὸς δέοντα τριήκοντα ἔτεα and 9.70.5 Λακεδαιμονίων...ἀπέθανον οἱ πάντες...εἶς καὶ ἐνενήκοντα.

ὑστέρησαν ἡμέρῃ μιῇ τῆς συγκειμένης: 'they arrived later than the time agreed by one day'. ὑστερέω with the gen. means 'come too late for', and ἡμέρῃ μιῇ is a dat. of manner used with comparatives to denote the degree of difference (Goodwin 1184). Cf. κεφαλῇ μείζων, 'taller by a head'. Here the comparative idea is contained in the verb ὑστερέω, in that the sense is 'be later than one ought to'.

90 Σούνιον: see note on ch. 87 above. The choice of Sunium will have been made not just because of its geographical suitability as a base of operations against Aegina by sea, but also because refugee Salaminians may have been settled here in the past. See W.S. Ferguson, 'The Salaminioi of Heptaphyle and Sounion', *Hesperia* 7, 1938, pp. 1-74; S.C. Humphreys, 'Phrateres in Alopeke and the Salaminioi', *Zeitschrift für Papyrologie und Epigraphik* 83, 1990, pp. 43-8. Opposition to the settlement may have come from Aristeides, if his name is correctly restored in an ostrakon which accuses some prominent citizen of rebuffing suppliants ([Ἀριστείδης ho Λυσιμ]άχο [hος τὸ]ς ἱκέτας [ἀπέοσ]εν); see M. Lang, *The Athenian Agora 25: Ostraka* (Princeton, 1990), cat. no. 44, p. 37. The belief of Figueira (*op. cit.*, p. 283) that Nicodromus and his supporters were granted Athenian citizenship is not supported by Herodotus' text; the wholesale enfranchisement of large groups of foreigners is unheard of at Athens before the grant of 427 in favour of the Plataeans (Isocrates 14.51; Demosthenes 59.104; Diod. 15.46.6).

ἔφερόν τε καὶ ἦγον: see note on 42.1 above.

91.1 ταῦτα μὲν δὴ ὕστερον ἐγίνετο: the chronology of the war between Athens and Aegina is unclear from Herodotus' narrative. Though he admits here that the settlement of the Aeginetans at Sunium is taken out of sequence, he still appears to date the rest of the narrative of the war to the year 491/0, apparently between the death of Cleomenes and Marathon. However it is difficult, perhaps impossible, to fit these additional events into a period already overflowing with incident (see note on 85.1 above), and the warfare between the Aeginetans and their exiles based at Sunium could belong anywhere between the accession of Leotychidas in 491 and the reconciliation of Athens and Aegina in the face of the Persian threat in 481 (7.145.1). The only real argument in favour of a date prior to Marathon is the size of the Athenian fleet, which amounted to 50 in 491 but which had increased to 70 by 489 (see ch. 132.1 below). For modern treatments of the problem, see N.G.L. Hammond, 'Studies in Greek Chronology of the Sixth and Fifth Centuries BC: the War between Athens and Aegina c.505-481', *Historia* 4, 1955, pp. 406-11, who argues for acceptance of Herodotus' dating; M. Amit, 'Great and Small Poleis: A Study in the Relations between the Great Powers and the Small Cities in Ancient Greece', *Latomus* 134, 1973, pp. 17-29, who favours a date of c. 488/7; T.J. Figueira, 'The Chronology of the Conflict between Athens and Aegina in Herodotus Book VI', *QUCC* 28, 1988, pp. 49-90 (reprinted in *Excursions in Epichoric History: Aeginetan Essays*, Lanham, 1993, pp. 113-49), who maintains that the the ambush of the Athenian *theoroi* took place in 489 or 488 and that the resulting war began in 488 or 487. Such a date is supported by the oracle cited by Hdt. at 5.89 promising victory to the Athenians if they wait 30 years, which seems to have been composed with prior knowledge of the Athenian triumph of 458/7 (Thuc. 1.105; Diod. 11.78.4). This points to a date of 488 or 487 for at least some of the fighting described by Hdt. in the present passage and suggests that the Athenian defeat recorded in ch. 93 below gave Themistocles the opportunity to introduce his navy bill of 483 (Hdt. 7.144.1; Thuc. 1.14.3; Plut. *Them.* 4).

ἐπαναστάντος τοῦ δήμου; 'the populace having risen', gen. abs. ἐπαναστάντος is 2nd. aor. part. of ἐπανίστημι, 'I cause to revolt', with intrans. meaning.

ἐξῆγον ἀπολέοντες: 'proceeded to lead them outside in order to put them to death', where ἀπολέοντες is Ionic fut. part. (= Attic ἀπολοῦντες), used to express purpose (see note on ch. 7 above).

τὸ ἐκθύσασθαι οὐχ οἷοί τε ἐγίνοντο: 'when they were unable to expiate by sacrifice'. ἐκθύω means 'atone for by making offerings to the gods'.

ἔφθησαν ἐκπεσόντες: 'they were driven out before they could do so'. φθάνω with the part. means literally 'anticipate' or 'get in first by taking some action'. See Goodwin 1586 and cf. 108.2, 115 and 116.1 below. ἐκπίπτω, literally 'fall out', is regularly found serving as a passive to ἐκβάλλω, 'expel' (Goodwin 1241).

πρότερον...ἤ σφι ἵλεων γενέσθαι τὴν θεόν: 'before the goddess could become well-disposed to them'. πρότερον ἤ (literally 'sooner than') is used as a temporal conj. equivalent to, and with the same construction as, πρίν (Goodwin 1474).

91.2 πρόθυρα Δήμητρος θεσμοφόρου: for πρόθυρα, see note on 35.2 above. This cult title of Demeter was widespread in the Greek world, including Athens (Paus. 1.31.1, 1.42.6), Thebes (Paus. 9.6.5, 9.16.5), Drymaea (Paus. 10.33.12) and Troezen (Paus. 2.32.8).

ἐπιλαβόμενος...τῶν ἐπισπαστήρων εἴχετο: 'seizing hold of the handles of the door, he clung to them'. For the gen. with verbs of holding and clasping, see Goodwin 1099. In Greek eyes, the grasping of the handles was enough to put the suppliant under divine protection, even if he was unable physically to enter the shrine, and the attempt to drag him away was as sacrilegious as it would have been were he actually within the temple's confines.

ἐμπεφυκυῖαι ἦσαν τοῖσι ἐπισπάστροισι: 'they remained clinging to the handles', the periphrastic form of the 3rd. pers. plur. plup. pass. from ἐμφύω, 'implant', with intrans./pass. meaning.

92.1 τοὺς αὐτοὺς καὶ πρότερον, 'Αργείους: 'the same people as they had called upon before, namely the Argives'. For ὁ αὐτός καί, 'the same as', cf.

4.109.1 Βουδῖνοι...οὐ τῇ αὐτῇ γλώσσῃ χρέωνται καὶ Γέλωνοι; 8.45.1 τωὐτὸ πλήρωμα παρείχοντο τὸ καὶ ἐπ' Ἀρτεμισίῳ. Herodotus here refers back to the incident described at 5.86.4, where the Argives lent support to Aegina in an earlier bout of hostilities with Athens.

Αἰγιναῖαι νέες ἀνάγκη λαμφθεῖσαι ὑπὸ Κλεομένεος: in the Sepeia campaign of 494. ἀνάγκη is intended to suggest that the Aeginetans had participated only under duress. The Argive change of policy was dictated in part by the advent of a new government after Sepeia (see notes on 83.1-2 above), which felt little affinity with the policies of the former aristocratic regime and which feared possible Spartan displeasure if an official force were to be sent. The volunteers were presumably adherents of the former government who felt a moral obligation to assist their old friends and allies.

ἔσχον: 'put in at', intrans. use of ἔχω, particularly common in the aor. (as here) and in the fut. σχήσω.

92.2 ἐπεβλήθη ζημίη, χίλια τάλαντα ἐκτῖσαι: 'a penalty was imposed on them that they should pay', where ἐκτῖσαι is an inf. standing in apposition to the noun ζημίη (see Goodwin 1517). Herodotus fails to explain under what authority the Argives were empowered to levy this fine, though the decision of Sicyon to make a partial payment demonstrates that their right to do so was legitimate. It may have originated at a time when Argos exercised some sort of suzerainty over 'the lot of Temenus' (Apollodorus 2.8.4-5; Strabo 8.3.33; Pausanias 4.3.4-5) which may have included both Aegina (Pausanias 2.29.5) and Sicyon (Pausanias 2.6.7, cf. 2.11.2, 2.13.1), and which their king Pheidon is said by Ephorus (Frag. 115) to have sought to reestablish (see R.A. Tomlinson, *Argos and the Argolid*, London, 1972, pp. 58-63). An alternative explanation would make Argos the leading state and president of a religious league or Amphictyony, possibly centred on the sanctuary of Apollo Pythaeus (either at Argos, Paus. 2.24.1 or at Asine, Paus. 2.36.5; cf. Thuc. 5.53). Alternatively, as argued by T. Kelly (*A History of Argos to 500 BC*, Minneapolis, 1976, pp. 68-9) the Amphictyony may have been based on a cult carried on at the Argive Heraeum.

Αἰγινῆται...οὔτε συνεγινώσκοντο, ἦσάν τε αὐθαδέστεροι: for οὔτε...τε, see notes on 1.1 and 16.2 above.

ἐθελονταὶ δὲ ἐς χιλίους: presumably these volunteers deplored the neutrality of the regime now in power and were adherents of the pre-Sepeia government who had survived the disaster. Given the current strength of Argive manpower, the new regime will have permitted their participation only because they were perceived as potentially disaffected, and their classification as volunteers will have helped to allay possible Spartan objections.

πεντάεθλον ἐπασκήσας: 'who had practised the pentathlon' and so presumably of the upper classes and out of sympathy with the *perioicoi* now in power. This victory was won at the Nemean Games (Paus. 1.29.5). The pentathlic events, at least for the Olympic games, were throwing the discus, jumping, throwing the javelin, running and wrestling (Simonides, Epigram 42 in D.L. Page, *Epigrammata Graeci*, Oxford 1975).

92.3 Σωφάνεος τοῦ Δεκελέος: so Paus. 1.29.5. Herodotus provides more information about Sophanes at 9.73-5, where we are told that he went on to distinguish himself at Plataea in 479, and subsequently met his death as *strategos* in battle with the Thracians in 465 in an attempt to colonise Ennea Hodoi, the site of the future city of Amphipolis.

93 αὐτοῖσι ἀνδράσι: 'crew and all'. See note on αὐτοῖσι τοῖσι ἱροῖσι at ch. 32 above.

94.1 Ἀθηναίοισι μὲν δὴ πόλεμος συνῆπτο πρὸς Αἰγινήτας: 'so then war had been engaged in by the Athenians against the Aeginetans', a formula marking the end of the digression on Aegina begun in ch. 85. συνῆπτο is plup. pass. of συνάπτω, 'join together', commonly found with an object such as μάχην or πόλεμον. For the resumptive μὲν δή, see Denniston, *GP*, pp. 225-7.

ὁ δὲ Πέρσης: continued from the narrative of ch. 49, after a long series of digressions. Whatever the chronology of the Aeginetan digression (see notes on 85.1 and 91.1 above), we are now back in the year 490.

τὸ ἑωυτοῦ ἐποίεε: literally 'was doing his own thing', i.e. 'continued to further his plans'.

ὥστε ἀναμιμνήσκοντός...τοῦ θεράποντος μεμνῆσθαί μιν: 'in that his servant was along reminding him'. For causal ὥστε, see note on 44.3 above, and cf. 52.3 and 136.2.

μεμνῆσθαί μιν τῶν Ἀθηναίων: see 5.105.2, where Darius orders a slave to repeat to him whenever he is about to dine the words, 'Remember the Athenians'. The reference is to his desire for vengeance on Athens for the burning of Sardis in the Ionian Revolt in 498.

Πεισιστρατιδέων: Darius had been pressing for the restoration of Hippias, son of Peisistratus, to Athens ever since he had sought refuge at his court following his overthrow in 510, and indeed Hippias was to accompany the Persian expedition to Greece later in the year (see ch. 102, 107-9). Which other Peisistratids were in residence at the Persian court is unclear. Of Hippias' known brothers, Hipparchus had been assassinated in 514, and nothing is known of the fate and current whereabouts, if still alive, of Thessalus, Iophon and Hegesistratus (see note on 39.1 above), nor are they recorded as having progeny (Thuc. 6.55.1). Herodotus is here presumably thinking of Hippias' five children, of whom three are totally unknown. A fourth, Archedice, was married to Aeantides, son of Hippoclus tyrant of Lampsacus, (Thuc. 6.59.3), while the fifth, the younger Peisistratus, who had held the archonship at Athens in 522/1, presumably accompanied his father to Darius' court, and is in all probability to be reckoned among the Peisisistatids who were at this time seeking Persian help in effecting their restoration.

ταύτης ἐχόμενος τῆς προφάσιος: 'seizing upon this excuse', a clear indication that in Hdt.'s view, Persian expansionism would have led to an invasion of Greece irrespective of any provocation from Athens. On the meaning of ἔχομαι, see note on 85.3 above.

τοὺς μὴ δόντας: the negative with the part. is here μή rather than οὐ because it is generic (i.e. it is equivalent to the generic conditional clause τούτους οἱ ἂν μὴ δῶσι). See Goodwin 1413, 1612.

94.2 Μαρδόνιον: on his parentage, see note on 43.1 above.

φλαύρως πρήξαντα: 'as having fared badly', 'as having enjoyed little success', with particular reference to the destruction of his fleet off Athos and to the setback his army had suffered at the hands of the Brygi (ch. 44-5). For the phrase φλαύρως ἔχω, cf. 135.1 below.

ἐπί τε Ἐρέτριαν καὶ Ἀθήνας: the two Greek states which had participated in the Ionian Revolt (5.99).

Δᾶτίν τε ἐόντα Μῆδον γένος: 'Datis, a Mede by race', acc. of respect or specification (Goodwin 1058). Though tributary like all the races of the empire apart from the Persians (3.92.1), Medes were close kin to the Persians, and held important military offices under the Achaemenids (e.g. Harpagus, 1.162 ff., Polyaenus 7.6.7, Diodorus 9.35; Mazares, 1.156 ff., Polyaenus 7.6.4). Cf. Balcer, *A Prosopographical Study of the Ancient Persians*, pp. 340-2. Nothing is known of Datis' parentage or earlier career, though it is possible that he commanded the Persian fleet at Lade in 494 (see note on 9.1 above), and he may be the father of Harmamithres and Tithaeus who commanded the Persian cavalry during Xerxes' invasion of Greece (7.88.1).

Ἀρταφέρνεα τὸν Ἀρταφέρνεος: also spelt Ἀρταφρένης, or in Persian Artafarnah, 'possessing righteous glory'. The elder Artaphernes (Balcer 35), son of Hystaspes, half-brother of Darius and slayer of Smerdis (Aeschylus, *Persians* 776), was given the satrapy of Lydia after the end of the Scythian expedition (5.25.1) and still held the post in 492 (see ch. 42.1 above). The younger Artaphernes (Balcer 148), Darius' nephew, who shared the command of this mission with Datis, later commanded the Lydian and Mysian contingents of Xerxes' army during the invasion of Greece in 480 (7.74.2).

95.1 τῆς Κιλικίης ἐς τὸ Ἀλήϊον πεδίον: 'the Aleian Plain in Cilicia', a 'topographical' or 'geographical' genitive. Cf. τῆς Ἐρετρικῆς χώρης κατὰ Ταμύνας at 101.1 below, and Thucydidean phrases such as τῆς Ἀττικῆς ἐς Οἰνόην at 2.81.1 and τὸ Κήναιον τῆς Εὐβοίας at 3.93.1. The fertile Aleian Plain was situated between the rivers Sarus (Seyhan) and Pyramus (Ceyhan) to the north of the city of Mallus (modern Kiziltahta). The plain, which is mentioned in the *Iliad* (6.201), as well as by Strabo (14.5.17) and Arrian (*Anab.* 2.5.8), is said by Stephanus of Byzantium to derive its name from the city of Alae.

ὁ ἐπιταχθεὶς ἑκάστοισι: 'which had been levied from each of the peoples'. See ch. 48.2 above.

95.2 οὐ παρὰ τὴν ἤπειρον: 'not along the (coast of the) mainland', the natural and safe route for shipping and that previously taken by Mardonius (see ch. 43).

παρά τε Ἰκάριον καὶ διὰ νήσων: 'past the Icarian Sea and through the islands', i.e. by cutting directly across the Aegean through the middle of the Cyclades. The Icarian Sea is the south eastern part of the Aegean from Chios to Cos, named from the island of Icaria to the south west of Samos. The mss. read Ἰκάριον (sc. πέλαγος), 'the Icarian Sea', which the *OCT* emends to read Ἴκαρον, thus giving the meaning 'alongside (the coast of the island of) Icarus/Icaria'.

ὡς...ἐμοὶ δοκέειν: 'in my view', the absolute inf. in a parenthetical phrase (Goodwin 1534, and cf. 8.66.1, 9.113.2). The expression also occurs as the more expected ὡς ἐμοὶ δοκέει.

τῷ προτέρῳ ἔτεϊ: an error on Hdt's part. The Athos disaster, narrated in ch. 44, in fact took place in 492, not 491, though the orders for the construction of new triremes and horse-transports intended to replace those destroyed on Mt. Athos, may well have been issued in 491.

τὴν κομιδὴν μεγάλως προσέπταισαν: 'they suffered a great disaster in the course of their passage'. πταίω, which means literally 'stumble' and metaphorically 'come to grief', is a favourite item in Hdt.'s vocabulary, especially with the adv. μεγάλως (cf. 1.16.2, 2.161.4, 5.62.2). τὴν κομιδὴν is acc. of specification or respect (Goodwin 1058).

πρὸς δὲ: 'and moreover', an adverbial use of the prep. See note on 61.3 above and cf. 125.5 below.

ἡ Νάξος...πρότερον οὐκ ἁλοῦσα: 'the fact that Naxos had not previously been captured', 'their previous failure to take Naxos'. The reference is to the earlier abortive attempt in 500 (see 5.34).

96 ἐπεῖχον στρατεύεσθαι: 'they intended to march', 'they directed their minds to marching', where τὸν νοῦν is to be understood as the object of ἐπεῖχον. The phrase occurs elsewhere in Hdt. (e.g. 1.80.4, 1.153.4).

97.1 Τῆνον: the largest island in the vicinity, some twelve miles to the north of Delos.

ἐν τῇ Ῥηναίῃ: Rheneia was the closest of the Cyclades to Delos, from which it was separated by a channel less than half a mile wide. It provided all the secular requirements of the sacred isle and served as its commercial centre (Thuc. 3.104.2; Hyperides, *Deliacus*, Frag. 70).

ἵνα ἦσαν οἱ Δήλιοι: 'where the Delians were'. ἵνα is here used in its local sense, 'where', with the indic.

97.2 οὐκ ἐπιτήδεα καταγνόντες κατ' ἐμεῦ: 'having condemned me for having friendly intentions', where καταγνόντες is 2nd. aor. part. of καταγιγνώσκω (Ionic καταγινώσκω), 'condemn', which is construed with the acc. of the charge and the gen. (here with the prep. κατά) of the person condemned.

ἐπὶ τοσοῦτό γε φρονέω: 'my own thoughts at least are enough'.

ἐκ βασιλέος ὧδε ἐπέσταλται: literally 'it has thus been ordered to me by the king', i.e. 'my insruction from the king are as follows', where ἐπέσταλται is perf. pass. of ἐπιστέλλω, 'order'. For ἐκ with the gen. expressing the agent, see note on 13.1 above.

οἱ δύο θεοὶ ἐγένοντο: 'the two gods were born', namely Apollo and Artemis. For accounts of their birth, see *Homeric Hymn* 3.45-128 (which places Apollo's birth on Delos and that of Artemis on Ortygia); Theognis 5-10; Pindar, Frag. 33c-d; Callimachus, *Hymn* 4.55 ff.; Apollodorus 1.4.1; Hyginus, *Fab.* 140).

μηδὲν σίνεσθαι: 'to do no harm'. σίνομαι, 'injure', is essentially poetic, though it does occur in both Plato (*Laws*. 936e) and Xenophon (*Anab*. 3.4.16; *Cyropaedia* 3.3.15, 5.5.4), and is a favourite word of Hdt. (e.g. 1.17.3, 4.123.1, 5.74.2, 7.147.1, 8.31, 9.49.2).

μετὰ δὲ: 'and afterwards', adverbial. See note on ch. 4 above, and cf. 38.1, 62.2, 103.2.

λιβανωτοῦ τριηκόσια τάλαντα κατανήσας: 'having heaped up 300 talents of frankincense'. Since the Aeginetan talent was equivalent to c. 26 kg. or 73$^1/_3$ lb, 300 talents would weigh about 7800 kg. or over 7$^1/_2$ tons. The burning of such a huge quantity would have caused comment at the time and been construed as ostentation rather than true piety.

98.1 Αἰολέας: the Aeolian Greeks lived on the the north west coast of Asia Minor to the north of the Ionians, roughly in the area between the Gulf of Adramyttium and the Hermus river. For the Aeolian cities, see Hdt. 1.149-53, and for their tribute to the Persians, see 3.90.

καὶ πρῶτα καὶ ὕστατα μέχρι ἐμεῦ σεισθεῖσα: 'shaken for the first and last occasion up to my time'. Thucydides (2.8.3) agrees that Delos had been struck by an earthquake only once in its history, but dates the event to a time just before the outbreak of the Peloponnesian War in 431. There are various possible explanations for this discrepancy, though there is much uncertainty as to whether both historians are referring to the same earthquake. If they are, Thuc. may be tacitly correcting an error on the part of his predecessor (for similar tacit corrections, cf. Thuc. 1.126.8 and Hdt. 5.71.2 on the identity of the officials who handled the Cylonian conspiracy; Thuc. 1.20.3 and Hdt. 9.53.2 on the Pitanate *lochos* in the Spartan army; and see note 57.5 above on the number of votes possessed by Spartan kings). Alternatively the quake may have occurred at some indeterminate date between 490 and 431, but was subsequently linked in the popular mind with any calamity taking place within this period, whether near in point of time or more remote. It is perhaps more likely that there was more than one quake (so A.W. Gomme, *Essays in Greek History and Literature*, Oxford, 1937, p. 122), and Hdt. may have written this passage before the occurrence of the earthquake of c.431 mentioned by Thucydides. However it is difficult to believe that Thuc. wrote in ignorance of Hdt.'s remark or out of forgetfulness, since his reference is to be found in a context concerning the interpretations that his contemporaries put upon omens, which echoes the comment made by Hdt. It may be that both Hdt. and Thuc. are paying lip service to the widespread belief that, since the island was situated in an earthquake-free zone (cf. Pindar, Frag. 33c, which refers to Delos as an ἀκίνητον τέρας, as contrasted with its previous status as a floating island), there must have been a connection between the quake and some major disaster, however loose the temporal link between the two.

98.2 ἐπὶ...Δαρείου...καὶ Ξέρξεω...καὶ Ἀρταξέρξεω: i.e. in the reigns of Darius I (522-486), Xerxes (486-65) and Artaxerxes I (465-24), covering roughly a century. It is unclear from Hdt.'s words whether Artaxerxes was already dead at the time of writing, but his text as a whole shows no knowledge of Artaxerxes' successor Darius II.

ἐγένετο πλέω κακὰ τῇ Ἑλλάδι ἢ ἐπὶ εἴκοσι ἄλλας γενεάς: Thucydides appears to have this passage in mind at 1.23.2-3, where he claims that the Peloponnesian War was the greatest ever, not least because of the number of calamities that befell the Greeks in this period.

τὰ μὲν ἀπὸ τῶν Περσέων...γενόμενα: Hdt. is here referring to the Ionian Revolt of 500-493, the Marathon campaign of 490, Xerxes' invasion of 480-79, and perhaps to losses incurred during the Delian League campaigns against Persia in the 470s and 460s.

ἀπ' αὐτῶν τῶν κορυφαίων: 'from the leading states themselves'. For the word κορυφαῖος, see note on 23.6 above. Herodotus has in mind the wars fought by the Spartans in Arcadia and Messenia in the 460s, those fought by Athens against her revolted allies Naxos, Thasos and Samos, and above all, those fought between Athens and Sparta (the First Pelponnesian War of 460-46 and possibly also the early years of the Peloponnesian War proper).

98.3 οὐδὲν ἦν ἀεικὲς: 'there was nothing extraordinary'. ἀεικής in prose normally means 'unseemly', 'disgraceful', but in Hdt. it can also bear the meaning 'strange', 'unusual', as at 3.33, οὐ νύν τοι ἀεικὲς οὐδέν ἦν τοῦ σώματος νοῦσον μεγάλην νοσέοντας μηδὲ τὰς φρένας ὑγιαίνειν.

χρησμῷ: source unknown, and as such omitted from consideration in the standard works on Greek oracles.

δύναται: in addition to the usual meaning 'have power', 'be able', this verb is also used in the sense of 'mean', 'signify'. This sentence is ill adjusted to its context and has every appearance of being in origin a gloss, whether or not composed by Hdt. Given the inaccuracy of the translations, one hopes that the sentence was not of his own composition, though his ignorance of the Persian language is revealed at 1.139, where he wrongly states that all Persian masculine proper names end in the letter S.

Δαρεῖος ἐρξίης: the word ἐρξίης may be derived either from εἴργω/ἔργω ('The Restrainer') or from ἔρδω ('The Doer'). In either event the Greek translation is distinctly inaccurate in that the Persian form of Darius' name, Darayavaush, is derived from dar- 'hold' and vau- 'good', and means something along the lines of 'Upholder of the Good'.

Ξέρξης ἀρήϊος: 'Xerxes' is the Greek transliteration of the Persian Xshayarsha, a compound of xshaya (thiya) ('king', cf. Modern Persian *shah)* and arshan ('male', 'masculine') and so meaning 'king who is a true male', 'hero among kings'. Herodotus' translation is thus somewhat free, but not all that wide of the mark.

'Αρταξέρξης μέγας ἀρήϊος: the Persian Artaxshacha is derived from arta ('law', 'justice', 'right') and xshacha ('kingdom') and means '(possessing a) kingdom based on justice'. Hdt.'s translation wrongly assumes that the word is merely an expanded or intensive form of Xerxes, though the two words are indeed based on the same root.

99.1 προσίσχον πρὸς τὰς νήσους: 'proceeded to put in at the islands', by visiting each in turn. προσίσχω is a variant form of προσέχω, 'bring a ship to port', obtained by reduplication of the stem (si-scho), with ναῦν to be understood as object.

99.2 Κάρυστον: a Euboean city on a bay on the south coast of the island, famous for a white and green marble popular under the Roman Empire.

οὐ γὰρ δή σφι οἱ Καρύστιοι οὔτε ὁμήρους ἐδίδοσαν οὔτε ἔφασαν... στρατεύεσθαι: 'for the Carystians neither offered to provide them with hostages nor expressed any willingness to march'. When a simple negative (οὐ) is followed by one or more compound negatives (οὔτε...οὔτε) in the same clause, the negative is strengthened (Goodwin 1619). For οὔτε ἔφασαν στρατεύεσθαι ('said they would not march'), see note on 1.1 above, and cf. 50.2, 52.4, 61.4 above. φημί is here followed by a prolative inf. rather than the fut. inf. of indirect statement because οὔτε ἔφασαν is equivalent to, and thus takes the same construction as, οὔτε ἤθελον, ('refused to march').

λέγοντες Ἐρέτριάν τε καὶ Ἀθήνας: 'meaning Eretria and Athens'.

ἐνθαῦτα: 'under these circumstances'. Cf. 32.1 above and 138.4 below.

ἐς ὃ καὶ οἱ Καρύστιοι παρέστησαν ἐς τῶν Περσέων τὴν γνώμην: 'until such time as the Carystians came over to the Persian way of thinking'. παρέστησαν is the intrans. 2nd. aor. of παρίστημι, which in the middle means 'come over to someone's way of thinking', 'submit to someone's will'.

100.1 Ἀθηναίων ἐδεήθησαν σφίσι βοηθοὺς γενέσθαι: 'they asked the Athenians to become their helpers', i.e. 'to come to their aid'. A predicative noun or adj. after εἰμί or γίγνομαι/γίνομαι which refers to a noun in the dat. is itself either assimilated to the dat. or put in the acc. to agree with the unexpressed subject of the inf. A predicative adj. referring to a noun in the gen. in similar circumstances is regularly itself assimilated to the gen., but a predicative noun usually stands in the acc. to agree with the omitted subject of the inf. (Goodwin 928). Hence Hdt. here has βοηθοὺς rather than βοηθοῖς in agreement with σφίσι.

ἀπείπαντο: on the 1st. aor. forms of this verb, see note on 61.5 and cf. 82.1 above.

τοὺς τετρακισχιλίους κληρουχέοντας τῶν ἱπποβοτέων Χαλκιδέων τὴν χώρην: 'the 4000 who had obtained plots of land that had belonged to the Chalcidian *hippobotai*'. Following the defeat of the Chalcidians who had invaded Attica in support of Cleomenes in 506, Athens deprived the Chalcidian aristocrats (called *hippobotai* or horse breeders), who were held responsible for the invasion, of their land, which they divided into plots and assigned to landless Athenians (see 5.77). If the word *cleruchs* is used here in the technical sense it bore in the 5th century, these will have retained their Athenian citizenship. The figure of 4000 looks suspiciously high for a cleruchy in that the largest number known to have settled abroad in the 5th century amounted to 2700 at Mytilene in 427 (Thuc. 3.50.2). More typical cleruchies consisted of 250 (as on Andros, Plut. *Pericles* 11.5) or 500 (as on Naxos, Diod. 11.88.3). For a good discussion, see T.J. Figueira, *Athens and Aegina in the Age of Imperial Colonisation*, Baltimore and London, 1991, Appendix C, pp. 256-60, who suggests that the 4000 who helped the Eretrians on the present occasion included native Chalcidians as well as Athenian settlers.

τῶν δὲ Ἐρετριέων ἦν ἄρα οὐδὲν ὑγιὲς βούλευμα: 'the plan of the Eretrians, as it happened, was not a sound one'. According to a fragment of the 4th century philosopher Heracleides Ponticus, quoted by Athenaeus (12.536F-537C = Heracleides frag. 58), the family of the Eretrian Diomnestus moved to Athens and entrusted to Hipponicus, son of Callias of the Ceryces, a treasure which Diomnestus had appropriated from a Persian commander during an earlier Persian attack on Eretria. Since no such attack is known either to Hdt. or to any other ancient historian, the story is generally rejected. The only earlier opportunity for such an attack would have been in 500, when Megabates' expedition attacked Naxos. On that occasion, Hdt. does state (5.31.3) that Aristagoras held out the conquest of Euboea as an attractive proposition to the satrap Artaphernes, but gives no indication that the policy was actually implemented. For a discussion, see A.B. Bosworth, 'Heracleides Ponticus and the Past: Fact or Fiction?', in Ian Worthington (ed.), *Ventures into Greek History*, Oxford, 1994, pp. 15-22.

ἐφρόνεον δὲ διφασίας ἰδέας: 'they set their minds on two distinct types of plan', i.e. 'they were divided on which of two alternative plans they should adopt'. Numeral adjs. in -φάσιος (διφάσιος, τριφάσιος) are essentially Ionic, and mean 'of two (three) kinds', as at 2.36.4, διφασίοισι γράμμασι χρέωνται, of the two kinds of Egyptian writing; αἰτίαι διφάσιαι, 3.122.1; μουνομαχίη τριφασίη, 'a duel consisting of three parts', 5.1.2. In the plur., they are also used as equivalent to the corresponding cardinal number, as at 1.18.1, τρώματα διφάσια ('two defeats'); 1.95.1, τριφασίας ἄλλας ὁδούς, 'three other ways'; 2.17.3, τριφασίας ὁδούς 'three ways'; 2.17.5 διφάσια στόματα, 'two mouths'. Cf. also τριφασίας ἰδέας at 119.2 below.

100.2 τὰ ἄκρα τῆς Εὐβοίης: only the peak of the Euboean Mt. Olympus, which lies some 5 miles to the north east of Eretria, and the long ridge of Mt. Dirphys, which lies beyond Mt. Olympus and runs along the east coast, will have afforded any measure of protection.

οἴσεσθαι: fut. middle of φέρω, in the sense of 'win', 'gain'.

τούτων ἑκάτερα:'each of these two designs', i.e. the alternative policies of withdrawal to the heights and betrayal of the city to the Persians.

ἐὼν τῶν Ἐρετριέων τὰ πρῶτα: 'being the leading man among the Eretrians'. The use of τὰ πρῶτα to refer to one specific individual occurs also at 9.78.1, Λάμπων ὁ Πυθέω...Αἰγινητέων ἐὼν τὰ πρῶτα, and for its use with reference to a plurality of chief men, see Euripides, *Medea* 917, *Orestes* 1247; Aristophanes, *Frogs* 421. Cf. the application to people of the neut. of οὐδείς, as in οὐδέν εἰμί (Sophocles, *Philoctetes* 951), οὐδὲν εἶ (Aristophanes, *Eccl.* 144), or με ἀντ' ἀνδρὸς ἐποίησας τὸ μηδὲν εἶναι (Hdt. 8.106.3).

ἀπαλλάσσεσθαί σφεας ἐς τὴν σφετέρην: (sc. γῆν, χώρην) 'to depart for their own country'.

ἵνα μὴ προσαπόλωνται: 'so that they might not perish as well', i.e. in addition to the Eretrians. For the retention of the subj. in a final clause referring to the past, see Goodwin 1367.

101.1 Ὠρωπὸν: a town on the eastern border of Attica and Boeotia just across the Euripus from Eretria in Euboea, claimed by both states and currently (since 506?) under Athenian control. Thucydides (2.23.3) describes the inhabitants as subject to Athens at the time of the Peloponnesian War. For its subsequent history, see S. Hornblower, *A Commentary on Thucydides*, Vol. I, Oxford, 1991, p. 279. Oropus was significant mainly because of the existence of a sanctuary of Amphiaraus on its territory.

κατέσχον τὰς νέας τῆς Ἐρετρικῆς χώρης κατὰ Ταμύνας καὶ Χοιρέας καὶ Αἰγίλια: 'puttting in their ships at Tamynae, Choereae and Aegilia in the territory of Euboea'. For the topographic gen., see note on 95.1 above. Tamynae, if a correct emendation of the mss. reading 'Temenos', was a town in Eretrian territory in the valley of the river Oxylido to the east of Euboean Olympus, best known as the site of a victory of the Athenian general Phocion over Callias of Chalcis in 348. Choereae and Aegilia are otherwise unknown.

παρεσκευάζοντο ὡς προσοισόμενοι: 'they prepared to attack'. προσοισόμενοι is fut. part. middle of προσφέρω, 'bring to', 'apply to', used in the middle and pass. in the sense of 'approach' or 'attack'. παρασκευάζομαι is usually followed (as here) by a fut part. with or without the particle ὡς (the usual construction in Hdt.; cf. 2.162.2, 5.34.1, 9.122.3). Other possible constructions are the simple inf. (as at 2.162.4) and ὅπως with the fut. indic.

101.2 οἱ δὲ Ἐρετριέες ἐπεξελθεῖν...οὐκ ἐποιεῦντο βουλὴν: 'the Eretrians had no intention of coming out'. For ποιέομαι with a noun as a periphrasis for the corresponding verb, see note on 27.3 above, and cf. 61.1 and 78.2.

εἴ κως...διαφυλάξαιεν τὰ τείχεα, τούτου σφι ἔμελε πέρι: 'they were concerned about this, namely if it might be possible for them to preserve their walls'. For εἴ κως, see note on 52.7 above. For τούτων πέρι, see note on 4.1 and cf. 57.4, and for the impers. μέλει see note on 19.2.

ἐνίκα μὴ ἐκλιπεῖν τὴν πόλιν: literally 'it prevailed (i.e. the prevailing opinion/majority decision was) not to leave the city'.

ἐπὶ ἓξ ἡμέρας: 'for six days'. ἐπί with the acc. is used in a temporal sense to indicate duration of time, with the meaning 'extending over 6 days'. According to Plato, *Menexenus* 240b, the siege lasted only 3 days.

101.3 τοῦτο μὲν...τοῦτο δὲ: see note on 27.2 above and cf. 44.1, 69.3, 107.2, 114.

ἀποτινύμενοι τῶν ἐν Σάρδισι κατακαυθέντων ἱρῶν: Hdt. here refers to Eretrian involvement in the burning of Sardis during the Ionian Revolt. See 5.101-2.

ἠνδραποδίσαντο κατὰ τὰς Δαρείου ἐντολάς: according to Plato (*Laws* 698d, *Menexenus* 240b) and Strabo (10.1.10), Persian propaganda spread the story that Eretria was 'netted' (see note on 31.2 above) and that not a single Eretrian escaped.

102 κατέργοντές τε πολλόν: κατέργω (Attic καθείργω) means literally 'shut in', 'enclose', as at 4.69.1 and 5.63.4. Here the verb seems to be used metaphorically in the sense of 'bring into a difficult situation', 'press hard', with τοὺς Ἀθηναίους from the following clause to be understood as its object.

δοκέοντες ταὐτὰ τοὺς Ἀθηναίους ποιήσειν τὰ καὶ τοὺς Ἐρετριέας ἐποίησαν: 'thinking that they would do to the Athenians what they had already done to the Eretrians', 'believing that they would treat the Athenians as they had treated the Eretrians'. For the double acc. with ποιέω, see note on 41.4 above.

Μαραθὼν: a deme on the east coast of Attica facing the southern tip of Euboea, some 26 miles from Athens.

ἐπιτηδεώτατον χωρίον τῆς Ἀττικῆς ἐνιππεῦσαι: 'the most suitable place in Attica for cavalry', because Marathon lay in the centre of one of the three Attic plains, though it covered a smaller area than the Athenian and Thriasian Plains. For the gen. τῆς Ἀττικῆς, see note on 95.1 above, and cf. 101.1. On the absence of Persian cavalry in the battle, see note on 112.1 below.

ἀγχοτάτω τῆς Ἐρετρίης: 'nearest to Eretria', where ἀγχοτάτω is an Ionic superl. of the adv. ἄγχι, 'near'. In fact both Rhamnus and Oropus were nearer to Euboea than was Marathon, but neither locality offered good facilities for cavalry operations.

ἐς τοῦτό σφι κατηγέετο Ἱππίης: a significant factor in the choice of landing place, since the former tyrant, who accompanied the expedition and who would have been restored to power in the event of a Persian victory, was influential in the area and could expect to attract a good deal of local support. In similar circumstances, Peisistratus had landed at Marathon when he established his third period of tyranny in 546 (Hdt. 1.62.1). For Peisistratid links with the later deme of Philaidae, see [Plato], *Hipparchus* 228b and Plut. *Solon* 10.2.

103.1 στρατηγοὶ δέκα: elected one from each of the ten Cleisthenic tribes since 501/0 ([Aristotle], *Ath. Pol.* 22.2).

τῶν ὁ δέκατος ἦν Μιλτιάδης: Miltiades the Younger, whose return from the Chersonese in 493 is recorded in ch. 41 above. Since his deme (Laciadae) belonged to the tribe Oeneis, which was sixth in the official tribal order, he cannot have been tenth in the literal sense. The phrase may be used much as the Thucydidean expression δέκατος αὐτός (literally 'himself tenth', i.e. 'with nine others'), found at Thuc. 1.116.1. 2.13.1 (cf. πέμπτος αὐτός, 'with four others' at Thuc. 1.61.1), to indicate a general who enjoyed a higher degree of repute but no greater powers than his colleagues on the board. See K.J. Dover, 'Dekatos Autos', *JHS* 80, 1960, pp. 61-77.

Κίμωνα...κατέλαβε φυγεῖν...Πεισίστρατον: 'it befell Cimon to flee Athens to escape from Peisistratus', i.e. 'to be exiled from Athens by Peisistratus', where καταλαμβάνει is used impersonally with the acc. and inf. in the sense of 'it happens to one to', 'it is the fate of one to'. Miltiades' father Cimon the Elder was the half-brother of the Elder Miltiades (ch. 38.1 above), who had founded the Athenian settlement in the Chersonese (see chs 35-6). Though this Cimon is not known to have had any political ambitions – and his nickname Koalemos ('the simpleton') suggests that he had none – his distinguished lineage was seen by Peisistratus as a potential threat should he ever be used as a figurehead by disaffected elements.

103.2 Ὀλυμπιάδα ἀνελέσθαι τεθρίππῳ συνέβη...: 'it so happened that Miltiades won an Olympic victory with his four horse team'.

τωὐτὸ ἐξενείκασθαι...τῷ...Μιλτιάδῃ: 'it happened also that he won this victory in the very same event as Miltiades', where συνέβη is to be supplied from the preceding clause.

μετὰ δὲ: 'and afterwards', adverbial. See note on 4.1 and cf. 38.1, 62.2, 97.2.

τῇ ὑστέρῃ Ὀλυμπιάδι: 'at the next Olympiad'.

ἀνακηρυχθῆναι: 'to be proclaimed', an inf. of purpose, common after verbs of choosing, giving, taking or receiving (Goodwin 1532). At the Olympic Games the victor's name, patronymic and city were proclaimed and, since an Olympic victory was one of the greatest honours that a Greek could attain, Cimon's act off self-effacement represented a significant gesture of conciliation with the tyranny, which duly brought him the desired political dividend. Cf. note on 70.2 above.

103.3 κατέλαβε ἀποθανεῖν ὑπὸ τῶν Πεισιστράτου παίδων: literally 'it befell him to die at the hands of the sons of Peisistratus', i.e. 'it was his lot to be killed by the Peisistratids'.

οὐκέτι περιεόντος αὐτοῦ Πεισιστράτου: 'Peisistratus himself no longer surviving', (gen. abs.), i.e. after Peisistratus' death in 528/7. Clearly Hippias and Hipparchus lacked their father's scruples and were insecure enough at the beginning of the new reign to feel threatened by such a triple victory. The three Olympic victories were presumably in 536, 532 and 528.

κατὰ τὸ πρυτανήϊον: for the prytaneum, see note on 38.2 and cf. 139.3 below. The building was situated on the north slope of the Acropolis (for a discussion of the site, see Miller, *The Prytaneum*, pp. 38-54).

ὑπείσαντες: literally 'placing under', 'placing secretly', aor. part. of ὑφίζω, used with the meaning 'causing to lie in wait', 'placing in ambush'. The simple form εἷσα is aor. of the poetic verb ἵζω ('seat', 'place', Attic καθίζω), and occurs at 3.61.3, τοῦτον...Πατιζείθης...εἷσε ἄγων ἐς τὸν βασιλήϊον θρόνον, 'Patizeithes took the man and set him on the royal throne'.

πέρην τῆς διὰ Κοίλης καλεομένης ὁδοῦ: 'on the other side of the road called "Through the Hollow"'. Cf. Marcellinus, *Life of Thucydides* 17, where Koile is said to be the site of the Philaid family burial ground close to the Melitean Gate. The area lay to the south west of Athens, between the city and the Philaid deme of Laciadae.

τετάφαται: 3rd. pers. plur. perf. pass. of θάπτω. For the form, see note on ἀπίκατο at 9.1 above.

103.4 Εὐαγόρεω: Poralla no. 288. This Euagoras is attested elsewhere only by Aelian (*De Natura Animalium* 12.40) and by Pausanias (6.10.8), who refers to his dedication of a chariot at Olympia.

οὐδαμαί: 'none', an Ionic adj. serving as the plur. of οὐδείς. The form οὐδένες, which in Attic may be used with reference to groups or sets of individuals, is restricted in Hdt. to the meaning 'nobodies', 'nonentities' (as at 9.58.2).

Στησαγόρης: see ch. 38 above.

104.1 Φοίνικες...ἐπιδιώξαντες μέχρι Ἴμβρου: see ch. 41 above.

περὶ πολλοῦ ἐποιεῦντο λαβεῖν: 'they set much store on capturing him'. For this phrase, see notes on chs 6 and 61.5 above, and cf. 134.1 below.

104.2 οἱ ἐχθροὶ...ἐδίωξαν τυραννίδος τῆς ἐν Χερσονήσῳ: in 493. The identity of Miltiades' prosecutors is not stated, but it is likely that they included members of the Alcmeonid family who were to prosecute him again, and with more success, in 489 (see ch. 136 below). The 493 prosecution was brought under the anti-tyrant law enacted after the expulsion of Hippias in 510, which prescribed a penalty of *atimia* (*Ath. Pol.* 16.10). Since this law can hardly have been applicable to exercising tyranny in the Chersonnese, Miltiades' opponents will have argued that the Chersonnese was in a sense Athenian territory and so within the scope of the law.

ἀποφυγὼν: 'having been acquitted', in the legal sense. Miltiades' acquittal on this occasion is usually ascribed to the influence of Themistocles, who was either archon or archon elect at the time of the trial, and who had in common with Miltiades a strong antipathy to the Persians.

στρατηγὸς...ἀπεδέχθη: for the year 490/89 (C.W. Fornara, 'The Athenian Board of Generals from 501 to 404', *Historia, Einzelschrift Heft* 16, pp. 41-2; Develin *AO*, p. 56).

αἱρεθεὶς ὑπὸ τοῦ δήμου: 'elected by the people'. The pass. of αἱρέω regularly has this meaning, with ἁλίσκομαι reserved for the sense 'be captured'. Generals were chosen one from each tribe from 501/0 (*Ath. Pol.* 22.2), though the identity of the electoral body is left vague. If Hdt. is correct, that body will

at this time have been the ecclesia, a view accepted by most scholars (e.g. C. Hignett, *A History of the Athenian Constitution*, Oxford, 1952, pp. 169-73; E.C. Stavely, *Greek and Roman Voting and Elections*, London, 1972, p. 41; E.J. Bicknell, *Studies in Athenian Politics and Genealogy*, Einzelschrift 19, Wiesbaden, 1972, pp. 101-12; N.G.L. Hammond, *Studies in Greek History*, Oxford, 1973, pp. 34-51; P.J. Rhodes, *A Commentary on the Aristotelian Athenaion Politeia*, Oxford, 1981, pp. 264-6; Develin, *AO*, pp. 3-4). For the contrary view, see Fornara, *op. cit.*, pp. 1-10, who maintains that at this time generals were elected by the members of their own tribe. In this event, Hdt. would be guilty of some inaccuracy, unless his purpose was to contrast the civic procedure of election with the judicial procedure of prosecution.

105.1 ἐς Σπάρτην: a distance of approximately 230 km. or 140 miles. Sparta was approached as the state with the highest military reputation in Greece. There is no suggestion that the two cities had any form of understanding, much less an alliance at the time, though Cleomenes' response to the Athenian charge against Aegina (see chs 49-50 above) makes it likely that Sparta was considered to be not unsympathetic to Athens' predicament.

Φειδιππίδην: the manuscripts are divided between Φειδιππίδην and Φιλιππίδην. Philippides is an attested Attic name, whereas Pheidippides is not found as a proper name in Attica except as that of a character in Aristophanes' *Clouds*, where it is specifically said to be a sort of compromise between Pheidonides (the name favoured by the bearer's father) and the mother's desire for an equestrian sounding name ending in -ippides (*Clouds* 62-7). This is presumably why the *OCT* prints Φιλιππίδην. However Pheidippides is found elsewhere in the Greek world as a genuine if somewhat rare personal name (see K.J. Dover's edition of *Clouds*, Oxford, 1968, pp. xxv-xxvi). Both names occur in the later tradition: Philippides at Plut. *Moralia* 862B, Pausanias 1.28.4, 8.54.6, and Lucian, *Pro Lapsu* 3; the name Pheidippides lies behind Nepos' 'Pheidippus' at *Miltiades* 4.3.

ἡμεροδρόμον: literally 'day runner', a courier sent on diplomatic missions where speed was paramount, as in the case of the Argive runner sent to warn Mardonius of the despatch of the Spartan army in 479 (Hdt. 9.12), or the messengers sent by Agesilaus to advise his fellow countrymen of Epaminondas' night march on Sparta in 362 (Diodorus 15.82.6). The Euchidas who ran from Plataea to Delphi and back (a round trip of some 180 km. or c.110 miles) in one day to fetch sacred fire from the Delphic public hearth (Plut. *Aristides* 20.5), only to die on his return may also have been a *hemerodromos*. See also Plato, *Protagoras* 335e, and cf. Lucian's tale (*loc. cit.*) of Philippides' death on his return to Athens, which clearly confuses Philippides' death with that of Euchidas.

ὡς αὐτός τε ἔλεγε: both here and at 106.1 below Hdt. appears reluctant to vouch for the credibility of the story. For similar scepticism, cf. his treatment of Epizelus' story at 117.2-3 below.

τὸ Παρθένιον οὖρος: a mountain ridge in the east of Arcadia to the north east of Tegea, which separates Arcadia from the plain of Hysiae in the Argolid.

ὁ Πὰν περιπίπτει: 'Pan encountered him', 'Pan fell in with him'. As the patron deity of flocks, herds, woods, mountains and the countryside in general, he was the recipient of a widespread cult in Arcadia. For a deailed account of the god and his cult, see P. Borgeaud, *The Cult of Pan in Ancient Greece*, tr. K. Atlass and J. Redfield, Chicago and London, 1988.

105.2 βώσαντα: the Ionic form of the Attic βοήσαντα, aor. part. of βοάω.

ἑωυτοῦ οὐδεμίαν ἐπιμέλειαν ποιεῦνται: 'they paid no attention to him'. Though Pan appears on Attic vases from c. 500, and his cult became popular only in the years after Marathon, there was certainly no official state cult of Pan in existence as early as 490.

105.3 καταστάντων σφίσι εὖ...τῶν πρηγμάτων: 'when their affairs were in a proper condition', i.e after Datis' departure from Athens. καταστάντων is the intrans. 2nd. aor. part. of καθίστημι, 'set up', 'establish'.

ἱδρύσαντο ὑπὸ τῇ ἀκροπόλι Πανὸς ἱρόν: 'they erected a shrine of Pan below the Acropolis', in a cave at the north western corner, which subsequently acquired erotic associations (cf. the site of Creusa's rape by Apollo at Euripides, *Ion* 492 ff., 938, and of Cinesias' and Myrrhine's projected tryst at Aristophanes, *Lysistrata* 721, 911). For Pan's shrine below the Acropolis, see also Pausanias 1.28.4; Lucian, *Bis Accusatus* 9; J. Travlos, *Pictorial Dictionary of Ancient Athens*, London, 1971, p. 93, 417-21; R. Garland, *Introducing New Gods*, London, 1992, pp. 59-62 and Plate 11; R. Parker, *Athenian Religion: A History*, Oxford, 1996, pp. 163-8. From 490, Pan's cult became widespread in Attica, usually in caves, and often in association with that of the nymphs.

ἀπὸ ταύτης τῆς ἀγγελίης: 'as a result of this news'.

θυσίῃσι τε ἐπετέῃσι καὶ λαμπάδι: 'with annual sacrifices and a torch race', i.e. Pan became the recipient of a state-sponsored cult, for which see Garland, *op. cit.*, pp. 58-62. Torch races, both for relay teams and for individual runners, were also prominent features of the Panathenaea, the Prometheia, the Hephaesteia and, on horseback, of the later Bendidia.

106.1 ὅτε...οἱ ἔφη καὶ τὸν Πανα φανῆναι: 'which was the occasion on which he said that Pan appeared to him'. ἐφάνθην, the lst aor. pass. of φαίνω, is generally used in the truly pass. sense of 'be shown', whereas the 2nd. aor. pass. ἐφάνην is normally used with the middle meaning 'show oneself', 'appear'. By narrating the various stages of Pheidippides' mission out of strict chronological order, Hdt. leaves unanswered the question of whether Pan's epiphany occured on the way to Sparta or on the return journey, but both Borgeaud (*op. cit.*, p. 133) and Garland (*op. cit.*, p. 49 note 2) argue for the latter as being psychologically more appropriate.

δευτεραῖος: 'on the second day'. Adjectives in -αῖος, derived from ordinal numbers (τριταῖος, τεταρταῖος etc.) indicate lapses of time and are best translated by prepositional phrases. δευτεραῖος serves as a synonym for the phrase τῇ ὑστεραίη (sc. ἡμέρᾳ). For a distance of some 150 miles, such a journey time was no mean achievement.

τοὺς ἄρχοντας: 'the magistrates', 'the authorities', probably here with reference to the ephors, who controlled most aspects of foreign policy, but not necessarily excluding the kings or even the *gerontes*.

106.2 ὑμέων δέονται σφίσι βοηθῆσαι: 'they beg you to help them'. For the use of σφίσι as indirect reflexive pronoun, see Goodwin 987-8.

πόλιν ἀρχαιοτάτην ἐν τοῖσι ῞Ελλησι: cf. 7.161.3, Thuc. 1.2.5, 1.6.3. The reference is to the Athenian claim to be autochthonous. On this, see esp. N. Loraux, *The Invention of Athens*, Cambridge (Mass.) and London, 1986, pp. 145-50; R. Thomas, *Oral Tradition and Written Record in Classical Athens*, Cambridge, 1989, pp. 217-18. For references in Greek literature, see Hdt. 7.161.3, Thuc. 1.2.5, and, above all, those occurring in the surviving *epitaphia* (Thuc. 2.36.1; Lysias 2.17; Plato, *Menexenus* 237a-b; [Demosthenes] 60.4; Hyperides 6.7).

πρὸς ἀνδρῶν βαρβάρων: 'at the hands of barbarians'. See note on 9.1. above.

᾿Ερέτριά τε ἠνδραπόδισται: see ch. 101.3 above.

106.3 τοῖσι...ἔαδε: 'it pleased them', i.e. 'they decided to', where ἔαδε is aor. of ἀνδάνω, 'please', used impersonally, as in the decrees of official bodies such as Cretan assemblies, as the equivalent of the Attic ἔδοξε (cf. 4.145.5; 4.153; 4.201.2; 7.172.1; 9.5.2).

ἱσταμένου τοῦ μηνὸς εἰνάτη: see note on 57. 2 above.

εἰνάτη δὲ οὐκ ἐξελεύσεσθαι ἔφασαν μὴ οὐ πλήρεος ἐόντος τοῦ κύκλου: 'they said that they would not march out on the ninth unless the course (sc. of the moon) was full'. On the syntax, see note on 9.1 above. Historians are divided on the issue of whether this was a genuine excuse or a mere pretext to explain the tardy Spartan departure. Unless the Spartan calendar was in complete confusion at the time, the full moon must have fallen on the fifteenth of the month and could not possibly ever have occurred on the ninth. Plutarch (*De Malignitate Herodoti* 26 = *Mor.* 861E-F) complains that Hdt. has maligned the Spartans on the grounds that, as they had campaigned on many earlier occasions in the first part of a month without waiting for the full moon, they must have set out on this occasion too if they arrived at Marathon soon after the battle, which he here dates to the 6th of the Attic month Boedromion. However he is undoubtedly guilty of confusing Boedromion 6, the anniversary of the battle ('Marathon Day') with the date of the battle itself, which took place earlier. Herodotus' accuracy, and the genuineness of the Spartan excuse, are vindicated if it is assumed that the reference is not to Spartan months in general but only to the sacred month of Carneius, corresponding roughly, as Plut. is only too well aware (*Nicias* 28.1), to the Attic month Metageitnion. During this month sacred to all Dorians, expeditions were banned for the duration of the Carnean festival which covered the 7th to the

15th of the month (see 7.206.1; Thuc. 5.54 and 75; Euripides, *Alcestis* 449-51). For Spartan inaction at the time of festivals, see also 7.206.2 (the Olympia), 9.7.1 and 9.11.1 (the Hyacinthia), and Thuc. 5.82.2-3 (the Gymnopaedia). If the Spartans set out on 16th Carneius, the earliest day on which they could have legally done so, the excuse they offered will have been perfectly genuine, and indeed was accepted as such by the Athenians at the time, though in the fourth century, Plato (*Laws* 698e) felt it necessary to justify the Spartan absence by synchronising Marathon with a helot revolt. If Cleomenes was in exile at the time of Marathon (see note on 85.1 above) and intriguing with the helots to procure his restoration, Herodotus' failure to mention this unrest is surprising. For the possibility of a helot revolt at the time of Marathon, see Burn, *PG*, pp. 271-2 and Huxley, *Early Sparta*, pp. 87-94 with note 606.

107.1 κατηγέετο: Ionic imperf. of καθηγέομαι, 'guide', 'lead'.

ἐς τὸν Μαραθῶνα: on the choice of landing place, see ch. 102 above.

τῇ μητρὶ τῇ ἑωυτοῦ: the name of Hippias' mother is unknown.

107.2 ἀνασωσάμενος: the middle of σῴζω, 'save', with the meaning 'save in one's own interest', i.e. 'recover'.

ἐν τῇ ἑωυτοῦ: (sc. γῇ or χώρῃ) 'in his native land'.

τοῦτο μὲν...τοῦτο δὲ: see note on 27.2 above, and cf. 44.1, 69.3, 101.3 and 114.

ἀπέβησε: 'he disembarked them'. βαίνω in verse has a fut. act. βήσω and a 1st. aor. ἔβησα which are used in the transitive sense of 'cause to go', a meaning supplied in Attic by βιβάζω. The causative aor. ἔβησα also occurs in Hdt. at 5.63.3 and 8.95.

Στυρέων: the citizens of Styra, a city in the south west of Euboea, practically due east of Marathon.

Αἰγίλειαν: an island in the Euripus lying just off the harbour of Styra.

καταγομένας: κατάγω, 'bring down', is also used in the act. in the sense of 'put a ship in to shore', and in the middle with the meaning 'put in to land', as opposed to ἀνάγομαι, 'put to sea'. Cf. 4.43.5.

διέτασσε: 'he set about getting the troops into position'. Cf. 16.2 above and 108.4 below.

107.3 οἱ...ἐπῆλθε πταρεῖν τε καὶ βῆξαι: 'it so happened that he sneezed and coughed', 'there came upon him a fit of sneezing and coughing', where ἐπέρχομαι is used impersonally. πταρεῖν is aor. inf. of πταίρω or πτάρνυμαι, 'sneeze'. A sneeze was regarded as an omen, whether favourable, as at *Odyssey* 17.541, Xen. *Anab.* 3.2.9, Catullus 45.8-9, 17-8, or unfavourable, as at Menander Frag. 620 (Koerte), line 9.

οἷα δέ οἱ πρεσβυτέρῳ ἐόντι: 'inasmuch as he was advancing in years', 'as might be expected in an older person'. For this use of οἷα, see note on 61.3 above.

τῶν ὀδόντων οἱ πλεῦνες ἐσείοντο: 'most of his teeth were shaking', i.e. 'were loose', where πλεῦνες is an Ionic form of πλείονες.

ἐς τὴν ψάμμον αὐτοῦ: 'there in the soil', where αὐτοῦ is adverbial.
ἐποιέετο πολλὴν σπουδὴν ἐξευρεῖν: 'he put a great deal of effort into finding out', 'he was extremely eager to find out', as at 3.4.2 and 7.205.3.
108.1 ἐξεληλυθέναι: see note on 82.1 above.

ἐν τεμένεϊ Ἡρακλέος : 'in a precinct of Heracles'. Prevailing scholarly opinion, which used to locate this precinct near Vrana on the slopes of Mt. Agrieliki at the chapel of Ayios Georgios or Ayios Demetrios, now favours a site to the south east, at the southern entrance to the plain between the eastern slopes of Mt. Agrieliki and the sea, close to the direct route leading from Marathon to Athens by way of Pallene, which the Athenians sought to block. See E. Vanderpool, 'The Deme of Marathon and the Herakleion', *AJA* 70, 1966, p. 319 ff.; A.R. Burn, 'Thermopylae Revisited and Some Topographical Notes on Marathon and Plataiai', in K.H. Kinzel (ed.), *Greece and the Eastern Mediterranean in Ancient History and Prehistory*, Berlin, 1977, pp. 89-105.

ἐδεδώκεσαν σφέας αὐτοὺς τοῖσι Ἀθηναίοισι: in 519, according to Thuc. 3.68.5, who dates the alliance 93 years before the Spartan destruction of Plataea in 427. This date is generally accepted, though some scholars find it implausible that the Spartans would have sought to embroil their friend Hippias in a war with Thebes or that Hippias himself would have wished to give offence to a city that had assisted his father's return (see Hdt. 1.61.3, [Aristotle], *Ath. Pol.* 15.2). Such doubts have led to suggestions that '93rd year' in Thucydides' text should be emended to read '83rd' year, thus dating the Plataean alliance to the beginning of the democracy in 509. However the Spartans need not have allowed their friendship with the tyrants to stand in the way of what they saw as their overall interest in sowing dissension between two potentially strong rivals, and the Alcmeonid seizure of the fort at Leipsydrium in 514 or 513 (Hdt. 5.62.1, *Ath. Pol.* 19.3), which can hardly have been achieved in the face of outright Theban opposition, suggests that relations between Hippias and Thebes may have grown distinctly chilly by then.

108.2 πιεζόμενοι ὑπὸ Θηβαίων: Thebes as the largest city in Boeotia had throughout her history sought to assert a domination over the other cities through the medium of a federated state (the Boeotian Confederacy), in which she enjoyed a predominant voice. The other cities were frequently coerced into membership, and could stay aloof only with outside support. A period of intense Theban pressure on the other Boeotian communities seems to have begun in the 520s. See R.J. Buck, *A History of Boeotia*, Edmonton, 1979, pp. 107-17.

ἐδίδοσαν...παρατυχοῦσι Κλεομένεϊ...καὶ Λακεδαιμονίοισι σφέας αὐτούς: 'they sought to hand themselves over to Cleomenes and the Spartans, who happened to be in the area', where ἐδίδοσαν is a conative imperf. (see notes on 2.1 and 5.1 above). We have no other knowledge of any Spartan presence in the area in 519, though it may have been occasioned by the enrolment of Megara into the Peloponnesian League (see A.H.M. Jones, *Sparta*, London, 1967, p. 49).

ἑκαστέρω: comparative of the adv. ἑκάς, 'far away'.

ἐπικουρίη ψυχρή: literally 'cold assistance'. i.e. help that would prove ineffectual. For the metaphorical use of ψυχρός, cf. ἐπαρθεὶς ψυχρῇ νίκῃ at 9.49.1.

φθαίητε...ἐξανδραποδισθέντες ἤ τινα πυθέσθαι ἡμέων: 'you would be enslaved before any of us ever heard'. For the use of φθάνω, see note on 91.1 above.

108.3 πλησιοχώροισί: the territory of Plataea marched with that of Attica along the western part of Mt. Cithaeron.

τιμωρέειν ἐοῦσι οὐ κακοῖσι: 'not bad at coming to the rescue', a litotes. For the epexegetic inf. after adjs., especially those denoting ability, fitness and willingness, see Goodwin 1526. Cf. Sophocles, *OT* 545, λέγειν σὺ δεινός, μανθάνειν δ' ἐγὼ κακός: and Thuc. 6.38.2 κακοὶ...προφυλάξασθαι.

οὐ κατὰ εὐνοίην οὕτω...ὡς βουλόμενοι: 'not so much out of good will as out of a desire...'.

συνεστεῶτας: 2nd. perf. part. of συνίστημι in the sense of 'join battle with', 'engage in fighting with'.

108.4 τοῖσι δυώδεκα θεοῖσι: the 12 gods to whom an altar was erected in the agora in 522/1 (Thuc. 6.54.6). See J.M. Camp, *The Athenian Agora*, London, 1986, pp. 40-2. The altar was traditionally a place of asylum (Plut. *Pericles* 31.2; Diodorus 12.39.1), as well as the place from which all distances within Attica were measured (Hdt. 2.7.1; IG²264). The gods to whom the altar was dedicated were Zeus, Hera, Poseidon, Demeter, Apollo, Artemis, Ares, Athene, Aphrodite, Hephaestus, Hermes and Dionysus.

ἐστρατεύοντο: 'they proceeded to march against them', an incohative imperf. See note on 16.2, and cf. διέτασσε at 107.2 above.

108.5 Κορίνθιοι: prior to the transformation of Athens into a major naval power in the late 480s, relations between Corinth and Athens had been good, largely because they had common enemies in Megara and Aegina. In 506, Corinth refused to participate in Cleomenes' threefold invasion of Attica (Hdt. 5.75), and several years later was instrumental in the abandonment of Spartan plans to restore Hippias to power (5.92). Moreover in the early 480s, she lent Athens 20 ships for use in her war with Aegina (see ch. 89 above). Presumably in 519 the Corinthians felt that it would be contrary to their interests to see Athens weakened by defeat in a possible war with Thebes.

καταλλάξαντες ἐπιτρεψάντων ἀμφοτέρων: 'reconciling them when both parties submitted the matter to their arbitration' (gen. abs.).

οὔρισαν τὴν χώρην: 'they laid down the boundaries of their territory', from οὖρος, the Ionic equivalent of the Attic ὅρος, 'boundary'.

ἐπὶ τοισίδε: 'on the following conditions'.

ἐὰν Θηβαίους Βοιωτῶν τοὺς μὴ βουλομένους ἐς Βοιωτοὺς τελέειν: 'that the Thebans should leave those Boeotians alone who did not wish to...'. The neg. with βουλομένους is μή because the clause is indefinite/generic (Goodwin 1612). For the phrase τελέω ἐς, see note on 53.1 above.

108.6 τὸν ᾿Ασωπὸν αὐτὸν ἐποιήσαντο οὖρον: 'they made the Asopus itself the frontier'. The Asopus flows east between the territoriy of Thebes and Plataea and flows into the Euripus between Delium and Oropus. We must infer that the Theban/Plataean frontier had previously lain farther to the south, and that the Parasopia (the land between the Asopus and the Cithaeron/Parnes range) had belonged in part to Thebes.

῾Υσιάς: a community in the Parasopia east of Plataea, to be identified with the site of the chapel of Pantanassa near the modern village of Kriekouki (Buck pp. 15-18; J.M. Fossey, *Topography and Population of Ancient Boeotia*, Chicago, 1988, pp. 112-15).

109.1 τοῖσι δὲ ᾿Αθηναίων στρατηγοῖσι: the known generals for the year are Miltiades and Stasileos (see ch. 114). More doubtfully attested are Aristeides, Themistocles, Polyzelus, and Cynegeirus the brother of the tragedian Aeschylus (Plut. *Arist.* 5.1, *Mor.* 305B). See A.J. Fornara, 'The Athenian Board of Generals from 501 to 404', *Historia, Einzelschrift Heft* 16, Wiesbaden, 1971, pp. 41-2; R. Develin, *AO*, pp. 56-7.

οὐκ ἐώντων συμβάλλειν: literally 'not allowing them to engage', i.e. 'forbidding an engagement'.

ὀλίγους...συμβαλεῖν: 'too few to engage'. The positive degree of the the adj. is used before an inf. (with or without ὥστε) to indicate unsuitability or inadequacy for the object in mind. Cf. Hdt. 7.207; Thuc. 1.50.5, 2.61.2; Xen. *Mem.* 3.13.3, *Cyr.* 4.5.15. The more usual use of the comparative with ἢ ὥστε may be avoided here because of the rarity of ὀλείζων, the comp. degree of ὀλίγος.

109.2 ἐνίκα ἡ χείρων τῶν γνωμέων: 'the worse of the two opinions prevailed'.

ὁ τῷ κυάμῳ λαχὼν ᾿Αθηναίων πολεμαρχέειν: 'the man who had drawn by lot the office of polemarch'. κύαμος, meaning literally 'bean', acquired the secondary meaning of 'lot' since offices selected by sortition were filled by the drawing of white beans. Candidates who drew black beans were unsuccessful (Plut. *Pericles* 27.2). λαγχάνω, when followed by an acc. or an acc. and inf. means 'obtain as one's portion', 'obtain an office by the casting of lots'. The polemarch was one of the nine archons whose duties, as the name implies, were originally mainly military, but in the later 5th century came to be largely civil and judicial ([Aristotle], *Ath. Pol.* 58). The military functions of the polemarch declined as the importance of the *stategoi* increased, particularly after the army reform of 501/0 (see note on 104.2 above), though he remained titular commander-in- chief and ceremonial head (*Ath. Pol.* 22.2), and in 490 was still able to exercise some influence on military decision making. The accuracy of Hdt.'s claim that the polemarch was selected by sortition is suspect. According to the *Ath. Pol.* 22, the tyrants substituted election for sortition as the method of selecting archons, and sortition was not reintroduced until 487/6. This belief is supported by the 3rd. century biographer Idomeneus, who states that Aristeides was elected archon for 489/8 (Plut. *Arist.* 1.8), as well as by Pausanias, who at 1.15.3 has Callimachus elected as polemarch for 490/89. It is possible that Hdt. wishes to sharpen the contrast between the polemarch and the elected board of generals.

τὸ παλαιόν: 'formerly', 'previously', an adverbial acc. (Goodwin 1060). The alternative translation 'in ancient times' would imply that generals had existed as such long before the military reform of 501/0. There is indeed evidence that such was the case (Hdt. 1.59.4; *Ath. Pol.* 17.2, 22.2; Plut. *Solon* 11.2), but these generalships may have been *ad hoc* creations for one specific task rather than annual boards of magistrates.

Ἁρμόδιός τε καὶ Ἀριστογείτων: the assassins of Hipparchus, brother of the tyrant Hippias, in 514. They were regarded after the fall of the tyranny in 510 as liberators despite being motivated by purely personal grievances (Thuc. 6.56.1; *Ath. Pol.* 18.2-3). Since, like Callimachus, they belonged to the deme Aphidna, Miltiades' appeal was particularly apt.

ἢν...ὑποκύψωσι τοῖσι Μήδοισι: 'if they bow down before the Medes', a conditional clause with ἄν and the subj. referring to the future (Goodwin 1463).

δέδοκται τὰ πείσονται: 'it has been decided what they would suffer', where πείσονται is fut. of πάσχω, not of πείθω.

παραδεδομένοι Ἱππίῃ: 'if they are handed over to Hippias', a conditional or temporal use of the part.

οἵη τέ ἐστι πρώτη...γενέσθαι: 'she is capable of becoming the first', a somewhat anachronistic prediction on Miltiades' part of the growth of imperial Athens later in the century. For the use of the inf. after οἷος, see Goodwin 1526.

109.4 ἐς σέ...ἀνήκει...τὸ κῦρος: 'it has devolved upon you to have the final say'.

ἔρχομαι φράσων: 'I'm going to tell you', where ἔρχομαι is virtually an auxiliary verb, as is its English equivalent in this construction. The expression is not unknown in Attic (Plato, *Euth.* 2c, *Phaedo* 100b; Xen. *Ages.* 2.7), but it is particularly common in Hdt. (e.g. 1.5.3, 2.35.1, 3.6.1, 4.99.2).

δίχα γίνονται αἱ γνῶμαι: 'our opinions are divided', 'our opinions are split in two'.

τῶν δὲ οὔ: (sc. κελευόντων) 'while others are forbidding it'.

109.5 τινα στάσιν: here the meaning is 'strife', 'dissension'.

ὥστε μηδίσαι: 'with the result that they will go over to the Persian side', a reference to the existence of a pro-Persian faction which had already made its presence felt in 507 or 506 (Hdt. 5.73), and which will have included the supporters of Hippias and, at least according to a widespread belief of the day, members of the Alcmeonidae (see chapters 115 and 123 below). Verbs in -ίζω and -ιάζω derived from the names of nations indicate either the ability to speak the language concerned (e.g. θρακίζω, φρυγίζω) or the desire to ape the customs of and/or political sympathies for that particular nation (e.g. ἀττικίζω, λακωνίζω). Some verbs (e.g. λυδίζω, σκυθίζω, βοιωτιάζω, αἰγυπτιάζω) are used in both senses.

πρίν τι καὶ σαθρὸν Ἀθηναίων μετεξετέροισι ἐγγενέσθαι: 'before something rotten falls upon some of the Athenians'. σαθρός, literally 'rotten', is also used metaphorically in the sense of 'hollow', 'unsound'. For the inf. with πρίν, see note on 22.1 above, and for μετεξέτεροι, see note on 71.1.

θεῶν τὰ ἴσα νεμόντων: see note on 11.3 above, where the phrase also occurs.

109.6 ἐς σὲ νῦν τείνει: 'it now belongs to you', 'it is now up to you', an impersonal use of τείνω.

ἢν δὲ τὴν τῶν ἀποσπευδόντων τὴν συμβολὴν ἔλῃ: (sc. γνώμην) 'but if you choose the view of those who are striving to avert the engagement'.

ὑπάρξει τοι...τὰ ἐναντία: 'you will have the opposite'. ὑπάρχω means 'begin', 'take the initiative in', followed by a noun in the gen. or by a part. With a dat., as here, the meaning is 'belong to', 'accrue to'.

110 προσκτᾶται: 'he won over', i.e. 'he acquired' Callimachus in addition to the support he already enjoyed on the board of generals.

ἐκεκύρωτο: 'it had been decided'. For the constitutional relation between polemarch and generals at the time, see C. Hignett, *A History of the Athenian Constitution to the End of the Fifth Century B.C.*, Oxford, 1952, pp. 170-3; N.G.L. Hammond, 'The Campaign and Battle of Marathon', *JHS* 88, 1968, pp. 48-50; P.J. Rhodes, *A Commentary on the Aristotelian* Athenaion Politeia, Oxford, 1981, pp. 264-5; Fornara, *op. cit.*, pp. 5-7 and 72-3.

μετὰ δὲ: adverbial (see note on 4.1 above).

τῶν ἡ γνώμη ἔφερε συμβάλλειν: 'whose view inclined towards joining battle', where ἔφερε is intrans. For another intrans. use of the verb φέρω, see note on 42.1 above.

πρυτανηΐη: 'the command', an Ionic use of the word which in Attic normally refers to the standing subcommittee of the *boule*. By analogy with the operation of the *boule*, πρυτανηΐη here refers to the presidency or chairmanship of the board of *strategoi*, which was held by each general in turn on a daily basis, though Hdt. also seems to have in mind a system whereby the command of the Athenian army was also exercised daily by each general in turn. Plutarch too believed this to be the case (παρ' ἡμέραν ἑκάστου στρατηγοῦ τὸ κράτος ἔχοντος, *Arist.* 5.2), and Diodorus assumes the principle of rotation of command to have been in operation even at Arginusae in 406 (13.97.6) and at Aegospotamoi in 405 (13.106.1).

οὔτι κω συμβολὴν ἐποιέετο, πρίν γε δὴ αὐτοῦ πρυτανηΐη ἐγένετο: 'he didn't yet attack until it was the day of his own presidency'. For the construction with πρίν, see note on 22.1 above, and for πρίν γε δή, see note on 79.1.

111.1 ὡς συμβαλέοντες: 'in order to engage'. See note an 28.2 above.

τοῦ μὲν δεξιοῦ κέρεος: 'the right wing', the traditional place of honour and, as such, the regular position in Greek armies of the commander (Hdt.

198

9.26.7, 9.46.1; Thuc. 5.71; Euripides, *Suppliants* 657; Xen. *Hell.* 6.4.14; Plut. *Arist.* 16; Arrian, *Anab.* 1.14.1, 2.8.9, 3.13.2. On the Ionic forms of κέρας, see note on 50.3 above.

ὁ γὰρ νόμος τότε εἶχε οὕτω: 'for such was the law in force at that time', as opposed to the practice in Hdt's own day when the polemarch no longer commanded the army. He was probably deprived of all but ceremonial duties at the time of the reform of the archonship in 488/7 (*Ath. Pol.* 22.5).

ἐξεδέκοντο ὡς ἠριθμέοντο αἱ φυλαί: 'the tribes succeeded according to their numerical order'. Herodotus may be referring to the official order of the ten tribes as established by Cleisthenes' reforms, though in this event it is not at all clear why Aeantis (the 9th tribe) should have been on the extreme right (Plut. *Mor.* 628E), unless it was because Aeantis was the tribe to which the polemarch himself belonged. However, if Plut. is correct in his assertion (*Arist.* 5.3) that Leontis (tribe 4) and Antiochis (tribe 10) fought side by side in the centre, the position of each tribe may have been determined by lot (as was the order of the prytanising tribes in the *boule*).

ἐχόμεναι ἀλλήλων: 'coming next one another'. For this use of the middle of ἔχω, cf. 8.1 above.

111.2 θυσίας ἀναγόντων: 'when offering sacrifices'.

πανηγύριας τὰς ἐν τῆσι πεντετηρίσι γινομένας: 'festivals which occur in five yearly cycles', or rather, by inclusive reckoning, every four years (cf. chapter 87 above). According to *Ath. Pol.* 54.7, there were five such festivals (Delia, Brauronia, Heracleia, Eleusinia and Panathenaea), but only the fifth was of major importance. Though held every year (the 'Lesser Panathenaea'), the festival was celebrated every fourth year with greater magnificence (the 'Greater Panathenaea'), with the addition of athletic and, from the time of Pericles, musical competitions.

111.3 ἐγίνετο τοιόνδε τι: 'something as follows was the result', 'the outcome was roughly as follows'.

τὸ στρατόπεδον ἐξισούμενον τῷ Μηδικῷ στρατοπέδῳ: 'making the army equal to the Persian army'. Since the Persians were numerically superior to the Athenians, the two lines can have been equal only if the former had been confined by the narrowness of the space available between the sea and the hills, and even then only where they faced the thinnest part of the Athenian line.

τὸ μὲν αὐτοῦ μέσον ἐγίνετο ἐπὶ τάξιας ὀλίγας : 'its centre was formed only a few ranks deep'. The Ionic forms of nouns in -ις retain the -ι of the stem throughout the declension.

τὸ δὲ κέρας ἑκάτερον ἔρρωτο πλήθει: literally 'each wing had been strengthened in number', where ἔρρωτο is plup. middle/pass. of ῥώννυμι, 'strengthen'. The meaning is not that the Athenians deliberately strengthened their wings by moving men from the centre but that the wings were strong at the time of deployment only in contrast to the thinner centre. Though Athenian armies were often drawn up eight deep (see, e.g. Thuc. 4.94.1,

Delium; 6.67.1, Syracuse), here the centre may have been weakened in order to achieve the eight-deep wings which were essential if the army was not to be outflanked.

112.1 τὰ σφάγια ἐγίνετο καλά: 'the sacrifices proved favourable'. σφάγια was the name for sacrifices offered by the *manteis* on each side just as the battle line was about to advance. Cf. Hdt. 9.61.3, 62.1 (Plataea), Thuc. 6.69.2 (Syracuse), Xen. *Hell.* 3.4.23 (Sardis), 4.2.20 (Nemea), 7.4.30 (Olympia).

ὡς ἀπείθησαν: 'when they were let go', temporal. ἀπείθησαν is the Ionic form of the aor. pass. of ἀφίημι (Attic ἀφείθησαν).

ἦσαν δὲ στάδιοι οὐκ ἐλάσσονες τὸ μεταίχμιον αὐτῶν ἢ ὀκτώ: 'the distance between the two armies was not less than 8 stades'. For μεταίχμιον, see note on 77.1 above. 8 stades would be approximately a little more than 1 1/2 km. or just under a mile (see note on 36.2 above). As it would have been impossible for the Athenians to run a mile in full armour without exhausting themselves, they probably advanced at a normal pace and did not break into a run until they were within bowshot of the enemy.

112.2 μανίην τε τοῖσι Ἀθηναίοισι ἐπέφερον: 'they began to ascribe madness to the Athenians'.

οὔτε ἵππου ὑπαρχούσης σφι οὔτε τοξευμάτων: 'since they had neither cavalry nor archers'. τόξευμα, meaning literally 'arrow', can also be used (as at Plut. *Pyrrhus* 21.6) to denote a company of archers. This remark is intelligible only if Persian cavalry were deployed in the battle, (so too the reason given in ch. 102 for the their choice of Marathon as their landing place). Yet the historian nowhere gives the slightest hint that Persian cavalry did participate in the battle. Athenian cavalry at Marathon are attested only in an unreliable passage of Pausanias (1.27.1) which is contradicted by Hdt. 9.21. If such a force even existed in 490, it can have comprised at most 96 men, two from each *naukraria* (Pollux, *Onomasticon* 8.108), if indeed the naukraries survived Cleisthenes' reform programme. A regular cavalry did not exist until later in the century, when a force of 300 was instituted (Andocides 3.5; Aeschines 2.173). It was enlarged by stages until it amounted to 1000 (Aristophanes, *Knights* 225; Philochorus Frag. 39; cf. Thuc. 2.13.8). See also G.R. Burgh, *The Horsemen of Athens*, Princeton, 1988, pp. 3-14; I.G. Spence, *The Cavalry of Classical Greece*, Oxford, 1993, pp. 9-17. If Hdt. is correct in stating that the Athenians had no archers at Marathon they were certainly able to provide a troop of bowmen for both Salamis in 480 (Aeschylus, *Persians* 460; Plut. *Them.* 14.1) and for Plataea the following year (Hdt. 9.22.1 and 60).

112.3 ταῦτα...οἱ βάρβαροι κατείκαζον: 'this was what the barbarians imagined'.

πρῶτοι...πάντων τῶν ἡμεῖς ἴδμεν δρόμῳ ἐς πολεμίους ἐχρήσαντο: 'they were the first of all the Greeks we know of to proceeed at a run against the enemy'. ἴδμεν is the Ionic equivalent of the Attic ἴσμεν, 1st. pers. plur. of οἶδα, where the ending -μεν is attached directly to the stem ἰδ-. For the attraction of the rel. pron. (τούς) to the case of its antecedent (τῶν), see note on 21.1 above and cf. chs 86β2 and 87 above.

πρῶτοι δὲ ἀνέσχοντο ἐσθῆτά τε Μηδικὴν ὁρέοντες: 'and first to endure the sight of Persian dress'. Presumably Hdt. is thinking of the mainland Greeks, since the Greeks of Asia Minor and Cyprus had faced Persians in battle as early as 545 (1.169) and, more recently, in the Ionian Revolt (5.102, 110ff., 120, and ch 28 above).

τέως δὲ ἦν τοῖσι Ἕλλησι καὶ τὸ οὔνομα τὸ Μήδων φόβος ἀκοῦσαι: 'at that time the Greeks were afraid even to hear the name of the Persians'. For the 6th century, see Theognis 764. The inf. is used after φόβος ἦν by analogy with the construction after a verb of fearing when the meaning is 'be afraid to' (Goodwin 1521).

113.1 τῇ Πέρσαι τε αὐτοὶ καὶ Σάκαι ἐτετάχατο: 'where the Persians themselves and the Sakai were stationed'. For ἐτετάχατο (Attic τεταγμένοι ἦσαν), see note on 9.1 above. Σάκαι is the Greek form of the Persian word Saka, a name given to the Iranian speaking nomads who inhabited the steppes to the north and north west of the Achaemenid Empire from the Danube to the Altai. The Greeks usually called them Scythians. Darius I lists Sakai as Achaemenid subjects in various inscriptions (Behistun I ll.16-7, V 22ff., Persepolis E line 18, Naqsh-i-Rustam A ll.25-6), as do Xerxes (Persepolis H ll-26) and Artaxerxes (Persepolis ll.14-15). Old Persian inscriptions regularly distinguish two Scythian subject peoples, the Saka Tigraxauda ('Scythians wearing pointed caps') and the Saka Haumavarga (interpretation doubtful, but perhaps to be understood as 'Scythians who manufacture/ drink/venerate haoma', the sacred fermented drink). Herodotus includes unspecified Sakai in the 15th satrapy of his list of provinces (3.93.3, cf. 8.113.2), and mentions Pointed-Cap Scythians as coming to Greece with Xerxes (7.64.2), but calls these 'Amyrgians', possibly a translation of the Persian haumavarga. He may here be confusing the two groups of Scythians, though it is possible that most Sakai, and not just the Tigraxauda, wore pointed caps, a view that derives some support from Achaemenid art. The Saka Haumavarga are usually located to the north east of the empire, somewhere beyond Bactria/Sogdiana, and the Tigraxauda either in the same area or in the vicinity of the Caspian and Black Sea (see M.A. Dandamev, *A Political History of the Achaemenid Empire*, tr. W.J. Vogelsang, Leiden, 1989, pp. 135-40; W.J. Vogelsang, *The Rise and Organisation of the Achaemenid Empire: The Eastern Iranian Evidence*, Leiden, 1992, pp. 106-9, 115-16, 192. A third group, the Saka Paradraya, 'the Scythians who live across/ beyond the sea, (Darius, Naqsh-i-Rustam A ll.28-9, cf. Xerxes Persepolis H l.24) were those encountered by Darius in the course of his Scythian campaign of c.513, but these remained unconquered and are unlikely to have fought at Marathon.

κατὰ τοῦτο: 'at this point', 'in this place'.

ἐνίκων...ἐδίωκον...ἐνίκων...ἐμάχοντο: this series of imperfects is used to indicate that the action lasted for some considerable time before being successfully completed.

113.2 τὸ μὲν τετραμμένον (sc. μέρος) τῶν βαρβάρων φεύγειν ἔων: 'they allowed the routed part of the barbarians to escape', where ἔων is the Ionic imperf. of ἐάω, corresponding to the Attic εἴων.

συναγαγόντες τὰ κέρεα: 'drawing the two wings together'. On the form κέρεα (Attic κέρατα), see notes on 50.3 and 111.1 above.

φεύγουσι: 'as they were fleeing', here dat. plur. of the part. in agreement with Πέρσῃσι.

ἐπελαμβάνοντο τῶν νεῶν: 'they proceeded to take hold of the ships', i.e. as they were being pushed out to sea by the Persian fugitives.

114 τοῦτο μὲν...τοῦτο δὲ: see note on 27.2 above, and cf. 44.1, 69.3, 101.3, 107.2.

ὁ πολέμαρχος: Callimachus was subsequently commemorated in Panaenus' famous painting in the Stoa Poikile (Pliny, *NH* 35.57; Paus. 1.15.3, 5.11.6; Aelian, *De Natura Animalium* 7.35).

ἀπὸ δ᾽ ἔθανε: by tmesis for ἀπέθανε, essentially a poetic construction, though not unparalleled in Hdt. (see 8.33, 8.89.1, 9.5.3).

Κυνέγειρος ὁ Εὐφορίωνος: brother of the tragic poet Aeschylus, who also fought in the battle. Cynegeirus too earned a place in Panaenus' painting in the Stoa Poikile (Pliny, *loc. cit.*).

τῶν ἀφλάστων: the sternpost, including the ornament affixed to it, often fan-like in appearance.

τὴν χεῖρα ἀποκοπεὶς: literally 'chopped off with respect to his hand', i.e. 'having had his hand chopped off', where ἀποκοπεὶς is aor. part. pass. of ἀποκόπτω.

115 ἐξανακρουσάμενοι: 'having pushed themselves away from land', by means of poles.

ἐκ τῆς νήσου: Aegilia (see 107.2 above).

φθῆναι τοὺς Ἀθηναίους ἀπικόμενοι ἐς τὸ ἄστυ: 'to reach the city in advance of the Athenians'. For φθάνω with the part., see note on 91.1 above and cf. 108.2 and 116.1.

αἰτίη δὲ ἔσχε: 'an accusation came to prevail', ingressive aor. (see note on 25.2) of ἔχω used intransitively.

Ἀλκμαιωνιδέων: one of the most illustrious families in Athens, which included in its membership Cleisthenes the reformer. The current head of the family was Cleisthenes' nephew Megacles, who was to be ostracised in 487/6 (*Ath. Pol.* 22.5). Hdt.'s defence of the Alcmeonidae in connection with the accusation of treachery follows at chapters 123-4 below.

ἀναδέξαι ἀσπίδα: 'displayed a shield', probably by holding it aloft to reflect the sunlight. The implausibilities of the story are exposed by Lazenby (*The Defence of Greece*, pp. 72-4). The charge may have been fabricated by the political enemies of the Alcmeonid family at the time of the series of ostracisms held during the next few years.

116 ὡς ποδῶν εἶχον: literally 'with what measure of feet (i.e. speed) they had', i.e. 'as fast as they could', 'as fast as their legs could carry them'. The gen. is used thus with adverbs of manner, especially with ἥκω and intrans. ἔχω. Cf. 5.62.3 χρημάτων εὖ ἥκοντες, 'being well supplied with money'; ἐδιώκων ὡς ποδῶν ἕκαστος εἶχον, 9.59.2. Some scholars doubt the ability of the army to rush back to Athens, a distance of 26 miles, on the very day of the battle. According to Plut. *Arist.* 5.4, only nine of the ten tribes returned and Aristeides and his tribe, Antiochis, were left on the field to guard the prisoners and the spoils.

ἔφθησάν...ἀπικόμενοι πρὶν ἢ τοὺς βαρβάρους ἥκειν: 'they succeeded in returning before the barbarians arrived'. For the construction with φθάνω, see note on 91.1 and cf. 108.2 and 115. For πρὶν ἤ, see note on 22.1 above. According to Plut. *Mor.* 347C, citing Heracleides Ponticus, the Athenian who first brought back news of the victory was either Thersippus of Eroeadae or one Eucles, who collapsed and died in the Council Chamber after gasping out the words χαίρετε· νικῶμεν. For Lucian's more melodramatic substitution of Philippides for Thersippus, see note on 105.1 above. Modern calculations of the time taken for the Athenians to return to Athens depend on which route was taken and offer estimates of from 8 to 10 hours (see e.g. Lazenby, *op. cit.* p. 74). In the case of the Persians, on the assumption that some ships were detached to collect the Eretrian captives, the remainder would have taken about 10 hours to sail from Marathon round Cape Sunium to Phalerum (see Lazenby, p. 74, citing J.S. Morrison and J.F. Coates, *The Athenian Trireme*, Cambridge, 1986, p. 74. For the speed of ancient ships, see also L. Casson, *Ships and Seamanship in the Ancient World*, Baltimore and London, 1971, pp. 281-96). On the basis of these calculations, it would have been anyone's guess as to who would reach Athens first.

Ἡρακλείῳ τῷ ἐν Κυνοσάργεϊ: Cynosarges lay outside the gates of Athens (Plut. *Them.* 1.2; Diogenes Laertius 6.113), somewhere in the south western suburbs (J. Travlos, 'The Gymnasium of Kynosarges', *Athens Annals of Archaeology* 3, 1970, pp. 6-14; R.E. Wycherley, *The Stones of Athens*, Princeton, 1978, pp. 229-30; D.G. Kyle, *Athletics in Ancient Athens*, Leiden, 1987, pp. 84-7). It was the site of a sanctuary of Heracles from an early date. In the classical period the sanctuary's chief claim to fame was the presence of a gymnasium on the site, albeit the least prestigious of the three which the city possessed, being associated above all with bastards, although it could also boast of the patronage of Themistocles. (see Kyle, *op. cit.* pp. 88-92, 99-101).

ὑπεραιωρηθέντες: literally 'being lifted above', i.e. 'anchoring off'. For the concept that the sea is 'up' or 'above' in relation to the land, see note on ἀνάγω at 12.1.

Φαλήρου (τοῦτο γὰρ ἦν ἐπίνειον τότε τῶν Ἀθηναίων): Phalerum, the old harbour of Athens, was some 3 miles distant from the city, but, being more exposed both to storms and to potential enemy attack than Piraeus, was less desirable from a military and commercial viewpoint. Construction of a new harbour at Piraeus, some 5 miles from Athens, was begun by Themistocles during his archonship in 493 (Thuc. 1.93.3; Plut. *Them.* 19.2). The present passage shows that construction work was by no means near completion in 490.

ἀνακωχεύσαντες τὰς νέας: literally 'holding back the ships', i.e. 'letting the ships ride at anchor', the Ionic form of the Attic ἀνοκωχέω, and connected with the root of ἔχω and ἀνέχω in the significance of 'hold back'. The related noun ἀνοκωχή, literally 'a holding back of arms', is regularly used with the meaning 'truce'.

117.1 κατὰ ἑξακισχιλίους καὶ τετρακοσίους ἄνδρας: 'about 6400 individuals', where κατά is used in the sense of 'approximately'. See notes on 44.3 and cf. 79.1 above. Though the Athenians are unlikely to have been too accurate in their estimate of enemy casualties, they presumably made some sort of tally when they burned them (Paus. 1.32.5), if only because, according to Xenophon (*Anab.* 3.2.12, cf. Plut. *Mor.* 862B), they had promised to sacrifice a she-goat to Artemis Agrotera for every enemy killed. In the circumstances, they were obliged to modify the promise by sacrificing 500 goats each year in lieu of the number due. Even so, Hdt.'s figure of 6400 compares favourably with the grossly inflated estimates of later writers (e.g. Lysias 2.20; Plato, *Menexenus* 240a; Nepos, *Miltiades* 4.1; Plut. *Mor.* 862B; Paus. 4.25.5; Justin 2.9.20): the number 20,000, according to the Suda, appeared already on an inscription in the Stoa Poikile.

'Αθηναίων δὲ ἑκατὸν ἐνενήκοντα καὶ δύο: this number is almost certainly accurate as the Athenians compiled names for an official casualty list which they had engraved on the monument (Paus. 1.32.3). According to Thucydides (2.34.1), war casualties were normally brought back to Athens for burial, but those slain at Marathon were given the exceptional honour of burial on the field. Modern scholars however incline towards the view that the burial of war casualties in Athens was not the regular practice until after the end of Xerxes' invasion (see F. Jacoby, 'Patrios Nomos: State Burial in Athens and the Public Cemetary in the Kerameikos', *JHS* 64, 1944, pp. 37-66, esp. 44-5; J.E. Ziolkowski, *Thucydides and the Tradition of Funeral Speeches at Athens*, New York, 1981, pp. 13-21; C. Clairmont, *Patrios Nomos*, Oxford, 1983, p. 9ff.; W.K. Pritchett, *The Greek State at War* IV, Berkeley and Los Angeles, 1985, pp. 249-50). At all events, the Athenians slain at Marathon were interred in the *soros* excavated in 1890. Herodotus gives no numbers for the Plataeans and slaves, though they too were buried at Marathon, albeit in a separate grave (Paus. *loc. cit.*), which has been identified, perhaps erroneously, with a grave discovered in the Vrana valley in 1970 (see J.A.G. Van der Veer, 'The Battle of Marathon: A Topographical Survey', *Mnemosyne* 34, 1982, pp. 301-4; Lazenby, *op. cit.* p. 75).

117.2 συνήνεικε...θώυμα γενέσθαι τοιόνδε: 'it happened that the following marvel occurred'. See note on 23.1 above.

τῶν ὀμμάτων στερηθῆναι: literally 'deprived of his eyes', i.e. 'of his sight'. For the gen. of separation after verbs of depriving and taking away, see Goodwin 117-18.

πληγέντα οὐδὲν τοῦ σώματος: 'struck on no part of his body'. πληγέντα is aor. pass. of πλήσσω and οὐδέν is acc. of specification or aspect (Goodwin 1058).

117.3 λέγειν δὲ αὐτὸν ἤκουσα...τοιόνδε τινὰ λόγον: 'I heard that he gave some such account as the following', a clear statement that the ultimate source of information goes back to Epizelus himself, though Hdt. does not claim to have talked to him in person. Epizelus earned himself inclusion in the painting in the Stoa Poikile on the strength of this incident (Aelian, *De Natura Animalium* 7.38). The Athenians too could claim to have heroes fighting on their side in the battle (Theseus and Echetlus, Paus. 1.15.3, 1.32.4).

118.1 Μυκόνῳ: an island of the Cyclades, situated to the north east of Delos.

ἐπυνθάνετο ὁκόθεν σεσυλημένον εἴη: 'enquired from what source it had been looted'. For the opt. in indirect questions in historic sequence, see Goodwin 1481.2. The subj. and opt. of the perf. middle and pass. are regularly expressed periphrastically by the part. with the relevant part of εἰμί. For the few synthetic forms in use, see Goodwin 722 and 734.

118.2 Δήλιον τὸ Θηβαίων: Delium, situated between Tanagra and Oropus and facing Eretria in Euboea across the Euripus, was famous mainly for its precinct of Apollo. It was subsequently the scene of a battle in 424, where the Boeotians defeated the Athenians. Since Delium was officially in Tanagran territory (Thuc. 4.76.4; Paus. 9.20.1), Hdt.'s description of it as 'Theban' is distinctly odd, and may indicate either that Tanagra lost it to Thebes some time before 490 or that it was Theban at the time Hdt. wrote the passage.

119.1 προσέσχον ἐς τὴν Ἀσίην: see note on 99.1 above.

πρὶν...αἰχμαλώτους γενέσθαι τοὺς Ἐρετριέας: on the construction with πρίν, see note on 22.1 above and Goodwin 1470-4.

ἀρξάντων ἀδικίης: the reference is to the Ionian Revolt (see 5.99.1).

119.2 Κισσίης: the eighth province of the Persian Empire (3.91.4), centred on Susa, generally known as Elam or, in Greek, as Susiana or Elymais.

ἐν σταθμῷ ἑωυτοῦ: 'in a township belonging to himself'. σταθμός, meaning originally 'resting place' on a road, where one could obtain food and a bed for the night, came, as further lodgings for the use of wayfarers were constructed on the site, to denote the entire complex of buildings thus established.

Ἀρδέρικκα: the destination of the deportees is variously reported. Whereas an epigram ascribed to Plato in the Greek Anthology (D.L. Page, *Epigrammata Graeca* 545-6) agrees with Hdt., Strabo (16.1.25) locates it in the eparchy of Gordyene in Armenia, and another epigram ascribed to Plato (Page *op. cit.* 547-8) places the deportees somewhere in Media:

> We are those who once leaving the Aegean's deep-roaring surge
> lie in the middle of Ecbatana's plain. Farewell, famous Eretrian
> motherland, farewell Athens, neighbour to Euboea, farewell,
> beloved sea.

δέκα καὶ διηκοσίους σταδίους ἀπέχοντι: 'distant by 210 stades', a distance of some 37 km. or 23 miles.

φρέατος τὸ παρέχεται τριφασίας ἰδέας: 'a well that provides three distinct kinds of product'. On τριφάσιος, see note on 100.1 above.

119.3 κηλωνηΐῳ: the Ionic form of the Attic κηλώνειον, as at 1.193.1, an irrigation tool in the form of a water-hoist or hand operated swing beam, consisting of a long pole with a water scoop (γαῦλος) at one end balanced by a counterweight at the other, revolving on a base, by means of which water could be transferred from a natural source. The scoop was dipped in the river or canal by hand, raised and emptied into a container or irrigation channel as appropriate, then lowered again into the river. The device, known in Arabic as a *shaduf*, is still employed to some extent in near eastern countries. For an illustration, see, for example, J. Barnes and J. Malek, *Atlas of Ancient Egypt*, Oxford, 1980, p. 17.

γαυλοῦ: see note on ch. 17 above.

ἥμισυ ἀσκοῦ οἱ προσδέδεται: 'half of a wineskin (i.e. a wineskin cut in half) is attached to it'.

ὑποτύψας δὲ τούτῳ ἀντλέει: 'dipping into the liquid with it, the operator draws it up', where some such noun as ἐργάτης is to be understood as the subject of ἀντλέει.

δεξαμενήν: 'tank', 'container', 'receptacle'. The aor. part. of δέχομαι (Ionic δέκομαι), 'receive', here used (with a change of accent) as the equivalent of a noun.

ἐς ἄλλο διαχεόμενον τράπεται τριφασίας ὁδούς: 'when it is poured through this container into another it turns three ways'. The second receptacle has three distinct outlets or channels through which the three liquids flow as the difference in their respective masses ensures their separation.

πήγνυνται: literally 'become fixed', i.e. 'solidify'.

συνάγουσι ἐν ἀγγηΐοισι: 'they collect it in buckets', the reading of the Sancroftian manuscript (? a guess by the copyist), where all others have a lacuna of a few words.

ῥαδινάκην: one of the few Persian glosses recorded by Hdt. (cf. ἀγγαρήϊον, 8.98.2; Ὀροσάγγαι, 8.85.3; τυκτά, 9.110.2).

ἔστι δὲ μέλαν καὶ ὀδμὴν παρεχόμενον βαρέαν: this description suggests that the oil in question is petroleum, and, if so, would locate Ardericca somewhere in the oilfields of southern Iran.

206

120 μετὰ τὴν πανσέληνον: see note on 106.3 above.

ἔχοντες σπουδὴν πολλὴν καταλαβεῖν: the object to be supplied for καταλαβεῖν is unclear: perhaps πρήγματα (to give the meaning 'participate in the action'), or a geographical name such as Ἀθήνας or Μαραθῶνα (in the sense 'reach').

τριταῖοι: 'on the third day'. For adjs. in -αῖος derived from ordinal numerals, see note on 106.1 above. According to Isocrates (*Panegyric* 87), they covered the distance in a march of three days and three nights.

ὕστεροι...ἀπικόμενοι: on the day after the battle, according to Plato (*Laws* 698e, *Menexenus* 240c).

θηήσασθαι τοὺς Μήδους: since the Athenians are said by Pausanias (1.32.5) to have buried the Persian dead, this statement lends some support to the tradition of a Spartan arrival the day after the battle, when the enemy were not yet buried.

μετὰ δὲ: 'and afterwards', adverbial. See note on 4.1 above.

121.1 οὐκ ἐνδέκομαι τὸν λόγον : Hdt. returns to the alleged medism of the Alcmeonidae which has already been mentioned in ch. 115 above. Plutarch (*Mor.* 862F-863A), who cites the phrase as proof of the historian's maliciousness, regards it as no more than the merest pretence of a defence. See also Daniel Gillis, 'Collaboration with the Persians', *Historia, Einzelschrift* 34, Wiesbaden, 1976, pp. 45-58, who argues strongly for Alcmeonid treachery and describes Hdt. as 'the house historian of the Alcmeonids'. If Hdt.'s defence is taken at face value, he will perhaps have felt that his silence on the story could he construed as tacit acceptance. Be that as it may, the twofold mention of the tale will seem to the modern reader to be both decidedly unfortunate and highly damaging to the Alcemeonid reputation.

Ἀλκμαιωνίδας ἄν κοτε ἀναδέξαι...ἀσπίδα: 'that the Alcmeonidae might possibly have displayed a shield'. Here ἄν with the inf. represents in indirect discourse what in direct speech would be ἄν with the opt., a construction used by Hdt. to represent hesitant or cautious assertions. Cf. 9.71.4 ταῦτα ἄν εἰποῖεν, 'they might possibly say this', and particularly common with the adv. τάχα, 'perhaps' (7.180, 8.136.3).

μᾶλλον ἢ ὁμοίως: literally 'more than equally', i.e. 'equally, or even more so'.

Καλλίῃ τῷ Φαινίππου: Davies *APF* no. 7826. Born c.590, he was later head of the aristocratic family of the Ceryces. Practically nothing is known of his career apart from what we are told in this and the following chapter.

Ἱππονίκου: equally obscure, other than being father of the 5th century diplomat Callias who married Cimon's sister Elpinice. Plutarch (*Mor.* 863A) taxes Hdt. with gratuitously including his name in order to flatter Callias.

φαίνονται μισοτύραννοι ἐόντες: Hdt. here conveniently forgets that Megacles had been responsible for the recall of Peisistratus after his first period of exile and had been, at least for a time, the tyrant's father-in-law

207

(1.60, cf. [Arist.] *Ath. Pol.* 15.1; Plut. *Mor.* 863B). In addition Megacles had links with the Lydian kings (chapter 125.2 below) and with the tyrants of Sicyon (ch. 126). The latter link was even advertised through the use in his family of personal names favoured by the Sicyonian tyranny (Cleisthenes, Aristonymus, Agariste). Cleisthenes' acceptance of the archonship from Hippias in 525/4 (Meiggs and Lewis 6) was presumably unknown to Hdt.

121.2 μοῦνος...ἐτόλμα: 'he was the only one to venture', since the purchaser of such property was likely to suffer in the event of Peisistratus' regaining power. In addition buying confiscated property was considered disreputable in the eyes of most members of the aristocracy.

ὅκως Πεισίστρατος ἐκπέσοι: 'when Peisistratus was expelled', a frequentative opt. (cf. 31.1, 61.3, 75.1, 77.3. 137.3) used with reference to the two exiles and restorations of the tyrant (see 1.60.1, 1.61.2).

κηρυσσόμενα ὑπὸ τοῦ δημοσίου: 'when it was advertised for sale by the public auctioneer'. With δημοσίου, the noun δούλου is to be understood, since public criers, along with certain other categories such as policemen (the Scythian archers) and the state executioner, were supplied from public slaves bought and owned by the state.

122.1 This chapter is generally considered to be an interpolation based on some marginal note on Callias which in the course of recopying was mistakenly assumed to be an integral part of the text. Not only is the chapter missing from the three best manuscripts, but it interrupts the syntax of Καλλίης τε at 121.2, ...καὶ οἱ Ἀλκμαιωνίδαι at the beginning of 123.1 and contains some non-Herodotean vocabulary (τὰ προλελεγμένα, where Hdt. regularly has τά μοι πρότερον εἴρηται; φανερόομαι in place of the Herodotean ἀπολαμπρύνομαι, as at 1.41.2 and ch. 70.3 above; δωρέη for the Herodotean φέρνη, as at 1.93.4), and some equally un-Herodotean syntax (ἔδωκέ σφι...ἐκείνῃσί τε ἐχαρίσατο).

πολλαχοῦ: here, exceptionally, used in a causal sense ('for many reasons'). The adv. is regularly local ('in many places').

τοῦτο μὲν...τοῦτο δὲ: see note on 27.1 above, and cf. 44.1, 69.3, 101.3, 107.2, 114.

τὰ προλελεγμένα: 'as has already been stated', adv. acc. for the more usual expression κατὰ τὰ προλελεγμένα.

ἵππῳ νικήσας: Callias' Olympic victory in the horse race was won in 564 (scholiast on Ar. *Birds.* 283). It was presumably pride in this victory that prevailed over filial piety in the naming of his son Hipponicus.

Πύθια...ἀνελόμενος: 'having won at the Pythian games'. For the syntax, see note on 36.1 above.

122.2 τοῦτο δὲ: 'in the third place'.

κατὰ τὰς...θυγατέρας...οἷός τις...ἐγένετο: literally 'what sort of man he became in the matter of his daughters'.

γάμου ὡραῖαι: 'of an age for marriage', a phrase borrowed from 1.196.1.

τὸν ἑκάστη ἐθέλοι: normally the father would select suitable husbands with an eye on the wealth and status of the bridegroom and the possible political benefits which the match would confer on himself. The bride would not normally be consulted, and indeed would in most cases be unlikely even to have seen her prospective husband prior to the betrothal. One of Callias' daughters may have married Lysimachus and become the mother of Aristeides, if the story told by Plutarch (*Arist.* 25) is true; a second may have been the wife of one Struthon (see Davies, *APF* p. 256).

123.1 οἵτινες ἔφευγόν τε τὸν πάντα χρόνον τοὺς τυράννους: 'inasmuch as they were exiled by the tyrants throughout the entire period', a causal relative clause (Goodwin 1461). φεύγω, literally 'flee', is also used as the pass. of ἐκβάλλω, 'expel', with the meaning 'be banished', 'be in exile'. This statement is in conflict with 1.60-1, where we are told that Megacles supported the first restoration of Peisistratus when the tyrant agreed to marry his daughter, as well as with 1.64.3, where it is made clear that the Alcmeonidae went into exile only after Peisistratus' third restoration. At least some members of the family returned after the accession of Hippias in 528/7, and Cleisthenes even held the archonship in 524/3 (see note on ch. 121.1 above), though the entire clan was in exile again by the time of Hippias' expulsion in 511/0, probably as a result of the assassination of Hipparchus in 514. Presumably after the establishment of the democracy the Alcmeonidae were embarrassed by their record of cooperation with the tyrants and tried to supress as much of it as they could.

ἐκ μηχανῆς...τῆς τούτων ἐξέλιπον οἱ Πεισιστρατίδαι τὴν τυραννίδα: a reference to the events that culminated in the expulsion of Hippias in 510, which, though effected by the Spartans, was to some extent set in motion by the Alcmeonidae (see 5.62-3).

123.2 οὗτοι ἦσαν οἱ ἐλευθερώσαντες πολλῷ μᾶλλον ἤπερ Ἁρμόδιός τε καὶ Ἀριστογείτων: Harmodius and Aristogeiton were the murderers of Hippias' brother Hipparchus in 514. As a result of their actions they acquired a reputation as liberators in the popular tradition as found in the *scolia* or drinking songs current at aristocratic symposia in the fifth century. For the text and translation of these scolia, see G.R. Stanton, *Athenian Politics c.800-500 B.C.: A Sourcebook*, London and New York, 1990, no. 711, p. 119; D.A. Campbell, *Greek Lyric*, Vol. 5, Loeb Classical Library, Cambridge Mass and London, 1993, nos. 894-6. For the political implications of the murder, see A.J. Podlecki, 'The Political Significance of the Athenian "Tyrannicide" Cult', *Historia* 15, 1966, pp. 129-41; C.W. Fornara, 'The Tradition about the Murder of Hipparchus', *Historia* 17, 1968, pp. 400-24; M. Ostwald, *Nomos and the Beginnings of the Athenian Democracy*, Oxford, 1969, pp. 121-36; C.W. Fornara, 'The Cult of Harmodius and Aristogeiton', *Philologus* 104, 1970, pp. 55-80; M.W. Taylor, *The Tyrant Slayers: The Heroic Image in the Fifth Century B.C. in Athenian Art and Politics*, New

York, 1981, pp. 51-77. Herodotus here agrees with Thucydides (6.54-9) in demonstrating the falsity of the tradition, which may have entered historiography through the account of Hellanicus in his *Atthis*.

τοὺς ὑπολοίπους Πεισιστρατιδέων: Hippias himself, together with the surviving members of his family. On the identity of these, see note on 94.1 above.

οὐδέ τι μᾶλλον ἔπαυσαν...τυραννεύοντας: Hippias continued to hold the tyranny for some three to four years after Hipparchus' death.

ὥς μοι πρότερον δεδήλωται : at 5.63, where Hdt. narrates how the exiled Alcmeonidae made use of the Delphic oracle to effect a Spartan intervention. For the use of the dat. of the agent after a perf. pass., see note on 53.2, and cf. 82.2 and 130.2.

124.1 ἀλλὰ γὰρ ἴσως τι...προεδίδοσαν τὴν πατρίδα: 'but perhaps it might be argued that they betrayed their country'. On the use of ἀλλὰ γάρ to introduce an imaginary objection, see Denniston, *GP*, pp. 104-5.

οὐ μὲν ὦν ἦσάν σφεων ἄλλοι δοκιμώτεροι: 'on the contrary there were no others held in greater repute'. On the use of μὲν οὖν to answer a previous objection, see Denniston, *GP*, pp. 478-9. Herodotus here chooses to ignore both the curse which had lain on the Alcmeonidae since the affair of Cylon (Hdt. 5.71, Thuc. 1.126, Plut. *Solon* 12.1-3) and the ostracism of Megacles in 487/6 (*Ath. Pol.* 22.5).

124.2 οὐδὲ λόγος αἱρέει: 'nor does reason prove...', 'nor is it in accord with rational probability that...', where αἱρέει is used absolutely, as at 2.33.2 (καὶ δὴ καὶ ὁ λόγος οὕτω αἱρέει), 2.43.3 (ὡς...ἐμὴ γνώμη αἱρέει), 3.45.3 (οὐδὲ λόγος αἱρέει).

ἀναδεχθῆναι ἔκ γε ἂν τούτων: 'would have been held up by them', a past unreal condition (Goodwin 1397). For the use of ἐκ with the gen. to denote the agent, see note on 13.1 above. For the separation of ἂν from the word with which it belongs (*hyperbaton*), see Goodwin 1311. Here Hdt. desires to lay emphasis on τούτων in order to make clear that, whoever did hold up the shield, it was not the Alcmeonidae.

ἐπὶ τοιούτῳ λόγῳ: 'on the basis of any reasoning of this sort', 'on such grounds as these'.

ἀνεδέχθη μὲν γὰρ ἀσπίς: 'for a shield was indeed held up'.

125.1 καὶ τὰ ἀνέκαθεν: 'from the very first' (literally 'from above'), i.e. in earlier times as well as at the time of Marathon. See note on 53.2 above.

ἀπὸ δὲ Ἀλκμαίωνος καὶ αὖτις Μεγακλέος: 'but from the time of Alcmeon and afterwards of Megacles'. This Alcmeon was the son of the Megacles of the Cylonian affair, and the Megacles in question is Alcmeon's son, who married Agariste of Sicyon (see chapter 126 ff. below).

125.2 Λυδοῖσι παρὰ Κροίσου ἀπικνεομένοισι ἐπὶ τὸ χρηστήριον: the reference is to the various oracular consultations made by Croesus, including the testing of the oracles at 1.46-9, the enquiries concerning war with Persia (1.53, 1.55), and those about his dumb son (1.85).

συμπρήκτωρ...ἐγίνετο: 'he became their helper'. Chronological difficulties make it impossible to accept the historicity of this statement. Since Croesus came to the throne in 560, his oracular consultations must belong to the 550s at the earliest, yet Alcmeon, as son of the Megacles who was archon at a date somewhere in the 630s or 620s, was politically active in the 590s (Olympic victor in 592 and commander of the Athenian forces in the First Sacred War of 595-86). By the 550s Alcmeon was either dead or politically inactive, and had yielded the headship of his family to his son Megacles (1.60; *Ath. Pol.* 13.4; Plut. *Solon* 29.1), who was already the father of a girl old enough to be married to the tyrant Peisistratus (1.61.1). If Alcmeon assisted any Lydian envoys to Delphi, it can only have been the delegation sent by Alyattes to enquire about his illness (1.19.2).

μιν Κροῖσος...μεταπέμπεται ἐς Σάρδις: if there is any truth to the story, Alcmeon will have visited Sardis in the reign of Croesus' father Alyattes (c.607-560), and if he met Croesus in the course of his visit, Croesus was crown prince and not king at that time (cf. the similar tale of Croesus' meeting with Alcmeon's contemporary Solon at 1.30-33). It is not impossible that Alcmeon went to Sardis in a diplomatic capacity to solicit support for the allied coalition during the First Sacred War, and if so, he might well have established the commercial links with the Lydian kingdom that may underlie the vast increase in the Alcmeonid family fortune which belongs to this period.

τὸν ἂν δύνηται...ἐξενείκασθαι: 'however much he might be able to carry out'. For ἄν with the subj. in a generalising or indefinite relative clause, see Goodwin 1431 and note on ch. 56.1 above.

ἐσάπαξ: 'at one time'.

125.3 πρὸς τὴν δωρεήν...τοιάδε ἐπιτηδεύσας προσέφερε: 'contriving the following scheme, he proceeded to apply it to the matter of the gift'.

ἐνδὺς κιθῶνα: 'putting on a tunic'. κιθών is the Ionic equivalent of the Attic χιτών, and ἐνδύς is the 2nd. aor. part. of ἐνδύω, 'clothe' which has a trans. 1st. aor. ἐνέδυσα, 'I clothed', and an intrans. 2nd. aor. ἐνέδυν, 'I clothed myself in', 'I put on'.

κόλπον: literally 'breast', used here in the sense of 'fold', formed by the girdle to serve as the equivalent of a modern pocket.

κοθόρνους...ὑποδησάμενος: 'putting on boots'. ὑποδέω, literally 'fasten something underneath', is used to mean 'put footwear on someone', and so in the middle, 'put shoes on oneself', i.e. 'wear shoes' (cf. τὰ ὑποδήματα, 'footwear'). The κόθορνος was a high boot which fastened well up the leg, as opposed to the ἀρβύλη, 'half boot', which came up only as far as the ankle. The κόθορνος ('buskin'), which was particularly associated with tragic actors, was capable of being worn on either foot, and hence came to be given as a nickname to the politician Theramenes, who could adapt himself equally to oligarchic and democratic constitutions (Xen. *Hell.* 2.3.31 and 47; Plut. *Nicias* 2.1).

125.4 σωρὸν ψήγματος: 'heap of gold dust'.

παρέσαξε παρὰ τὰς κνήμας τοῦ χρυσοῦ ὅσον ἐχώρεον οἱ κόθορνοι: 'he stuffed alongside his legs as much gold as his boots could contain'.

μετὰ δὲ: 'and afterwards', adverbial, balancing πρῶτα μέν.

πλησάμενος: aor. middle part. of πίμπλημι, 'fill'.

διαπάσας τοῦ ψήγματος: 'sprinkling the gold dust', aor. part. of διαπάσσω. Verbs that are normally trans. may be followed by the gen. when the action affects only part of the object (Goodwin 1097). The use of the acc. here would imply that Alcmeon sprinkled all of the dust in the treasure chamber over his hair and not just some of it.

παντὶ δέ τεῳ οἰκὼς μᾶλλον ἢ ἀνθρώπῳ: literally 'looking more like anything else rather than a human being', where οἰκώς is the Ionic form of the perf. part. from ἔοικα (Attic ἐοικώς or εἰκώς), and τεῳ is the Ionic form of the dat. of the indef. pron. τις (Attic τινί or τῳ).

τοῦ τό τε στόμα ἐβέβυστο: causal relative, 'inasmuch as his mouth was crammed full'. ἐβέβυστο is pluperf. of βύω, 'stuff'.

125.5 καὶ πρὸς ἕτερα δωρέεται οὐκ ἐλάσσω ἐκείνων: 'and in addition he gave him another sum no less than that', i.e. 'he gave him as much again as he was able to bring out'. For adverbial πρός, see notes on 61.3 and 95.2 above.

ἐπλούτησε: 'he became rich', ingressive aor. See note on 25.2 above.

Ὀλυμπιάδα ἀναιρέεται: 'he won a victory at the Olympic Games'. See note on 70.3 above. This victory, which belongs to the year 592, is mentioned also by Isocrates (16.25).

126.1 μετὰ δὲ: adverbial.

γενεῇ δευτέρῃ ὕστερον: 'later, in the next generation'.

Κλεισθένης...ὁ Σικυῶνος τύραννος ἐξήειρε: 'Cleisthenes the tyrant of Sicyon exalted it', where ἐξήειρε is the aor. of ἐξαίρω, ' raise up'. Cleisthenes was tyrant of Sicyon in the first third of the sixth century, and a member of the dynasty founded by Orthagoras in the 7th century.

Κλεισθένεϊ...τῷ Ἀριστωνύμου τοῦ Μύρωνος τοῦ Ἀνδρέω: Herodotus' genealogy (supported by Paus. 2.8.1) leaves no room for Orthagoras, who is said by Aristotle (*Politics* 1315b 14-5) to have established the dynasty along with his sons (? = 'grandsons', 'descendants'), and by Plutarch (*Mor.* 553B) to have been the predecessor of Myron and Cleisthenes in the tyranny. Moreover it appears that there were two Myrons in the family, Myron the Elder, son of Andreas and grandfather of Cleisthenes, who is probably to be identified with the Myron who won an Olympic victory in 648 (Paus. 6.19.2), and who was never himself tyrant, and Myron the Younger, descendant of Orthagoras and Cleisthenes' elder brother, who held the tyranny between Orthagoras and Cleisthenes (Nicolaus of Damascus, Frag. 61 Jacoby). If all the information preserved about the dynasty is true, the only possible reconstruction of the family tree is that of Audrey Griffin (*Sicyon*, Oxford, 1982, pp. 40-1), where the names of tyrants are printed in capitals:

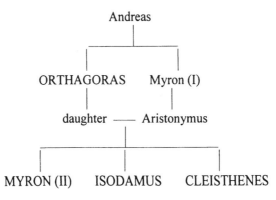

Andreas

ORTHAGORAS   Myron (I)

daughter —— Aristonymus

MYRON (II)   ISODAMUS   CLEISTHENES

For other possible stemmata, see N.G.L. Hammond, 'The Family of Orthagoras', *CQ* 6, 1956, pp. 45-53; D.M. Leahy, 'The Dating of the Orthagorid Dynasty', *Historia* 17, 1968, pp. 1-23.

126.2 νικῶν...τεθρίππῳ: from the likely ages of Megacles' children by Agariste, Cleisthenes' victory should probably be dated to 596 or 592. See M.F. McGregor, 'Cleisthenes of Sicyon and the Panhellenic Festivals', *TAPA* 72, 1941, pp. 266-87, esp. 276 ff; Griffin, *op. cit.*, pp. 43-4.

ὁ Κλεισθένης κήρυγμα ἐποιήσατο: since the Olympic festival was attended by people from all over the Greek world who would afterwards return to their individual cities, such a proclamation was the best method of ensuring that the message reached as many areas in the shortest possible time. For the periphrasis κήρυγμα ἐποιήσατο (= ἐκήρυξε), see note on 63.3 above.

γαμβρὸν: here 'son-in-law', as at 5.30.2 and 5.67.3, though elsewhere in Hdt. (e.g. at 1.73.2) the word means 'brother-in-law'. Cf. the use of κηδεστής in Attic prose to denote any male relation by marriage.

ἐς ἑξηκοστὴν ἡμέρην ἤ καὶ πρότερον: 'by the sixtieth day or even earlier'.

ὡς κυρώσοντος Κλεισθένεος τὸν γάμον ἐν ἐνιαυτῷ: 'in order that Cleisthenes might confirm the marriage within a year'.

126.3 ὅσοι σφίσι τε αὐτοῖσι ἦσαν καὶ πάτρῃ ἐξωγκωμένοι: 'as many as took pride in themselves and in their country', i.e. only men of aristocratic birth from one of the more significant Greek states need apply.

ἐπ' αὐτῷ τούτῳ εἶχε: 'kept them exclusively for this very purpose'. Some scholars, taking εἶχε as intrans., translate 'devoted himself to this very purpose', but this sense of ἔχω does not occur elsewhere in Hdt. The tale of the wooing of Agariste seems to be modelled on the myth of Tyndareus and the suitors of Helen, though the latter were numbered greatly in excess of the thirteen who came to woo Agariste (the number varies from 29 to 99). See [Hesiod], *Catalogue of Women* Frags. 196-204; Euripides, *Iphigeneia at Aulis* 49-71; Apollodorus 3.10.8; Pausanias 3.20.9; Hyginus, *Fabulae* 81).

127.1 Σμινδυρίδης: later writers describe how Smindyrides travelled from Sybaris in his own ship, bringing with him to Sicyon a retinue of 1000 cooks, birdcatchers and fishermen (Timaeus Frag. 9; Aelian, *VH* 12.24; Athenaeus 273a-c, 541c), and possessing enough wealth to entertain not only his fellow suitors but Cleisthenes as well (Diodorus 8.19). He is also alleged to have complained that the bed of roses on which he slept was so uncomfortable that it gave him blisters (Seneca, *De Ira* 2.25; Aelian, *op. cit.*, 9.24).

Συβαρίτης: as Hdt. says, Sybaris was at this time at the height of its prosperity. For its destruction in 510, see ch. 21.1 above.

ἐπὶ πλεῖστον δὴ χλιδῆς εἰς ἀνὴρ ἀπίκετο: 'he reached the greatest degree of luxury that a single individual was capable of attaining'. The numeral εἰς, like the Latin *unus* is used with superl. adjs. and advbs. for emphasis. Cf. Thuc. 8.68.1, τοὺς μέντοι ἀγωνιζομένους καὶ ἐν δικαστηρίῳ καὶ ἐν δήμῳ πλεῖστα εἰς ἀνηρ...δυνάμενος ὠφελεῖν.

Σιρίτης: a citizen of Siris, a Colophonian colony situated in a fertile plain on the north west coast of the Gulf of Tarentum and lying between Metapontum to the north east and Sybaris to the north west. It ceased to have an independent existence at the end of a war with its neighbours Metapontum, Sybaris and Croton in the mid-6th century (Justin 20.2.4), but was in the time of Cleisthenes second only to Sybaris in luxury (Athenaeus 523c). It was subsequently refounded as Heracleia by the Tarentines in 432 (Antiochus, Frag. 11; Diod. 12.36.4).

Ἀμύριος τοῦ σοφοῦ λεγομένου: according to Timaeus (Frag. 50), Amyris was a Sybarite who was sent as envoy to Delphi to enquire if his city's prosperity would continue. Apollo's reply that it would last until the Sybarites revered a mortal more than a god, though interpreted at the time to be an equivalent to 'never', was fulfilled when a citizen flogged a runaway slave who had sought sanctuary in a temple but declined to renew the flogging when that same slave later fled for asylum to the tomb of his owner's father (PW no. 73; Fontenrose *DO*, Q122). Presumably the story referred originally to the destruction of Siris, but was transferred to Sybaris after its fall in 510. It may have been Amyris' belated recognition of the unwitting fulfilment of the oracle that earned him his nickname.

127.2 Ἐπιδάμνιος: a citizen of Epidamnus, a joint colony of Corinth and Corcyra on the Adriatic some 150 miles north of Corcyra, the modern Durazzo or Durres. Possessed of a good harbour, it was well adapted to the short sea crossing to Italy. It also served as terminus of the main trans-Balkan route later developed by the Romans as the Via Egnatia. Trade with the Illyrian interior helped to increase the prosperity which the city enjoyed because of its strategic position.

Αἰτωλός: Aetolia was a tribal state to the north of the Corinthian Gulf, opposite Achaea in the Peloponnese, and in classical times one of the most backward in Greece.

Τιτόρμου τοῦ ὑπερφύντος...Ἕλληνας ἰσχύϊ: 'Titormus who excelled the Greeks (i.e. all the Greeks) in strength'. ὑπερφύντος is intrans. 2nd. aor.

part. of ὑπερφύω, 'outgrow', 'surpass'. According to Aelian (*VH* 12.22 and 14.47b), he was a cowherd and strongman capable of performing feats such as lifting huge rocks and holding stationary two bulls simultaneously. In both exploits he is supposed to have outperformed the celebrated athlete Milon of Croton. Since Milon's career spanned the years 540-516, Aelian's tale is improbable on chronological grounds, and certainly any contemporary of Milon is unlikely to have had a brother of marriageable age in the 570s.

127.3 Φείδωνος τοῦ 'Αργείων τυράννου παῖς Λεωκήδης: Aristotle (*Politics* 1310b) and Pausanias (6.22.2) agree with Hdt. in calling Pheidon a tyrant, though the former may be trying to reconcile different traditions in regarding him as a tyrant who started his career as a king. Moreover the word *tyrannos* is occasionally used in Greek of hereditary rulers who are strictly speaking kings. R. Drews (*Basileus*, New Haven and London, 1983, p. 61) thinks that in using the word *basileus*, Aristotle here has in mind an elected magistrate who held a military command. In antiquity however Pheidon was generally seen as a hereditary king of the Temenid dynasty (Ephorus, Frag. 115; Theopompus Frag. 393). Pheidon's date was a matter of controversy even in antiquity: whereas the *Marmor Parium* puts him in the 9th century (Jacoby *FGH* 239, A30), and Pausanias dates him to the 8th (6.22.2), Hdt.'s account places him in the late 7th/early 6th century. For modern discussions of his date, see R.A. Tomlinson, *Argos and the Argolid*, London, 1972, pp. 78-87; W.S. Kelly, *A History of Argos to 500 B.C.*, Minneapolis, 1976, pp. 94-129. His son Lacedas, who apparently succeeded him as *basileus* (Plut. *Mor.* 89E), is probably to be identified with the Lacedas whose son Meltas, the last hereditary *basileus* of Argos, was deposed by the people (Paus. 2.19.2) in circumstances narrated by Diodorus (7.13, where Meltas is not mentioned by name).

τοῦ τὰ μέτρα ποιήσαντος Πελοποννησίοισι: 'who introduced a system of measures for the Peloponnesians', an addition made to distinguish this Pheidon from other individuals with the same name, such as Pheidon of Corinth, known from Aristotle (*Politics* 1265b 12) as a lawgiver. The word μέτρα is often translated as 'weights and measures', and indeed the later tradition does have Pheidon introduce weights as well as measures, and even a coinage (Ephorus, Frags. 115, 176; *Marmor Parium* A.30; Heracleides Ponticus Frag. 152; Strabo 8.3.3, 8.16.6; Pollux, *Onomasticon* 9.83). However μέτρα in Greek means 'measures', while weights are denoted by σταθμά, and the version of Hdt. is supported by *Ath. Pol.* 10.2. In the light of the intimate connection between weights and the currency, it is not impossible that a Pheidon contemporary with Cleisthenes of Sicyon could have introduced the latter into the Peloponnese, since the earliest coins appearing on the Greek mainland, the 'turtles' of Aegina, are currently dated around the second quarter of the 6th century (see T.J. Figueira, *Aegina: Society and Economy*, New York, 1981, pp. 88-106, and cf. Aelian, *VH* 12.10), and it was on Aegina that tradition has Pheidon mint his coinage (Ephorus, Frag. 176). However it is difficult to believe that Argos could have exercised any control over Aegina at a time when Aegina's links were with Epidaurus rather than with Argos (Hdt. 5.83). The only link we know of between Argos and Aegina was an alliance of uncertain date implied by the help sent by Argos to Aegina during the latter's war with Athens c. 500 (Hdt. 5.86.4). It is thus preferable to accept the earlier tradition of Hdt. and the *Ath. Pol.* that Pheidon introduced only a system of measures. If the iron spits allegedly dedicated by Pheidon in the Argive Heraeum (Heracleides Ponticus, Frag. 152; *Etymologicum Magnum* s.v. *obeliskos*) were intended to be official standards of length, Pheidon's new measures could have been linear: more probably Hdt. is thinking of measures of capacity, in that Pollux (*Onomasticon* 10.179, citing Aristotle, Frag. 480), refers to 'Pheidonian' measures for oil, and there are references to 'Pheidonian' measures of capacity being used at both pre-Solonian Athens (*Ath. Pol.* 10.2) and Apollonia (Tod, *GHI* I 140, 11.80-87).

ἐξαναστήσας τοὺς Ἠλείων ἀγωνοθέτας: 'having removed the Elean Commissioners of the Games', trans. 1st. aor. part. of ἐξανίστημι. The *agonothetai* were the officials in charge of the games in various Greek cities, though the technical term for the officals who presided over the Olympic Games was *hellenodikai*. Prior to the 5th century these were two in number, selected from the most distinguished Elean citizens. Among their duties were the enforcement of the regulations, the scrutiny of the candidates' qualifications, the maintenance of discipline and the umpiring of the contests. By his expulsion of the *hellenodikai* Pheidon was denying the right of the Eleans to run the games, and asserting his own claim. The rights of Elis had been challenged by the citizens of Pisa, a neighbouring city to the east of the Olympic sanctuary, when it was free of Elean control. In some versions of the story (Strabo 8.3.30; Pausanias 6.22.2; Eusebius, *Chron.* 1.196), Pheidon was called in by the Pisans and celebrated the games in conjunction with them. Pausanias' date for the event, the 8th Olympiad (i.e. 748), cannot be reconciled with that of a Pheidon whose son was a suitor for the hand of Agariste in the 570s, any more than can the dates offered for Pisan control of the Games by either Strabo (an unspecified period commencing in 672) or Eusebius (Pisan control in 668 and from 660 until 572). According to T.J. Figueira, 'Aeginetan Independence', *CJ* 87, 1983, p. 11, note 13 (reprinted in *Excursions in Epichoric History: Aeginetan Essays*, London, 1993, p. 13), Hdt. is guilty of confusion between Lacedas the son of Pheidon (whom Figueira dates to the early 7th century) and a later member of the family bearing the same name, who was at the time living in exile and, as such, hostile to the current Argive regime. This would certainly explain why an Argive would have been an acceptable suitor in the eyes of a strongly anti-Argive ruler such as Cleisthenes.

ἐκ Τραπεζοῦντος: Trapezus was a city in the south west of Arcadia, due east of the Lycaeus range, on the route from Sparta to Heraea and Olympia.

Ἀζὴν ἐκ Παίου: Azania was the most northerly district of Arcadia, border-ing on Elis and Achaea. Paeus was an insignificant town roughly equidistant from the two larger northern cities of Psophis and Cleitor.

Διοσκούρους: Castor and Polydeuces, sons of Zeus and Leda daughter of Tyndareus king of Sparta, whose subsequent epiphanies in various parts of the Greek world are attested at Sparta (Paus. 3.16.3), in Messenia (Paus. 4.16.9) and at Aegospotamoi (Cicero, *De Div.* 1.34.75; 2.32.68).

127.4 τοῦ παρὰ Κροῖσον ἀπικομένου: see ch. 125 above.

Ἱπποκλείδης Τισάνδρου: a member of the aristocratic family of the Philaidae, who traced their ancestry back to Telamonian Ajax through his son Philaeus (Marcellinus, *Life of Thucydides* 3). Hippocleides survived his rejection as a suitor to become archon at Athens in 566/5 (see R. Develin, *AO*, p. 41).

Ἐρετρίης ἀνθεύσης: finds of Eretrian pottery indicate that the city flourished in the 7th century, and the evidence of Hdt. would show that this prosperity lasted into the following century. It was due at least in part to the city's status as one of the major trading powers of the day, and to her role as mother city of several colonies on the Macedonian and Chalcidican coast (Methone, Mende, Scione, Dicaea).

Σκοπαδέων Διακτορίδης Κραννώνιος: the Scopadae were one of the leading aristocratic families of Thessaly, with a power base at Crannon in the hilly western part of the tetrarchy of Pelasgiotis. The eponymous ancestor Scopas was remembered as the originator of the war tax payable by the perioecic communities (Xenophon, *Hell.* 6.1.19).

ἐκ δὲ Μολοσσῶν Ἄλκων: the Molossians were one of the major Epirot tribes who occupied the central and eastern parts of the country. Of mixed Greek and Illyrian blood, they were of little significance politically until the 4th century. In the classical period the royal family, the Aeacidae, claimed descent from Achilles and advertised this claim in the use of personal names such as Neoptolemus, Pyrrhus, Aeacides, Phthia and Deidameia. Presumably in view of the high lineage of the other suitors, Alcon must be assumed to have had royal blood in his veins, but he is not attested outside this passage, and is conspicuously absent from the king list preserved by Julius Valerius (1.43). If Alcon is a historical character, he must have been a collateral member of the royal family whose exact pedigree was soon forgotten; it is surely significant that he is the only suitor whose patronymic Hdt. does not record.

128.1 τὴν προειρημένην ἡμέρην: 'the appointed day', where προειρημένην is perf. part. pass. of προλέγω, 'proclaim', with reference to the end of the sixty day period allotted by Cleisthenes for the suitors to come to Sicyon (see 126.2).

μετὰ δὲ: 'and afterwards', 'but then', adverbial.

τῆς ὀργῆς: here 'temper', 'disposition', rather than the more usual 'anger', 'passion'.

ἐξαγινέων: 'leading them forth', the Ionic equivalent of Attic ἐξάγων.

ἐν τῇ συνιστίῃ: 'in the social gathering', 'at the entertainment', a noun occurring only here, if the correct reading. Some manuscripts offer συνεστοῖ, dat. of the otherwise unattested noun συνεστώ, from σύνειμι. Cf. ἀπεστώ, 'absence' (9.85.3), εὐεστώ, 'prosperity' (1.85.1).

ὅσον γὰρ κατεῖχε χρόνον αὐτοὺς, τοῦτον (sc. χρόνον) πάντα ἐποίεε: 'for throughout the time he kept them, he did those things'.

128.2 ἐκρίνετο: literally 'was being judged', i.e. 'was coming to be preferred'.

τὸ ἀνέκαθεν τοῖσι...Κυψελίδῃσι ἦν προσήκων: 'he was related to the Cypselids further back in his genealogy'. The Cypselids were the family (Cypselus, Periander and Psammetichus) who ruled as tyrants of Corinth in the second half of the 7th century and early 6th (traditional dates 657/6-584/3). The Athenian Cypselus, who was archon in 597/6 and father of the elder Miltiades (see ch. 34.1 above), was probably, but not certainly, the son of a daughter of the Corinthian Cypselus and brother of Hippocleides' father Tisander (see Davies, *APF* pp. 294-6).

129.1 τῆς τε κατακλίσιος τοῦ γάμου: 'the celebration of the marriage feast'. κατάκλισις means literally 'a lying down', i.e. on a couch for the purpose of dining, from the verb κατακλίνω, 'cause to recline', as at 1.126.3, cf. 9.16.1. τοὺς Πέρσας κατακλίνας ἐς λειμῶνα εὐώχεε.

θύσας βοῦς ἑκατόν: 'having sacrificed one hundred cattle'. Clearly Cleisthenes does everything on a grand scale. The phrase is intended to suggest the epic word *hecatomb*, though the sacrifice of 100 cattle would be extravagant even by heroic standards. (Helenus at *Iliad* 6.93 is content with a sacrifice of 12 cattle, and Peleus at 23.146 offers a *hecatomb* of 50 rams.)

129.2 ἔριν εἶχον ἀμφί τε μουσικῇ καὶ τῷ λεγομένῳ ἐς τὸ μέσον: 'they had a contest in music and on a subject spoken for everyone to hear', i.e. 'in public speaking'. In Attic the prep. ἀμφί normally takes the acc. (with the meaning 'around', 'about', 'concerning'), but in Ionic prose the dat. is also found, in the sense of 'about', 'for the sake of'. See note on 62.1 above.

κατέχων πολλὸν τοὺς ἄλλους: 'virtually holding the others spellbound'.

ἐμμέλειαν: properly speaking, a tragic dance or the music with which this dance was associated (Aristoxenus, cited by Bekker, *Anecdota Graeca* p. 101), but also used more generally to mean 'a dance tune'.

κως ἑωυτῷ μὲν ἀρεστῶς ὠρχέετο: 'he danced in a manner pleasing to himself', i.e. 'to his own satisfaction'.

Κλεισθένης ὁρέων ὅλον τὸ πρῆγμα ὑπώπτευε: the association in the Graeco-Roman world of dancing with drunkenness (e.g. Aristophanes, *Wasps* 1476ff.; Demosthenes 2.18-9; Theophrastus, *Characters* 12; Cicero, *Pro Murena* 6.13) will have led Cleisthenes to question his earlier assessment of Hippocleides' suitability as a son-in-law.

129.3 μετὰ δὲ ἐπισχὼν...χρόνον: 'but after a time', where μετά is adverbial (see note on 4.1). The separation of the object from its verb with the insertion of ὁ Ἱπποκλείδης is an example of the figure of speech termed *hyperbaton*.

218

ἐσενεῖκαι: Ionic aor. inf. of εἰσφέρω. See note on 27.2 above.

Λακωνικὰ σχημάτια: 'Laconian steps'. σχημάτιον is the diminutive of σχῆμα, 'figure', here with reference to the steps or movement of a dance. What we know of Spartan music (e.g. Polybius 4.20.6; Plut. *Lyc.* 21; Cicero, *Tusc. Disp.* 2.16.37) suggests that the movement originated in a kind of war-dance.

μετὰ δὲ ἄλλα Ἀττικὰ: 'and afterwards Attic steps as well'. Since Hippocleides has not previously displayed his proficiency in Attic dances, ἄλλα here cannot mean 'other', but must be used in the sense of 'besides', 'moreover', 'in addition' (Goodwin 966.2). Cf. Xen. *Hell.* 2.4.9, τοὺς ὁπλίτας καὶ τοὺς ἄλλους ἱππέας; *Anab.* 1.5.5 οὐ γὰρ ἦν χόρτος οὐδὲ ἄλλο οὐδὲν δένδρον.

τὴν κεφαλὴν ἐρείσας ἐπὶ τὴν τράπεζαν: literally 'propping his head against the table', i.e. 'standing on his head on the table'.

τοῖσι σκέλεσι ἐχειρονόμησε: 'he gesticulated with his legs'. The verb means literally 'wave one's hands about', but the meaning is here extended, through the figure known as *catachresis*, to cover the idea of waving legs in the air.

129.4 τὰ μὲν πρῶτα καὶ τὰ δεύτερα ὀρχεομένου: 'while he was dancing the first and the second of these movements', gen. abs.

ἀποστυγέων γαμβρὸν ἄν οἱ ἔτι γενέσθαι Ἱπποκλείδην: 'loathing the thought of Hippocleides becoming his son-in-law', an unparalleled use of the acc. and inf. construction after this verb.

οὐ βουλόμενος ἐκραγῆναι ἐς αὐτὸν: 'not wanting to make an outburst against him', where ἐκραγῆναι is aor. pass. inf. of ἐκρήγνυμι, 'cause to break out', used intransitively in the sense of 'indulge in a public outburst', 'lose one's temper'.

οὐκέτι κατέχειν δυνάμενος: 'no longer able to control himself'. κατέχειν is here used intransitively instead of the more usual κατέχειν ἑωυτόν found in the previous sentence.

ἀπωρχήσαό γε μὴν τὸν γάμον: 'yes indeed, you've just danced away your marriage'. For the affirmative meaning of the particle combination γε μέν, see Denniston, *GP* p. 348. The verb ἀπορχέομαι occurs only here, and is presumably a coinage on the analogy of phrases like ἀποδακρύω τὴν γνώμην, 'I weep away my resolution'. (Aristophanes, *Wasps* 983), ἐκκυβεύομαι, 'gamble away', 'lose at dice', (Plut. *Art.* 17.5), and the similar ἐξορχέομαι, 'dance away' at Aelian, *NA* 16.23. D. Ogden (*The Crooked Kings of Greece*, London, 1997, p. 117) is of the opinion that Cleisthenes' use of ἀπωρχήσαο puns upon the word ὄρχεις ('testicles'), which Hippocleides will have inadvertently displayed while standing on his head, and offers a translation along the lines of 'you've made a balls up of your marriage'.

οὐ φροντὶς Ἱπποκλείδῃ: literally 'this is of no concern to Hippocleides', i.e. 'Hippocleides couldn't care less'.

130.1 ἀπὸ τούτου...τοῦτο ὀνομάζεται: 'it is from this incident that the phrase passed into common usage', where ὀνομάζεται is used in the sense of 'take one's name', 'become proverbial'. Despite what Hdt. says, the saying is not attested elsewhere in Greek literature. For the probable origin of the story in folklore, see Introduction, p. x-xi. Attempts to explain the origin of the saying will have resulted in the application of a less specific story to one particular individual.

πᾶσιν ὑμῖν, εἰ οἷόν τε εἴη, χαριζοίμην ἄν: 'I would gratify you all, if it were to be possible'. This construction (opt. in protasis, opt. with ἄν in apodosis) is normally used in future conditions expressed in the less vivid form (Goodwin 1408), though here the phrase is practically equivalent to a present unreal condition. Hdt. seems to be influenced by the Homeric construction in present unreal conditions where the opt. is preferred to the imperf. indic. that is regular in later Greek. It is also possible that he is trying to convey something of Cleisthenes' tact in implying that circumstances might conceivably arise in the future when he might once again be able to gratify the unsuccessful suitors.

μήτε τοὺς λοιποὺς ἀποδοκιμάζων: 'nor rejecting the others'. ἀποδοκιμάζω refers properly speaking to the rejection of candidates for political office at the official scrutiny (*dokimasia*) to which they submitted before taking up their post.

130.2 ἀλλ᾽ οὐ γὰρ οἷά τέ ἐστι: 'but since this is impossible'. For the use of ἀλλά...γάρ to indicate the non-fulfilment of a condition, see Denniston, *GP* p. 104, and cf. 2.120.1, εἰ ἦν Ἑλένη ἐν Ἰλίῳ, ἀποδοθῆναι ἂν αὐτὴν τοῖσι Ἕλλησι...ἀλλ᾽ οὐ γὰρ εἶχον Ἑλένην ἀποδοῦναι, 'if Helen had been in Troy, she would have been given back to the Greeks...but in fact they were unable to give Helen back'. See also 5.3.1, 7.143.2, 9.113.2.

τοῖσι...ὑμέων ἀπελαυνομένοισι τοῦδε τοῦ γάμου: literally 'to those of you who are driven (i.e. 'excluded', 'rejected') from this marriage'.

δωρεὴν:'as a gift', in apposition to τάλαντον ἀργυρίου, though the word is also used, as is its synonym προῖκα, in the acc. (an adverbial acc., Goodwin 1060) in the sense of 'gratis', 'as a free gift' (cf. 5.23.1).

τῆς ἀξιώσιος εἵνεκεν τῆς ἐξ ἐμεῦ γῆμαι: literally 'because of your deeming it proper to marry from my house', i.e. 'because of the honour you have conferred on me by desiring to marry into my family', where ἀξιώσιος is construed with the inf. γῆμαι on the analogy of the kindred verb ἀξιόω.

νόμοισι τοῖσι Ἀθηναίων: 'in accordance with the laws of the Athenians'. Herodotus seems to have in mind the situation in Athens at the time of writing, when under the Periclean citizenship law of 451, Athenians could contract legal marriage only with the daughters of other citizens ([Arist.] *Ath. Pol.* 26.4; Plut. *Pericles* 37.3), and is at pains to point out that, in the 6th century the validity of Megacles' marriage to Agariste was not in doubt. (See D. Ogden, *Greek Bastardy in the Classical and Hellenistic Periods*, Oxford, 1996, pp. 32-69.)

φαμένου δὲ ἐγγυᾶσθαι Μεγακλέος: 'when Megacles said that he was betrothed', i.e. accepted the betrothal. The act. ἐγγυάω,'betroth', 'plight', is used of the role of the father, whereas the middle ἐγγυάομαι is used of the bridegroom, 'have a woman betrothed to one', 'be betrothed'.

ἐκεκύρωτο ὁ γάμος Κλεισθένεϊ: 'the marriage stood ratified by Cleisthenes once and for all'. Here the plup. denotes an event which took place so soon after another that their accomplishment is virtually simultaneous ('plup. of immediate occurrence'). For the dat. of the agent after a perf. or plup. pass., see note on 53.2 above.

131.1 ἀμφὶ...κρίσιος: 'about the decision'.

ἐβώσθησαν: 'became famous', 'were celebrated', Ionic aor. pass. of βοάω, 'shout'.

Κλεισθένης...ὁ τὰς φυλὰς καὶ τὴν δημοκρατίην...καταστήσας: Cleisthenes the reformer, whose programme of reforms in 508/7 strengthened the democratic element in the Athenian constitution (see 5.66-73; [Arist.] *Ath. Pol.* 20.1).

131.2 Ἱπποκράτης: nothing is known of Hippocrates apart from what we are told in the present passage.

Μεγακλέης: the head of the Alcmeonid family in the 480s, ostracised in 487/6 ([Arist.] *Ath. Pol.* 22.5), and victor in the chariot race at the Pythian Games of 486, for whom Pindar wrote the Seventh *Pythian*. He was also remembered as the maternal grandfather of Alcibiades (Lysias 14.39; Plut. *Alc.* 1.1).

Ξανθίππω τῷ 'Αρίφρονος: prosecutor of Miltiades in 489 (see chap. 136 below) and subsequently ostracised in 485/4 (*Ath. Pol.* 22.6), he was recalled to meet the Persian threat and went on to lead the Athenian contingents at Plataea (8.131.3), Mycale (9.114) and Sestos (7.33). He is last heard of in 477/6 (Diodorus 11.42.2).

ἐδόκεε...λέοντα τεκεῖν: 'she seemed to give birth to a lion'. This, the only reference to Pericles in the text of Hdt., is of uncertain interpretation. Scholars who believe this entire section to be a glorification of the Alcmeonids, naturally understand the lion to be symbolic of greatness and magnificence; others see Pericles depicted as an absolute ruler (cf. the lion symbolism applied to tyrants like Hipparchus at 5.56 and Cypselus at 5.92. β3), and interpret the lion as a symbol of destruction (as, e.g. at Aeschylus, *Agamemnon* 717-36). It may not be entirely accidental that Hdt. does not offer any personal interpretation of the dream, and is apparently content to leave the story ambiguous. On Herodotus' attitude to Pericles, see F.D. Harvey, 'The Political Sympathies of Herodotus', *Historia* 15, 1966, pp. 254-5 (favourable); K.H. Waters, 'Herodotus and Politics', *Greece and Rome* 19, 1972, pp. 136-50 (unfavourable). Cf. C.W. Fornara, *Herodotus: an Interpretative Essay*, Oxford, 1971, pp. 53-4.

132 μετὰ δὲ τὸ ἐν Μαραθῶνι τρῶμα: the narrative is resumed from chapter 120. τρῶμα is the Ionic form of the Attic τραῦμα, meaning literally 'wound', but commonly used by Hdt. in the sense of 'defeat', 'disaster' (cf. 1.18.1, 4.160.4, 8.66.1, 9.90.1). Here a word such as Περσέων is to be understood.

The events narrated in the following chapters belong to 489.

αἰτήσας δὲ νέας...καὶ στρατιήν τε καὶ χρήματα ’Αθηναίους: ‘having asked the Athenians for ships, as well as an army and money’, in his capacity as one of the *strategoi* of the year. Verbs of asking, depriving, teaching, clothing, unclothing, concealing and reminding are regularly followed by two accusatives, one of the person and the other of the thing (Goodwin 1069).

οὐ φράσας σφι, ἐπ’ ἣν ἐπιστρατεύσεται χώρην: ‘without telling them against which country he would campaign’.

φὰς αὐτοὺς καταπλουτιεῖν, ἤν οἱ ἕπωνται: ‘saying that he would enrich them if they followed him’. According to Nepos (*Miltiades* 7.1), the pretext for the expedition was the need to punish the islanders who had supported Persia in the previous year. It was as much the prospect of wealth as Miltiades’ prestige as the victor of Marathon that induced the Athenians to approve such an ill-defined proposition, just as in the previous decade the hope of booty was as important a motive for involvement in the Ionian Revolt as were the intrigues of Aristagoras (5.97.1). Cf. the extortion of money from Andros, Paros and Carystus in the aftermath of Salamis (8.111-2). For the part. φάς (Attic φάσκων), see note on 58.3.

ἐπὶ...χώρην τοιαύτην δή τινα ἄξειν: ‘he would lead them to a land of such great wealth, or so he claimed’. For the ironical use of δή, see Denniston, *GP* p. 234 and note on 41.3 above.

χρυσὸν...ἄφθονον οἴσονται: ‘they would win an abundance of gold’. οἴσονται is the fut. middle of φέρω, with the meaning ‘acquire for oneself’.

133.1 ἔπλεε: ‘he proceeded to sail’. See note on 16.2 above.

Πάρον: one of the Cyclades, to the west of its larger neighbour Andros, important to the Athenians because of the considerable revenues it enjoyed from the exploitation of its high quality marble (see 3.57.4, 5.62.3). When a member of the Delian League, Paros was to be assessed at the high tribute rate of 16-18 talents, three times the rate paid by its larger neighbours Naxos and Andros, and the third highest in the entire confederacy.

οἱ Πάριοι ὑπῆρξαν πρότεροι στρατευόμενοι: ‘the Parians had initiated (sc. the present situation) by previously campaigning’. ὑπάρχω, in the sense of ‘begin’, ‘take the lead in’, is followed by a part. or by a noun in the gen. Here the idea is that the animosity between Athens and Paros was initiated by the latter when it supplied Datis with a ship for use in the Marathon campaign of the previous year. After ὑπάρχω some such noun as ἀδικίης is to be understood. Cf. ὑπάρξαντα ἀδίκων ἔργων at 1.5.3 and ἀρξάντων ἀδικίης at ch. 119.1 above.

στρατευόμενοι τριήρεϊ: for the Persian campaign of the previous year in the Cyclades, see ch. 96 above. Presumably Paros is to be included among τὰς ἄλλας νήσους.

ἔγκοτον εἶχε τοῖσι Παρίοισι: ‘he was malevolently disposed towards the Parians’, ‘he had a grudge against the Parians’.

222

Λυσαγόρην τὸν Τισίεω: not otherwise known.

διαβαλόντα μιν πρὸς Ὑδάρνεα: 'who had slandered him to Hydarnes'. It is unclear whether this Hydarnes is to be identified with the Hydarnes who participated in Darius' coup of 522 (3.70.2) or to his homonymous son, who was later to command the Immortals during Xerxes' invasion (7.83.1) and subsequently served as 'general over the men of the coast' (7.135.1). These are variously identified with Hellespontine Phrygians (Burn, *op. cit.*, pp. 136, 321) or with Lydians (D.M. Lewis, *Sparta and Persia*, Leiden, 1977, p. 84). If the reference is to the elder Hydarnes, the slander may have concerned Miltiades' alleged disloyal behaviour in the course of the Scythian expedition of c.513 (see 4.137); if to the younger Hydarnes, the slander may have been related to Miltiades' behaviour during the Ionian Revolt or to the excessively independent stance he took in annexing the island of Lemnos (see ch. 140 below), both of which served to precipitate his flight from the Chersonese to Athens in 493 (see ch. 41 above).

133.2 αἴτεε ἑκατὸν τάλαντα: 'he proceeded to demand 100 talents', or roughly six times the annual amount of tribute which Paros was later to pay to the Delian League.

ἢν μή οἱ δῶσι: 'unless they paid it to him', a condition referring to the future (Goodwin 1403).

πρὶν ἢ ἐξέλῃ σφέας: 'until he had destroyed them'. For the construction, see note on 82.1 above. For πρὶν ἢ, see notes on 22.1 and 116 above.

133.3 ὅκως μέν τι δώσουσι...ἀργυρίου, οὐδὲ διενοεῦντο: 'they did not as much as give thought to the notion of giving him any money'. διανοέομαι, 'intend', regularly takes the inf. (e.g. at 2.121. 4, 2.126.1 and in ch. 86δ above), but it is also found followed by ὅπως and the fut. indic. by analogy with verbs denoting striving and effort (Goodwin 1372-3).

καὶ τῇ...ἔσκε ἑκάστοτε ἐπίμαχον τοῦ τείχεος: 'and whatever point in the wall was from time to time vulnerable to attack'. τῇ, here adverbial, is to be construed with τοῦ τείχεος (partitive gen.). For the iterative ending -σκε, see note on 12.1 above.

διπλήσιον τοῦ ἀρχαίου: 'twice as high as it was originally', 'twice as much as its original height'. Adjectives in -πλήσιος (Attic -πλάσιος) formed from numerals are proportionals that indicate 'so many times as large' or 'so many times as numerous', followed by a gen. of comparison. Though not comparatives in form, they are in effect comparatives in sense (see Goodwin 1154).

134.1 ἐς...τοσοῦτο τοῦ λόγου: 'as far as this point in my account'.

ἐοῦσαν...Παρίην γένος: 'being a Parian by birth', where γένος is an acc. of respect or specification (Goodwin 1058).

Τιμοῦν: fem. nouns ending in -ώ , mostly proper names, do not in Attic distinguish the acc. from the nom., but in Hdt. generally have an acc. in -οῦν (Λητοῦν, 2.156.5; Ἰοῦν,1.1.3), though the acc. form πειθώ occurs at 8.111.2.

ὑποζάκορον τῶν χθονίων θεῶν: 'an assistant temple servant of the infernal goddesses', i.e. of Demeter and Persephone. The word ὑποζάκορον is rare, but ζάκορος is common in the sense 'temple servant', as opposed to a genuine priest or priestess (ἱερεύς, ἱέρεια).

εἰ περὶ πολλοῦ ποιέεται Πάρον ἑλεῖν: 'if he regarded it of importance to capture Paros'. For this phrase, see note on 61.5 above, and cf. chs 6 and 104.1. **134.2** μετὰ δὲ: adverbial (see note on 4.1).

τὸ ἕρκος θεσμοφόρου Δήμητρος: 'the fence running round the precinct of Demeter the Lawgiver'. ἕρκος is used with reference both to the fence or wall surrounding an enclosure and to the ground that is enclosed. *Thesmophoros* is a common epithet or cult title of Demeter in various Greek cities (see note on 91.2 above), just as *Thesmophoria* is a common name for her festival (as at 16.2 above).

ὅ τι δὴ ποιήσοντα ἐντός: 'in order to do something or other inside'. For the indef. ὅστις δή, see note on 62.2 above, and for the use of the fut. part., see note on 28.2.

κινήσοντά τι τῶν ἀκινήτων: 'to remove one of the objects that must not be removed', i.e. one the removal of which would constitute an act of sacrilege. Presumably Miltiades believed that the loss of whatever religious object he sought would have a disastrous effect on Parian morale.

πρὸς τῇσι θύρῃσί τε γενέσθαι, καὶ...φρίκης αὐτὸν ὑπελθούσης: 'no sooner was he at the door than a shudder crept over him', where τε...καί expresses simultaneous action.

πρόκατε: a form of the Ionic adv. πρόκα, 'straightaway', with the addition of the indef. suffix τε.

ὀπίσω τὴν αὐτὴν ὁδὸν ἵεσθαι: 'he rushed back by the same way'. αὐτὴν ὁδόν is an adverbial acc. (Goodwin 1060).

καταθρώσκοντα δὲ τὴν αἱμασιὴν: 'as he jumped down from the wall'. αἱμασιὰ refers properly to a wall of dry stone, but is also used of walls in general. Here the reference is to the ἕρκος already mentioned.

τὸν μηρὸν σπασθῆναι: 'he wrenched his thigh', literally 'he was wrenched in respect of his thigh'.

οἱ δὲ αὐτὸν τὸ γόνυ προσπταῖσαι λέγουσι: 'there are those who say that he injured his knee', i.e. by knocking it against some object as he fell. **135.1** φλαύρως ἔχων: 'in poor shape', 'in a bad way', 'in a sorry condition', (cf. 94.2 above). For ἔχω with an adv., see note on 49.2.

ἀπέπλεε ὀπίσω: according to Nepos (*Miltiades* 7.3-4), Miltiades abandoned the siege when he mistook a fire that had broken out in a nearby grove for a signal from the Persian fleet to announce its imminent arrival. **135.2** κατηγήσατο: 'guided', for the Attic καθηγήσατο.

θεοπρόπους: the regular word in Hdt. for delegates chosen to consult the Delphic oracle. Cf. 1.48.2, of the messengers sent to Delphi by Croesus.

ὡς σφεας ἡσυχίη τῆς πολιορκίης ἔσχε: literally 'when respite from the siege took possession of them', i.e. 'when they were free from preoccupation with the siege'.

εἰ καταχρήσονται τὴν ὑποζάκορον: 'if they should put the under-priestess to death'. καταχράομαι in Attic normally means 'apply', 'use up', 'abuse', but is common in Hdt. in the sense of 'dispose of', 'make away with' (e.g. 1.82.8, 1.117.2, 4.146.3, 9.120.4). For this oracular consultation, see PW no. 91; Fontenrose *DO*, Q143.

ὡς ἐξηγησαμένην τοῖσι ἐχθροῖσι τῆς πατρίδος ἅλωσιν: literally 'as having shown the capture of her country to the enemy', i.e. 'on the grounds that she had shown to the enemy how to capture her country'.

τὰ ἐς ἔρσενα γόνον ἄρρητα: 'sacred objects forbidden to the male sex', literally 'things not to be spoken of'.

135.3 φᾶσα οὐ Τιμοῦν εἶναι τὴν αἰτίην τούτων: 'saying that it was not Timo who was responsible for these things'. When the clause introduced by φημί is neg., the neg. is usually taken out of its own clause and attached to φημί (see, e.g. 1.1, 50.2, 52.4, 61.4, 99.2), but it remains in the subordinate clause when it is closely linked in sense with a particular word within that clause (see notes on 65.3 and 69.2 above).

δέειν γὰρ Μιλτιάδεα τελευτᾶν μὴ εὖ: 'but since Miltiades was fated to come to a bad end', where μὴ εὖ is a litotes equivalent to κακῶς. For this use of γάρ, see notes on 11.2 and 130.2 above. For this use of δεῖ, see note on ch. 64 above.

φανῆναί οἱ τῶν κακῶν κατηγεμόνα: 'she had appeared to him (merely) to introduce him to his wickedness'. For φαίνομαι, 'appear', see notes on 61.3 and 106.1 above.

136.1 ἔσχον ἐν στόμασι: literally 'had him in their mouths', i.e. 'constantly talked about him'. The mss. are divided between ἔσχον (aor.) and εἶχον (imperf.). At 3.157.4 they are unanimous in reading εἶχον.

Ξάνθιππος: see note on 131.2 above. Xanthippus and/or his Alcmeonid in-laws may have been behind the unsuccessful prosecution of 493 (see 104.2 above).

θανάτου ὑπαγαγὼν ὑπὸ τὸν δῆμον: 'had brought him before the people (i.e. the *ecclesia*) on a capital charge'. For this use of ὑπάγω, cf. 9.93.3 as well as chapters 72.2 and 82.1 above.

ὅς...ἐδίωκε τῆς Ἀθηναίων ἀπάτης εἵνεκεν: 'who initiated a prosecution against him on the ground that he had deceived the people'. The charge was ἀπάτη or ἀπάτη τοῦ δήμου. The democracy operated on the principle that the *demos* was not itself accountable for its errors, and that, if a policy which it had approved were subsequently to be revealed as a failure, the fault must lie, not with those who had voted for it but with those who had promoted it. Nepos (*Miltiades* 7.5) makes the charge one of treason, allegedly because he had been bribed by the Persians to abandon the siege. It is by no means improbable that more than one charge was brought, in the hope that, even if

Miltiades was to be acquitted on one charge, he might be condemned on the other.

136.2 ὥστε σηπομένου τοῦ μηροῦ: 'inasmuch as his thigh was beginning to rot', i.e. because of the effects of gangrene. For causal ὥστε, see note on 44.3, and cf. 52.3 and 94.1 above. The act. σήπω is trans., 'cause to rot', 'make rotten', while the middle σήπομαι (together with the aor. pass. ἐσάπην and perf. act. σέσηπα) is used intransitively in the meaning 'rot'.

τῆς μάχης...πολλὰ ἐπιμεμνημένοι καὶ τὴν Λήμνου αἵρεσιν: 'recalling much about the battle and about the capture of Lemnos'. Verbs of recalling and remembering are followed in Hdt. by either the acc. or the gen. (with or without περί); here both constructions are used in the same sentence. Lemnos is a volcanic island in the northern Aegean some 70 miles to the south of Abdera and 460 miles to the west of the Troad.

τισάμενος τοὺς Πελασγούς: 'having punished the Pelasgians'. The word is associated with various places in the Greek world and used with particular reference to the aboriginal or pre-Hellenic inhabitants. See especially 2.51-2. The pre-Hellenic Lemnians are also described as Pelasgian at 5.26.1, and at Thuc. 4.109.4 as Pelasgians of the Tyrrhenian race. Tyrrhenian was a another label used loosely of pre-Greeks in general, as well as of the Etruscans in particular. Nepos on the other hand, adopting an alternative tradition (cf. Hdt. 1.171.2; Thuc. 1.4.1, 1.8.1), asserts that the pre-Hellenic Lemnians were Carian (*Miltiades* 2.5). In fact epigraphical evidence (the Siva inscription or Lemnos Stele), indicates that the inhabitants of Lemnos prior to its annexation by Miltiades spoke a language that was very close to Etruscan, if not an actual dialect of that language. For text and possible translation of the Siva inscription, see J. Best and F. Woudhuizen, *Lost Languages from the Mediterranean*, (Publications of the Henri Frankfort Foundation, Vol. 10), Leiden 1989, pp. 139-51.

136.3 προσγενομένου...τοῦ δήμου αὐτῷ κατὰ τήν ἀπόλυσιν τοῦ θανάτου: 'the people having come to his support at least to the extent of freeing him from the death penalty'. προσγί(γ)νομαι with the dat. in a political context means 'range oneself on the side of', 'attach oneself to', 'lend one's political support to'. According to Plato (*Gorgias* 516d), the Athenians originally decided to throw him into the *barathron*, but were dissuaded by the presiding officer.

ζημιώσαντος...πεντήκοντα ταλάντοισι: a huge sum, affordable only by citizens in or close to millionaire status, and surpassed as a fine, so far as is known, only by the 100 talent penalty imposed on Timotheus in 356/5 (Isocrates 15.129; Deinarchus 1.14, 3.17), and by the 80 talent fine perhaps inflicted on Pericles in 430, according to Diod. 12.45.4 (though, in his case, Plutarch states (*Pericles* 35.4) that writers offered various estimates ranging from 15 to 50 talents). Nepos (*Miltiades* 7.6) claims that the fine was intended to recoup the losses incurred by the state in financing the expedition. According to the later tradition (Diod. 10.30; Nepos, *Miltiades* 7.6; Plutarch, *Cimon*

4.3), Miltiades was unable to pay the fine and was thrown into prison as a state debtor.

σφακελίσαντός τε τοῦ μηροῦ καὶ σαπέντος: 'his thigh having gangrened and rotted away'. σφακελίζω is derived from the noun σφάκελος, 'gangrene'.

ἐξέτισε...Κίμων: according to Ephorus (Frag. 64), Cimon was able to pay the fine thanks to his marriage to a rich woman. This is presumably a reference to Cimon's wife Isodice, a member of the Alcmeonid family. However it is doubtful if the Alcmeonidae, who had a feud with Miltiades and had precipitated the events that led to the imposition of the fine in the first place, would have displayed such generosity after his fall. More plausible is the version of Plutarch (*Cimon* 4.3), who states that the fine was paid by Callias of the Ceryces, one of the wealthiest men in Athens, who had married Cimon's sister Elpinice. It may be that Ephorus (or his excerptor) was under the mistaken impression that the marriage in question was that of Cimon himself rather than that of his sister. The account of Diodorus (10.31), who seems to think that the Callias who paid the fine was Cimon's son, not his brother-in-law, is thoroughly muddled. There is no hint of Cimon's financial problems in Hdt., and indeed his belated entry into politics (ambassador in 480/79, Plut. *Arist.* 10.8; strategos in 478/7, Plut. *Arist.* 23.1, *Cimon* 6.1) is just as likely to be due to his comparative youth as to inability to pay the fine.

137.1 ἔσχε: 'took possession of', ingressive aor. (see note on 25.2 above).

Ἑκαταῖος: the well known logographer Hecataeus of Miletus, author of the *Genealogies* and of the *Periodos* (*Periegesis*) *Ges*. He was a literary predecessor of Hdt. who also pursued a political career in his native city at the time of the Ionian Revolt (see 5.36 and 5.125-6). The passage in question occurred in Book I of his *Periodos Ges* (Jacoby, *FGrH* 1, Frag. 127). For Hecataeus' place in the logographic tradition, see L.Pearson, *Early Ionian Historians*, Oxford, 1939, pp. 25-108.

137.2 ἐπείτε γὰρ ἰδεῖν τοὺς Ἀθηναίους: 'for when the Athenians saw'. The passage is in indirect speech since Hdt. is summarising the story as narrated in Hecataeus' work. The rules of Greek grammar applicable to indirect speech require that a dependent clause in the indic. in historic sequence should remain in the indic. (Goodwin 1497.2, hence εἶδον οἱ Ἀθηναῖοι) but a relative or temporal clause may in such circumstances be put in the acc. and inf. by way of assimilation to the construction of the clause on which it depends (here λαβεῖν). See Goodwin 1524.

ὑπὸ τὸν Ὑμησσόν: Mt. Hymettus, a mountain ridge some six miles to the east and south-east of Athens, famous in antiquity for the excellent quality of its marble and honey.

μισθὸν τοῦ τείχεος τοῦ περὶ τὴν ἀκρόπολίν κοτε ἐληλαμένου: 'as payment for the wall at one time constructed around the Acropolis'. ἐληλαμένου is perf. part. pass. of ἐλαύνω in the sense of 'build'. The Pelasgian Wall was the name given to the fortification which from the Mycenaean period onwards surrounded and protected the Acropolis until its replacement in the time of Cimon. See Cleidemus, Frag. 16; Pausanias 1.28.3; J. Travlos, *Pictorial Dictionary of Ancient Athens*, London, 1971, p. 52.

οὐδεμίαν ἄλλην πρόφασιν προϊσχομένους: 'offering no other justification'.

137.3 Ἐννεάκρουνον: literally 'The Nine Springs', a fountainhouse constructed under the tyrants at the spring of Callirhoe by the Ilissus (Thuc. 2.15.5). On the identification of the site, see Travlos, *op. cit.*, p. 204; J.S. Camp, *The Athenian Agora*, London, 1986, pp. 42-4. The word Enneacrounos is anachronistic when applied to pre-Peisistratid Athens.

οὐ γὰρ εἶναι τοῦτον τὸν χρόνον...οἰκέτας: since slaves are well attested both in the Linear B Tablets and in Homer, this statement is false, but Hdt. is probably seeking to contrast the simpler households of bygone days, when only the wealthy and powerful had servants, with the practices of his own time, when even some of the lesser families had a slave or two to undertake menial tasks of this sort.

ὅκως δὲ ἔλθοιεν αὗται: 'and whenever these women came', indefinite opt. indicating repetition (see note on 31.1 above).

σφι οὐκ ἀποχρᾶν ποιέειν, ἀλλὰ: 'nor were they satisfied with just doing this, but...'.

ἐπιβουλεύοντας ἐπιχειρήσειν ἐπ' αὐτοφώρῳ φανῆναι: 'but were revealed in the very act of plotting to attack'. For φανῆναι, see notes on 61.3 and 106.1 above. ἐπιβουλεύω is regularly followed by a prolative pres. or aor. inf., but, as with other verbs indicating will or desire, it may take the fut. inf. by analogy with the construction after verbs of hoping, promising etc., if the author wishes to stress that the action is to follow without delay. See Goodwin 1277.

137.4 ἑωυτοὺς δὲ γενέσθαι τοσούτῳ ἐκείνων ἄνδρας ἀμείνονας: 'they said that they were so much better men than these (i.e. the Lemnians). τοσούτῳ ἀμείνονας means literally 'better by so much', a dat. of manner indicating the degree of difference (Goodwin 1184).

παρεὸν αὐτοῖσι ἀποκτεῖναι τοὺς Πελασγοὺς: 'it being in their power to slay the Pelasgians', an acc. absolute from an impers. verb. See note on 72.1 above, and cf. 82.1.

ἄλλα τε σχεῖν χωρία καὶ δὴ καὶ Λῆμνον: literally 'they took possession of other places and Lemnos as well', i.e. 'among the places they captured was Lemnos'. See note on 21.2, and cf. 49.1, 73.2. The 'other places' Hdt. has in mind presumably included at least some of those mentioned elsewhere in the text as inhabited by Pelasgians in his own day, such as Creston in Chalcidice (1.57.1), Placia and Scylace on the Hellespont (1.57.2), Samothrace (2.51.3), Imbros (5.26) and Antandros in the Troad (7.42.1).

ἐκεῖνα...Ἑκαταῖος ἔλεξε, ταῦτα δὲ Ἀθηναῖοι λέγουσι: 'the former is the account of Hecataeus, the latter that of the Athenians'. When ἐκεῖνος and οὗτος are contrasted, the former usually refers to the more remote object, the latter to the nearer.

138.1 Ἀρτέμιδι ἐν Βραυρῶνι ἀγούσας ὁρτὴν τὰς...γυναῖκας: Brauron was a village situated near the east coast of Attica and the site of a cult of Artemis, at which a curious rite was performed by girls aged between five and ten who played the part of bears, ostensibly in order to appease the wrath of the goddess for the killing of a bear in her sanctuary in the distant past. A shrine of Artemis Brauronia (the Brauronion) also existed on the Athenian Acropolis, from which the women of Athens processed each year to celebrate the Brauronia. See J. Pollard, *Seers, Shrines and Sirens*, London, 1966, pp. 57-8; H.W. Parke, *Festivals of the Athenians*, London, 1977, pp. 139-40; Erika Simon, *Festivals of Attica: an Archaeological Commentary*, Madison, Wisconsin and London, 1983, pp. 83-8.

παλλακὰς εἶχον: 'kept them as concubines', where παλλακάς stands in apposition to σφεας.

138.2 τέκνων...ὑπεπλήσθησαν: literally 'were filled with children', i.e. 'gave birth to numerous children', where ὑπεπλήσθησαν is aor. pass. of ὑποπίμπλημι.

γλῶσσάν τε τὴν Ἀττικὴν...ἐδίδασκον τοὺς παῖδας: 'they taught their children the Attic tongue'. For the double acc. after verbs of teaching, see note on ch. 132 above.

εἴ τε τύπτοιτό τις αὐτῶν: 'if ever any of them was struck', a general conditional clause denoting repetition. See Goodwin 1393.2 and notes on 31.1 and 75.1.

καὶ δὴ καί: 'moreover', 'indeed','and in particular'. See Denniston, *GP* p. 255, and cf. chs 64 and 86.2.

ἐδικαίευν: 'thought it right', 'claimed', 'saw fit'. See notes on 15.2 and 86.1 above.

138.3 ἑωυτοῖσι λόγους ἐδίδοσαν: 'proceeded to take thought with one another', 'pay attention to', 'consult with'. For the use of the reflexive pronoun ἑωυτούς as equivalent to the reciprocal ἀλλήλους, see Goodwin 996 and notes on 12.2 and 42.1 above.

δεινόν τι ἐσέδυνε: literally 'something terrible was insinuating itself into them', i.e. 'a terrible thought struck them'.

εἰ...διαγινώσκοιεν σφίσι τε βοηθέειν οἱ παῖδες...τί δὴ ἀνδρωθέντες δῆθεν ποιήσουσι: 'if they were absolutely determined to support one another (now) while they were (still) children, whatever would they do once they became men?', a mixed condition with the protasis referring to the present and the apodosis referring to the future. The verb in the protasis is here opt. because the sentence reflects the thoughts and fears of the Pelasgians and accordingly is subject to the rules of indirect discourse (see Goodwin 1497 and 1503).

πρὸς τῶν κουριδιέων γυναικῶν: 'from wedded wives', i.e. 'born in wedlock', 'legitimate', a Homeric expression (e.g. *Iliad* 1.114, 19.298), found elsewhere in Hdt. at 1.135 and 5.18.2..

138.4 ἐνθαῦτα: 'under such circumstances', 'such being the case'. Cf. 32, 99.2 above.

προσαπολλύουσι: 'kill in addition', for προσαπολλύασι, derived from the collateral form ἀπολλύω.

Θόαντι: a mythological king of Lemnos, son of Dionysus and Ariadne. According to the myth, Aphrodite, in her anger against the Lemnian women for their neglect of her worship, cursed them with such a foul odour that their husbands refused to sleep with them and imported Thracian concubines as a substitute. In revenge, the women slaughtered all the male inhabitants of the island, but Thoas, warned by his daughter Hypsipyle, escaped to the mainland. When the other women learned of her treachery, they sought to kill her, but she succeeded in escaping, only to fall into the hands of pirates who sold her into slavery in Greece. There she was eventually rescued by her two sons, Euneus and Nebrophonus, who restored her, along with her father, to her native island (Apollonius, *Argonautica* 1.609-26; Apollodorus 1.9.17). In Hdt's. version of the tale, Thoas too was slain by the women.

νενόμισται...τὰ σχέτλια ἔργα...Λήμνια καλέεσθαι: 'it has been the custom that atrocious deeds should be called Lemnian'. For other references to 'Lemnian deeds', see Aeschylus, *Choephoroi* 631-4; Plut. *Mor.* 755C; Scholiast on Aristophanes, *Lysistrata* 299; Suda s.v. Λήμνιον κακὸν βλέπων.

139.1 ὁμοίως...καί: 'equally as', 'to the same extent as'. The conj. καί is used to introduce a comparative clause after adjs. and advs. indicating sameness, similarity and their opposites (ἴσος καί, ὁ αὐτὸς καί etc. Cf. Latin *idem ac*, *aeque ac*, *similis ac* etc.).

πρὸ τοῦ: 'formerly', 'in the past'. See note on 84.2 above.

λύσιν...αἰτησόμενοι: 'to ask for release'. See note on 28.2, and cf. 33.2, 34.1, 35.2, 81, 111.1, 134.2.

139.2 ἡ δὲ Πυθίη...ἐκέλευε Ἀθηναίοισι δίκας διδόναι ταύτας, τὰς ἂν αὐτοὶ Ἀθηναῖοι δικάσωσι: 'the Pythia bade them give such satisfaction as the Athenians might determine'. For ἄν with the subj. in generic or conditional relative clauses, see Goodwin 1431 and 1434. This Delphic response appears as PW no. 83 and Fontenrose *DO*, Q132.

ἐπηγγέλλοντο βουλόμενοι διδόναι: 'they announced that they were willing to give'. ἀγγέλλω and its compounds usually take the acc. and inf. construction, but are occasionally followed by the part. instead of the inf., by analogy with verbs of perception (see Goodwin 1588).

139.3 πρυτανηΐῳ: see note on 38.2 and cf. 103.3.

στρώσαντες: aor. part. of στορέννυμι (in Hdt. usually στόρνυμαι), 'spread', 'strew'.

οὕτω ἔχουσαν: 'being thus', i.e. 'being in the same condition'. For ἔχω with an adv., see note on 49.2 above.

139.4 εἶπαν: Attic preferred the 2nd. aor. εἶπον except in the 2nd. pers. sing. of the indic. and imper., whereas forms of the 1st. aor. εἶπα are widely used in Ionic. See note on 61.5, and cf. 82.1 and 100.1.

ἐπεὰν...νηῦς ἐξανύσῃ: 'when a ship arrives at'. For temporal clauses referring to the fut., see Goodwin 1434. ἀνύω is usually used transitively in the sense of 'accomplish' or 'destroy', while the commonest intrans. meaning is 'make haste', often in the part. ἀνύσας, where it is best translated 'quickly' (Goodwin 1564). Here it means 'finish one's journey', 'attain one's destination', 'arrive'. Cf. the use of κατανύσας in 140.1 below.

ἐπιστάμενοι τοῦτο εἶναι ἀδύνατον γενέσθαι: conditional acceptance of an oracle is unusual, but even odder is the setting of a condition by the Pelasgians which they believe to be impossible.

ἡ γὰρ Ἀττικὴ πρὸς νότον κέεται πολλὸν τῆς Λήμνου: 'Attica lies far distant from Lemnos to the south'. i.e. 'far to the south of Lemnos', in fact by some 140 miles. πολλόν, 'by far', 'by much', is an adverbial acc. (Goodwin 1060). τῆς Λήμνου may be taken with πρὸς νότον, though Hdt. is also influenced by the use of the gen. after verbs such as ἀπέχω or διέχω to indicate distance.

140.1 ἔτεσι...πολλοῖσι ὕστερον: a vague phrase, especially since both the Pelasgians' offer and Miltiades' conquest are themselves left undated. Lemnos was still inhabited by Pelasgians at the time of the Persian conquest in 513/2 (see 5.26-7), but though the date of Miltiades' annexation is unknown, it probably happened at a time when Persia was preoccupied with the Ionian Revolt. A date around 495, if the historian rightly places Miltiades' return to the Chersonese about this time (see 40.1 above), is as likely as any.

ὡς ἡ Χερσόνησος...ἐγένετο: ὡς is here temporal, with the meaning 'when'.

ἐτησίων ἀνέμων κατεστηκότων: 'while the etesian winds were prevalent', i.e. at some time between July and September.

νηΐ κατανύσας ἐξ Ἐλαιοῦντος...ἐς τὴν Λῆμνον: 'having arrived at Lemnos by ship from Elaeus'. For this use of ἀνύω, see 139.4 above. Elaeus, a city near the southern tip of the Chersonese lying opposite to Sigeum in the Troad, had been an Athenian possession since the middle of the 6th century.

ἀναμιμνήσκων σφέας τὸ χρηστήριον: 'reminding them of the oracle'. For the double acc. with verbs of reminding, see Goodwin 1069 and note on ch. 132 above.

140.2 Ἡφαιστιέες: the inhabitants of Hephaestia (modern Palaeopoea), the wealthier of the two cities on Lemnos, situated in the north-east of the island. Under the Delian League, it paid an annual tribute of 3 talents, as contrasted with the 1.3 talents paid by Myrrhina. The name is derived from the island's patron god Hephaestus, and was probably given after Miltiades' conquest. Its pre-Greek name seems to have been Serona, mentioned in the Siva inscription (see note on 136.2 above). According to the post-Herodotean tradition preserved by Diodorus (10.6) and Charax of Pergamum (Frag. 18J), Hermon, the Pelasgian leader who negotiated the surrender, did so through fear of Persia. The reason for this fear is not stated, but may have been connected with involvement in the murder of the Persian appointed governor of Lemnos, Lycaretus the brother of Maeandrius the former tyrant of Samos (see 5.27; and H. Berve, 'Miltiades', *Hermes, Einzelschrift* 2, Berlin, 1937, p. 49). Diodorus goes on to state that the expression 'Lemnian favours', applied to gifts made under duress, became proverbial as a result of this incident.

ἔσχον: 'acquired', 'took possession of'. See note on 25.2 above.